CAMBRIDGE CLASSICAL STUDIES

General editors: M.I.Finley, E.J.Kenney, G.E.L.Owen

SENECA THE ELDER

Seneca the Elder

JANET FAIRWEATHER

CAMBRIDGE UNIVERSITY PRESS
Cambridge
London   New York   New Rochelle
Melbourne   Sydney

Published by the Press Syndicate of the University of Cambridge
The Pitt Building, Trumpington Street, Cambridge CB2 1RP
32 East 57th Street, New York, NY 10022, USA
296 Beaconsfield Parade, Middle Park, Melbourne 3206, Australia

First published 1981

Printed in Great Britain by Redwood Burn Limited, Trowbridge

British Library Cataloguing in Publication Data

Fairweather, Janet
Seneca the elder. - (Cambridge classical studies).
1. Seneca, Lucius Annaeus, b.55 B.C. - Criticism
and interpretation
I. Series
878'.01'09   PA6659   79-41469 ✓

ISBN 0 521 23101 9

To my mother

CONTENTS

The English-speaking world was without a monograph on Seneca the
Elder until the end of 1978. Now it has two, but I trust that no
reader will consider this, the second to appear, wholly superfluous. Certainly the recently published book by Professor L.A.
Sussman, *The elder Seneca* (Leiden, 1978), is in no way dependent
on any work of mine. For my part, I have for a considerable time
had access to Sussman's doctoral dissertation of 1969, but it only
became available to me three years after I had begun my Senecan
researches, by which time I had passed the stage when it might
have had a formative effect on my views. Certain points of organization in Section III of this book were suggested to me by
Sussman's dissertation, but I am not otherwise substantially indebted to it. As a consequence of the publication of Sussman's
new book I have added many references to it in footnotes, but have
made only three minor alterations to my main text. Inevitably our
fields of investigation overlap, but we have to a surprising extent
chosen to concentrate our attention on different aspects of the
elder Seneca. Unlike Sussman, I have not attempted to say much
about the Senecan historical fragments of the *Nachleben* of the
declamatory anthology, but I *have* ranged over a number of areas
outside the scope of his book. Some, it may fairly be alleged, are
rather remote from the person of Seneca the Elder. Students of
classical Greek and Hellenistic education may, I hope, find something of interest in these pages, as may those interested in the
rhetoric of Cicero's day, in the Greco-Roman biographical tradition, or in Roman elegy. Thanks to the generosity of the editors
of this series I have been allowed to include in my book complex
discussion of some highly technical matters. Consequently I am
able to present an analysis of the processes involved in the
composing and declamation of *controversiae* and *suasoriae* much more
detailed than any available till now, to demonstrate how far

research into the authenticity and style of the declamatory fragments may be carried without the aid of systematic lexicography,
and to give serious consideration to the ways in which the elder
Seneca as a literary critic differed from Cicero and Quintilian in
aims and presuppositions.

This book is a revised version of a Ph.D. dissertation sub-
mitted to the University of London in 1977. To Dr J.B. Hall, my
former supervisor, I owe a particular debt of gratitude for his
seemingly inexhaustible good cheer, his detailed and patient
criticism of my work, and for various helpful suggestions for the
restoration of the elder Seneca's text. The authorship of these
conjectures is duly acknowledged wherever they are considered, as
is my indebtedness to Dr Miriam Griffin and Dr M. Winterbottom for
discussion of various points of interpretation. I am grateful to
Dr Winterbottom and Professors E.J. Kenney and C.O. Brink for
reading and commenting on my work and for recommending its acceptance by the editors of Cambridge Classical Studies. I must also
express gratitude to the Department of Education and Science for
the award of a Major State Studentship (1967-70) and to the
Mistress and Fellows of Girton College, Cambridge who, by electing
me to the Jex-Blake Research Fellowship for 1973-6, enabled me,
after a period spent chiefly in Canada engaged in Greek studies,
to resume work on a project which could hardly otherwise have been
completed. Finally, the kindness and generosity shown to me in
the darker days of my career by my mother, to whom this book is
dedicated, should not go without recognition.

Cambridge   J.A.F.

June 1979

Postscript.

I wish to thank Mrs Janet Chapman and the officers of the Cambridge
University Press for their part in the production of this book and
also Dr Marie Lovatt and Dr J.C. McKeown for their assistance with
proof-reading.

Brugnoli	Suetonius, *De grammaticis et rhetoribus*, ed. G. Brugnoli (Leipzig, 1963)
Diels/Kranz, *Vorsokr.*[6]	*Die Fragmente der Vorsokratiker*, ed.[6] H. Diels, W. Kranz, 3 vols. (Berlin-Grunewald, 1951-2)
FGrHist	*Die Fragmente der griechischen Historiker*, ed. F. Jacoby (Berlin/Leiden, 1923-58)
GL	*Grammatici Latini*, ed. H. Keil, 8 vols. (Leipzig, 1855-80)
GRF	*Grammaticae Romanae Fragmenta*, ed. H. Funaoli (Leipzig 1907)
HRR	*Historicorum Romanorum Reliquiae*, ed. H. Peter (Leipzig, 1870-1906; vol.I ed.[2] 1914-16)
LSJ	*A Greek-English Lexicon*, ed.[9] H.G. Liddell, R. Scott, H.S. Jones, with supplement (Oxford, 1968)
OLD	*Oxford Latin Dictionary* (Oxford, 1968 -)
ORF[3]	*Oratorum Romanorum Fragmenta liberae rei publicae*, ed.[3] H. Malcovati (Turin, 1967)
PIR[2]	*Prosopographia Imperii Romani saec.I, II, III*, ed.[2] E. Groag, A. Stein (Berlin/ Leipzig, 1933)
RE	*Paulys Real-Encyclopädie der classischen Altertumswissenschaft* (Stuttgart, 1894 -)
RLM	*Rhetores Latini Minores*, ed. K. Halm (Leipzig, 1863)
Rh.Gr. Rabe	*Hermogenis Opera (Rhetores Graeci VI)*, ed. H. Rabe (Leipzig, 1913, repr. Stuttgart, 1969)
Rh.Gr. Spengel	*Rhetores Graeci*, ed. L. Spengel, 3 vols. (Leipzig, 1853-6, repr. Frankfurt, 1966)
Rh.Gr. Spengel-Hammer	*Rhetores Graeci ex recognitione Leonardi Spengel* (Leipzig, 1894)
Rh.Gr. Walz	*Rhetores Graeci*, ed. C. Walz, 9 vols. (London and elsewhere, 1832-6, repr. Osnabrück, 1968)
ThLL	*Thesaurus Linguae Latinae* (Leipzig, 1900 -)

Note: For an explanation of symbols used in references to the text
of Seneca the Elder and other ancient authors see p.377.

PART I

THE PLACE OF SENECA THE ELDER IN LITERARY HISTORY

The elder Seneca had every reason to consider himself singularly
well-equipped for the task he was undertaking when he compiled the
work which has come down to us under the title *Oratorum et
rhetorum sententiae divisiones colores*.[1]* This task was to provide a detailed record of the rise of the type of rhetorical declamation which had become a remarkably important feature of the
literary life of Rome in the early years of the Empire, that is,
the declamation of *controversiae* (speeches for the prosecution or
defence in imaginary court cases) and *suasoriae* (speeches offering
advice to mythical or historical figures as they face crucial de-
cisions), in public as well as in private, by adult amateurs -
often eminent men - as well as by schoolboys and professional
teachers of rhetoric.

Born most probably in the fifties B.C.,[2] at any rate back in
the days when Cicero had still been alive, by the time he came to
write his work on the declaimers the elder Seneca was able to draw
on an unusually intimate knowledge of his subject acquired over
seventy years or more. He could remember the days before public
declamation by non-professionals had become accepted practice
(*Contr.* X pr. 4: ...*nondum haec consuetudo erat inducta*), and he
knew that it was in the last years of the Republic, when he was a
child, that the word *declamare* had first been used as a technical
term to describe the habit, newly popular among Roman orators, of
delivering practice speeches in the privacy of their homes (*Contr.*
I pr. 12). He therefore felt able to refer to the declamation
with which his readers would be familiar as something which had
been born within his own life-time: ...*facile est mihi ab incunabulis nosse rem post me natam* (*ibid.*).

Actually, most of the features of modern declamation had been
emerging long before its birth in its final form.[3] Many of the
declamation themes recorded in Seneca's collection show signs of

having been invented for use in Greek schools of rhetoric, probably several centuries earlier,[4] and there is evidence that judicial themes of the *controversia* type were already being set as
exercises for Roman schoolboys in the earlier half of the first
century B.C.[5] We also have the testimony of Suetonius that the
grammaticus Antonius Gnipho was giving regular public declamations
in Latin and Greek to distinguished audiences in the year of
Cicero's praetorship, 66 B.C.[6]

Seneca was aware that some kind of declamation had been known
before his time, but he seems to have underestimated the degree of
continuity between old and new. In *Contr.* I pr. 12 he presents an
account of Roman declamation according to which it had gone
through three distinct phases: in the first the *thesis* had been
the dominant type of exercise; then came the exercises which
Cicero called *causae*; finally the *controversia* had come to the
fore. This account over-simplifies the facts, and is in some ways
positively misleading.[7] It does not tell us, for instance, that
Cicero in his maturity came to regard the *thesis* as preferable to
less abstract types of exercise as a means of educating the orator,[8] or that themes of the *controversia* type had been invented
long before that name had been applied to them. In ignorance of
this last fact, Seneca could set about his task with a light heart,
not worrying that declaimers active earlier than his life-time
might have anticipated his contemporaries in their treatment of
the standard themes.[9]

The one great speaker he regretted not having heard was
Cicero. Age alone had not prevented him but, because of the extreme difficulty of travel between Spain and Italy during the
Civil Wars, he had been kept at home as a child in Corduba, his
birth-place,[10] instead of being sent to Rome for his entire education, as was to be, and may already have been, the custom with
children in his family:[11]

omnes autem magni in eloquentia nominis excepto Cicerone videor
audisse; ne Ciceronem quidem aetas mihi eripuerat, sed bellorum
civilium furor, qui tunc orbem totum pervagabatur, intra coloniam
meam me continuit: alioqui in illo atriolo in quo duos grandes
praetextatos ait secum declamasse, potui adesse illudque ingenium,
quod solum populus Romanus par imperio suo habuit, cognoscere et,
quod vulgo aliquando dici solet, sed in illo proprie debet, potui

vivam vocem audire. (*Contr.* I pr. 11)

Even supposing Seneca had been in Rome in the late Republic,
it is improbable that a mere provincial boy would really have been
admitted to the *atriolum* where Cicero and the consuls-designate
declaimed, about as probable as the ancient tradition, with which
Seneca's wishful thinking about overlapping chronology may be
compared, that Demosthenes (384-322 B.C.) had been known by his
great predecessor Lysias (*c*.459-*c*.380 B.C.).[12] As it was, by
staying in Spain he had the chance to meet at a very early age a
boy who was to become the leading declaimer in Rome in the years
that followed Cicero's death. Seneca's close friendship with
Porcius Latro, which lasted *a prima pueritia usque ad ultimum eius
diem* (*Contr.* I pr. 13), must have been one of the main reasons for
the enthusiastic interest in declamation which he retained as an
adult.

Seneca and Latro went as *condiscipuli* to the school of a mediocre rhetorician called Marullus (*Contr.* I pr. 22). Whether his
school was in Spain or Rome is unclear, but the former hypothesis
is by no means improbable.[13] According to Suetonius, *grammatici*
had long been active in the western provinces (*De gramm. et rhet.*
3.6 Brugnoli), and in the Republican period their curriculum had
often included rhetoric in addition to the usual grammatical
studies (4.6). Even supposing that rhetoric had never been taught
in Corduba before the elder Seneca's boyhood, the educational
emergency brought about by the Civil Wars, when the sons of even
the wealthiest families could not be sent to Rome, was just the
kind of situation likely to prompt an enterprising rhetorician to
set up a school there. The outstanding gifts of the two boys were
apparent from early days. Seneca displayed a prodigious capacity
for memorizing vast quantities of unrelated data:

nam et duo milia nominum recitata quo erant ordine dicta reddebam,
et ab his qui ad audiendum praeceptorem mecum convenerant singulos
versus a singulis datos, cum plures quam ducenti efficerentur, ab
ultimo incipiens usque ad primum recitabam. (*Contr.* I pr. 2)

At declamation itself he was out-shone by Latro, who worked his
way to the top of Marullus' class (*Contr.* I pr. 24), but he had
just the talents to fit him to play Boswell to Latro's Johnson.

However, when Latro set himself up in Rome as a professional

rhetorician, Seneca did not confine his attention to his friend's
school alone. Rome in the last three decades B.C., the time when
Latro was active there, was full of men more or less eager to display their declamatory skills to the public, and Seneca, to judge
from the number of declaimers cited in his work, seems to have had
plenty of leisure to go and hear as many of them as he wished.

We do not know exactly how often the leading professional
rhetores would declaim to the public, but that five or six times a
year was thought infrequent can be deduced from what Seneca says
about Albucius:

Instatis mihi cotidie de Albucio: non ultra vos differam, quamvis
non audierim frequenter, cum per totum annum quinquiens sexiensve
populo diceret <et> ad secretas exercitationes non multi in-
rumperent; quos tamen gratiae suae paenitebat. (*Contr.* VII pr. 1)

Antonius Gnipho, according to Suetonius, had declaimed *non nisi*
nundinis.[14] Some of the professionals liked to demonstrate their
virtuosity by declaiming for very long stretches of time: when
Albucius did declaim to the public, he might go on for hours on
end: *saepe declamante illo ter bucinavit* (*Contr.* VII pr. 1),[15]
and we hear of one occasion when Latro, incensed by hostile criticism of his eloquence, declaimed a *suasoria* for three days (*Contr.*
II.4.8). Some of these professional recitals were the occasion of
distinguished social gatherings. For instance, one of Latro's
declamations was attended by Augustus in the company of Agrippa
and Maecenas (*Contr.* II.4.12f.). They rivalled poetry recitations
(a parallel development in the social life of Rome)[16] for the
attention of the city's literary connoisseurs.

It was often possible to listen to declamations by up-and-
coming students in the schools, as well as the masters, but different *rhetores* differed in the extent to which they let their
pupils perform. Latro refused even to listen to his pupils'
efforts, let alone to correct their work or allow them to declaim
publicly in his school - *declamabat ipse tantum et aiebat se non*
esse magistrum sed exemplum - but he and the Greek declaimer
Nicetes were alone in being able to take this egotistical line
(*Contr.* IX.2.23). Their pupils were obliged to display their talents elsewhere. Thus Seneca heard Latro's pupil Florus declaiming,
but *non apud Latronem* (*ibid.*). Other rhetoricians let their

students perform in their own schools, and ran the risk of being
up-staged by them. Among these was Cestius Pius, one of whose
young pupils, Alfius Flavus, attracted such large audiences that
the master hardly dared declaim immediately after him (*Contr.*
I.1.22).

Sometimes adult amateurs, including men well established in
public life, were invited to declaim in a school to an audience of
students and other interested people. Aietius Pastor, according
to Seneca, declaimed a certain *controversia* in Cestius' school
when he was already a senator (*Contr.* I.3.11). Probably declamations were also given by amateurs to invited guests in private
houses: if M. Lepidus, before whom the senator Scaurus declaimed
(*Contr.* X pr. 3 W), was the consul for A.D.11 he can hardly have
kept a regular school, even if he is identical to the teacher of
Nero (son of Germanicus) mentioned in *Contr.* II.3.23. Other
public figures were more self-effacing about their declamatory
pursuits, viewing declamations as mere exercises for the real
business of forensic speaking (*Contr.* III pr. 1: *domesticas
exercitationes*), rather than as an excuse for self-advertisement
(*Contr.* X pr. 4: *frivolae iactationis*). Their motives for adopting this view-point were, according to Seneca, usually mixed: good
orators could be disappointing as declaimers, sometimes they
realized this and acted accordingly (*Contr.* III pr. 1; IV pr. 2);
they might also reject public declamation as part of an effort to
present themselves as defenders of old-fashioned austerity (*Contr.*
X pr. 4).

Seneca somehow managed to hear even the most reluctant declaimers at their private exercises. He was probably among those
who barged in (*inruperent*) to hear the private declamations of
Albucius; at least, he gives quite a detailed account of why it
was a waste of effort to do so (*Contr.* VII pr. 1). He was able to
criticize the declamatory manner of Cassius Severus (*Contr.* III
pr. 1ff.), who declaimed only *raro...et non nisi ab amicis coactus*
(*Contr.* III pr. 7), and of T. Labienus, who never admitted the
public (*Contr.* X pr. 4). He even had the chance to see Asinius
Pollio as an old man giving a lesson in declamation to his grandson Marcellus Aeserninus (*Contr.* IV pr. 3) - a remarkable

privilege, perhaps to be explained by a friendship between Pollio
and Seneca's family originating in the Civil Wars when, in 43 B.C.,
Pollio had his headquarters in Corduba.[17]

What Seneca was doing in these years apart from listening to
declamations is unclear. There is no evidence that he was ever a
rhetorician himself. Any plans he may have had for a political
career were abortive, and how serious his aspirations in that direction may have been cannot be determined now. In a digression
addressed to Mela, his youngest son, in *Contr*. II pr. 3f., he
refers to his elder sons' entry into politics *in quibus ipsa quae
sperantur timenda sunt*, and then has this to say about himself:
*ego quoque eius alioqui processus avidus et hortator laudatorque
vel periculosae dum honestae modo industriae duobus filiis
navigantibus te in portu retineo*.[18] There is a certain ambiguity
in the word *alioqui*. Does it have a purely temporal sense here,
in which case does it mean 'at one time', so that we have a confession here on the elder Seneca's part of early political ambitions, or merely 'at other times'? Or does it mean 'otherwise',
that is, either 'if circumstances were different' (i.e. if politics were not so dangerous), or 'in other cases' (pointing a contrast between his ambitiousness with regard to other people's
careers and his contentment with Mela's lack of ambition)?

In her recent work on the Senecas[19] Mrs M. T. Griffin assumes
that it means 'at one time' and that Seneca the Elder is recalling
that he once had eager political ambitions himself. The strongest
argument in favour of this view is that *avidus* + genitive seems
not to be used of mere warm approval for other people's actions,
but rather has to mean 'greedy on one's own behalf';[20] an octogen-
arian, such as the elder Seneca must have been by the time of
writing, could hardly be 'otherwise' or 'at other (recent) times'
eager for his own advancement. Against this view it must be objected that in none of the other instances of the use of *alioqui*
by Seneca the Elder or the declaimers he quotes which are cited in
the *Thesaurus Linguae Latinae*,[21] does it appear to have unambigu-
ously a temporal sense equivalent to *olim*.[22] Most often in their
usage it seems to mean 'otherwise', 'if this were not so'.[23*] So
perhaps we ought to argue that greed on behalf of one's family was

not so far removed from personal greed that *avidus* could not be
used with reference to it. Also worth considering is the recent
suggestion of J. B. Hall[24]* that *et* should be deleted after *avidus*,
so that we should read: *ego quoque eius alioqui processus avidus
hortator laudatorque vel periculosae dum honestae modo industriae
...* The difficulty of *avidus* is removed if it qualifies *hortator*.

It is clear that Seneca the Elder remained an *eques*,[25] for
whatever reason, all his life, but there is nothing to show that
he was involved in any of the standard occupations of his class,
private business or public financial administration. For all we
know, the running of his family's estates may have been his only
responsibility. His wide knowledge of the Roman schools shows
that he must have spent a good deal of time in the capital, but it
is possible that he travelled quite frequently between there and
Corduba, witness in particular his interest in Spanish orators,
*quibus, quo minus ad famam pervenirent, non ingenium defuit sed
locus* (*Contr.* X pr. 13).[26] The journey need not have been unduly
arduous in peace-time. When the elder Pliny (*NH* XIX.1.4) declares
that the voyage from Gades to Ostia could be made under sail in
less than seven days, he is assuming perfect weather conditions,
but the winds would have had to be consistently adverse for it to
take as long as a month.[27] In view of this we need not assume
that a man, having arrived in Rome from Spain, would necessarily
stay there for years on end. It is therefore even more futile
than is generally recognized to attempt to trace the elder
Seneca's movements over the years. We do know that at least one
of his three sons by Helvia, the lady, very much his junior,[28] to
whom we find him married in the last decade B.C., was born in
Corduba, but that this child, the future philosopher, was in due
course taken to Rome by an aunt, '*illius manibus in urbem perlatus
sum*'.[29]

Seneca's interest in declamation lasted well past the time of
Latro, who tragically took his own life to escape from a quartan
fever, according to St Jerome, two years before the birth of
Christ.[30] The occasion on which Seneca heard Asinius Pollio,
already an old man (*iam senem*), giving a lesson to his grandson
(*Contr.* IV pr. 3) may have been within Latro's life-time,[31] given

that Pollio had been born in 76 B.C., but several of his references to declaimers belong to a rather later period. The incident
in which Cestius Pius unkindly criticized the young Quinctilius
Varus, son of the general, at the time when he was *Germanici gener
ut praetextatus* (*Contr.* I.3.10) can hardly have happened before
A.D.16.[32] The education of his sons gave him an excuse, if one
were needed, for keeping in touch with the world of rhetoric in
his old age. He refers with disgust to the style of Musa, a
rhetorician whom his sons occasionally went to hear (*Contr.* X pr.
9); he tells us that he had actually been with them, evidently on
more than one occasion, to hear Scaurus declaim (*Contr.* X pr. 2).
In the latter years of his life he must have found some compen-
sation for the loss of Latro in friendship with another distinguished declaimer, Iunius Gallio. Repeatedly in addressing his
sons he refers to him as *Gallio noster* or *vester*.[33] He rates him
among the four greatest declaimers of his day, indeed as Latro's
only serious rival:

primum tetradeum quod faciam, quaeritis? Latronis, Fusci, Albuci,
Gallionis. hi quotiens conflixissent, penes Latronem gloria
fuisset, penes Gallionem palma. (*Contr.* X pr. 13)

Novatus, Seneca's eldest son, later assumes the name of Iunius
Gallio,[34] presumably adopted by his father's friend. One of the
lost prefaces must surely have been devoted to praise of Gallio as
a declaimer.

About the political inclinations of his family and friends in
these years he is uncommunicative.[35] His two references to
Sejanus, key figure in the politics of Tiberius' reign, are not
illuminating: in *Contr.* IX.4.21 it is with the wit of Asilius
Sabinus, who happened to encounter in prison certain *Seianianos
locupletes*, that he is primarily concerned, and in *Suas.* 2.12
his main intention is to praise the eloquence of Attalus the
Stoic; the fact that this philosopher was exiled by Sejanus is
only mentioned in an aside. We do know that Iunius Gallio suffered exile on the grounds (unsubstantiated) of association with
Sejanus, after the disastrous misfiring of something which Tacitus
classed as *meditata adulatio* (*Ann.* VI.3). Events of this kind
must have left a mark on the elder Seneca's attitudes and have to

be considered as part of the background to his memorable words on
politics 'in which the very objectives which are sought after are
to be feared' in *Contr*. II pr. 4.

The digression in the second preface in which these sentiments are expressed is a most interesting passage, full of clues
(unfortunately open to varying shades of interpretation) about the
elder Seneca's outlook at the time when, surprisingly late in
life, Novatus and Seneca were setting out on the *cursus honorum*.

haec eo libentius, Mela, fili carissime, refero, quia video
animum tuum a civilibus officiis abhorrentem et ab omni ambitu
aversum hoc unum concupiscentem, nihil concupiscere.   tu[36]
eloquentiae tamen studeas: facilis ab hac in omnes artes discursus
est; instruit etiam quos non sibi exercet. nec est quod insidias
tibi putes fieri, quasi id agam ut te bene cedentis studii favor
teneat. ego vero non sum bonae mentis impedimentum: perge quo
inclinat animus, et paterno contentus ordine subduc fortunae magnam tui partem. erat quidem tibi maius ingenium quam fratribus
tuis, omnium bonarum artium capacissimum: est et hoc ipsum
melioris ingenii pignus, non corrumpi bonitate eius ut illo male
utaris. sed quoniam fratribus tuis ambitiosa curae sunt foroque
se et honoribus parant, in quibus ipsa quae sperantur timenda
sunt, ego quoque eius alioqui processus avidus et hortator
laudatorque vel periculosae dum honestae modo industriae duobus
filiis navigantibus te in portu retineo. sed proderit tibi in
illa quae tota mente agitas declamandi exercitatio, sicut Fabiano
profuit: qui aliquando cum Sextium audiret nihilominus declamita-
bat, et tam diligenter ut putares illum illi studio parari, non
per illud alteri praeparari. (*Contr*. II pr. 3f. W)

Seneca the Elder here breaks off from his pen-portrait of Fabianus,
declaimer turned philosopher, and suggests that what he has been
saying (*haec*) ought to be of special interest to his youngest son
Mela. Why this should be so does not emerge till the last sentence of the passage quoted. It appears that Mela had decided to
live a life of philosophical quietude, far from the world of politics, and therefore could see no point in continuing his rhetorical studies. His father puts the case of Fabianus before him as
an object lesson: here was a distinguished philosopher who had
continued declaiming after his philosophical conversion, and with
no diminution of effort.

The contrast between the unambitious Mela and his brothers
with their political aspirations calls forth some remarkably
interesting observations from their father, the exact implications
of which, however, are often far from clear. Mrs Griffin in her

recent work on the Senecas has taken *Contr.* II pr. 3-4 as evidence
that the elder Seneca, frustrated in his own early ambitions for a
political career, looked upon public life as *honesta industria*
and, having perhaps gone as far as to resort to plots (*insidias*)
in order to ensure that Novatus and Seneca should be well trained
as orators, gave them whole-hearted backing when they decided to
embark on their 'noble voyage'.[37] A. Vassileiou[38] has also recently asserted that Seneca the Elder was very ambitious on his
sons' behalf, though he does not view these ambitions as the outcome of an early disappointment in his own career. Neither of
these two interpretations of the passage pays sufficient attention
to the fact that it is Mela, the philosophical quietist, whom
Seneca the Elder is explicitly commending in the passage, and that
in doing so he says things which are extraordinarily ungenerous to
the two elder brothers. What had they done to deserve the as-
persions cast on their intellects and the use they were making of
their talents in the words *est et hoc ipsum melioris ingenii
pignus, non corrumpi bonitate eius ut illo male utaris*? Nevertheless, elsewhere in the same passage the elder Seneca does appear to
suggest that he gave strong backing to his elder sons' ambitions.

The suggestion that Seneca's denial of plots indicates that
he had gone to all lengths to ensure that Novatus and Seneca entered politics may readily be discounted: all that he denies in
Contr. II pr. 3 is that he wants Mela to keep up his study of
rhetoric merely because it is something which he is good at; in
the next sentence he makes it clear that he regards rhetoric as a
useful training for other occupations besides public life. It is
in the sentence where he refers to public life and *honesta
industria* that we find him expressing himself in such a way that
it seems difficult to argue, as one might have done on the
strength of his previous remarks, that he approved of Mela, but
not of his two elder sons.

Three problems of interpretation are raised by this long sentence. What is the precise significance of the opening words, *sed
quoniam*? What is the meaning of *alioqui*? And why does the sentence end without any expression of pleasure by Seneca the Elder
at the prospect of keeping Mela in harbour?[39] To start with the

second question, we have noted the difficulty of finding examples
in the usage of Seneca and the declaimers quoted by him of the use
of *alioqui* as equivalent to *olim*, so that unless one is convinced,
as I am not completely, by the argument that *eius...processus
avidus* cannot possibly refer to the elder Seneca's avidity for any
but his own advancement, it seems hazardous to interpret *alioqui*
in this narrowly restricted sense to the exclusion of any other,
and view the words *eius...avidus* as an unambiguous confession of
early political ambitions on his part. The most natural interpretation does seem to be that *alioqui* means 'otherwise', 'in
other cases', i.e. in particular, 'in the case of my other
sons',[40] even though, as we have seen, he casts doubts on the wis-
dom of their ambitions in previous sentences. The interpretation
of *alioqui* as meaning 'otherwise' in the sense 'if public life
were not so dangerous' (referring back to the words, *in quibus
ipsa quae sperantur timenda sunt*) has a certain attraction, as it
would make the elder Seneca's avidity for political advancement
conditional on circumstances not found in the Rome of his day, and
hence not inconsistent with his praise of Mela's quietism. But it
is difficult to make sense of *ego quoque* if one adopts this
interpretation.

The problems raised by the beginning and the end of the sentence are best considered together. The only solution to them, I
suggest, is to postulate that the text at least at the end of the
sentence is corrupt. Some expression there of warm indulgence for
Mela seems demanded by the context: perhaps between *navigantibus
te* and *retineo* the word *libenter* has dropped out, owing to its
slight resemblance to *...tibus te*, or, to adopt an alternative
suggested by J. B. Hall, *retineo* is a corruption of *retin<ere
gaud>eo* or the like.[41] If we accept that some such supplement is
required at the end of the sentence, *quoniam* at the beginning
becomes much more intelligible. *Sed* before *quoniam* still seems
puzzling. A connective meaning 'and' or 'therefore' might have
been expected. Perhaps it is a corruption of *et*[42]* or *ita*[43]*
(the intrusive *s* being the product of dittography of the last
letter of the preceding word *utaris*), in which case *quidem* in the
previous sentence is picked up by *sed* not here but later on, in

the emphatic words *sed proderit tibi...declamandi exercitatio...*

Translate then, perhaps:

'But' (or 'And' or 'Therefore') 'since your brothers are busying themselves with ambitious aims and preparing themselves for the forum and public careers, in which the very objectives which are sought after are to be feared, even I, though in other cases eager for this advancement and an encourager and praiser of hard work, however dangerous' (or, deleting *et*,[44] 'though in other cases an eager encourager of this advancement and a praiser of hard work, however dangerous') '<am glad to> keep you in harbour.'

The difficulty remains that the elder Seneca does not seem consistent in the attitude he expresses towards public office in *Contr.* II pr. 3-4, one moment implying that it is a bad use of the intellect, and the next representing himself as an enthusiast for it despite its dangers. Prolonged consideration of the passage leaves me with an uneasy feeling that Seneca the Elder, thoroughly familiar with the arguments for and against the *thesis*, 'an capessenda sit sapienti respublica',[45] was all too ready to be deflected from a clear expression of his views into phrase-making appropriate to whichever side of the debate he happened to be touching on.[46]

But, whatever his true attitude was towards his elder sons' ambitions, two interesting facts do come to light in *Contr.* II pr. 3-4 which we could not have learnt from any other source, first, that it was Mela and not Seneca who was regarded when young as the philosopher of the family, and secondly that when the elder sons entered politics their father was to some extent conscious of the dangers into which their aspirations might lead them. He was not to know that Mela's decision to remain *paterno contentus ordine* would not save him from the calamity which was to befall the whole family.[47]

The *Oratorum et rhetorum sententiae divisiones colores* was one of two literary projects to which the elder Seneca devoted himself in the last years of his life, the other being a study of recent Roman history, starting from the beginning of the Civil Wars, which he kept up to date practically until the day he died.[48] He probably regarded this other work as much the more important, being well aware that historiography was a weightier matter than scholastic rhetoric (see *Suas.* 5.8; 6.16).

That the declamatory anthology was composed at least in part
in the last years of his life, is shown by various references
which could not have been made before the 30s A.D.: an allusion to
the fall of Sejanus in 31 (*Contr.* IX.4.21); another to the death
of Scaurus in 34 (*Suas.* 2.22). The fact that he refers to the
writings of Cassius Severus (*Contr.* III pr. 3) and Cremutius
Cordus (*Suas.* 6.19, 23), whose books were publicly burnt in A.D.
12 and 25 respectively, not to be republished until early in
Caligula's reign, has been adduced as evidence that the passages
in question were not written before 37.[49] This is open to doubt,
for it is unlikely that any attempts in antiquity to suppress
books were rigorous enough to stop their circulation in private
hands, and Seneca, who was over eighty in the 30s A.D., might have
thought it an old man's privilege to write about anything he
chose, and to leave it to his literary executors to decide the
right time for publication. But as one historical fragment which
may well be by the elder Seneca describes the death of Tiberius,[50]
a date in the reign of Caligula for the compilation of the declamatory anthology is by no means to be ruled out.

It seems that after his death, which we know has to be dated
before 41,[51] the younger Seneca decided to suppress at least some
of his father's works, though in the biography which he wrote *De
vita patris*, now lost except for one fragment, he was full of
praise for them:

si quaecumque composuit pater meus et edi voluit, iam in manus
populi emisissem, ad claritatem nominis sui satis sibi ipse pro-
spexerat: nam nisi me decepit pietas, cuius honestus etiam error
est, inter eos haberetur, qui ingenio meruerunt ut puris titulis
nobiles essent.[52]*

The elder Seneca's decision to work in his old age on two
very different projects - the political history and the work on
the declaimers - is one of several pieces of evidence that he was
a much more complex character than is commonly supposed. Even
within the declamatory anthology we find indications that he was
one of those people who have, in private life, an irrepressible
charm and sense of humour which it takes only friendships, or
even the memory of friendships, to keep alive, but who are at the
same time profoundly pessimistic and austere in outlook when they

consider the state of the world as a whole. The younger Seneca has this to say about his father's *Histories*:

quisquis legisset eius historias ab initio bellorum civilium, unde primum veritas retro abiit, paene usque ad mortis suae diem, magni aestimaret scire, quibus natus esset parentibus ille, qui res Roma<nas...[53]*

The parenthesis, *unde...abiit*, is interesting. It has to be taken as the younger Seneca's own comment, but he would surely not have made it if it did not reflect a dominant theme in his father's work. The phraseology should be compared with *Contr.* I pr. 6:

...*ut possitis aestimare, in quantum cotidie ingenia decrescant et nescio qua iniquitate naturae eloquentia se retro tulerit.* It is of course hazardous to speculate on the character of Seneca's historical work,[54] now so hopelessly lost, but it seems very unlikely that it was wholly cheerful in tone. True, in the declamatory anthology he has some kind things to say about Augustus as a 'most clement man' (*Contr.* IV pr. 5) and as a ruler who allowed himself to display human feelings and friendliness in his letters (*ibid.*), while allowing others to insult his right-hand men without fear of retribution: *tanta autem sub divo Augusto libertas fuit, ut praepotenti tunc M. Agrippae non defuerint qui ignobilitatem exprobrarent* (*Contr.* II.4.13). It also seems that he had come to terms in some ways with the fact that the Republic was no more: *mihi videtur admiratione dignus divus Augustus, sub quo tantum licuit, sed horum non possum misereri, qui tanti putant caput potius quam dictum perdere* (*ibid.*); he finds it remarkable that Labienus retained his enthusiasm for the Pompeian cause *in tanta pace* (*Contr.* X pr. 5). On the other hand, against book-burning, the punishment unknown in the Republic which Labienus was the first to suffer, he vents great fury (*Contr.* X pr. 6f.), only equalled by that with which he inveighs against the young men of his day who have neglected eloquence and chosen instead to aim for *turpia multo honore quaestuque vigentia* (*Contr.* I pr. 7). We have seen in *Contr.* II pr. 4 his realization of the dangers which faced men entering public life in post-Augustan Rome.

In a historical fragment ascribed to 'Seneca' by Lactantius, the rise and fall of Rome is described in terms of the stages in a human life; the Empire with its return to monarchy is reckoned as the second childhood of the state:

haec fuit prima eius senectus, cum bellis lacerata civilibus atque intestino malo pressa rursus ad regimen singularis imperii recidit quasi ad alteram infantiam revoluta. amissa enim libertate, quam Bruto duce et auctore defenderat, ita consenuit, tamquam sustentare se ipsa non valeret, nisi adminiculo regentium uteretur. (Fr. hist. 1 = Lact. *Inst. div.* VII.15.14)

It is open to dispute whether this gloomy assessment of Roman history belongs to Seneca the Elder or his son the philosopher.[55] In my view there is a limit to the lengths to which one should go in order to deny the elder Seneca's authorship of it. True, it can be argued of this, as of any other piece of historical analysis or narrative, that it could have originated as an *exemplum* in a philosophical work, but seeing that it is known that the elder Seneca wrote *historias ab initio bellorum civilium*..., and we have famous parallels in, for example, the first book of Thucydides, and the beginning of Tacitus' *Annals* for the inclusion of a summary of the history of a state from its origins in works otherwise devoted to recent history, it seems unreasonable to argue that the fragment is *more* likely to be by Seneca the philosopher than his father. Again, it is not at all self-evident what moral point could have been illustrated by the second of the Senecan historical fragments printed by Müller, a graphic account of the death of Tiberius:

Seneca eum scribit intellecta defectione exemptum anulum quasi alicui traditurum parumper tenuisse, dein rursus aptasse digito et compressa sinistra manu iacuisse diu immobilem subitoque vocatis ministris ac nemine respondente consurrexisse nec procul a lectulo deficientibus viribus concidisse. (Suet. *Tib.* 73.2)

The historical sentiments in the fragment preserved by Lactantius accord well enough with what we know about the elder Seneca's outlook from his extant work;[56] note that, even if there is no place in its bleak scheme for kind words about Augustus, the author's view is that there has been a deterioration since Rome's *prima senectus*. This fragment could well have formed the preface of his lost work. We simply do not have enough information on which to base a denial that the elder Seneca's *Histories* were ever published. Remember that it would only need one scholar to read through a manuscript, excerpting as he went along, for fragments of it to enter the literary tradition.

To be on the safe side, however, we must restrict our attention to the declamatory anthology when looking for evidence of the
elder Seneca's character. In this work the prevailing tone is one
of cheerful bonhomie and wit, as Seneca reminisces about people
who had been dear friends to him, and others who at least had impressed or amused him, in years gone by. The work was a pleasure
to him, as he declares in the first preface:

est, fateor, iucundum mihi redire in antiqua studia melioresque ad
annos respicere et vobis querentibus, quod tantae opinionis viros
audire non potueritis, detrahere temporum iniuriam. (*Contr.* I pr.
1)

It was particularly pleasant to have a chance to recall his
friendship with Latro:

in aliis autem an beneficium vobis daturus sim nescio, in uno ac-
cipio: Latronis enim Porcii, carissimi mihi sodalis, memoriam
saepius cogar retractare et a prima pueritia usque ad ultimum eius
diem perductam familiarem amicitiam cum voluptate maxima repetam.
(*Contr.* I pr. 13)

Having been on extremely close terms with Latro and other leading
figures responsible for the promotion of public declamation, he
was not at all disposed to adopt a censorious attitude towards
rhetoricians and their activities, though he knew perfectly well
that there were some people who took the view that it was misguided to regard declamation as more than useful private practice
for true public oratory, and others who even doubted the educative
value of *controversiae*. Indeed, he quotes the arguments of two
such critics at length (*Contr.* III pr. 8ff.; IX pr. 1ff). But he
was himself convinced of the usefulness of a rhetorical education
even for people who had no intention of becoming public speakers
of any kind in later life: *facilis ab hac in omnes artes discursus
est; instruit etiam quos non sibi exercet* (*Contr.* II pr. 3). He
voices no objection to the practice of public declamation - to
have done so would have been disloyal to the memory of Latro.
That he was far from outraged by the scholastic outlook is evident
when he expresses a preference for a *bona fide scholasticus* over a
declaimer who aped the manner of forensic speakers (*Contr.* X pr.
12). The tolerance which is characteristic of his criticisms of
the declaimers is summed up by some words in the tenth preface:
nec sum ex iudicibus severissimis, qui omnia ad exactam regulam

derigant:[57]* *multa donanda ingeniis puto; sed donanda vitia, non
portenta sunt* (*Contr*. X pr. 10). Some of the more stupid declaimers' efforts call forth caustic rebukes. For instance, just
before his declaration of tolerance in *Contr*. X pr. 10 he has been
saying of Musa, *non ergo, etiamsi iam manu missus erat, debuit de
corio eius nobis satis fieri?* But on other occasions he suffers
fools remarkably gladly, making such whimsical comments as *non
minus stulte Aemilianus quidam Graecus rhetor, quod genus stultorum amabilissimum est, ex arido fatuus, dixit...* (*Contr*. X.5.25)
and *nihil est autem amabilius quam diligens stultitia* (*Contr*.
VII.5.11).

Very occasionally, though, a powerful outburst of pessimism
breaks through for a while, and disrupts the easy-going geniality
which is the usual mark of his literary criticism. On the two
main occasions when this happens the style becomes far more agitated and much nearer to the manner of the rhetoricians than
usual. A long section of the first preface is given over to a
heated discourse on the decline of eloquence since Cicero's time.
The following is a typical sample:

torpent ecce ingenia desidiosae iuventutis nec in unius honestae
rei labore vigilatur: somnus languorque ac somno et languore
turpior malarum rerum industria invasit animos, cantandi saltandi-
que obscena studia effeminatos tenent; [et] capillum frangere et
ad muliebres blanditias extenuare vocem, mollitia corporis certare
cum feminis et inmundissimis se excolere munditiis nostrorum
adulescentium specimen est. quis aequalium vestrorum quid dicam
satis ingeniosus, satis studiosus, immo quis satis vir est?
(*Contr*. I pr. 8-9)

The only other passage in the work at all comparable with this
comes in the tenth and last preface (*Contr*. X pr. 6-7), a tirade
perhaps deliberately placed there as a counterbalance to the one
on the decline of eloquence at the beginning of the work. Several
other motifs which first appear in the first preface are certainly
taken up in the tenth, with the evident intention of unifying the
work.[58] This time the subject of Seneca's anger is book-burning:

bono hercules publico ista in poenas ingenio<rum ver>sa crudelitas
post Ciceronem inventa est; quid enim futurum fuit, si triumviris
libuisset et ingenium Ciceronis proscribere? sunt di immortales
lenti quidem, sed certi vindices generis humani et magna exempla
in caput invenientium regerunt, ac iustissima patiendi vice quod
quisque alieno excogitavit supplicio saepe expiat suo. quae vos,

dementissimi homines, tanta vecordia agitat? (*Contr.* X pr. 6)

Modern writers on the elder Seneca have had a tendency, when describing his character, to stress the sterner side of it,[59] his 'old fashioned austerity',[60] to the exclusion of all else. There is no denying that he had such a side. Admittedly, it needs to be taken into consideration that the first of his major pessimistic tirades is on a theme, known as *convicium saeculi* (*Contr.* II pr. 2) or *insectatio temporum* (*Suas.* 6.9), which was a well-known rhetorical commonplace, and that attacks on book-burning were likewise part of the declaimers' repertoire, required notably when one was declaiming *Suasoria* 7: *deliberat Cicero, an scripta sua conburat, promittente Antonio incolumitatem si fecisset.* Seneca will therefore not have needed to think as hard as usual when composing these passages, and his memories of other people's treatments of the themes may have given him more than his usual fluency. But that does not mean that he was insincere when he wrote them.

However, bitter reflections on Roman decadence and the loss of free speech do not bulk very large in Seneca's books on declamation, and it is a mistake to blind ourselves to the evidence provided by these books that he was a man of considerable tolerance and geniality, and, at least in his literary tastes, a modernist. We must be wary of sweeping statements by modern writers to the effect that he was the personification of all the ideals which made Rome great, a latter-day Cato, weighed down with *gravitas* and stiff with *antiquus rigor*, statements such as are the key-note of the somewhat rhapsodic accounts of his character given by Bornecque and Edward: '*il est profondément pénétré de l'esprit de l'ancienne Rome: aussi bien son idéal est-il le type parfait du vieux Romain, Caton l'Ancien*';[61] 'Seneca's character has undoubtedly the *gravitas*, *dignitas* and *constantia* of the old Roman.'[62]

In fact, especially in his literary preferences, he appears deeply affected by the spirit of the new era in which he lived. If he had been a straightforward *strictus Cato* he would hardly have had much patience with a man so devoted to art for art's sake as Porcius Latro, or made remarks so attuned to the Ovidian age[63] as his facetious comments on dry stylists in *Contr.* II.1.24:

aridi declamatores fidelius quos proposuerunt colores tuentur:
nihil enim illos sollicitat, nullum schema, nulla sententia. sic
quae malam faciem habent saepius pudicae sunt: non animus illis
deest sed corruptor.

We have in the elder Seneca the curious phenomenon of a *laudator
temporis acti se puero* whose youth had been spent in a milieu far
from austere.

The idea that the elder Seneca was a man of antique severity,
devoted to old Roman traditions and contemptuous of new-fangled
philosophy, derives from no less an authority than his second son,
but there is some reason to doubt whether the younger Seneca's
references to his father can be trusted to provide more than a
conventional portrait of what an aged *paterfamilias*, born back in
the good old days of the Republic, ought to have been like. It
seems to have been the rule, rather than the exception, among the
Annaei Senecae, to present stylized portraits of any members of
their family mentioned in their writings. The elder Seneca leads
the way by representing his sons throughout his work on the
declaimers (with the notable exception of *Contr.* II pr. 3-4, where
he refers to their choice of careers) as thoroughly immature young
men, interested only in scholastic *sententiae*, unwilling to apply
their minds to the serious study of history (*Suas.* 6.16, 27) or
even to the drier aspects of declamation (*Contr.* I pr. 22). He
never mentions that his second son was interested in philosophy.
Again, the younger Seneca, when writing about his mother, uses
language suspiciously reminiscent of the standard declamatory descriptions of female types. Compare, for example, *Cons. Helv.*
16.4, *non faciem coloribus ac lenociniis polluisti: numquam tibi
placuit vestis, quae nihil amplius nudaret, cum poneretur*, with
some words from a declamation by Latro (*Contr.* II.7.4), *prodite
mihi fronte in omne lenocinium composita, paulo obscurius quam
posita veste nudae*.[64] He also represents his father as contemptuous of philosophy (*Ep. mor.* 108.22: *philosophiam oderat*). Here he
is totally misleading: there is inescapable evidence that the
elder Seneca shared his son's admiration for the philosopher
Fabianus and the *sanctis fortibusque praeceptis* to which he dedicated himself, and for the Stoic Attalus, for his *subtilitas* as
well as for his eloquence (*Suas.* 2.12).[65] On another occasion the

younger Seneca asserts that his father had not wished Helvia to
immerse herself too deeply in philosophical learning:

itaque illo te duco, quo omnibus, qui fortunam fugiunt, confugi-
endum est, ad liberalia studia: illa sanabunt vulnus tuum, illa
omnem tristitiam tibi evellent. his etiam si numquam adsuesses,
nunc utendum erat; sed quantum tibi patris mei antiquus rigor permisit, omnes bonas artes non quidem comprendisti, attigisti tamen.
utinam quidem virorum optimus, pater meus, minus maiorum consuetudini deditus voluisset te praeceptis sapientiae erudiri potius quam
imbui! non parandum tibi nunc esset auxilium contra fortunam sed
proferendum. propter istas quae litteris non ad sapientiam
utuntur sed ad luxuriam instruuntur, minus te indulgere studiis
passus est. beneficio tamen rapacis ingenii plus quam pro tempore
hausisti. (*Cons. Helv.* 17.3f.)[66]

These remarks are best taken as telling us more about the elder
Seneca's attitude towards women than towards philosophy, that is,
supposing we do not take this passage as just one more case of
Senecan persiflage, intended to excuse a son for preaching to his
mother, rather than as certain evidence that Helvia's desire for
philosophic enlightenment was discouraged by her husband. Certainly the younger Seneca felt no more obliged to tell the whole
truth when referring to his father's character in his philosophical works than the elder Seneca had done when referring to the
tastes of his sons in his declamatory anthology. Seneca the
Younger never mentions his father's interest in scholastic rhetoric, which would not have been consistent with the picture he
wished to present of his father as a man *maiorum consuetudini
deditus*, distinguished for his *antiquus rigor* (*Cons. Helv.* 17.
3-4).

Modern scholars have added two main embellishments to the
younger Seneca's picture of the old man, both of which deserve re-
examination. First, we are to believe that his devotion to the
consuetudo maiorum included an attachment to traditional re-
ligion.[67] For all we know this may have been the case, but surely
the one sentence adduced as evidence (*Contr.* X pr. 6): *sunt di
immortales lenti quidem, sed certi vindices generis humani* etc.,
coming as it does from one of his untypically declamatory passages
(the tirade against book-burning), and expressing, albeit elo-
quently, a fairly commonplace sentiment, is not necessarily sufficient basis for an assumption that he paid more than lip-service

to the immortal gods.

The other main characteristic modern writers are fond of
attributing to him is intense patriotism. According to W. A.
Edward, 'He is a provincial; but for Rome and things Roman he has
a burning enthusiasm that surpasses that of the true sons of the
eternal city.'[68] However, Mrs Griffin in a recent article has
taken a new look at the evidence, and, finding the elder Seneca
less thoroughly Romanized than his philosopher son, has laid more
emphasis than is usual on signs of his attachment to his native
province.[69] One assertion commonly made about him that needs to
be questioned more than it has been, is that he was prejudiced
against the Greeks.[70] Now, it is true that he once pits the
achievements of Roman eloquence in the Ciceronian age against
'insolent' Greece: *quidquid Romana facundia habet, quod insolenti
Graeciae aut opponat aut praeferat, circa Ciceronem effloruit
(Contr.* I pr. 6). But before we lay too much weight on this
remark, we might note that it had a close parallel in a *sententia*
from a declamation by Cestius Pius, a Greek declaimer notorious
for his contempt for Cicero:[71] *iniuriam illum facturum populo
Romano, cuius linguam <in locum pr>incipem extulisset, ut
insolentis Graeciae studia tanto antecederet eloquentia, quanto
fortuna (Suas.* 7.10 M).[72] It looks as if *insolens Graecia* was a
standard phrase, a famous quotation, maybe, whose source is no
longer known, which one might use with no particular depth of
feeling. Another of the elder Seneca's expressions of patriotism,
taken seriously by Edward, though not so much so by Bornecque,[73]
sed nolo Romanos in ulla re vinci (Contr. X.5.28), would be less
ambivalent if the contest in which he is pitting Romans against
Greeks at this point were not a competition for the most insane
sententia. It is necessary to notice these facts about these
supposed key passages, because detailed study of Seneca's criticisms of individual Greek *sententiae* does not reveal undue harshness of judgement, as A. F. Sochatoff[74] was the first to point
out. J. Buschmann, who wrote two papers about Seneca the Elder,
one dealing with the Greek declaimers mentioned by him and another
with what he calls his '*enfants terribles*', ought to have made the
point that these two classes of declaimers overlap very little.[75]

When Seneca criticizes samples of bad taste by the Greek declaimers he is no harder on them, as a rule, than on their Roman
counterparts.[76] Such a departure from mildness as the use of the
superlatives *corruptissime* and *furiosissime* against two Greek
declaimers in *Contr.* X.5.21 is very exceptional. Elsewhere we
find him giving as high praise as he ever awards to a declamatory
sententia to one by a Greek: *Diocles Carystius dixit sententiam,
quae non in declamatione tantum posset placere sed etiam in
solidiore aliquo scripti genere... (Contr. I.8.16).*[77] Nor does
such cautious weighing up of merits as we find, for example, in
the same section, when he considers a *sententia* by Dorion, betoken
blind prejudice: *Dorion dixit rem paulo quidem elatiorem, quam
pressa et civilis oratio recipit, sed qua egregie attonitos patris
adfectus exprimeret...* In the several passages where he considers
the relative merits of Greek and Latin *sententiae* on the same
theme,[78] Roman declaimers are just as likely to win the prize for
corruptum or obscenity as for excellence. In the international
competition of *Contr.* I.4.10-12 which opens with the words, *ex
altera parte multa sunt pulcherrime dicta; sed nescio an Graecis
nostri cessuri sint*, it is Albucius who finally emerges as victor,
but the opposition, in Seneca's opinion, was strong:

Vibius Rufus dixit: adulter meus exit et commodo suo. Hybreas
hunc sensum optime dixit:... Dionysius, filius eius Dionysii, qui
Ciceronis filium docuit, elegans magis declamator quam vehemens,
hunc sensum et vehementer dixit et eleganter: ...Vibius Rufus
dixit: quam otiosi, quam securi adulteri transierunt praeter
oculos meos, praeter filii manus! Latro cum exeuntis adulteros
descripsisset adiecit: adulescens, parentes tuos sequere. Nicetes
illam sententiam pulcherrimam, qua nescio an nostros antecesserit:
... sed illud Albuci utique Graecos praeminet: cum pugnantem se
<in> acie descripsisset, dixit: me miserum quas manus adulter
effugit! et illud Albuci: 'non potui' inquit 'matrem occidere.'
quo excusatior sis, adice: 'et patrem'. (*Contr.* I.4.11f. M)

And in *Contr.* I.4.12 the contest ends with a reference to a most
stupid imitation of a Greek *sententia* by one of Seneca's Roman
'*enfants terribles*':

dixerat Nicetes:... Murredius dum hanc sententiam imitari vult,
stultissimam dixit: reliqui in acie pugnantes manus.

In *Contr.* I.2.22 Seneca takes pains to ensure that we do not gain
the impression that obscenity was a fault peculiar to Greek declaimers. After citing a sweeping statement by Scaurus on the

subject, *hoc autem vitium aiebat Scaurus a Graecis declamatoribus tractum, qui nihil non et permiserint sibi et inpetraverint*, and two Greek examples, he goes on to remark: *in hac controversia de sacerdote non minus obscene dixit Murredius: fortasse dum repellit libidinem, manibus excepit* (*Contr.* I.2.23). A protracted contest between Greeks and Romans in *Contr.* X.4.18-23 opens with the words:

celebris haec apud Graecos controversia est; multa ab illis pulchre dicta sunt, a quibus non abstinuerunt nostri manus, multa corrupte, quibus non cesserunt nec ipsi.

The last stages of this competition deserve close consideration, as they lead up to one of Seneca's rare generalizations, which is often quoted in isolation and in context is rather puzzling. In §22-3 Seneca shows how two corrupt *sententiae* by Glycon met their match in three equally bad Latin ones:

ΓΛΥΚΩΝ[79*] corruptam dixit sententiam: κρουσάτω τις τὴν θύραν τῶν ἐχόντων <ἵνα> προσαγάγῃ τις. et illam: ἄγε, σὺ δὲ κλαῖε, σὺ δὲ θρήνει. ὦ κακῶν συμφωνιῶν! sed nostri quoque bene insanierunt. Murredius dixit: producitur miserorum longus ordo, maior pars se sine se trahit. et Licinius Nepos: ut solvendo sis, in poenas quotiens tibi renascendum est? illud Sparsus dixit, quod non corruptum tantum sed contrarium dicebat esse Montanus: 'solus plura habes membra quam tot hominibus reliquisti.' ita enim hic potest videri laesisse rem publicam, si multi sunt debilitati; apparet autem non esse multos, si plura habet membra quam debilitatis reliquit. et illud aeque aiebat ab illo corrupte dictum: 'prodierunt plures mendici quam membra.'

It is at this juncture that we read:

Graecas sententias in hoc refero, ut possitis aestimare, primum quam facilis e Graeca eloquentia in Latinam transitus sit et quam omne, quod bene dici potest, commune omnibus gentibus sit, deinde ut ingenia ingeniis conferatis et cogitetis Latinam linguam facultatis non minus habere, licentiae minus.

This conclusion seems in its latter part quite out of joint with what has come immediately before. One might have expected Seneca to say rather: *et cogitetis Latinam linguam facultatis minus habere, licentiae non minus.*[80*] Perhaps he did, and our text is at fault.

To sum up, Seneca the Elder was very much a man of his time, not the embodiment of all the old Roman virtues and prejudices which he is sometimes made out to have been. While he occasionally expressed pride in Roman achievements, patriotism did not

seem to him so serious a matter that he could not make jokes about
it,[81] and he did not let his judgement of individual Greek *sententiae* be distorted by a general bias against *Graeculi* - a term
which, significantly, he uses only once, and then with good humour
and in a passage where he may well be quoting Cestius (*Suas.*
1.6).[82] He shows no sign anywhere in his extant writings of the
disdain for philosophy attributed to him by his second son.[83]
With regard to literature he was a modernist. This is not only
apparent from his enthusiastic interest in the activities of the
rhetoricians and in the intricacies of the art taught in what a
really old-fashioned Roman would have called their schools of
impudence,[84] but also from the range of his references to the
higher forms of literature: with the single exception of his quotation from Cato in *Contr.* I pr. 9 he makes no reference to any
pre-Ciceronian Roman orator;[85] nor does he mention any Latin
historians or poets earlier than Sallust and the Neoterics.[86]
Where politics were concerned, he appears to have had a certain
amount of admiration for Augustus, though, if the Senecan fragment
preserved by Lactantius (fr. hist. 1) comes from his *Histories*, he
viewed the return of Rome to the rule of one man as in itself a
sign of an advanced stage of decline. Certainly in his opinion
that Roman rhetoric had degenerated seriously during his life-time
(*Contr.* I pr. 6ff.), in his awareness of the dangers which faced
men of his sons' generation entering public life (*Contr.* II pr.
3), and in his fulminations against the suppression of literature
(*Contr.* X pr. 6f.), he reflects some of the disillusionment
typical of the era in which he was writing.

The elder Seneca mentions several reasons why he came to write
about declamations and declaimers. First, he will have us believe
that the theme of his work was suggested by his sons:

Seneca Novato, Senecae, Melae filiis salutem.
Exigitis rem magis iucundam mihi quam facilem: iubetis enim quid
de his declamatoribus sentiam, qui in aetatem meam inciderunt,
indicare et si qua memoriae meae nondum elapsa sunt ab illis dicta
colligere, ut, quamvis notitiae vestrae subducti sint, tamen non
credatis tantum de illis sed et iudicetis. (*Contr*. I pr. 1)

This request from his sons is perhaps fictional or semi-fictional.
To claim that one was writing at the request of some person was,
like the epistolary greeting, a standard convention among ancient
writers of prefaces to works whose utility needed to be emphasized.[1] To make out that one's purpose in writing was to give
information to some member of one's family had been a cliché in
classical didactic writing ever since Hesiod had addressed the
Works and days to his brother. To take two Roman instances, Cato
in, for example, the dictum quoted by Seneca in *Contr*. I pr. 9:
orator est, Marce fili, vir bonus dicendi peritus, and Cicero in
his *Partitiones oratoriae*, had addressed rhetorical precepts to
their sons, the latter in a baby-simple catechistic fashion which
his rebellious offspring can hardly have appreciated.[2] Admittedly
Cicero's son was only thirteen when it was written. On the other
hand Novatus, Seneca and Mela were adults by the time they are
supposed to have made their request (see *Contr*. II pr. 4), and
their father had no reason besides literary convention to talk
down to them in the way he sometimes does (e.g. *Contr*. I pr. 22;
Suas. 6.16), as if they were foolish youths, uninterested in the
intricacies of argument or the serious study of history, uninterested in anything, in fact, except *sententiae*. The way he
refers to his sons' request as a command (*exigitis...iubetis...*)
is in line with old-established conventions of preface-writing.

Precedents are to be found in Hellenistic technical writings:
Janson[3] cites Archimedes, *De sphaera et cylindro* II pr. *init.*,
ἐτέστειλάς μοι γράφαι τῶν προβλημάτων τὰς ἀποδείξεις, as a typical example. Among Roman writers the 'command' was absolutely
conventional, as one of the younger Pliny's anecdotes, about an
elegist called Passenus Paulus, shows:[4]

is cum recitaret, ita coepit dicere: 'Prisce, iubes...' ad hoc
Iavolenus Priscus (aderat enim ut Paulo amicissimus): 'ego vero
non iubeo.' cogita qui risus hominum, qui ioci. est omnino
Priscus dubiae sanitatis. (*Ep.* VI.15.1ff.)

Seneca represents his work on the declaimers as a collection
of rhetorical specimens for his sons to examine with a view to
imitation. Anticipating Quintilian in this,[5] he argues that it is
not a good idea to take a single writer, however excellent, as
one's only model:

Facitis autem, iuvenes mei, rem necessariam et utilem, quod non
contenti exemplis saeculi vestri prioris quoque vultis cognoscere:
primum quia, quo plura exempla inspecta sunt, plus in eloquentiam
proficitur. non est unus, quamvis praecipuus sit, imitandus, quia
numquam par fit imitator auctori. haec rei natura est: semper
citra veritatem est similitudo. (*Contr.* I pr. 6)

He does not, however, exclude examples of bad taste from his collection, arguing that there was something to be learnt from exam-
ining even these:

omnia autem genera corruptarum quoque sententiarum de industria
pono, quia facilius et quid imitandum et quid vitandum sit docemur
exemplo. (*Contr.* IX.2.27)

As it turned out, at least one of his sons did learn something
from his collection. Several studies have revealed close parallels between turns of phrase in the younger Seneca's works and
sententiae recorded in his father's anthology.[6] It is as well to
remember that the younger Seneca was not dependent solely on his
father's work for his knowledge of declamation, so that one can
never be sure that a declamatory-sounding phrase in his works is
not based on something remembered from his school-days, rather
than from his father's books. That he did take a considerable
interest in his father's work on declamation is proved, however,
by some obvious imitations of his father's literary criticism he
makes in the description of Fabianus' style in *Ep. mor.* 100.

Although he dedicates the anthology to his sons, the elder

Seneca makes it clear early on that he has reasons for writing it
other than their alleged demands for *sententiae*. It seems that he
was depressed by the lack of any comprehensive or accurate written
record of the work of the declaimers famous in his youth. The
situation had arisen where new declaimers could plagiarize the
sententiae of their predecessors with impunity, as few people
could remember who had originally composed them. This was a situation he aimed to rectify by the publication of his work:

sententias a disertissimis viris iactas facile in tanta hominum
desidia pro suis dicunt et sic sacerrimam eloquentiam, quam praestare non possunt violare non desinunt. eo libentius quod exigitis faciam et quaecumque a celeberrimis viris facunde dicta
teneo, ne ad quemquam privatim pertineant, populo dedicabo. ipsis
quoque multum praestaturus videor, quibus oblivio inminet, nisi
aliquid, quo memoria eorum producatur, posteris tradetur. fere
enim aut nulli commentarii maximorum declamatorum extant aut, quod
peius est, falsi. itaque ne aut ignoti sint aut aliter quam debent
noti, summa cum fide suum cuique reddam. (*Contr.* I pr. 10-11 W)

It is evident that all along he had a wider readership than his
immediate family in view.

The *Oratorum et rhetorum sententiae divisiones colores* is a
work of a curious design, unparalleled in extant ancient literature. From certain things Seneca says, it appears that its form
was suggested by the arrangement of a gladiatorial show, and it is
probably best to take him at his word and look no further for
possible sources of its inspiration.[7] The task Seneca had set
himself was two-fold: on the one hand, he wanted to give general
descriptions of the style and personal traits of the leading declaimers of his acquaintance, and on the other, he wanted to provide a detailed record of the treatment by as many declaimers as
possible of particular *controversiae* and *suasoriae*. How to combine these two aspects of his work in a unified scheme was a problem. The solution he adopted was this: he would introduce the
leading declaimers by means of pen-portraits, not all together at
the beginning of the work, but in a series of prefaces to separate
books, which would provide at intervals welcome diversions from
the series of detailed surveys of declamations which would make up
the bulk of the work. The first preface would be rather more diverse in content, and longer, than the others, and would serve as
an introduction to the whole, like the opening procession at the

Circus, to which he whimsically alludes at the end of the preface:
sed iam non sustineo diutius vos morari: scio, quam odiosa res
mihi sit Circensibus pompa (*Contr.* I pr. 24). This first preface
would have as a prominent feature a portrait of his great friend
Latro; later ones would serve to introduce one declaimer or several. He would keep his readers waiting right to the end for the
formal introduction of some of the celebrities quoted in his surveys. In doing this he was adopting a technique for holding an
audience's attention familiar to anyone in show-business:

quod munerarii solent facere, qui ad expectationem populi detin-
endam nova paria per omnes dies dispensant, ut sit, quod populum
et delectet et revocet, hoc ego facio: non semel omnes produco;
aliquid novi semper habeat libellus, ut non tantum sententiarum
vos sed etiam auctorum novitate sollicitet. acrior est cupiditas
ignota cognoscendi quam nota repetendi. hoc in histrionibus, in
gladiatoribus, in oratoribus, de quibus modo aliquid fama pro-
misit, in omnibus denique rebus videmus accidere: ad nova homines
concurrunt, ad nota non veniunt. (*Contr.* IV pr. 1)

After each of the ten prefaces came surveys illustrating the
way in which about eight *controversia* themes were treated by various declaimers, some of whom would have been formally introduced
in previous prefaces, others not. Particular prominence tends to
be given in these surveys to any declaimer introduced in the preface immediately before: thus Latro, introduced in the first preface, dominates book I, but is less frequently quoted as the work
progresses; Fabianus is repeatedly quoted in book II. At the end
of the preface Seneca usually makes an effort to point forward to
some feature in the surveys to follow: thus he tells us at the end
of the first preface that the first *controversia* in the collection
will be one which he remembers having heard Latro declaim as a
schoolboy (*Contr.* I pr. 24), and at the end of the second preface,
in which he describes Fabianus, he makes the promise, '*in hunc*
ergo libellum quaecumque ab illo dicta teneo conferam' (*Contr.* II
pr. 5).[8]

The surveys of *controversiae* all have the same basic plan,
the threefold structure of which, *sententiae*, *divisiones*, *colores*,
is alluded to in the title of the work. After quoting in full the
theme of the *controversia* and the laws under which it was to be
tried, Seneca first assembles, normally without comment,[9] samples,

very diverse in kind, extracted from a number of declaimers'
treatments of the theme. Presumably these samples comprise the
sententiae mentioned first in the title, as *divisiones* and *colores*
are dealt with in the second and third sections of the surveys
respectively. It cannot be, however, that any of these substan-
tial extracts taken as a whole could have been called a *sententia*,
for this word is not used in a technical sense by Latin writers on
rhetoric to mean anything much longer than a single sentence,[10]
except when they are referring to the delivery of verdicts - which
is *not* the function of by any means all the extracts in the first
section of the Senecan surveys[11] - or to a type of *progymnasma*
akin to the *chria* (Quint. I.9.3). Rather, Seneca's extracts give
us series of *sententiae*, and very little but *sententiae*, if we
give that name to all the types of sentence so called by Quintilian in VIII.5.1ff.[12] together with the descriptive sentences
which, it would appear from *Contr.* IX.2.24, Seneca was prepared to
describe loosely as *sententiae* as well.

   The logical sequence between the sentences in the samples is
sometimes extremely tortuous, and the question arises whether
Seneca is presenting continuous prose exactly as first delivered
by the declaimer, or whether he is stringing together particularly
notable sentences which did not follow one another so closely in
the original declamation. No certain answer can be given in every
case, but careful and detailed consideration has been given to the
matter by both Bornecque and Winterbottom, who in their editions
place dashes (Bornecque in both text and translation, Winterbottom
in the translation only) wherever there is discontinuity of
thought between adjacent *sententiae*. It does not seem as if
Seneca's usual practice was to string together single *sententiae*
which had borne no relation to one another in the declamation as
originally delivered. Usually at least two or three sentences in
succession do seem to be linked closely together, and perhaps some
of the jerky transitions marked by Bornecque and Winterbottom with
dashes ought to be attributed to the declaimers rather than to
Senecan excerpting. Occasionally, for example in the long extract
from Latro's declamation of *Contr.* II.7,[13] it seems clear that
Seneca was quoting continuous prose at considerable length.[14]

The *sententiae* recorded in the opening section of Seneca's surveys are of many different kinds. They were taken, one suspects, from all the different parts of a declamation, some from the *prooemium*, some from the *narratio*, and so on. Just occasionally it is indicated that he is quoting from the narrative of the case, thus: *CESTI PII narratio* (*Contr.* I.2.7), but usually only the name of the rhetorician is given (in the genitive). Normally most of the extracts treat the *thema* from whichever point of view, whether that of the prosecution or the defence, was most favoured by the declaimers, but often, though not invariably, the section devoted to *sententiae* ends with a few extracts from treatments of the less popular side of the case under the heading, *pars altera*.

After the *sententiae* comes a section devoted to *divisio*. Here we are given analyses of the scheme of argument used by a few of the leading *rhetores*, notably Latro, with whose perceptiveness in the detecting of basic issues Seneca wished to impress us (*Contr.* I pr. 20f.). He outlines the main questions at issue, and the subsidiary ones arising from them with admirable clarity, but very concisely, using a very few standard terms and phrases to guide the reader, too few for the liking of H. Bardon,[15] a censorious critic of the elder Seneca's style, vocabulary and critical techniques. Seneca makes it clear from the outset that the scope of the sections on *divisio* in his surveys is to be strictly limited: he will state the main questions raised by each declaimer, but it will be no part of his plan to give any detailed account of the way in which separate lines of argument were developed, '*nec his argumenta subtexam, ne et modum excedam et propositum*', since, so he alleges, his sons would not be interested (*Contr.* I pr. 22). He nevertheless does sometimes quote a few sentences of argumentation to show how some of the basic questions were treated.

It is in the third and final section of the surveys that we find the only extensive passages of literary criticism outside the prefaces. In the surveys of *controversiae* this section begins with consideration of the *colores* used by each declaimer. *Color* was a technical term meaning the complexion which one gave to the past actions of the litigants in a *controversia*.[16] For, as long

as he did not actually contradict the given facts of the case, the
declaimer was free to give whatever damning, or mitigating, interpretation he chose, to actions described in the *thema*. Seneca
does not, however, restrict himself to the discussion of *colores*
in the closing section of his surveys. He usually digresses into
other, often more interesting, topics. There is much comparative
criticism. Seneca shows a great interest in the question who imitated whose *sententia*, and whether the imitation was an improve-
ment on, or a frigid over-working of, the original idea. Usually
he is concerned with imitations by one rhetorician of another, but
sometimes he also enlightens us about the debt owed by certain
declaimers to the poets, and by certain poets to the rhetoricians
(e.g. *Contr*. II.2.8; *Suas*. 3.5). Occasionally he turns aside from
the subject of declamation altogether and recalls discussions of
modern poetry in which some of the leading critics and patrons of
Augustan Rome took part (e.g. *Contr*. VII.1.27; *Suas*. 1.12), or
momentarily lets his interest in historiography come to the fore,
as in *Suas*. 6.14-25, where he compares recent historians' accounts
of the death of Cicero. Sometimes in this section too, Seneca
feels prompted, on mentioning some declaimer's name, to sketch his
character or to tell some illuminating anecdote about him.

        Usually at the very end of the section, but sometimes earlier
in it too (e.g. *Contr*. IX.1.12ff.; X.5.19ff.), we find a few *sententiae* by Greek declaimers quoted, sometimes set out for comparison with Latin *sententiae* on similar themes. The comparison of
Greek with Latin *sententiae* may follow fairly naturally from what
has come before, but quite often the Greek examples seem almost to
be thrown in as an afterthought. (The nearest parallel for this
rather strange arrangement comes in Valerius Maximus' presentation
of history for rhetoricians, the *Facta et dicta memorabilia*, where
in each section a few foreign *exempla* are added after the more
numerous Roman ones.) The medieval scribes made valiant attempts
to cope with the unfamiliar Greek script where Seneca required it,
but sometimes gave up the unequal struggle and left the names of
Greek declaimers without their *sententiae*. Seneca, then, allotted
more space to Greek declaimers than is now apparent. But it is
improbable that he originally devoted as much attention to them as

to their Latin counterparts. The survey of *Contr*. X.5, which
seems to be complete, and is unusually rich in Greek *sententiae*,
contains no Greek quotation more than thirteen words long. We
ought perhaps to question whether Seneca relegated as many Greek
sententiae right to the end of the surveys as we find there now in
our texts. The surveys often end with what seems like a rag-bag
of *sententiae*, sometimes probably consisting of displaced addenda,
miscellaneous sentences which some scribe, correcting his manuscript, noted as omitted earlier in the survey. However, it is
usually rather difficult to see where those Greek *sententiae* left
till last could have been placed earlier, and in *Contr*. I.5.9, if
the text is to make good sense, a transposition is required which
actually restores some Greek *sententiae* to the end of the survey.[17]*

   As well as dealing with *controversiae* in ten books, Seneca
compiled surveys of *suasoriae*. Seven of these are extant, and
more, it seems, were part of Seneca's plan, for in *Contr*. II.4.8
he promises an account of a *suasoria* not among those we have. It
is uncertain, though, whether any more surveys of *suasoriae* than
are now extant were actually written or published. The colophon
which follows the *suasoriae* in some manuscripts, *lannei senecae*
oratorum et reto(retho V)rum sententiae divisiones colores suas-
oriarum liber primus (I B) explicit incipit liber secundus (II
<feliciter> B), to give the version of BV, cannot be regarded as
evidence for a second book of *suasoriae*.[18] The order and number-
ing of the books in the manuscripts which preserve the fuller version of the text of Seneca's collection, are as follows:

   Suasoriae = *liber* I *suasoriarum*
   Contr. I = *liber* II
   Contr. II = *liber* III
   Contr. VII= *liber* IV
   Contr. IX = *liber* V
   Contr. X = *liber* VI.

The *liber secundus* promised in the colophon to the *suasoriae* in
these manuscripts is none other, then, than the first book of
controversiae, and *suasoriarum* is to be taken as a genitive of
definition, not as a partitive genitive.

   One question which seems never to be considered seriously,

but ought to be, though it is probably unanswerable, is where in
the plan of the whole work Seneca intended the surveys of *suasoriae* to fit. The manuscripts which give them, place them, as we
have seen, before the *controversiae*; modern editors print them
after *Contr.* X. Neither position seems very satisfactory. The
problem is that the preface to *Contr.* I is unquestionably intended
to act as an introduction to the whole collection, and the preface
of book X seems just as obviously intended to draw the work towards its close. In the first preface Seneca has expressed de-
light at the opportunity which his sons' request has given him, to
relive happier years, *redire in antiqua studia melioresque ad
annos respicere* (*Contr.* I pr. 1), and has accepted the task with
the words: *fiat quod vultis: mittatur senex in scholas* (*Contr.* I
pr. 4). In the tenth preface he harks back to his initial enthusiasm, but now professes to be weary of his task:

Quod ultra mihi molesti sitis, non est: interrogate, si qua vultis, et sinite me ab istis iuvenilibus studiis ad senectutem meam
reverti. fatebor vobis, iam res taedio est. primo libenter ad-
silui velut optimam vitae meae partem mihi reducturus: deinde iam
me pudet, tamquam diu non seriam rem agam. hoc habent scholasticorum studia: leviter tacta delectant, contrectata et propius ad-
mota fastidio sunt. sinite ergo me semel exhaurire memoriam meam
et dimittite vel adactum iureiurando, quo adfirmem dixisse me quae
scivi quaeque audivi quaeque ad hanc rem pertinere iudicavi.
(*Contr.* X pr. 1)

Though one may be sure that this passage is packed with literary
convention, and it seems quite possible that Seneca, far from
being weary of declamation, went indefatigably on, after writing
book X of the *controversiae*, to compile his surveys of *suasoriae*,[19]
it seems inconceivable that book X, prefaced as it was by all
these protestations of weariness and reminiscences of *Contr.* I pr.
1ff., was not intended to be the final book of the collection. On
the other hand, the character of the first preface, and Seneca's
promise in *Contr.* II.4.8 of a survey of the *suasoria* about Theodotus '*cum ad suasorias venero*', make it clear that the manuscripts
are wrong in placing the *liber suasoriarum* before the *controversiae*.

Some radically different speculation is required, and one
line to consider is this. Perhaps Seneca's original plan was that
each preface should serve as an introduction to surveys of both

controversiae and *suasoriae*. (The *controversiae* would have to
come first, for, as we have seen, Seneca leads into them at the
end of the prefaces.) However, his editors failed to recognize
his intention, perhaps because he had left writing the surveys of
suasoriae till last, and had died without completing them or making it clear where in the scheme of the whole work they were to
go. I suggest this because our extant '*liber suasoriarum*' looks
suspiciously like two fragments wrongly linked together.

A notable feature of *Suas.* 2, 3 and 4 is that they contain a
series of curiously laboured reminiscences of Seneca's description
of Arellius Fuscus in the second preface (*Suas.* 2.10, 23; 3.7; 4.5
cf. *Contr.* II pr. 1). *Suas.* 1 also contains the only extant quotation in the collection outside the second book of *Controversiae*
from a declamation by Fabianus, of whom Seneca has said at the end
of the second preface, *in hunc ergo libellum quaecumque ab illo
dicta teneo conferam* (*Contr.* II pr. 5). Can it be, then, that the
first five *suasoriae* – five, because the reference to Fuscus in
Suas. 4.5 points forward to the fifth *suasoria* – were originally
intended to follow the *controversiae* of book II and share the same
preface? The main objections to such a theory are that the *suasoria* on Theodotus, promised in *Contr.* II.4.8, is not to be found,
and that the surveys we have contain no quotations from *suasoriae*
declaimed by Ovid in his youth, which one might have expected in
view of Seneca's words in *Contr.* II.2.12: *declamabat autem Naso
raro controversias et non nisi ethicas; libentius dicebat suasorias*. The only plausible ways to counter both these objections
are to surmise either that some other *suasoria*-surveys preceded
our *Suas.* 1 in the hypothetical continuation of book II, or that
Seneca turned to the *suasoriae* he intended to add to book II (our
Suas. 1-5) considerably later than the *controversiae* in it; that
he only re-read the preface of the book before setting to work on
the *suasoriae*, and had forgotten the promise given in *Contr.*
II.4.8 and the expectations which might be aroused by his remarks
in *Contr.* II.2.12.

Suasoriae 6 and 7 stand rather apart from the rest: Fuscus
does not feature nearly so prominently in them. These two long
surveys would follow happily after the *controversiae* of book IV:

Haterius, introduced in the fourth preface, is given the prominent
first position in both surveys; Pollio, who is contrasted with
Haterius in *Contr.* IV pr. 2ff. also figures conspicuously in the
historiographical digression of *Suas.* 6 (14f., 24f.). Both *suasoriae* concern the death of Cicero, and would follow easily after
the last *controversia* of book IV, which was also about a victim
of the proscriptions:

Bello civili patronus victus et proscriptus ad libertum confugit.
receptus est ab eo et rogatus, ut operas remitteret. remisit con-
signatione facta. restitutus indicit operas. contradicit.
(*Contr.* IV.8 *thema*)

The surveys of *suasoriae* follow much the same plan as those
of *controversiae*: *sententiae* are followed by *divisiones*. The only
difference is that, as *colores* are a feature peculiar to judicial
rhetoric and are therefore not found in *suasoriae*, the surveys end
with a section which is even more of a mixed bag than usual, and
includes unusually long and intriguing digressions.

One of the most vexed questions about the elder Seneca is how
far he relied on his memory when compiling his anthology. The
question arises because, in the section of the first preface
where, in accordance with a well-known convention of prefatory
writing, he expresses doubts about his ability to undertake the
projected work,[20] he discourses at length about his memory, once
miraculously tenacious, but now weakened by old age. The implication is that it is on this faculty that he is expecting to have
to rely:

memoria est res ex omnibus animi partibus maxime delicata et
fragilis, in quam primam senectus incurrit. hanc aliquando <adeo>
in me floruisse, ut non tantum ad usum sufficeret sed in miraculum
usque procederet, non nego... [Remarkable examples follow]
...nunc et aetate quassata et longa desidia, quae iuvenilem quoque
animum dissolvit, eo perducta est ut, etiamsi potest aliquid praestare, non possit promittere. diu ab illa nihil repetivi: nunc
quia iubetis quid possit experiar et illam omni cura scrutabor.
ex parte enim bene spero: nam quaecumque apud illam aut puer aut
iuvenis deposui, quasi recentia aut modo audita sine cunctatione
profert; at si qua illi intra proximos annos commisi, sic perdidit
et amisit ut, etiamsi saepius ingerantur, totiens tamen tamquam
nova audiam... controversiarum sententias fortasse pluribus locis
ponam in una declamatione dictas, non enim <semper> dum quaero
aliquid invenio, sed saepe quod quaerenti non comparuit aliud
agenti praesto est... (*Contr.* I pr. 2-5 W)

Many scholars have been quite willing to countenance the idea that

Seneca's only source, or at least his main source, was his memory, and they have a number of good reasons for doing so. The examples Seneca gives of the miraculous memory of his youth - his ability to recall two thousand separate names in the correct sequence, or over two hundred isolated lines of poetry in reverse order - are impressive, and we must not be over-sceptical about his claims, for a glance at any encyclopaedia's entry on memory or mnemonics will convince one that the human memory is capable of almost anything, especially when trained in a discipline in which memorizing is regarded as a necessity or a virtue. And doubtless many a specialist in geriatrics would attest that Seneca's account of his ability to recall things heard in youth better than those of more recent years, is psychologically convincing. Boissier in his article, 'Les écoles de déclamation à Rome', and Bonner in *Roman declamation*, show themselves firm believers in Seneca's memory,[21] and Winterbottom has recently reaffirmed their view, though he refers us in a footnote to Bornecque for evidence that Seneca 'certainly had some written sources'.[22]

Bornecque expresses scepticism about Seneca's memory in no uncertain terms: '*enfin sa memoire, si extraordinaire fût-elle, ne pouvait suffire à un pareil effort*',[23] and proceeds to list a number of written sources which Seneca mentions and could have used. Other doubters have included G. L. Hendrickson[24] and O. Immisch,[25] who seem to have arrived independently at the view that it is naïve to regard Seneca's picture of himself racking his brains for memories of declamations long ago as anything but a preface-writer's convention taken over from the tradition followed by writers of dialogues. Their view has been elaborated in a recent American thesis, C. W. Lockyer's 'The fiction of memory and the use of written sources: convention and practice in Seneca the Elder and other authors',[26] a careful piece of work in which, however, the evidence as to Seneca's possible use of written sources is pressed much further than it will go.

Here is a dispute that will never be settled conclusively. We have seen plenty of evidence that Seneca was fully conscious of prefatory conventions. In the vexed passage about his memory he is adopting at least one such. To express misgivings about one's

capacity to undertake the task at hand had been standard practice
among the Attic orators, and had become enshrined in the Greco-
Roman theory about *prooemia*: *benevolentia...comparatur...si quae
incommoda acciderint aut quae instent difficultates, proferemus...*,
as Cicero puts it (*De inv.* I.16.22). So it is not unreasonable to
be somewhat sceptical about the extent of Seneca's powers of recollection, when one considers that far-fetched claims about reliance
on memory were commonplace among writers of dialogues and related
types of literature. It is true that Seneca writes about his
memory at surprising length, which makes one less disposed to regard the passage as a mere prefatory cliché than if he had dismissed the matter briefly, but we should bear in mind that he was
capable of alluding to the fiction of his sons' frivolous tastes
more than once in his work. Note too that even some of the observations in *Contr.* I pr. 2-5 which look most like the fruit of
Seneca's own experiences may in fact have been traditional in
mnemonic theory. We should compare Quintilian's remarks in
XI.2.6f. on the vagaries of memory:

quid? non haec varietas mira est, excidere proxima, vetera in-
haerere? hesternorum inmemores acta pueritiae recordari? quid
quod quaedam requisita se occultant et eadem forte succurrunt?
nec manet semper memoria sed aliquando etiam redit?

Two questions arise, if we adopt a sceptical view of Seneca's
claims about his memory, and it is important to distinguish between them. First, did he make use of written records of the
declaimers' work published by his contemporaries? Secondly, did
he draw on private written records which he had collected himself?

Seneca did not pretend that there was no information about
the declaimers active in his life-time available to him except
that which was stored in his head: in *Contr.* I pr. 11 he openly
recognizes the existence of various published works in his field
of interest. However, he is scathingly critical of them. The
value of his work, as he sees it, will be that, by drawing on his
private store of information, he will be able to supplement and
correct the inadequate, and often misleading, data contained in
these books, where they relate to the declaimers who had been
known to him personally.

It ought therefore to come as no surprise to find Seneca

occasionally making passing references to written records, and to
find that these references are sometimes accompanied by hostile
criticism. In *Contr.* X pr. 12, for instance, he assigns a declamation, falsely ascribed to Latro, to its true author: *Capitonem,
cuius declamatio est de Popillio, quae misero Latroni subicitur*,
and in *Contr.* I.3.11 he finds a stupid *color* used by Iunius Otho
all the more intolerable because the man had written books about
colores.

The extent to which Seneca actually *used* such sources is
tantalizingly unclear. Take, for example, one of the most
interesting instances discussed by Lockyer:[27]

Montanus Votienus Marcellum Marcium, amicum suum, cuius frequenter
mentionem in scriptis suis facit tamquam hominis diserti, aiebat
hanc dixisse sententiam... (*Contr.* IX.6.18)

Lockyer jumps to the conclusion that 'Here Seneca is drawing on a
written work which records the sayings of someone else', and notes
also, on *aiebat*, 'The word itself suggests reporting by word of
mouth, although here written sources are being used.' Now, there
is absolutely nothing here to prove that Seneca took the *sententia*
in question from a book by Montanus, and we are free to take him
at his word and believe that he had heard Montanus orally ascrib-
ing it to his friend. On the other hand, Lockyer's instinct could
very well be right.

Seneca's explicit references to contemporary works on declamation are very brief and scattered. They are not of a kind which
would lead one to assume that he kept the works in question by his
side as he wrote. Indeed, even if one is sceptical about Seneca's
memory, it is unnatural to suppose that he went through the cum-
brous process of looking up references in a wide selection of
papyrus rolls every time he wished to refer to a modern authority.

This brings us to the other question: whether Seneca's work
could have been based on some private written record he had kept
of declamations heard throughout his long life. I do not find
this hypothesis improbable. Quintilian refers to a practice,
current among schoolboys of his time, of collecting noteworthy
extracts from other people's declamations: *commentariis puerorum
in quos ea quae aliis declamantibus laudata sunt regerunt*

(II.11.7). It is not inconceivable that an adult enthusiast might
continue to keep his collection up to date. We may have a tell-
tale sign that Seneca's anthology is an edited version of such
commentarii, in his occasional remark, in lieu of criticism, that
such and such *sententia* 'was praised': *hoc loco dixit Latro rem
valde laudatam* (*Contr.* VII.1.18); *hoc loco dixit Gallio illam
sententiam, quae valde excepta est* (*Contr.* X.2.10). For the keeping of collections of literary extracts on a very large scale by
adults there is clear evidence in the younger Pliny's description
of his uncle's private notes:

electorumque commentarios centum sexaginta mihi reliquit, opistho-
graphos quidem et minutissimis scriptos; qua ratione multiplicatur
hic numerus. (*Ep.* III.5.17)

The elder Pliny in the preface to his *Naturalis historia* takes
great pride in the number of obscure sources he has perused, but
it does not occur to him to write about the menial processes of
excerpting and sorting his material which he must have gone
through before producing the final version of his work, except in
so far as these processes are implied in the word *lectione* (*NH*
pr. 17). It may well have been the case that considerations of
literary dignity, the idea that it would be unthinkable to confess
in an artistic preface to the use of a private cache of declamatory extracts - *res omnium sordidissimae*, lacking even the
distinction of having originated in recondite writings - may have
been sufficient to persuade Seneca the Elder to throw a smoke-
screen around his methods in the shape of an elaborate disquisition on his memory. Unwillingness to admit to the usefulness of
writing as an aid to the memory was a time-honoured theme in
ancient literature; it is well summed up by the Egyptian myth of
Theuth, discoverer of writing, related by Plato in *Phaedrus* 274c-
275b.[28] As Lockyer's dissertation has made clear, claims to have
remembered vast quantities of material are commonplace in antiquity, and, though it is fair to believe that people then took
more pains to train their memories and use them than we do, no one
will be credulous enough to believe, for instance, Athenaeus when
he claims to be reporting in the *Deipnosophists* the conversations
at a banquet at which he was personally present[29] (*Deip.* I.2a).

Athenaeus' epitomator recognizes the fact of the matter when he
says of Athenaeus' claim to have been present: δραματουργεῖ δὲ τὸν
διάλογον ὁ Ἀθηναῖος ζήλῳ Πλατωνικῷ (*Deip.* I.1f.). Seneca's
disquisition in *Contr.* I pr. 2-5, though surely containing some
genuine personal reminiscences, has to be viewed against the background of the old Platonic tradition of hostility towards the
written word.

More important than the question of what written sources, if
any, the elder Seneca used, is the question whether the samples of
eloquence he attributes to the various declaimers are in fact
accurate records of the styles of these individuals. Bornecque,
citing the work of M. Sander and H. T. Karsten, and adducing some
additional arguments of his own, assures us that they are.[30]
Unfortunately, though his conclusion is unlikely to be wrong, we
find that he arrived at it on the basis of untrustworthy and inadequate data. The reader will scarcely need to have it pointed
out that the parallel he notes between the versions of a *sententia*
by Gallio given by Seneca in *Contr.* II.3.6 and Quintilian in
IX.2.91 is no evidence at all for Seneca's reliability: modern
editors of Seneca have drawn on Quintilian's version, and editors
of Quintilian on Seneca's, to reconstruct the text, and even then
they cannot make the ancient authorities agree over which past
tense Gallio used, *eras* or *fuisti*. It is less obvious that
Bornecque's discussion of the *clausulae* used by Seneca and the
declaimers is riddled with errors, and that very little of the
work of Sander and Karsten, to which he refers, is of any relevance to the question of the authenticity of the declamatory
fragments.

Bornecque claims to be able to show that different declaimers
varied in the extent to which they kept to the canonical rhythms
for sentence-endings, and that they differed again from Seneca,
who was more negligent in this respect than any of them. But if
we look closely, for example, at Bornecque's selection of alleged
irregular *clausulae* from the fragments of Votienus Montanus' declamations, we find that they include some examples from the analysis of his *divisio* in *Contr.* IX.2 (not X.2, as Bornecque's
printers will have us believe), for which Seneca is responsible,

not Montanus; in one of the cases cited Seneca is actually quoting
Montanus in indirect speech (*Contr*. IX.2.18: *responsurum*).
Bornecque also assumes that the rhythm ————∪∪ is objectionable,
whereas in fact it was one much favoured by Cicero. De Groot
gives the figures: Cicero's speeches - 9.7%; 'normal' - 5.4%.[31]

Here is a subject which requires complete re-examination - a
difficult undertaking, for when an analyst of prose-rhythm tackles
the Latin of Seneca's declaimers he is faced, not only with the
usual hazards of his occupation,[32] but with the difficulty of
deciding just how many of the paratactic *cola* and *commata* in which
their extracts abound end with sufficiently strong breaks in the
sense to warrant strong *clausula* rhythms. An element of subjec-
tivity inevitably intrudes. It is with some hesitation therefore
that I offer tentatively a few conclusions derived from study of
samples, selected and analysed as honestly as lay within my capa-
bilities, of 100 *clausulae* each from Seneca (prefaces), Porcius
Latro and Arellius Fuscus.[33]

Most of the *clausula* rhythms found in each of these samples
either belong to five types strongly favoured by Cicero (however
un-Ciceronian in effect the Silver Latin versions may be owing to
the preponderance of short words at the cadence), or may be regarded as resolutions of these types, viz.:

    −∪−−∪
    −∪−∪
    −∪−−∪∪
    −∪−∪∪
    ————∪∪

The figures are as follows: Seneca - 72% (inclusive of 23% resolutions); Latro - 72% (17% resolutions); Fuscus - 80% (15% resolutions).

However, of the eight *clausula* rhythms which occur five or
more times in any one of the samples, two are of types generally
avoided by Cicero,[34] viz.:

    −−−∪
    −−∪∪∪

Occurrences (%)

	Seneca	Latro	Fuscus	Cicero (speeches)	'Normal'
—◡——◡	16	12	13	16.2	7.4
———◡	16	13	6	6.4	23.5
—◡—◡	12	11	18	25.3	17.2
—◡——◡◡	10	13	15	8.3	2.9
—◡—◡◡◡	10	3	4	2.8	2.2
——◡◡◡	7	4	2	1.8	6.2
—◡—◡◡	6	13	12	4.9	4.4
————◡◡	5	6	7	9.7	5.4

Several points emerge from these provisional findings which suggest that *clausula* study on a larger scale might prove valuable.[35] It would be interesting if Fuscus proved to be significantly fonder throughout of the unresolved standard *clausulae* than Seneca in his prefaces; also if, unlike Seneca and Latro, he consistently followed Cicero in abjuring the double spondee and the rhythm ——◡◡◡. One might have predicted that the friends Seneca and Latro would agree to a large extent in their rhythmic preferences: the apparent discrepancy in their attitude towards the rhythms —◡—◡◡, —◡—◡◡◡ and ——◡◡◡ would seem all the more significant if it were sustained consistently throughout a larger sample. It does look very much as if we are dealing with three distinct stylists.

Bornecque[36] was over-generous in his estimate of the work of M. Sander and H. T. Karsten on the language of Seneca the Elder and the declaimers. Sander's *Sprachgebrauch des Rhetors Annaeus Seneca*,[37] though obviously the product of enormous labours, gives us little help in deciding whether or not the declamatory extracts are authentic, as no clear distinction is made in his lists of usages between the Latin of Seneca and that of the men quoted by him. The one observation by Sander on the question of authenticity which Bornecque refers to, namely that Latro alone uses the term *idcirco* whereas the others use *ob hoc*, *ob illud* etc., appears similarly in isolation in the introduction of *Sprachgebrauch* I.[38] We are referred back for further examples to Sander's earlier dissertation, *Quaestiones in Senecam Rhetorem syntacticae*

(Greifswald, 1872), a work which Bornecque does not appear to have
used. As copies of this dissertation are rare, and the question
of the authenticity of the fragments is treated less cursorily in
it than elsewhere, though still not at all adequately, it seems
worth quoting Sander's observations in full, only bringing the
system of reference up to date:[39]

...non pauca vocabula sunt, quae Seneca singulos rhetores pro-
nuntiantes faciat, a quibus tamen ipse abhorreat, ipse rursus
saepius talibus vocibus utitur quas rhetores aliis eiusdem
notionis verbis circumscribunt. utriusque rei ex permultis
exemplis nonnulla eligam. Latro enim locutionibus *naturale est ut*
(*Contr.* VII.2.8), *facile est ut* (*Contr.* IX.2.3), *idcirco* (*Contr.*
II.7.8) utitur, quae apud Senecam ipsum non inveniuntur.[40] item
Asinius Pollio duobus locis *namque* (*Suas.* 6.24), *quando* vi causali
(*ibid.*), item Albucius Silus *expecto ut* (*Contr.* VII.4.1), *mereo ut*
(*Contr.* VII.8.1) scribit; item Papirius Fabianus *enimvero* (*Contr.*
II.1.11); Arellius Fuscus *mos est ut* (*Contr.* I.5.8), *aequum est ut*
(*Contr.* IX.3.1);[41] Cestius Pius (?) *licet ut* (*Contr.* IX.4.10);[42]
Pompeius Silo *iubeo ut* (*Contr.* I.2.15);[43] Cremutius Cordus *aliter
ac* (*Suas.* 6.19);[44] Titus Livius *ut* cum participio futuri con-
iunctum (*ibid.* 17), aliaque multa quae Seneca ipse evitavit. e
contrario Seneca (*Contr.* I pr. 15f.) *ideoque* locutione utitur,
ceteri rhetores constanter *et ideo*; *lex est ut* (*Contr.* I pr. 7);[45]
spero ut (*Contr.* IX.2.18); *iam vero* (*Contr.* I pr. 17; III pr. 4).

Unfortunately the value of these observations, promising though
they may seem, is limited. Presumably this summary lists the
variations of usage which Sander found most significant '*ex permultis exemplis*', but it is marred by inaccuracies: the words in
Contr. I.2.15, *iubemur ut*, are surely to be attributed to Seneca,
not Pompeius Silo; the attribution of the phrase *speramus ut* in
Contr. IX.2.18 to Seneca is probable but uncertain; the attribution of *licere...ut* in *Contr.* IX.4.10 to Cestius, which he marks
as doubtful, is indeed pure guess-work, and Cestius is found elsewhere (*Suas.* 2.6) using *licere* + infin.; it also needs pointing
out that if Seneca is quoting Latro verbatim in *Contr.* I.1.13,
II.6.5 and VII.6.13, Latro used *ob hoc* and *ob id* in his *divisiones*.
Moreover, the expressions cited by Sander as peculiar to particular stylists in Seneca's anthology are all very rare ones; where
one example of a usage is cited it is probably the only example
Sander could find; at any rate, when attempting to check his
claims, I found that one could not expect to find in a single
declamation-survey more than one of the abnormal usages he refers

to in *Quaestiones* 5f. It does not seem that we have a large
enough sample of the writing of Seneca the Elder to be sure that
he would always have avoided all the expressions which Sander
reckons to have been peculiar to the declaimers quoted by him.

H. T. Karsten makes some attempt in his *Elocutio rhetorica
qualis invenitur in Annaei Senecae Suasoriis et Controversiis*[46]
to distinguish between the usage of Seneca and the various declaimers when listing abnormal expressions, but only in the case
of very rare ones; in the case of commoner abnormalities, the
distribution of which might be of much interest to us, he gives us
just book and section references and expects us to be content with
the information (given after a list of abbreviations of rhetoricians' names in capital letters) that '*verba ac nomina, quibus
litteras maiusculas non adscripsi, pleraque ab ipso Seneca nonnulla a compluribus rhetoribus usurpata sunt.*'[47] Even in the case
of great rarities he sometimes lapses from his good intentions,
omitting to tell us, for instance, that the phrase *supplex
accadens genibus* in *Suas.* 6.3 for which he found no parallel, was
Latro's. His introductory observations on linguistic differences
between the declaimers are quite untrustworthy – note in particular that he is quite wrong when he suggests that Latro used the
word *alioquin* in a sense peculiar to himself[48] – and his method of
listing rarities, like Sander's, seems calculated to exhaust the
patience of the best-intentioned reader. The fundamental trouble
with the approach of these two scholars is that they never make it
clear to what extent their presentation of material is selective.
What is needed before any serious work on the language of the declaimers can be done is nothing short of a complete *index verborum*
to Seneca the Elder, in which usages of Seneca himself are clearly
distinguished from those attributed to the various declaimers and
again from those found in passages where Seneca appears to be
reporting the words of critics or declaimers either obliquely or
verbatim. Until such a work exists there seems little hope of
pin-pointing subtle differences between the usages of the various
declaimers in a way which will convince the sceptical reader that
Seneca recorded their words faithfully.[49]

There is certainly some general correlation between the

styles of the declaimers as they are described by Seneca in his
prefaces and the styles found in the extracts attributed to them.
Particularly striking in the extracts are certain peculiarities of
the rhetorician Arellius Fuscus and his independent-minded pupil
Fabianus to which Seneca refers in the second preface.[50] However,
that there is such a correlation is not necessarily proof of the
complete authenticity of the fragments: a fraudulent or imprecise
anthologist would have been certain to make the extracts he presented display the stylistic qualities he had mentioned when
criticizing the writers to whom they were attributed. In view of
this, it seems worth drawing attention to two correspondences of a
type which it is hard to account for if Seneca has not given us
authentic fragments. In *Contr*. VII pr. 4f. Seneca mentions that
Albucius used sometimes to imitate Fabianus and Hermagoras. It is
interesting to find that parallels between Albucius' and Fabianus'
sententiae occur, not in the *controversiae* which one imagines
Seneca treated while the seventh preface was still fresh in his
mind, but in the first *Suasoria* (*Suas*. 1.3, 9-10), and that we
have to wait until *Contr*. X.1 for the one clear parallel between
Albucius and Hermagoras (*Contr*. X.1.1, 15).[51]

To the general rule that the declamatory extracts confirm
well enough what Seneca the Elder says in his prefaces about the
men to whom they are attributed, there appears, however, to be one
glaring exception. The case of Votienus Montanus obliges us to
question our most fundamental assumptions about the soundness of
the elder Seneca's methods. In *Contr*. IX pr. 1 we read: *Montanus
Votienus adeo numquam ostentationis declamavit causa ut ne
exercitationis quidem declamaverit*. Seneca then reports how, when
he asked him why he took this line (*rationem quaerenti mihi*), he
answered with an uncompromising tirade against the pretensions of
the schools of rhetoric (§1-5). Yet in *Contr*. VII.5.12 we are
told that Votienus Montanus was *toto animo scholasticus*, and
furthermore, books IX and X of the *Controversiae* contain twenty-
two references to his treatment of declamations.[52]

No attempt yet made to account for this contradiction is at
all convincing. O. Gruppe,[53] in an attempt to eliminate the
phrase *toto animo scholasticus* from *Contr*. VII.5.12, had recourse

to the wildest of conjecture, and even if one accepted his theory
one would still have to explain away the presence of declamatory
extracts attributed to Montanus in *Contr.* IX and X. R. Hess[54] and
Bornecque[55] looked for a third reason, apart from the two he is
said in *Contr.* IX pr. 1 to have rejected, why Montanus might have
treated declamatory themes. The explanation of Hess that he did
not deliver full declamations but frequented the schools *ut
disputaret*[56] has surely to be discounted in view of *Contr.* IX.4.14:
Montanus partem accusatoris declamavit. Bornecque's suggestion,
'*il déclama non par ostentation ou pour s'exercer, mais vrai-
semblablement pour faire comme tout le monde*', fails to take into
account the fact that *ostentatio* and *exercitatio* mark opposite
poles in the range of possible reasons for declaiming, and that
the effect of Seneca's use of polar expression in the crucial
sentence is to lead the unbiased reader to conclude that Montanus
did not declaim at all. The hypothesis advanced by W. Hoffa[57]
that *illud 'Montanus Votienus adeo numquam ostentationis declamavit
causa, ut ne exercitationis quidem declamaverit' magis ad verba
Votieni quam ad facta spectat, ut ipsius Votieni verba hoc loco
tamquam suo ore reddere Senecam censeamus*, and that the origin of
Seneca's statement in *Contr.* IX pr. 1 lay in a claim, '*ego non
declamo*' made by Montanus himself, seems totally implausible,
though it points the way towards an explanation of the mystery
which is perhaps not so incredible. This is that in the ninth
preface Seneca derived his material not, as he suggests, from an
actual conversation he had once had with Montanus, but from one of
the *scripta* to which he refers in *Contr.* IX.6.18,[58] perhaps a
dialogue in which Montanus, though himself *toto animo scholasticus*,
presented an interlocutor who declared that he never declaimed,
even for the most austere of educational motives, and proceeded to
inveigh against the schools in the words reported by Seneca in
Contr. IX pr. 1-5. Such an explanation does not do much credit to
poor Seneca, and one may hope it is not the right one. An
alternative perhaps worth considering is that the attribution to
Votienus Montanus of a hard line against the schools is the result
of textual corruption in *Contr.* IX pr. 1, most likely arising from
an ambiguous abbreviation in Seneca's original manuscript or an

early copy of it. One would expect the man introduced in the
ninth preface to have been quoted perhaps elsewhere by the elder
Seneca as a critic, but never as a declaimer. Very few people
mentioned by him come into this category, but interestingly enough
they include two whose names, if abbreviated, might well have been
confused with that of Votienus Montanus, namely, Valerius Messala,
who shared his initials, and the poet Iulius Montanus.[59]*

The question whether Seneca's quotations give us authentic
records of the declaimer's words must remain unanswered at least
until there exists a full *index verborum* to the work, and the
prose rhythm of Seneca and the men quoted by him has been studied
more thoroughly. Nevertheless, it is surely justifiable to adopt
the working hypothesis that, before the text became corrupt in the
course of transmission, the extracts were accurate. One fails to
see why Seneca the Elder, if he did not possess a reliable record,
memorized or written, of the actual words of the multitudinous
declaimers he quotes, would have undertaken the labour of compiling the type of anthology which he has given us. It seems
about as plausible that he should have set out to forge thousands
of declamatory fragments as that Athenaeus, for instance, should
have forged all his quotations from Greek comedy. If the elder
Seneca had been content with partially accurate remembrances, or
had a taste for forgery, why did he not, for example, take on the
much easier task of passing off as Latro's some complete declamatory compositions of his own, with or without a Latronian core?
It will be assumed in my discussion of declamatory styles that
Seneca recorded the words of the declaimers faithfully, though
textual corruption has inevitably diminished the reliability of
his record.

The chief glories of Seneca's criticism are the pen-portraits,
mainly to be found in the prefaces. These remarkable psychological and critical descriptions have been more often imitated than
discussed. Fine imitations of his manner were produced in this
country particularly in the seventeenth century, when English
prose had an incisiveness and luminosity strangely akin to
Seneca's, and hard to recapture now. Following the example of
Montaigne who, for instance in his essay *Du parler prompt ou
tardif*, had looked to the elder Seneca for reflections from which
morals could be drawn –

On recite de Severus Cassius, qu'il disoit mieux sans y avoir
pensé; qu'il devoit plus à la fortune qu'à sa diligence; qu'il luy
venoit à profit d'estre troublé en parlant, et que ses adversaires
craignoyent de le picquer, de peur que la colere ne luy fit re-
doubler son eloquence. (Cf. *Contr*. III pr. 6)[1] –

English essayists took to adapting Seneca's anecdotes. Here is
Abraham Cowley imitating *Suas*. 2.17 in his essay *On greatness*:

...he would eat nothing but what was great, nor touch any Fruit
but Horse-plums and Pound-pears. He kept a concubine that was a
very Gyantess, and made her walk, too, alwaies in *chiopins*, till
at last, he got the surname of *Senecio Grandio*, which, as Messala
said, was not his *Cognomen*, but his *Cognomentum*.[2]

But earlier than Cowley, and probably more out of admiration for
Seneca the Elder as a sensitive observer of literary qualities
than as a purveyor of anecdotes suitable for moralization, Ben
Jonson in his commonplace book, the *Discoveries*, had paraphrased
several passages from Seneca's prefaces, for example:

One, though hee be excellent, and the chiefe, is not to bee imitated alone. For never no Imitator, ever grew up to his *Author*;
likeness is alwayes on this side Truth: Yet there hapn'd, in my
time, one noble *Speaker*, who was full of gravity in his speaking.
His language (where hee could spare, or passe by a jest) was nobly
censorious. No man ever spake more neatly, more presly, more
weightily, or suffer'd lesse emptinesse, lesse idleness, in what
hee utter'd. No member of his speech, but consisted of the owne
graces: His hearers could not cough, or looke aside from him,

without losse. Hee commanded where hee spoke; and had his Judges angry, and pleased at his devotion. No man had their affections more in his power. The feare of every man that heard him, was, lest hee should make an end.[3]

Though Jonson is paraphrasing, after the initial comments on imitation based on *Contr.* I pr. 6, Seneca's description of Cassius Severus (*Contr.* III pr. 4, 1f.), a marginal note, '*Dominus Verulanus*' (i.e. Francis Bacon, Lord Verulam), assures us that he did indeed have a particular contemporary in mind. Later he actually adapts Senecan criticisms (*Contr.* III pr. 6; I pr. 6) to English statesmen named in the body of his text:

Lo: *Egerton*, the Chancellor, a grave, and great Orator; and best, when hee was provok'd. But his learned and able (though unfortunate) *Successor* is he, who hath fill'd up all numbers; and perform'd that in our tongue, which may be compar'd, or preferr'd, either to insolent *Greece*, or haughty *Rome*.[4]

Seneca's phrase *insolenti Graeciae* (*Contr.* I pr. 6) appealed to Jonson so much that elsewhere in some famous verses he compares Shakespeare's comedies favourably with

> all that insolent *Greece*, or haughtie *Rome*
> Sent forth, or since did from their ashes come.[5]

Thus Seneca's prefaces served as an important model for Jonson's attempts at a type of writing uncommon then in English, the description of the literary qualities of contemporaries.

But, inspiring though they once proved to be to eminent moralists and critics, Seneca's character sketches do not lend themselves to systematic analysis or classification.[6] They vary enormously in length; they are also very diverse in their constituents. Some give us mainly biographical information; others contain quite extensive literary description. For example, the fourth preface consists of the introduction of a contrasting pair of men, Asinius Pollio and Q. Haterius. The pen-portrait of Pollio consists almost entirely of reflections on his character and pleasing anecdotes about his private life; true literary criticism is restricted to one sentence:

floridior erat aliquanto in declamando quam in agendo: illud strictum eius et asperum et nimis iratum ingenio suo iudicium adeo cessabat ut in multis illi venia opus esset quae ab ipso vix inpetrabatur. (*Contr.* IV pr. 3)

On the other hand, Haterius' introduction, though it opens with an

anecdote illustrative of his character, consists mainly of a long
and detailed analysis of his declamatory manner: we are told about
his excessively rapid delivery, his inability to refrain from
developing each point in an argument at inordinate length, the
lack of order in his declamations which resulted from this failing, and the eccentricity of his diction in relation to the canons
of taste usually accepted in the schools (*Contr.* IV pr. 7-11).

The techniques by which Seneca brings to our attention the
salient characteristics of the declaimers range from the simplest
to the most oblique. Most often, of course, he describes character and style in simple direct statements: the sentence quoted
above on Pollio, *floridior...impetrabatur* (*Contr.* IV pr. 3), will
serve as one example. His talent for the analysis of style by
direct means is perhaps best illustrated by his description of the
declamatory manner of Arellius Fuscus (as compared with that of
his pupil, Fabianus) in *Contr.* II pr. 1:

erat explicatio Fusci Arelli splendida quidem, sed operosa et implicata, cultus nimis adquisitus, conpositio verborum mollior,
quam ut illam tam sanctis fortibusque praeceptis praeparans se
animus pati posset; summa inaequalitas orationis, quae modo exilis
erat, modo nimia licentia vaga et effusa: principia, argumenta,
narrationes aride dicebantur, in descriptionibus extra legem
omnibus verbis, dummodo niterent, permissa libertas; nihil acre,
nihil solidum, nihil horridum; splendida oratio et magis lasciva
quam laeta.

Though this passage shows that Seneca was quite capable of vivid
evocation of style by means of a densely packed collection of
specifically critical nouns and adjectives, he did not usually go
about criticism in this way. He does not blind us with the excessive use of technical terminology which can make some ancient
critics heavy reading. His critiques normally come mixed with
illustrative examples and anecdotes. For instance, he could have
dismissed the declaimer Musa with a few insulting adjectives,
tumidus, *corruptus*, *insanus*, or the like. Instead, he gives us
specific examples of his bad taste:

omnia usque ad ultimum tumorem perducta, ut non extra sanitatem,
sed extra naturam essent. quis enim ferat hominem de siphonibus
dicentem 'caelo repluunt' et de sparsionibus 'odoratos imbres'...?
(*Contr.* X pr. 9)

Anecdotes serve to add precision to critical statements otherwise

open to more than one interpretation, and may incidentally shed
light on aspects of the subject's character which are nowhere
described in plain terms. Thus an anecdote intended to illustrate
Latro's fondness for *sententiae* tells us much also about his
relationship with the master who taught him rhetoric:

hoc quoque Latro meus faciebat, ut sententias amaret. cum condiscipuli essemus apud Marullum rhetorem, hominem satis aridum,
paucissima belle, sed non vulgato genere dicentem, cum ille
exilitatem orationis suae imputaret controversiae et diceret:
'necesse me est per spinosum locum ambulantem suspensos pedes
ponere', aiebat Latro: 'non mehercules tui pedes spinas calcant,
sed habent'; et statim ipse dicebat sententias, quae interponi
argumentis cummaxime declamantis Marulli possent. (*Contr.* I pr. 22)

As an alternative to his practice of illustrating direct
statements with examples or anecdotes, Seneca sometimes prefers to
allude to criticisms made by the declaimers and members of their
audiences, without always making it clear whether he agrees with
the critic quoted or not. For example in *Contr.* II.3.22 Cestius
finds fault with a *color* used by Fuscus in a *controversia* about a
raptor who has received pardon from the father of the raped girl
within the prescribed time-limit, but not from his own:

Fuscus Arellius dixit: magnam partem legis consumpsi nec de mora
queror: raptae pater rogabatur. Cestius non probabat, et hac
sententia usus est cum hunc colorem argueret: dum vult videri
rogatum diu raptae patrem, efficit ut videatur suum diu non
rogasse; malo autem videri huius patrem tarde exorari quam tarde
rogari.

Seneca gives us no indication what he personally thought of the
color, and, seeing that neither rhetorician cited is one for whom
he expresses whole-hearted approval, it is impossible to be sure
whether or not he approved of anything in Cestius' criticism
beyond the neat manner in which it was expressed. That he was by
no means always in agreement with criticisms which he quoted without comment is evident from the extreme case of the third preface,
eleven sections of which (8-18) are devoted to an attack by Cassius
Severus on the pretensions of the rhetoricians, to which he makes
no answer, although it seems clear from other evidence, notably
from *Contr.* II pr. 4, that he himself firmly believed in the value
of an extended rhetorical education. Fortunately he does sometimes indicate his disapproval of other people's criticisms, as
for example in *Contr.* I.3.10 where he condemns Cestius' cruel jibe

at Quinctilius Varus the younger, and similarly he does sometimes
note when a criticism he is quoting seems to him to contain the
mot juste, as, for example, when he quotes Pollio on Albucius'
style in *Contr.* VII pr. 2: *sententiae, quas optime Pollio Asinius
albas vocabat, simplices, apertae, nihil occultum, nihil in-
speratum adferentes, sed vocales et splendidae.*

Uncertainty whether Seneca shared the views of the critics he
quotes is one of the problems which we have to face when discussing his criticism. The only safe policy to adopt is not to regard
as Senecan any quotation from another critic which he does not (as
he does in the case of Pollio's adjective, *albas*) specifically
praise. Not that it is always a simple matter to tell whether
Seneca is quoting someone else, or criticizing on his own account.
A grammatical idiosyncrasy worth watching for in his writing is
his apparent tendency to mix direct with indirect speech. It
often seems unlikely that a change to direct speech signifies that
he has stopped reporting. A good example comes in his report of a
lecture[7] by Cestius on the different varieties of *suasoriae* (*Suas.*
1.5):

aiebat Cestius hoc genus suasoriarum \<alibi\> aliter *declamandum
esse* [quam suadendum]. non eodem modo in libera civitate *dicendam*
sententiam, quo apud reges, quibus etiam quae prosunt ita tamen,
ut delectent, suadenda sunt. et inter reges ipsos *esse* discrimen:
quosdam minus, alios magis osos veritatem; facile Alexandrum ex
iis *esse*, quos superbissimos et supra mortalis animi modum in-
flatos *accepimus*. denique, ut alia dimittantur argumenta, ipsa
suasoria insolentiam eius *coarguit*; orbis illum suus non *capit*.
itaque nihil *dicendum aiebat* nisi cum summa veneratione regis, ne
accideret idem, quod praeceptori eius, amitino Aristotelis,
accidit...

It would be unnatural to take the sentence, *denique...capit*, as
other than part of Cestius' disquisition, even though it is wholly
cast in direct speech, especially as its logical consequence,
introduced by *itaque*, is definitely ascribed to him.

Seneca's willingness to stand back, as it were, and let other
critics air their views, is a sign that he has given us a remarkably objective survey of the literary circles in which he moved.
However, to someone attempting to pin-point the place of the elder
Seneca's literary criticism in relation to that of more self-
assertive critics like Cicero and Quintilian it poses something of

a problem to find that he does not invariably cap the opinions of
others by a statement making his own opinion on the issues quite
clear.

Also, though it is possible, as we shall see, to form a picture of the types of teaching which he accepted on many issues of
rhetorical theory which fall within the five topics into which the
orandi ratio was customarily divided, *inventio*, *dispositio*,
elocutio, *memoria*, *actio* (cf. Quint. III.3.1), this can only be
done by collecting very scattered references from all parts of the
work, most of which are descriptive of a particular declaimer's
approach to a particular *thema*, rather than being cast in the form
of didactic generalizations. Hence, before we can compare his
views with those of, for example, Cicero and Quintilian, we have
to impose a framework on his criticism which bears no relation to
the way in which it was originally set out. For Seneca the Elder
is unusual among ancient critics in feeling no desire to arrange
his criticism according to the rigid divisions of oratory prescribed in the rhetorical handbooks.

When Dionysius of Halicarnassus, who was living and working
in Rome in Seneca's younger days, wanted to discuss an orator's
style, he did so with a certain thorough-going professionalism and
according to 'a system so rigorously defined that it may be set
out in tabular form'.[8] S. F. Bonner, in his monograph on this
critic, actually sets out a table showing how Dionysius aimed, by
considering in turn word-choice, composition, and figures, and by
weighing up the writer's virtues and failings, to assign his style
to one of three categories: plain, middle, or grand.[9] Seneca, by
contrast, shows no desire to be systematic. He alludes, of
course, in passing, to diction, *compositio*, figures, and *genera
dicendi*, but he evidently felt no need to discuss each aspect of
style in turn when writing about a declaimer, and certainly had no
desire to categorize anyone's style as plain, middle, or grand.
Of course, unlike Dionysius, he was writing about men he had known
personally, not about classical orators of three or four hundred
years before. That made a difference. Seneca could start his
descriptions with a *tabula rasa*, uninhibited by any accumulation
of critical tradition. Still, a less independent spirit would

probably have fallen back on the three-style system of literary classification, even when describing contemporaries.

Seneca's independence from the Hellenistic and Ciceronian tradition of didactic writing on rhetoric is evident again in the absence from his criticism of generalizations about certain large literary polemics which other critics found of absorbing interest, and in his lack of concern to tell us plainly where he stood in relation to the opposing parties in any battle of books. The controversy between Atticists and Asianists which had seemed so important to Cicero is mentioned by Seneca surprisingly rarely. He applies the epithet *Asianus* to a mere handful of declaimers and only on one occasion refers to any *Attici*.[10] Similarly he makes only a few references to the followers of Apollodorus of Pergamum and Theodorus of Gadara, whose disagreements were certainly a live issue in the schools of the early Empire, and does not swear allegiance to the ideals of either party.[11] Probably it was chiefly because he assumed adequate knowledge of these polemics on the part of his readers that he felt no need to pontificate on the questions being disputed, for he was not to know that future generations would be almost wholly dependent on his books for a knowledge of the Latin rhetoric of his time.

Perhaps the elder Seneca, as a critic, may be likened, if not to the proverbial man who cannot see the wood for the trees, then to one who assumes that the topography of the wood is common knowledge (the wood in question - the whole Greco-Roman rhetorical tradition - having been mapped out adequately by other men before him) and prefers to examine a few single trees in detail; this he does with an artist's eye, relying on instinct to show him the important peculiarities which make each an individual, rather than approaching them with systematic flora in hand, as a man like Dionysius of Halicarnassus might, with a view to determining genus and species.

There are certain recurring themes to be found in Seneca's pen-portraits, but they have nothing to do with classifications set out in rhetorical handbooks.

We find he is particularly intrigued, for example, by people's inconsistencies. He devotes a long section of the first

preface (*Contr*. I pr. 13-15) to a description of Latro's unalter-
able habit of working too hard and playing too hard: *in utramque
partem vehementi viro modus deerat: nec intermittere studium
sciebat nec repetere* etc. In the second preface Arellius Fuscus'
extreme unevenness of style occasions comment: *summa inaequalitas
orationis, quae modo exilis erat, modo nimia licentia vaga et
effusa...* (*Contr*. II pr. 1). The main theme of the third preface
is the phenomenon, exemplified by Cassius Severus, of men who made
good orators, but mediocre declaimers: *quosdam disertissimos cognovi viros non respondentes famae suae cum declamarent, in foro
maxima omnium admiratione dicentes, simul ad has domesticas
exercitationes secesserant desertos ab ingenio suo* (*Contr*. III
pr. 1). He remarks also on a certain discrepancy between Severus'
character and his oratorical manner: *nec enim quicquam magis in
illo mirareris, quam quod gravitas, quae deerat vitae, actioni
supererat* (*Contr*. III pr. 4). In the fourth preface, Pollio's
unwillingness to declaim in public is contrasted with his important contribution to the rise of public literary performances of
another kind; his declamatory style is contrasted with his oratorical manner (*Contr*. IV pr. 2f.). Haterius' theoretical attitude towards the arrangement of argument is contrasted with his
practice: *dividere controversiam putabat ad rem pertinere, si
illum interrogares, non putabat, si audires* (*Contr*. IV pr. 9).
Albucius, introduced in the seventh preface, changed his manner
according to the size of his audience, so Seneca tells us (*Contr*.
VII pr. 1), and his style was marred by his mixing of incompatible
types of vocabulary: *splendidissimus erat: idem res dicebat omnium
sordidissimas* (*Contr*. VII pr. 3). In the tenth preface, Scaurus'
potential as an orator is contrasted with his actual achievements
(*Contr*. X pr. 2-3); the censorious image Labienus wished to project is contrasted with his true character (*ibid*. 4); Musa is represented as talented enough, but deficient in other respects
(*ibid*. 9).

Seneca is also interested in the extent to which external
factors enhanced or damaged a man's literary reputation. We are
told of Alfius Flavus: *semper autem commendabat eloquentiam eius
aliqua res extra eloquentiam: in puero lenocinium erat ingenii*

aetas, in iuvene desidia (*Contr.* I.1.22). Cassius Severus, we
learn, owed a good deal of his reputation to his physical presence: *primum tantundem erat in homine quantum in ingenio: corporis
magnitudo conspicua, suavitas valentissimae vocis...* (*Contr.* III
pr. 3). The minor declaimer L. Magius would hardly have attracted
an audience if he had not been the son-in-law of Livy (*Contr.* X
pr. 2); on the other hand, distinguished family connections could
prove disastrous for one's career, as happened in the case of
Asinius Gallus: *...magnum oratorem, nisi illum, quod semper
evenit, magnitudo patris non produceret, sed obrueret* (*Contr.* IV
pr. 4). Nevertheless a really exceptional man might rise to emi-
nence from the most unpromising beginnings. Seneca marvels at the
way Labienus overcame his many disadvantages:

magnus orator, qui multa impedimenta eluctatus ad famam ingeni
confitentibus magis hominibus pervenerat quam volentibus. summa
egestas erat, summa infamia, summum odium. magna autem debet esse
eloquentia, quae invitis placeat, et cum ingenia favor hominum
ostendat, favor alat, quantam vim esse oportet, quae inter ob-
stantia erumpat! (*Contr.* X pr. 4)

Another theme which Seneca harps on is the way in which declaimers abused, or improved on, their natural gifts. Neglect of
vocal exercises, together with inadequate sleep, ruined Latro's
originally sound voice: *vox robusta, sed surda, lucubrationibus et
neglegentia, non natura infuscata* (*Contr.* I pr. 16); in general,
his irregular habits of life undermined his health:

iam vero quin rem inimicissimam corpori faceret, vetari nullo modo
poterat: post cenam fere lucubrabat nec patiebatur alimenta per
somnum quietemque aequaliter digeri, sed perturbata ac dissipata
in caput agebat; itaque et oculorum aciem contuderat et colorem
mutaverat. (*Contr.* I pr. 17)

Alfius Flavus was another man careless of his natural vigour, but
in his case it was simple indolence, together with a taste for
poetry, that brought about his downfall (*Contr.* I.1.22). The
choice of a life of philosophic calm, involving as it did the suppression of excessive emotions, was in itself an admirable thing,
but could ruin one as an effective declaimer. This was the case
with Fabianus: *cum veros conpressisset adfectus et iram doloremque
procul expulisset, parum bene imitari poterat quae effugerat*
(*Contr.* II pr. 2). On the other hand people sometimes made an
effort to improve their natural rhetorical talents. Latro

improved his memory by learning mnemonic techniques: *memoria ei natura quidem felix, plurimum tamen arte adiuta* (*Contr.* I pr. 17). In general, the way to overcome mediocrity was by hard work: *diligentiam, maximum etiam mediocris ingenii subsidium* (*Contr.* III pr. 7).

It is clear that the elder Seneca's criticism is of a kind set apart from the main stream of ancient writing on rhetoric to which Cicero's *Rhetorica* and Quintilian's *Institutio oratoria* belong. Seneca's most characteristic type of criticism is the pen-portrait in which the subject's human foibles are usually given as much attention as his style. In addition there is technical analysis of argumentation in the sections about *divisio*, and comparative criticism of varying complexity in the closing stages of his surveys of declamations. One important respect in which he differs fundamentally from Cicero and Quintilian is that he does not set out to give straightforward instruction to the student of rhetoric. His approach is only didactic to the extent that his examples are intended to serve as models for imitation or warnings of faults to be avoided. He rarely lays down any general rules about the way the various parts of a declamation should be treated. Still less is his aim to theorize about the qualities of the hypothetical ideal orator. To adopt a convenient modern division of literary criticism into three categories,[12] Seneca's criticism is primarily 'descriptive', rather than 'legislative' or 'theoretical'.

Most of the classics of ancient criticism belong to the latter two categories. Indeed, scant recognition has been given in histories of the critical tradition to the fact that descriptive criticism existed in antiquity at all. It did exist, but its practitioners tend not to be given the name of 'critics': we know them rather as philosophers, *grammatici*, scholiasts, epistolographers, historians or biographers. It is with the biographical tradition that the elder Seneca's work has most affinity. This becomes clear if we look at passages in Suetonius' *Lives of the Caesars* in which the literary preferences of the various emperors are described.

For example, in the *Life of Augustus* straightforward

description of Augustus' style of speaking is enlivened by allusions to his *ipsissima verba* on the types of rhetoric he tried
to avoid:

genus eloquendi secutus est elegans et temperatum, vitatis
sententiarum ineptiis atque concinnitate et 'reconditorum
verborum', ut ipse dicit, 'fetoribus', praecipuamque curam duxit
sensum animi quam apertissime exprimere. (*Aug*. 86.1)

Suetonius also illustrates the emperor's tastes by quoting disparaging remarks he made about named individuals:

cacozelos et antiquarios, ut diverso genere vitiosos, pari
fastidio sprevit, exagitabatque nonnumquam; in primis Maecenatem
suum, cuius 'myrobrechis', ut ait, 'cincinnos' usque quaque per-
sequitur et imitando per iocum irridet. sed nec Tiberio parcit et
exoletas interdum et reconditas voces aucupanti. M. quidem
Antonium ut insanum increpat, quasi ea scribentem, quae mirentur
potius homines quam intellegant. (*Ibid*. 2)

There is no closer parallel in Roman literature than this for the
way Seneca so often enlivens his criticism by recording illuminating comments made by a declaimer about himself, or vituperation
flung by one *rhetor* at another. Suetonius, like Seneca, is not
content with stereotyped generalizations about style: indeed, in
his efforts to pin down the essential qualities of Augustus'
writing, he goes into even more detail than Seneca ever does, not
only listing colloquialisms he was prone to use, but even noting
peculiarities of his orthography (*Aug*. 87f.). Like Seneca,
Suetonius thought it as important to discuss a man's delivery and
memory as his diction and style, and tried to find a psychological
explanation for the manner he adopted in public. Seneca had discussed with interest Albucius' unwarranted fear of improvisation
(*Contr*. VII pr. 2) and the lack of self-confidence which made him
unable to give up imitating other people's styles and settle on
one of his own (*Contr*. VII pr. 4f.). Suetonius tells us (*Aug*. 84)
that Augustus also avoided impromptu speaking, and was so afraid
of memory lapses that he took to preparing anything important he
had to say in writing, even his more serious conversations with
his wife.

Suetonius, of course, wrote later than the elder Seneca, and
seems to have known his work, at least in an epitomized form,[13] so
it would be more satisfactory if one could find an equally close
parallel for the mixture of stylistic analysis and psychological

description characteristic of Seneca's pen-portraits in earlier
biographical writing. Unfortunately the remains of such pre-
Suetonian biography as would be of interest to us are extremely
fragmentary.[14]

Parallels may be adduced between the elder Seneca and certain
Greek biographical miscellanists who, like him, chose to write
about their contemporaries. A certain similarity between Seneca's
manner and that of Antigonus of Carystus, who wrote in the third
century B.C. about recent philosophers, was noted by Wilamowitz.[15]
Georg Misch[16] has looked even further back and seen Ion of Chios
as a representative of an allied tradition.

Ion's *Epidemiai*, an anecdotal record of personalities to be
encountered in the fifth century B.C., included verbatim accounts
of literary conversations, such as the one in which Sophocles took
part about the correct language in which to describe rosy cheeks.
Ion concludes this anecdote (*FGrHist* 392 F 6) with a reflection on
an inconsistency in Sophocles' character: he did not, so we are
told, show in public life the same cleverness he displayed in
poetry and witty conversation. A remark of Plutarch (*Pericles*
5.3) confirms that Ion, like Seneca, delighted in presenting personalities as two-sided, ὥσπερ τραγικὴν διδασκαλίαν ἀξιοῦντα τὴν
ἀρετὴν ἔχειν τι πάντως καὶ σατυρικὸν μέρος.

How far the parallel noted by Wilamowitz between Antigonus
and Seneca is valid can be illustrated by two fragments in particular. A fine example of the theme of contradictions in character was to be found in his pen-portrait of Menedemus. This philosopher's violence in debate was contrasted with his mildness in
private life, and the generosity which he extended even to his
academic enemies:

ἐν δὲ ταῖς ζητήσεσι, φησίν, ὧδε μάχιμος ἦν ὥσθ' ὑπώπια φέρων
ἀπῄει. ὅμως δ' οὖν τοιοῦτος ἐν τοῖς λόγοις ὑπάρχων ἐν τοῖς ἔργοις
πρᾳότατος ἦν. Ἀλεξῖνον γοῦν πολλὰ καταπαίζων καὶ σκληρῶς
ἐπισκώπτων ὅμως αὐτὸν εὖ ἐποίησε τὴν γυναῖκα παραπέμψας ἐκ Δελφῶν
ἕως Χαλκίδος, εὐλαβουμένην τὰς κλωπείας τε καὶ τὰς καθ' ὁδὸν
λῃστείας. (Diog. Laert. II.136)

Another fragment, on Polemon (Diog. Laert. IV.17), may be compared
with Seneca's marvelling at the way the young Fabianus suppressed
his emotions (*Contr.* II pr. 2): τοσοῦτον δὲ ἐπιτεῖναι τὸ ἦθος

ἀρξάμενον φιλοσοφεῖν, ὥστ' ἐπὶ ταὐτοῦ σχήματος τῆς μορφῆς πάντοτε
μένειν.

Whether there existed any comparable descriptions of rhetoricians by Hellenistic writers is something of a mystery. The
first book of Philostratus' *Lives of the sophists*, which one might
have expected to draw on any such works as there were, proves to
be the reverse of informative on this point. In the text as we
have it, the gap in the succession of sophists between Aeschines,
who was in Philostratus' view the founder of the 'second sophistic', and Nicetes of Smyrna, a rhetorician of the first century
A.D., is bridged only by a meagre *praeteritio* in which three minor
rhetoricians, Ariobarzanes of Cilicia, Xenophron of Sicily, and
Peithagoras of Cyrene, are dismissed as unimportant (*Vit. soph.*
I.511). Whether this extraordinary gap is due to a lacuna in the
text, or the unavailability to Philostratus of any sources relating to the last three centuries B.C. is an open question.

Certainly the Hellenistic writers who wrote compendious works
on famous men included in their works biographical sketches of
orators and rhetoricians. For instance, Hermippus 'the Calli-
machean'[17] wrote books about Aristotle and his pupils, who included the orator Demetrius of Phalerum, and about Isocrates and
his school, which included Isaeus, Demosthenes, Hyperides, and
many minor orators and rhetoricians. However, to reconstruct the
life story of a great man already dead, using secondary sources and
his own writings, which is what Hermippus and most Hellenistic
biographers were usually doing, requires quite different methods
from those employed by an anecdotist who is describing his contemporaries, and may result in a very different kind of end-product.
A certain amount of literary criticism will have been mixed with
the biographical narrative in such *Lives*, but it may have been of
low quality and very negligible in scope, very much less important
in these *Lives* than the establishing of chronology and master-
pupil successions, matters which rarely interested Seneca the
Elder. The pseudo-Plutarchan *Lives of the ten orators*, which may
be regarded as reflecting the more serious side of Hellenistic
biography, serve to show how it was possible for an ancient bio-
grapher to write about an orator's life and works without bearing

any great resemblance to Seneca the Elder or Suetonius.

The elder Seneca nowhere leads us to suppose that he was widely read in Greek prose literature, so that any resemblance between his *Barockstil* (to use Wilamowitz' expression)[18] and that of Antigonus of Carystus and others is, if not completely coincidental, most likely the result of his knowledge of Latin imitations of Hellenistic biographical writings. He could very well have read some works of this type in the course of his study of Roman history. The problem is to know which Latin authors could possibly have influenced him.

We happen to know that Seneca was interested in the way that the pen-portrait had become an increasingly important motif in historiography:

quotiens magni alicuius <viri> mors ab historicis narrata est, totiens fere consummatio totius vitae et quasi funebris laudatio redditur. hoc, semel aut iterum a Thucydide factum, item in paucissimis personis usurpatum a Sallustio, T. Livius benignus omnibus magnis viris praestitit; sequentes historici multo id effusius fecerunt. Ciceroni hoc, ut Graeco verbo utar, ἐπιτάφιον[19] Livius reddit. (*Suas*. 6.21)

The character sketches of Sallust and Livy may well have influenced him to some extent: antithetical presentation of conflicting traits is certainly to be found in them. In Livy's 'epitaph' for Cicero, quoted with admiration by Seneca in *Suas*. 6.22, we read:

ingenium et operibus et praemiis operum felix, ipse fortunae diu prosperae; sed in longo tenore felicitatis magnis interim ictus vulneribus...omnium adversorum nihil ut viro dignum erat tulit praeter mortem...

Sallust's pithy description of Catiline comes rather nearer to Seneca's manner than the rotund period from which the Livian antithesis above has been excerpted:

L. Catilina, nobili genere natus, fuit magna vi et animi et corporis, sed ingenio malo pravoque...animus audax subdolus varius, cuius rei lubet simulator ac dissimulator: alieni adpetens, sui profusus, ardens in cupiditatibus: satis eloquentiae, sapientiae parum: vastus animus inmoderata, incredibilia, nimis alta semper cupiebat. (*Cat*. 5)

Note here, in addition to the antitheses, the way the portrait is built up in places by means of nouns and adjectives in the nominative, devoid of verbs. We have seen something similar in Seneca's description of Fuscus (*Contr*. II pr. 1: *summa inaequalitas*

orationis etc.). There is no frivolity, though, in the pen-
portraits of Sallust and Livy, no jotting down of revealing anecdotes and clever witticisms remembered from the time when the men
described were alive. The models, if any, for these features of
Seneca's technique, must have lain elsewhere, most likely in anecdotal records of earlier writers' lives.

Four Latin authors are listed by St Jerome (*De viris ill.*
praef.) as eminent predecessors of Suetonius in the writing of
works *De viris illustribus*, namely Varro, Santra, Nepos and
Hyginus. Varro, who wrote a book *De poetis* (*GRF* 209ff.) which was
used by Suetonius and may have influenced his biographical technique, also composed a work called the *Imagines* (*GRF* 214f.),[20]
comprising descriptions of seven hundred famous men, some of whom
must surely have been orators. Santra, cited by Suetonius as an
authority on poets, certainly wrote something about the history of
rhetoric, for Quintilian (XII.10.16 = Santra fr. 13, *GRF* 388)
cites an account by him of the rise of Asianism. Two of Nepos'
works on famous Romans, the brief *Life of Cato* and the longer
Atticus are extant; he also wrote a *Life of Cicero* (*GRF* 405ff.)
and other works containing biographical material (*HRR* II 26ff.).
Hyginus wrote a work called *De vita rebusque illustrium* and
another entitled *Exempla* (*HRR* II 72f.).

It is unfortunate that so little survives of Hyginus' biographical works, for he was a Spaniard, and a great friend of Ovid
(Suet. *De gramm. et rhet.* 20.2 Brugnoli), and on both these counts
Seneca the Elder might well have taken an interest in his writings.
It appears that Hyginus did occasionally touch on literary topics
(fr. 1, *HRR* II 72), but the main interests he displays in his
meagre extant fragments - in the property of great men (frs. 2f.),
in the *origines* of cities (frs. 5ff.) and in the rationalizing of
myths (frs. 15f.) - were not ones shared by the elder Seneca as
far as we know. It must be doubted whether Varro greatly influenced Seneca. The fragments of his works on literary history reveal him as a scrupulous user of the more cautious (if sometimes
misguided) methods evolved by Hellenistic scholars for recon-
structing the past. Nothing suggests that he was capable of vivid
metaphorical description of style, or exuberant anecdotal writing,

and, however fluent a writer he may have been, it seems unlikely
that he could have given nearly as much individual attention to
each of the seven hundred men in his *Imagines* as Seneca gives to
his rhetoricians. As for Santra, we lack evidence that he took an
interest in the details, as opposed to the broad outlines, of the
history of rhetoric. But it is unsafe to argue from silence.
Nepos, in the *Lives* of Atticus and Cato which have survived complete, emerges as one of those biographers who keep more or less
closely to the conventional form of classical eulogy: a survey in
chronological order of a man's achievements is followed by a
string of paragraphs singling out his particular virtues. Nothing
could be further from Senecan informality. Literary description
does find some place in these *Lives*, as it is permissible to eu-
logize a man for being *cupidissimus litterarum* (*Cato* 3) or
antiquitatis amator (*Atticus* 18), but though Nepos displays in
these *Lives* a certain gift for outlining the contents of books
succinctly, he makes only the most perfunctory and colourless
remarks about style. On the other hand a fragment of another of
Nepos' works (*De inl. viris* fr. 17, *HRR* II 40) gives us praise of
Cicero expressed in terms strikingly close to Seneca's talk of
Cicero's *viva vox* (*Contr.* I pr. 11) and the challenge of Roman
oratory to insolent Greece (*ibid.* 6):

Cornelius Nepos in libro de historicis Latinis de laude Ciceronis:
non ignorare debes, unum hoc genus Latinarum litterarum adhuc non
modo non respondere Graeciae sed omnino rude atque incohatum morte
Ciceronis relictum. ille enim fuit unus, qui potuerit et etiam
debuerit historiam digna voce pronuntiare, quippe qui oratoriam
eloquentiam rudem a maioribus acceptam perpoliverit, philosophiam
ante eum incomptam Latinam sua conformarit oratione.

We are not actually obliged to look to Nepos in order to find an
explanation for the fulsomeness of Seneca's expression when he
praises Cicero: there are sufficient parallels for it in the declaimers' treatments of *Suas.* 6 and 7. But this, as we shall
see,[21] is not the only case where we find in a fragment of one of
Nepos' lesser-known works a close analogue for the type of data,
and manner of presenting it, found in those rare passages in
Seneca's anthology where he refers to the rhetoric of the late
Republic. Such works as Nepos' *libellus quo distinguit litteratum
ab erudito*[22] and perhaps his *Exempla*[23] were evidently richer in

detailed linguistic investigation and literary allusion than his
extant *Lives* of Atticus and Cato. However, there is nothing in
his fragments that seems to bear a striking resemblance to the
pen-portraiture of contemporaries in Seneca's prefaces.

Of course, Varro, Nepos, Santra and Hyginus were not the only
pre-Suetonian authors to write about the life and works of famous
Romans. For instance, Atticus wrote a work called *Imagines* along
the same lines as Varro's work of the same name (Nep. *Att.* 18).
How much biographical speculation and criticism had accumulated
around Republican poets by the time of Seneca the Elder is particularly well illustrated by the Suetonian *Life of Terence* in
which we find cited variously as authorities on Terence's life and
as critics of his comedies, not only Nepos, Varro, and Santra, but
Fenestella, Porcius Licinus, Volcacius, C. Memmius, Q. Cosconius,
Afranius, Cicero and Caesar. Prose writers seem to have been less
thoroughly discussed by grammarians than poets. However, Cicero
in his *Brutus* had ensured that the achievements of his predecessors
in Roman oratory would not wholly be forgotten, and provided the
elder Seneca with precedents for his use of the σύγκρισις in *Contr.*
IV pr. 2ff. and *Suas.* 2.15. Tiro (*GRF* 390ff.), as well as Nepos,
wrote a *Life of Cicero*; he was also the author of *Epistulae de
rebus grammaticis rhetoricisque*, which included (fr. 6) analysis
of a speech by Cato. Certainly known to Seneca the Elder was a
work by Votienus Montanus in which he made frequent reference to
the eloquence of his friend Marcius Marcellus (*Contr.* IX.6.18).
This isolated reference to books by Montanus, the existence of
which is nowhere else attested, should warn us of our hopeless
ignorance of the true amount of written literary criticism which
may have been available to Seneca. There may have been many works
written in the early Empire containing a mixture of biographical
and literary information which, however, enjoyed too limited a
circulation for any record of them to be preserved. It should be
noted, for instance, that Suetonius must have had a second source,
in addition to an epitomized version of the elder Seneca's seventh preface, for his *Life of Albucius Silus* (*De gramm. et rhet.*
30 Brugnoli).[24]

There is no evidence, though, that any author wrote character-

sketches of the rhetoricians of the late Republic resembling those
in Seneca's prefaces. The index of Funaioli's *Grammaticae Romanae
fragmenta*, which lists Roman grammatical works, including biographical writings, from the period up to, and including, the
reign of Augustus,[25] records no work entitled *De rhetoribus*. It
is noteworthy that the Republican rhetoricians, only four in number, whose lives are sketched by Suetonius (*De gramm. et rhet.*
26-9 Brugnoli) are not treated in nearly as much detail as
Albucius. So, in the absence of any obvious precursor to Seneca
the Elder in his mode of pen-portraiture, we have to treat him as
an individualist and innovator, which maybe is indeed what in some
respects he was.

Individualists are, of course, the most difficult of all literary figures to discuss. In the elder Seneca's case the chief
difficulty, as we have seen, lies in the fact that, as he is primarily a writer of 'descriptive' criticism, he does not lend himself to comparison with either his main predecessor or his main
successor in the tradition of Roman rhetorical criticism, Cicero
or Quintilian, whose work belongs chiefly to the categories of
'legislative' and 'theoretical' criticism. Even the *Brutus*, with
its multitude of brief descriptions of Republican orators, is a
vehicle for Cicero's theorizing, notably his polemic against the
Atticists and his search for the ideal orator. No whimsical anecdotes or references to the peculiar quirks of individuals, such as
were acceptable in the Senecan or Suetonian pen-portrait, were
allowed, even in this work, to disrupt the smooth classicism which
Cicero thought appropriate for literary theory. The result is
that some modern readers have been disappointed by the lack, in
Cicero's descriptions of orators in the *Brutus*, of the liveliness
prevalent in Seneca's prefaces.[26]

Before we can make any useful comparisons or point out contrasts between the elder Seneca and the literary theorists, we
therefore have to process his criticism, to reconstruct, as far as
possible, the type of Art of Rhetoric he would have written, had
he chosen to write in that form. Two attempts to isolate theories
about the proper treatment of a declamation implicit in Seneca's
criticism have indeed already been made by the American scholars,

A. F. Sochatoff and L. A. Sussman, but as neither Sochatoff's observations in his all too brief article, 'Basic rhetorical theories of the elder Seneca',[27] nor the relevant chapters in
Sussman's doctoral dissertation and recent book,[28] provide a
wholly satisfactory treatment of the subject, a new and independent study along similar lines will not come amiss.[29]

There is a danger, though, that if we sort Seneca's criticism
into a rigid scheme far removed from his own informality, we shall
lose sight of the sort of critic he was. To counteract this
danger some attempt must also be made to use the pen-portraits as
Seneca the Elder intended them to be used, as an aid to the appreciation of the fragments of the major declaimers.[30]

I shall not be following, in my study of Seneca's criticism,
the lines mapped out by H. Bardon in his book, *Le vocabulaire de
la critique littéraire chez Sénèque le Rhéteur*,[31] and his article,
'Mécanisme et stéréotypie dans le style de Sénèque le Rhéteur',[32]
because, as no critical reader can fail to notice, his approach is
flawed by a fundamental misconception. Bardon regrets, basically,
that Seneca the Elder was not Cicero. The most important part of
his book consists of a *'Lexique'*, in which he lists critical terms
used by the elder Seneca, and notes where these terms were used by
Cicero and Quintilian, and occasionally other critics, and where,
significantly, they were not used by them. This *'Lexique'* has
some usefulness as a source of cross-references, but it is marred,
unfortunately, by many serious omissions and errors.[33] It is also
unfortunate that in the chapters which follow, Bardon takes the
line that it is totally deplorable that, after all the hard work
expended by Cicero in building up a Latin critical vocabulary of
considerable richness, Seneca does not use all the terminology put
at his disposal by the great master. Bardon's demonstration that
Seneca's critical vocabulary is very different from Cicero's is
valuable, but his complaints about Seneca's sins of omission are
in many ways unfair.[34] First, he does not pause to consider that
Cicero's coinages of critical terms are not all uniformly successful, and that not all were thought worthy of re-use even by his
keenest admirers. G. M. A. Grube has noted Cicero's use in *De or.*
III.52.199 of three alternative terms to designate a 'type' of

style, as an example of Cicero's 'impatience with precise technical terminology'.[35] It is easy to see why later critics were
likely to reject two of the three terms, *habitus, color, figura*,
when writing about style in general terms. *Figura* was increasingly to take on the very specific technical sense of figure of
speech, figure of thought; *color*, among the rhetoricians of the
early Empire, has a meaning which is unrelated to stylistics.
Rejection of some Ciceronian terms might mean a certain lessening
of the richness of critical language, but it did not mean any
diminution of clarity. It should be noted that Quintilian sometimes rejects as imprecise pure Latin critical terms, such as
Cicero always tried to use, and prefers to revert to the Greek
word his predecessors had been trying to translate: ...*enthymema*
(quod nos commentum sane aut commentationem interpretemur, quia
aliter non possumus, Graeco melius usuri)... (Quint. V.10.1). So
Seneca is in good company when he uses latinized forms of Greek
terms.

In his strictures on the elder Seneca, Bardon does not make
due allowance for the fact that Cicero's rhetorical criticism is
far greater in bulk than the purely critical sections of the declamatory anthology. It is quite unreasonable of him, on this
count alone, to complain that, '*Une autre faiblesse du vocabulaire*
critique chez Sénèque consiste dans le petit nombre des termes qui
le constituent par rapport à celui de Cicéron',[36] and to illustrate this statement by totting up the number of adjectives Seneca
applies to the word *vox*, and contrasting the total arrived at
unfavourably with the number of epithets applied by Cicero to the
same word. But even if Seneca's criticism were equal in bulk to
Cicero's, it would still not be fair to expect him to use an
identical and equally large selection of critical terms. It is
not just that the language of criticism was bound to evolve with
the passing of time, and that it would not be appropriate to write
about school rhetoric in exactly the same terms as were applied to
true oratory. The fact is simply that descriptive criticism
requires a different vocabulary from - in particular far fewer
strictly technical terms than - legislative or theoretical
criticism.

The last four hundred years of English criticism, it has been observed, have been marked by the gradual ousting of the latter two types of criticism, for example, books of rhetoric offering instruction to the writer, and essays on literary aesthetics, by descriptive criticism, 'the youngest' in English 'of the three forms, by far the most voluminous, and the only one which today possesses any life and vigour of its own'.[37] Parallel with this trend, it is noticeable that 'the terminology of criticism diminishes steeply'.[38] This decline is connected with the increasing horror with which formal rhetoric has come to be regarded by English writers, a phenomenon which was not paralleled in the Roman world, where the scholastics saw to it that rhetoric survived, whatever else might decline, and the situation was never reached where a man sufficiently well educated to write descriptive criticism would do so completely without reference to the standard body of rhetorical terminology. But there is something inherent in the nature of literary description which makes it unlikely that a descriptive critic would use the whole range of terms found in school text-books and theoretical essays, and this applies to the ancient world as much as to the modern. The descriptive critic may want to allude to someone's fondness for a particular rhetorical figure: it does not follow that he will feel called upon to mention all the *figurae* listed in the standard handbooks, however well-acquainted with their definitions he may have been. He may want to find an adjective to describe the voice of a particular man whose delivery contributed significantly to his success or failure: it does not follow that he will want to survey exhaustively all the possible types of vociferation. It is unreasonable of Bardon, then, to complain of Seneca's vocabulary that, '*il existe des mots du vocabulaire critique qui ne sont absolument pas representés*'.[39]

Nor would the ancient descriptive critic, if he had any imagination at all, restrict himself to the vocabulary provided for him by writers of Arts of Rhetoric. It would not, for example, be a sign of the best critic if, when assessing the essential qualities of an individual's style, he kept rigidly to the standard epithets attached by theorists to the *genera dicendi*.

The more gifted critic will draw much of his vocabulary from non-scholastic sources, applying to the written word images of light and shade, or density and fluidity, and transferring to criticism nouns and adjectives originally applied to extra-literary pursuits, the martial arts, for example, or crafts involving skilful constructive processes, building, carpentry, weaving and so on. This is what the elder Seneca does, not, of course, without Ciceronian precedent,[40] but choosing a new selection of words in which the love of the striking and colourful, characteristic of Silver Latin, is apparent. Bardon, who seems to have felt he must exclude from his '*lexique*' any words which were not strictly technical terms or metaphors well established in criticism by Cicero, does the richness of Seneca's language much less than justice. Take, for example, a remarkable sentence from his description of Fabianus: *deerat illi oratorium robur et ille pugnatorius mucro, splendor vero velut voluntarius non elaboratae orationi aderat* (*Contr.* II pr. 2). Bardon includes in his list *oratorius*, *splendor*, *elaboratus*, and of course, *oratio*, but not *robur*, *pugnatorius*, *mucro*, or *voluntarius*.

Bardon's selection of words is unnecessarily perverse, but there is a real difficulty in distinguishing, in Seneca's writing, between truly critical vocabulary and words of biographical description. Such a distinction is of doubtful validity anyway, in view of the ancient saying, *talis hominibus...oratio, qualis vita* (Sen. *Ep. mor.* 114.2). For this reason, no select list of his critical terminology is likely to be wholly satisfactory. Once more one feels the need for a complete *index verborum* to the elder Seneca's work.

The elder Seneca was not a great stylist. Schott[41] was being over-indulgent towards him when he wrote, *de cuius scriptoris stylo ita iudicare non dubitem, nihil esse in lingua Latina cum a Cicerone Fabioque discesseris scriptum purius aut elegantius.* He belongs to a period of stylistic transition: he seems to have been feeling his way towards that finesse of pointed expression for which his son was to be famous, but he is not uniformly successful in achieving it. One has to agree with Bardon that sometimes his striving after effect seems naïve, as for example, when he says of the child prodigy Alfius Flavus, *cum praetextatus esset, tantae opinionis fuit, ut populo Romano puer eloquentia notus esset* (*Contr.* I.1.22), and when he records how a certain Dionysius, *elegans magis declamator quam vehemens hunc sensum et vehementer dixit et eleganter* (*Contr.* I.4.11).[42] Sometimes also, as we have seen, he obscures his exact standpoint on moral issues by writing too much declamatory verbiage about them.

Yet one could fairly apply to his prose-writing the assessment with which he concludes a pen-portrait of one of the declaimers: *redimebat tamen vitia virtutibus et plus habebat quod laudares quam cui ignosceres...* (*Contr.* IV pr. 11). Mixing of metaphors, a feature of style carried to excess by some of his contemporaries, for example Valerius Maximus, occurs in his writing too: his references in quick succession to oratorical oakwood and a combative dagger in *Contr.* II pr. 2 provide a good example. But whereas in the hackneyed moralizing of Valerius Maximus in such a passage as VI.9 ext. 7,

caduca nimium et fragilia, puerilibusque consentanea crepundiis sunt ista quae vires atque opes humanae vocantur. affluunt subito, repente dilabuntur: nullo in loco, nulla in persona stabilibus nixa radicibus consistunt; sed incertissimo flatu fortunae huc atque illuc acta, quos sublime extulerunt, improviso recussu destitutos profundo cladium miserabiliter immergunt,

the effect of muddling together allusions to children's toys, rising tides, firm roots, blasts of fortune and so on, is decidedly tasteless, in the elder Seneca's underivative type of literary criticism a certain unconventionality in the deployment of imagery seems a positive virtue. The younger Seneca in *Ep. mor.* 100, where he echoes a number of his father's criticisms of Fabianus,[43] may show greater refinement of taste than his father when he paraphrases the words, *deerat...mucro* (*Contr.* II pr. 2), thus: *deest illis oratorius vigor stimulique quos quaeris et subiti ictus sententiarum* (§8), but this version is surely much less memorable than the original.

Nor is the elder Seneca's colourfulness in the language of his literary descriptions the only feature of his writing which one would not necessarily want to sacrifice in favour of the greater smoothness and refinement cultivated by some other classi-

cal writers of criticism and *belles lettres*. One also senses a
great charm and obvious warmth pervading his writing as he reminisces about his friends among the declaimers. In particular one
notices that he has an admirable capacity to sympathize with them
in the misfortunes which they brought upon themselves by an
approach to life which he recognized to be dangerously unbalanced.
His heart goes out to Latro, for instance, whose unremitting intellectual exertions caused him, in addition to physical suffering
(*Contr.* I pr. 17), another type of exhaustion, *ingenii lassitud-
inem, quae non minor est quam corporis sed occultior* (*ibid*. 15),
and to Albucius, who after the miscalculated use of a declamatory
device in a law-suit had lost him his case, felt obliged to retire
permanently from the courts, being, as Seneca explains, *homo
summae probitatis, qui nec facere iniuriam nec pati sciret* (*Contr.*
VII pr. 7). Besides, by such anecdotal digressions as the one
about the megalomaniac Seneca Grandio (*Suas.* 2.17), later to be
paraphrased so enjoyably in Abraham Cowley's essay *On greatness*,
and by such wry comments as his quasi-Ovidian strictures on dry
stylists in *Contr.* II.1.24, he earns a high rank among the wits of
the ancient world.

PART II

SENECA THE ELDER ON THE HISTORY OF ELOQUENCE

1 ORATORY AND RHETORICAL THEORY UP TO HIS OWN TIME

The extent of the elder Seneca's familiarity with the classics of
Greek and Roman oratory and rhetorical theory cannot be estimated
with any hope of accuracy but if, as seems probable, he had not
nearly the same depth of knowledge as Cicero of the rhetorical
traditions of Greece and the Roman Republic, this is nothing to be
wondered at in view of the contrast between the kinds of education
which the two men received in their youth. Seneca the Elder, confined in his formative years to a remote and war-torn western
province, and unfortunate in having to learn the elements of rhetoric from the uninspired Marullus, had none of the educational
experiences which were to enable Cicero to write about oratory
with his air of incontrovertible authority. Not for him, unless
our information is grossly misleading, anything comparable to the
old-fashioned *tirocinium fori*, the prolonged study of Greek philosophy, the travels around the schools of distinguished rhetoricians in Greece and Asia Minor, which Cicero describes in the
autobiographical section of the *Brutus* (89.304ff.).

Nevertheless Seneca the Elder was able to overcome to a certain extent the limitations of his formal education. As an adult
enthusiast in the *auditoria* of the declaimers he had the chance to
learn much, just by listening to the discussions and quips of the
rhetoricians and distinguished members of their audience, which
would sharpen his critical sensitivity. His study of history must
have further broadened his outlook. On the other hand it is
questionable whether he ever made any considerable study of the
works which we consider the classics of rhetorical theory, or of
the speeches of Greek, or pre-Ciceronian Roman orators. Of
course, we must beware of relying too much on an argument from
silence: the fact that Seneca does not mention a book does not
mean that he had never read it; his subject-matter does not call
for constant reference to the more venerable orators and

theorists. But references to rhetoric before his own time are
strikingly rare in his criticism, and it seems indicative of a
decided modernity in his outlook that when he wants to give extra
authority to a critical pronouncement he tends to refer to what
Latro said on the matter, or Pollio, or Messala - men he had actually heard airing their views - never, for example, to what Cicero
said in the *De oratore*. The frame of reference of Seneca's criticism is for the most part his own life-time. On the few occasions
when he looks back beyond his personal experience one needs always
to ask whether he could not have been relying on hear-say and
secondary sources for his information.

Consider first his references to Greek rhetoric outside the
schools of declamation. Seneca the Elder was by no means ignorant
of Greek, for he was clearly able to listen to declamations by
contemporary Greeks with discrimination. It is true that his quotations from their work are much briefer than those from Latin
declamations, but it cannot be argued that his familiarity with
their declamations could have been confined to an acquaintance
with *sententiae* which had been singled out for praise or condemnation by their Latin-speaking contemporaries, as in *Suas.* 3.6 he
explicitly refers to a visit which he and Gallio had made to
Nicetes' school: *memini una nos ab auditione Nicetis ad Messalam
venisse*. It is all the more remarkable that his allusions to the
great days of Attic oratory are so few, and so little suggestive
of first-hand knowledge of the authors concerned.

In *Contr.* III pr. 8 he quotes an unappreciative criticism of
Plato's *Apology* by Cassius Severus: *eloquentissimi viri Platonis
oratio, quae pro Socrate scripta est, nec patrono nec reo digna
est*. Severus is arguing that Plato was among those who could only
be successful in one genre; he was not as good an orator as a
philosopher. Of the Attic orators proper only Demosthenes and
Aeschines receive mention. Demosthenes was famous enough as a
historical figure to have his life-story pillaged for *exempla* even
by Latin rhetoricians. Musa, for instance, in *Contr.* VII.3.4 recalls Demosthenes' suicide: *'habuit' inquit 'Demosthenes venenum
et bibit.' idem ego tibi pater quod Demostheni Philippus?*
Seneca, then, may be displaying no more than the general knowledge

any Roman might have when he objects to Nicetes' anachronistic use of an imitation of Demosthenes' Marathon oath in a *suasoria* about Xerxes (*Suas.* 2.14). Another reference, however, the startling implications of which will be discussed later,[1] concerns Demosthenes' style. We are told of Calvus: *compositio quoque eius in actionibus ad exemplum Demosthenis viget:*[2] *nihil in illa placidum, nihil lene est, omnia excitata et fluctuantia* (*Contr.* VII.4.8). This is a striking critical remark, but whether it implies first-hand familiarity with Demosthenes' speeches is questionable. Demosthenes' vehemence must have been well known, and, as we shall see,[3] there is some reason to believe that in *Contr.* VII.4.8 Seneca is recalling remarks he had heard Latro make. Seneca's one reference to Aeschines is an insignificant one. At pains to distinguish the famous orator from a minor rhetorician called Aeschines active in his own day, Seneca says in passing that declamation was not known in the great man's time: *Aeschines, non ille orator - tunc enim non declamandi studium erat -, sed hic ex declamatoribus novis dixit...* (*Contr.* I.8.16). Evidently he did not know of the tradition that the origins of modern declamation belonged to the time of Aeschines (Quint. II.4.41: *circa Demetrium Phalerea*), or even in his school (Philostr. *Vit. soph.* I.481).[4]

These are the elder Seneca's only references to Attic oratory, unless one counts the sentence from ps.-Demosthenes, *In ep. Phil.* 13 (based on *Ol.* II.20), which he quotes with only slight deviation from the received text, but, misled by Arellius Fuscus, wrongly attributes to Thucydides (*Contr.* IX.1.13). There is absolutely no mention of Antiphon, Andocides, Lysias, Isocrates, Isaeus, Lycurgus, Hyperides, or Dinarchus. Greek rhetorical theorists before his own time are similarly neglected: we find no allusion to the fifth-century sophists, nothing, if we except Cassius Severus' opinion of the *Apology* (*Contr.* III pr. 8) and a garbled[5] reference by Cestius to Aristotle's cousin Callisthenes in *Suas.* 1.5, about Plato or Aristotle, no mention by name of Theophrastus, or Hermagoras, the second-century theorist whose views on the scope of the orator's work, and methods of analysing forensic argument, exercised so much influence on Cicero and Quintilian.[6] Even granted that as a writer of descriptive

criticism, Seneca had no compelling need to make constant reference to works of rhetorical theory, the number of famous names
conspicuous by their absence is remarkable.

His neglect of contemporary Greek rhetorical theorists is not
so complete, as he does make just a few references to the dogmatic
disagreements between the followers of Apollodorus of Pergamum and
Theodorus of Gadara (neither of whom he cites as a declaimer).[7]
We learn from him about one of the major issues over which Apollodorus and Theodorus differed: whether it was invariably necessary
to narrate the facts of a case.[8] The orator Vallius Syriacus,
criticized during a trial by his opponent Bruttedius Niger for
omitting to account for the movements of the accused, is reported
to have explained: *primum non apud eundem praeceptorem studuimus:
tu Apollodorum habuisti, cui semper narrari placet, ego Theodorum,
cui non semper* (*Contr.* II.1.36). Seneca notes the debilitating
effect that a rigid adherence to Apollodorean dogma could have on
an orator: *sed Turrinus pater multum viribus dempserat, dum Apollodorum sequitur ac summam legem dicendi sectam putat* (*Contr.* X pr.
15). He also reports minutiae of the Apollodoreans' theory: their
views on ambiguous *controversia* themes, of which *Contr.* I.2 is an
example: *aiebat* [sc. *Latro*] *Apollodoreis quidem fixa esse themata
et tuta, sed hic non repugnare controversiam huic suspicioni; non
enim ponitur adhuc virginem <esse> et multa sunt propter quae
credibile sit non esse* (*Contr.* I.2.14);[9] and on the treatment of
themes where the question arose whether a *beneficium* had been
received: Dionysius Atticus, a pupil of Apollodorus, agreed with
Gallio that if it were at all possible to get an adversary to concede that no benefit had been received, we should try to achieve
this, but that otherwise we should pass the matter over *quasi
donemus et possimus quidem facere controversiam, sed nolimus*
(*Contr.* II.5.11). Dionysius also pointed out that one could argue
in some cases that, though a benefit had been received, it was an
insignificant one (*ibid.*), and another Apollodorean, Moschus, produced a further quibble as to whether one could speak of *beneficia*
received by a husband from his wife and vice versa: *non est beneficium, sed officium facere quod debeas* (*Contr.* II.5.13).

On the Theodoreans Seneca has less to say, merely noting, in

addition to their views on the dispensability of *narratio*, the
fact that Tiberius was among their number: *Tiberius ipse Theo-*
doreus offendebatur Nicetis ingenio... (Suas. 3.7). He does not
explain what connection there was, if any, between Theodorean
doctrine and Tiberius' prejudice against the ecstatic rhetoric of
Nicetes.[10]

Seneca does not commit himself to allegiance to either
school. Though he shows a certain lack of sympathy for the Apollodoreans in *Contr.* X pr. 15, it does not follow that he was a Theodorean. He seems to have been tolerant, like the *Theodorei*, of
the omission of *narratio* (*Contr.* I.2.19, cf. IX.2.18) in certain
circumstances, but does not, for example, adopt the idiosyncratic
terminology they used for the analysis of argumentation: Seneca
uses the term *quaestiones*, following in this the usage of
Hermagoras et Apollodorus et alii plurimi scriptores (Quint. III.
11.3), where a Theodorean would have spoken of *capita generalia*
and *capita specialia* (*ibid.*).

Among Seneca's references to the two schools there is nothing
that need imply that he had read any critical work by Apollodorus
or Theodorus. He owes his information about the Apollodoreans'
insistence on water-tight *controversia* themes to Latro. The
reference to Tiberius' connection with the Theodoreans comes from
a long report of gossip about Nicetes. It is never to Apollodorus
and Theodorus themselves that he refers, but to their pupils, men
whose opinions it was quite possible to learn about without con-
sulting books, just by listening to lectures, the gossip of the
declamation halls, and repartee in the law-courts.

Similarly, the sprinkling of Greek critical terms to be found
in his books could have been gleaned here and there from the lectures and gossip of the schools. There is no reason to suppose
that Seneca owes a particular debt to any single Greek theorist
for his terminology, which includes, as is only to be expected,
words from every stratum of the language, from old-established
terms like *tragoedia* and *historia* to others which were much more
recent coinages (though, given the gaps in our evidence, we cannot
know quite how recent) like *idiotismus* and *metaphrasis*.[11] Some
are loan-words well entrenched in Latin, e.g. *comicus*,[12] others,

like *ethicos* and *problemata philosophumena* appear monstrous in the
Latin garb in which they appear in our texts. (But perhaps it was
a copyist, rather than Seneca himself, who was responsible for the
transliteration in such cases.)[13] No consistent criterion[14] can
be seen to determine the preference for Greek terms over Latin by
Seneca and the critics quoted by him: there seems no particular
reason why they should so often use the terms *prooemium* and
epilogus when there existed well-established pure Latin terms for
all the standard sections of a speech; again, Seneca seems just as
happy using *figura*[15] as its Greek equivalent *schema*, and it seems
legitimate to regard *insania* and *corrupte* as synonymous in his
criticism with *cacozelia* and *cacozelōs*.[16] So, although some of
his Greek terms are words for which no adequate, all-embracing and
unambiguous Latin equivalent had been coined, e.g. *tragoedia*, no
rational process of selection called for the use of all of them.
Now, irrational selection is what is to be expected if Seneca's
grecisms are derived from random reminiscences of a jargon originally used in impromptu, unwritten criticism. That this is their
origin becomes quite clear if we observe that in his prefaces, the
most formal and carefully composed parts of his work, Greek terms
are relatively less frequent than in the surveys of declamations,[17]
where he is less concerned with smooth artistic finish, and if we
note how in a number of passages Seneca quotes other people using
Greek terms which he elsewhere adopts for his own use, for example:
Contr. VII pr. 8: *clamabat Albucius: non detuli condicionem;
schema dixi*, and *Contr.* X.4.25: *P. Vinicius...hunc aiebat sensum
disertissime apud Nasonem Ovidium esse positum...occiso Achille
hoc epiphonema poni...* It is not surprising to find a free use of
Greek terms in the conversation of the Latin critics of Seneca's
time, for we may deduce from the frequent appearance of Greek expressions in the letters of Cicero and his friends where they are
discussing literature, that conversations about rhetoric and
poetry in the late Republic would also have been full of them.

It seems quite possible, then, that the whole of the elder
Seneca's knowledge of Greek oratory and rhetorical theory could
have been picked up at second hand from his friends and acquaint-
ances in and around the declamation halls. Significantly, he

said of Latro, whose formal education had been identical with his
own: *Graecos...et contemnebat et ignorabat* (*Contr.* X.4.21) – this
with reference to contemporary Greek rhetoricians. It would not
be fair to say that the same was true of Seneca, who was at least
a frequenter of Greek declamations, but this statement is indicative of the extent to which these two men, who were to exercise,
the one through his offspring, the other through his pupils, a
considerable influence on the development of Silver Latin, were
cut off from the main stream of Greco-Roman literary tradition by
an uninspired and perhaps wholly provincial[18] education.

There is a remarkable scarcity in Seneca's criticism of allusions to Republican Roman orators other than Cicero. The only
orator before Cicero's generation to receive mention is the elder
Cato, who is invoked in grand style in *Contr.* I pr. 9:

erratis, optimi iuvenes, nisi illam vocem non M. Catonis, sed
oraculi creditis. quid enim est oraculum? nempe voluntas divina
hominis ore enuntiata; et quem tandem antistitem sanctiorem sibi
invenire divinitas potuit quam M. Catonem, per quem humano generi
non praeciperet, sed convicium faceret? ille ergo vir quid ait?
'orator est, Marce fili, vir bonus dicendi peritus.'

The quotation is no proof that Seneca had read Cato's works. Not
only was Cato occasionally the subject of declamatory *exempla*[19]
but the particular dictum cited is one to be found quoted in handbooks of rhetoric after Seneca's time, and may well have been
excerpted for scholastic use earlier. It is given great prominence by Quintilian, who in his final book bases his whole discussion of the qualities of the orator on Cato's definition (XII.
1.1ff.) and by Fortunatianus, who quotes it right at the beginning
of his rhetorical catechism: *Quid est rhetorica? bene dicendi
scientia. quid est orator? vir bonus dicendi peritus* (*RLM*
81.4f.).

Seneca never alludes at all in his criticism to any of the
other oratorical worthies of the second century B.C., praised in
Cicero's *Brutus*. It may be suspected that his view of early Roman
oratory was similar to that of Velleius Paterculus (I.17.3):

at oratio ac vis forensis perfectumque prosae eloquentiae decus,
ut idem separetur Cato (pace P. Crassi Scipionisque et Laelii et
Gracchorum et Fanii et Servii Galbae dixerim) ita universa sub
principe operis sui erupit Tullio, ut delectari ante eum

paucissimis, mirari vero neminem possis nisi aut ab illo visum aut
qui illum viderit.

Certainly his conception of literary history resembles that
of Velleius in other respects: remember his desire to be numbered
amongst those who could have seen Cicero (*Contr.* I pr. 11), and
his contention that the only Roman oratory to rival the Greeks
circa Ciceronem effloruit, and that *omnia ingenia, quae lucem
studiis nostris attulerunt, tunc nata sunt* (*Contr.* I pr. 6-7). It
seems that Seneca wished to glorify the first generation of literary men he had known - misguidedly, one may think, in the case of
the rhetoricians whom he must have had primarily in mind - by
associating them with the Ciceronian age. About the orators who
might truly be described as *circa Ciceronem* he has little to say,
and, though his outrageous failure to qualify the statement in
Contr. I pr. 11, *omnes autem magni in eloquentia nominis excepto
Cicerone videor audisse*, may be blamed on a momentary lapse of
concentration combined with a taste for pithy expression, it will
not come as a surprise if we find no evidence that Seneca had any
very profound or extensive familiarity with late Republican
oratory.

Seneca professes to be a great admirer of Cicero, but then,
it was normal in the schools of rhetoric to revere Cicero uncritically. No matter how violent a reaction the declaimers' own rhetoric represented against the Ciceronian ideal, they were prepared
to declaim with enormous fervour on themes based on (more or less
apocryphal) stories about the great orator's life and death:

Contr. VII.2: De moribus sit actio.
Popillium parricidii reum Cicero defendit; absolutus est. pro-
scriptum Ciceronem ab Antonio missus occidit Popillius et caput
eius ad Antonium rettulit. accusatur de moribus.

Suas. 6: Deliberat Cicero, an Antonium deprecetur.

Suas. 7: Deliberat Cicero, an scripta sua conburat promittente
Antonio incolumitatem, si fecisset.

The death of Cicero may seem a surprisingly dangerous topic for
the declaimers of the early Empire to deal with. Perhaps part of
its charm lay in the danger. The rhetoricians were aware which
were the most sensitive issues, and generally avoided mention of
them. The extracts given by Seneca from *Contr.* VII.2 include

none where the declaimer explicitly mentions that Cicero had once
been hailed *Pater Patriae*, despite the fact that the theme of this
controversia almost cries out for *sententiae* complaining that
Popillius, having killed his own father, had gone on to murder the
Father of his Country.[20] The declaimers were normally careful,
when speaking of the proscription in which Cicero was doomed, to
lay the blame entirely on Antony. Seneca remarks on Albucius'
treatment of *Suas.* 6, ...*solus ex declamatoribus temptavit dicere
non unum illi esse Antonium infestum* (*Suas.* 6.9).

Cicero was undoubtedly read, if not always with any degree of
concentration, by the average student in the schools of the early
Empire. His diction already seemed old-fashioned: Seneca finds it
remarkable that the declaimer Haterius ...*quaedam antiqua et a
Cicerone dicta, a ceteris deinde deserta dicebat...* (*Contr.* IV pr.
9). Yet his reputation remained unassailable. The egotistical
Cestius might rate his own eloquence above Cicero's, and win his
pupils over to his point of view, but public opinion was against
him. Cassius Severus complains:

pueri fere aut iuvenes scholas frequentant; hi non tantum
disertissimis viris, quos paulo ante rettuli, Cestium suum praeferunt sed etiam Ciceroni praeferrent, nisi lapides timerent.
quo tamen uno modo possunt praeferunt; huius enim declamationes
ediscunt; illius orationes non legunt nisi eas quibus Cestius
rescripsit. (*Contr.* III pr. 15)

But it was not just the fear of a stoning that kept the scholastics from expressing open contempt for Cicero. The need to praise
him uncritically in declamations perpetuated an unnaturally high
regard for him through a period when in reality all his ideals in
oratory and politics were being rejected. The declaimers inter-
larded their *sententiae* in *Contr.* VII.2, *Suas.* 6 and *Suas.* 7 with
allusions to Cicero's speeches, sometimes direct quotations.[21]
Their favourite speeches seem to have been the last of the
Verrines,[22] the *Catilinarians*,[23] the *Pro Milone*, to which Cestius
had done the honour of providing an answer,[24] and above all the
second *Philippic*, the speech which Juvenal was later to single out
as the prime example of Ciceronian eloquence: *te, conspicuae divina
Philippica famae | volveris a prima quae proxima* (10.125f.).[25]
Thus the declaimers of the elder Seneca's time anticipated in

their choice of Ciceronian allusions the view of one of the inter-
locutors in Tacitus' *Dialogus*:

nec Ciceronem magnum oratorem P. Quinctius defensus aut Licinius
Archias faciunt: Catilina et Milo et Verres et Antonius hanc illi
famam circumdederunt... (*Dial*. 37.6)

To the rhetoricians these speeches were a quarry of resonant expressions of righteous indignation: *tuis verbis, Cicero, utendum
est: 'o tempora, o mores!'*,[26] and of dicta about the proper attitude towards death: *mors nec immatura consulari nec misera
sapienti;*[27] *mori enim naturae finis est non poena*,[28] which one
could imagine Cicero recalling as he faced the prospect of execution. They also provided lurid invectives against tyrannical
opponents which the declaimers might re-use when condemning
Popillius' evil deed: *ut uno ictu pereat tantum dabo: pro Cicerone
sic liceat pacisci?* (Sepullius Bassus in *Contr*. VII.2.1 cf. *Verr*.
II.5.118), or recall when dissuading Cicero from submission to
Antony:

videbis ardentes crudelitate simul ac superbia oculos; videbis
illum non hominis, sed belli civilis vultum; videbis illas fauces,
per quas bona Cn. Pompei transierunt, illa latera, illam totius
corporis gladiatoriam firmitatem; videbis illum pro tribunali
locum, quem modo magister equitum, cui ructare turpe erat, vomitu
foedaverat: supplex accadens genibus deprecaberis? eo ore, cui se
debet salus publica, humilia in adulationem verba summittes?
(Latro in *Suas*. 6.3; cf. *Phil*. II.63-4; *Verr*. II.5.161)

Sometimes, but not often, less famous speeches of Cicero are alluded to. Cestius quotes from the *Pro Roscio Amerino*: *quid tam
commune quam spiritus vivis, terra mortuis, mare fluctuantibus,
litus eiectis?* (*Contr*. VII.2.3 = *Rosc. Amer*. 72 - a somewhat notorious piece of Cicero's early oratory, whose faults he recognizes himself in *Or*. 30.107). Another *sententia* of Cestius' could
have been suggested by the first *Philippic*, or the *Pro Marcello*
(*Suas*. 6.4).[29] Varius Geminus in an unusual treatment of *Suas*. 6
gave Cicero what Cassius Severus approvingly called *vivum
consilium*, pointing out that innumerable people in the provinces
were indebted to Cicero and would shelter him if he fled from
Italy:

Siciliam dixit vindicatam esse ab illo, Ciliciam a proconsule
egregie administratam, familiares studiis eius et Achaiam et
Asiam, Deiotari regnum obligatum beneficiis, Aegyptum et habere
beneficii memoriam et agere perfidiae paenitentiam. sed maxime

illum in Asiam et in Macedoniam hortatus est in Cassi et in Bruti
castra. (*Suas.* 6.11)

Here is an allusion to the *Pro rege Deiotaro*, as well as one to
his prosecution of Verres. Varius Geminus also declaimed the
altera pars of this *suasoria*, recommending that Cicero should
yield to Antony. He pointed out, among other things, how enemies
often are persuaded to give up their hostility, instancing how
Cicero himself had been prevailed upon to defend Vatinius, whom he
had attacked in an earlier speech (*Suas.* 6.13 W).[30] Varius
Geminus' imaginative grasp of the details of Cicero's career seems
to have been exceptional: ...*Cassius Severus aiebat alios
declamasse, Varium Geminum vivum consilium dedisse* (*Suas.* 6.11),
but presumably Latro and others would at least have been able to
reel off Cicero's achievements *cursu* (see *Contr.* I pr. 18).

Were the declaimers familiar with any writings of Cicero
other than speeches? Some at least of Cicero's correspondence was
certainly accessible in the early Empire: in *Suas.* 1.5, perhaps
quoting from a lecture by Cestius, Seneca gives an explicit reference to a letter from Cassius to Cicero (*Ad fam.* XV.19.4). The
quotation, though not exact, is close to the original.[31] But none
of the other possible verbal echoes of the letters found in the
declaimers' utterances is so close as to be unquestionably the
product of actual reading of the originals. History books and
school tradition could have transmitted all that the average declaimer knew of them. For example, though it is interesting to
note the parallel between Haterius' *sententia* in *Suas.* 6.1, *in hac
causa etiam Ciceronem verba deficient*, and expressions in *Ad fam.*
II.11.1, *putaresne umquam accidere posse, ut mihi verba dessent...?*
and XIII.63.1, *non putavi fieri posse, ut mihi verba dessent*, the
verbal similarity is not close enough to prove that Haterius had
read the *Ad familiares*, though he may have done.[32] Nor can his
use of the words *iam nostra peracta sunt* (*Suas.* 6.1) be regarded
as firm evidence that he knew the letter to Brutus in which Cicero
quotes from Plautus' *Trinummus*: *mihi quidem aetas acta ferme est:
tua istuc refert maxime* (*Trin.* 319 = Cic. *Ad Brut.* 8.2 Watt).
Similarly, where the declaimers refer to topics to be found discussed in Cicero's philosophical and rhetorical treatises, the

inspiration for their words need not have come directly, or even indirectly, from Cicero. Fuscus' resounding words in *Suas*. 6.5, *non te ignobilis tumulus abscondet* etc., could have been inspired by any number of sources (given that Fuscus, if not a Greek himself, was much inclined to imitate Greek originals)[33] besides Cicero's *De senectute* 82, with which they have been compared.[34] Declamatory references to the oratory of the Republic may or may not imply knowledge of the *Brutus*. Varius Geminus could have learnt of Cicero's studies in Achaia and Asia from this source, but his reference to them (*Suas*. 6.11) is of too general a kind for us to be sure. Capito may have derived the knowledge he displays in *Contr*. VII.2.6 about Pompey's relations with Hortensius from the reference to the speech *Pro Cn. Pompei bonis* in *Brut*. 64.230, but it would be unnatural to suppose that Cicero was the only authority to mention this presumably quite important speech.

How familiar Seneca himself was with Cicero's works can hardly be determined, seeing that his subject-matter was not such as to require constant reference to them, but it is important to notice that the majority of his Ciceronian allusions could very well have been picked up from secondary sources, oral and written.

Some of what he says about Cicero has a highly rhetorical flavour untypical of his criticism. Probably he was influenced by the declaimers' eulogistic treatment of Cicero[35] when he wrote in *Contr*. I pr. 11:

illudque ingenium quod solum populus Romanus par imperio suo habuit, cognoscere et, quod vulgo aliquando dici solet, sed in illo proprie debet, potui vivam vocem audire.

As we have seen,[36] in the passage where he pits the Roman eloquence of Cicero's time against insolent Greece (*Contr*. I pr. 6) his expression is closely paralleled by a *sententia* by Cestius in *Suas*. 7.10.

Other references are more or less certainly reports of what other critics had said about Cicero. In *Contr*. VII.3.8-9 he acknowledges his debt to Cassius Severus for an account of the history of Roman humour, in which Cicero figures prominently. Another important Ciceronian allusion comes in the course of a passage throughout which it may be suspected that Seneca is

quoting Cestius (*Suas.* 1.5-8).[37] This is the passage discussed
earlier as an example of Seneca's eccentric mixing of direct and
indirect speech. If we set this allusion, an explicit reference
to a letter from Cassius to Cicero, in its context, it will be
apparent that we cannot use it as firm evidence that the elder
Seneca had read any of Cicero's correspondence. Cestius is talking in this passage about the way one ought to address a monarch
like Alexander:

...nihil dicendum aiebat nisi cum summa veneratione regis, ne
accideret idem, quod praeceptori eius, amitino Aristotelis,
accidit, quem occidit propter intempestive liberos sales; nam cum
se deum vellet videri et vulneratus esset, viso sanguine philosophus mirari se dixerat, quod non esset ἰχώρ οἶός πέρ τε ῥέει
μακάρεσσι θεοῖσιν. ille se ab hac urbanitate lancea vindicavit.
eleganter in C. Cassi epistula quadam ad M. Ciceronem missa
positum: multum iocatur de stultitia Cn. Pompei adulescentis, qui
in Hispania contraxit exercitum et ad Mundam acie victus est;
deinde ait: 'nos quidem illum deridemus, sed timeo, ne ille nos
gladio ἀντιμυκτηρίσῃ.' in omnibus regibus haec urbanitas
extimescenda est. aiebat itaque apud Alexandrum esse <sic>
dicendam sententiam, ut multa adulatione animus eius per-
mulceretur... (*Suas.* 1.5f.)

After *eleganter...positum* we should perhaps understand *esse aiebat*
rather than *est*.[38]

Worth considering as a group are three passages concerned
with rhetorical schools and amateur declamation in the late
Republic: *Contr.* I pr. 11; *ibid.* 12 and II pr. 5. These passages
have two things in common besides similarity of subject-matter:
they contain detailed information which could only have been
obtained from the writings of Cicero or sources contemporary with
him, and they are closely paralleled by passages in Suetonius' *De
grammaticis et rhetoribus.* *Contr.* I pr. 12, the main Senecan
passage to deal with the history of Roman declamation before his
own time, will be discussed at length in relation to other ancient
evidence, including that of Suetonius, in the next chapter.[39] The
Suetonian parallel passage is *De gramm. et rhet.* 25.8f. Brugnoli.
The reference to Cicero as a declaimer in *Contr.* 1 pr. 11, *alioqui
in illo atriolo in quo duos grandes praetextatos ait secum
declamasse potui adesse...* has a counterpart in *De gramm. et rhet.*
25.3:

Cicero ad praeturam usque etiam Graece declamitavit, Latine vero

senior et quidem cum consulibus Hirtio et Pansa quos discipulos et
grandes praetextatos vocabat.

The information recorded here seems of a type likely to have been
derived from Cicero's correspondence. Such was certainly the
ultimate source of the information given in *Contr*. II pr. 5,
primus omnium Latinus rhetor Romae fuit puero Cicerone Plotius, as
we see from the parallel passage in *De gramm. et rhet*. 26.1:

L. Plotius Gallus. de hoc Cicero in epistula ad M. Titinium sic
refert: equidem memoria teneo pueris nobis primum Latine docere
coepisse Plotium quendam. ad quem cum fieret concursus quod
studiosissimus quisque apud eum exerceretur, dolebam mihi idem non
licere. continebar autem doctissimorum hominum auctoritate qui
existimabat Graecis exercitationibus ali melius ingenia posse.

Sometimes in this group of related passages Seneca gives us
details which are not in Suetonius, for example the reference to
Cicero's *atriolum* in *Contr*. I pr. 11, and in the history of declamation in §12, among other things, a quotation illustrative of
Calvus' use of the term *declamare*. On other points, however,
Suetonius provides us with fuller information, which he could not
have derived from Seneca. It looks very much as though the two
authors were using data derived from a common source, presumably a
grammatical work dealing with the history of Roman declamation.[40]
If this is the case, *Contr*. I pr. 11 and II pr. 5 provide no more
certain proof that Seneca had read any of Cicero's correspondence
than does the reference to a letter of Cassius to Cicero in *Suas*.
1.5.[41]

But Seneca the Elder was not incapable of original research.
At least his discussion of the events surrounding the death of
Cicero, a subject which must certainly have come within the scope
of his *Histories*, looks like the fruit of his own investigations.[42]
In *Contr*. VII.2.8 he criticizes the declaimers for assuming that
Popillius was the assassin of Cicero, having previously been de-
fended by him on a charge of parricide:

Popillium pauci ex historicis tradiderunt interfectorem Ciceronis
et hi quoque non parricidi reum a Cicerone defensum, sed in
privato iudicio: declamatoribus placuit parricidi reum fuisse.
sic autem eum accusant tamquam defendi non possit, cum adeo possit
absolvi, ut ne accusari quidem potuerit.

This passage provides us with an important insight into the relationship between declamation themes and historiography. Note

that Seneca relies here on secondary sources, *historici*, for all
his information, but maybe this was inevitable, for there may
never have existed primary written documentation for the identity
of Cicero's assassin, and any there was is likely to have been
suppressed; Cicero's speech for Popillius may have been so unimportant that it was never published. We must not underrate
Seneca's carefulness as a historical investigator when he did have
access to primary evidence. In *Suas.* 6.14ff. he makes a study of
narratives of Cicero's death and estimates of his career by a variety of historians and poets. One extract he examines is a passage, damaging to Cicero's reputation, from Pollio's speech, *Pro
Lamia*. At least, this passage was to be found in the *published*
version of this speech, but Seneca tells us that he had learnt
from people actually present at the trial that it had not been in
the speech as Pollio delivered it; he also notes that Pollio had
not had the audacity to include his libellous allegations in his
Histories, and deduces from this that they were quite baseless:

...adieceratque his alia sordidiora multo, ut [tibi] facile
liqueret hoc totum adeo falsum esse ut ne ipse quidem Pollio in
historiis suis ponere ausus sit. huic certe actioni eius pro
Lamia qui interfuerunt, negant eum haec dixisse - nec enim mentiri
sub triumvirorum conscientia sustinebat - sed postea conposuisse.
(*Suas.* 6.15 W)

Here is a warning to us that, while we must make due allowance for the elder Seneca's sponge-like capacity for absorbing
other people's criticisms, and for the likelihood that in *Contr.* I
pr. 12 and allied passages he was dependent on a grammatical
source, it cannot be assumed that he was totally without independence as a researcher into matters outside his own experience. It
might seem quite legitimate to suggest, on the strength of the
available evidence, that Seneca could have written such literary
criticism as he gives us without having any more knowledge of
Cicero's orations than the average declaimer had, if as much. It
would be easy to argue that his quotation in *Suas.* 6.27 from the
Pro Archia, one of the less famous speeches, *Sextilius Ena fuit...
talis, quales esse Cicero Cordubenses poetas ait, <pingue> quiddam
sonantis atque peregrinum* (= *Arch.* 26) must have been one which
every Corduban schoolboy knew. But it would be unsafe to go so

far as to suggest that, for example, his passing observations relating to Ciceronian diction in *Contr.* IV pr. 9 need not imply any
careful reading of Cicero, being perhaps a reminiscence of anti-
Haterian gossip in the schools. The man who was interested enough
in the last years of the Republic to compare versions of Pollio's
Pro Lamia was quite probably much more widely read in Cicero's
oratory than we can judge on the evidence of his criticism.[43]

Nobody will expect the elder Seneca to draw heavily on
Cicero's philosophical works. There is, as it happens, a passage
in *Contr.* I pr. 19 which it is relevant to compare with *Tusc.
disp.* I.24.59: Seneca denies that the feats of memory ascribed to
Hortensius and Cineas are anything to be unduly amazed by, whereas
Cicero marvels at these two men as examples of brilliant memor-
izers, along with Simonides, Theodectes and Metrodorus Scepsius.
It need not be, however, that Seneca in *Contr.* I pr. 19 is consciously challenging Cicero's opinion. The fact seems to be that
the same examples of mnemonists were cited automatically by any
teacher of rhetoric when dealing with the topic of *memoria*. Quintilian was later to cite Simonides and Hortensius in this connection (XI.2.11ff.); the elder Pliny (*NH* VII.88) cites Cineas.

How familiar Seneca was with Cicero's rhetorical treatises is
another, and a more important, matter. Possible verbal echoes of
these works are extremely scarce. One is found in *Contr.* II pr.
5, just before one of the references paralleled in Suetonius:

...Blandum rhetorem...qui <primus> eques Romanus Romae docuit;
ante illum intra libertinos praeceptores pulcherrimae disciplinae
continebantur, et minime probabili more *turpe erat docere quod
honestum erat discere*. nam primus omnium Latinus rhetor Romae
fuit puero Cicerone Plotius.

The echo is of *Orator* 42.145:

num igitur...est periculum ne quis putet in magna arte et gloriosa
turpe esse docere alios id quod ipsi fuerit honestissimum discere?

It is possible that this verbal reminiscence was transmitted by
the grammatical source which told Seneca about Plotius, even
though it is not paralleled in the extant part of the *De gramm. et
rhet.*, which is also lacking in any reference to Blandus. For
though the scrappiness of Suetonius' text poses insoluble problems, and it is impossible now to discover for certain the

identity of the grammatical work from which he and Seneca seem to
have derived information about Republican schools and declaimers,
one observation at least will be appropriate here. A serious candidate for the role of author of the lost source – he would not
have liked to be called a *grammaticus* – is Cornelius Nepos, whose
minor work *quo distinguit litteratum ab erudito* was known to
Suetonius, and included pernickety differentiation between literary terms which may be compared with the drawing of the distinction between *dicere* and *declamare* and other terminological
niceties in *Contr.* I pr. 12:[44]

> Cornelius quoque Nepos libello quo distinguit litteratum ab
> erudito, litteratos vulgo quidem appellari ait eos qui aliquid
> diligenter et acute scienterque possint aut dicere aut scribere,
> ceterum proprie sic appellandos poetarum interpretes, qui a
> Graecis grammatici nominentur. (Suet. *De gramm. et rhet.* 4.2 =
> Nepos, *De inl. vir.* fr. 18*, *HRR* II 40)

Now, in another fragment quoted by Suetonius, Nepos displays an
interest, shared by Seneca in the remarks on Blandus where the
Ciceronian phrase comes, in a highly unusual subject, the breaking
of class barriers by men of letters:

> L. Voltacilius Pilutus...primus omnium libertinorum, ut Cornelius
> Nepos opinatur, scribere historiam orsus non nisi ab honestissimo
> quoque scribi solitam ad id tempus. (Suet. *De gramm. et rhet.*
> 27.1f. = Nepos, *De inl. vir.* fr. 16*, *HRR* II 40)

Nepos, of course, must have had a very wide familiarity with
Cicero's writings, being intimate with his circle, and the author
of a *Life of Cicero* as well as one of Atticus. And it is not out
of the question that Nepos could have referred to the unusual
career of Blandus, as he himself lived on into the twenties B.C.
and the knightly *rhetor* was one of the older generation of
Seneca's declaimers.[45]

Another briefer echo of Cicero's rhetorical theory is found
in *Contr.* I pr. 12, one of the passages which certainly have
Suetonian parallels. Cicero had written in *De or.* I.34.157:
educenda deinde dictio est ex hac domestica exercitatione. In
Contr. I pr. 12 we are told that Calvus explicitly distinguished
between *declamare* and *dicere*, and an illustrative quotation is
elucidated by the gloss, *alterum putat domesticae exercitationis
esse, alterum verae actionis.* This elucidation may in this case

be the work of Seneca's missing source, but the phrase reappears
in pure Senecan criticism in *Contr.* III pr. 1: *simul ad has
domesticas exercitationes secesserant, desertos ab ingenio suo.*
However, it is uncertain whether Seneca remembered Cicero's use of
this phrase, which may well have been a watch-word in his day
among people who adopted an old-fashioned attitude towards declamation.

Another, very different, possible case of Ciceronian influence is to be found at the very end of Seneca's tenth preface. At
the end of the *De oratore* we find commendation of the young
Hortensius, whose great promise was already evident at the dramatic date of the dialogue, first by Catulus, his father-in-law,
and then by his friend Crassus (III.61.228f.). Similarly, Seneca
the Elder closes his last preface with praise of a promising young
man, the son of Clodius Turrinus, an intimate friend of the
family:

inde filius quoque eius, id est meus - numquam enim illum a vobis
distinxi -, habet in dicendo controversiam paternam diligentiam,
qua vires ingenii sui ex industria retundit. hoc et in ipso
genere vitae sequitur, ad summa evasurus iuvenis nisi modicis
contentus esset, et ideo dignus est cuius tam modestis
cupiditatibus Fortuna praestet fidem. (*Contr.* X pr. 16)

Both Cicero and Seneca the Elder seem to be aligning themselves
with a tradition which went back to Plato, who introduces praise
of the young Isocrates at the end of the *Phaedrus* (278e-279b). Of
course we do not know how widely this Platonic device was used
among Roman writers of the late Republic and early Empire, but *De
or.* III.61.228f. must surely have been the most famous example of
its use. Even if not directly inspired by this passage, *Contr.* X
pr. 16 is a tantalizing reminder that Seneca the Elder must have
read much in the course of his long life to which he never refers
in his extant books. The fact remains that any study he may have
made of Cicero's rhetorical treatises left surprisingly little
mark on either his critical ideals or his vocabulary.[46]

Another debatable question is whether he had a first-hand
knowledge of the speeches and criticism of Calvus. He once quotes
a remark by Calvus about declamation, but it comes in one of the
passages (*Contr.* I pr. 12) where he may be suspected of depending

on a grammatical source. That the quotation is to be ascribed to
Calvus rather than to Cicero seems clear, despite a certain ambiguity in the text of the sentence which introduces it.

...ipsa 'declamatio' apud nullum antiquum auctorem ante Ciceronem
et Calvum inveniri potest, qui declamationem <a dictione>
distinguit; ait enim declamare iam se non mediocriter, dicere
bene; alterum putat domesticae exercitationis esse, alterum verae
actionis.

> <a dictione> *add. Gertz*; <ab oratione> *Bursian*.   declamare
> iam se *Bonnet;* declamare iam ne *M* (est *add. in marg.* M^3);
> declamare est *P;* declamare iam *NSα;* declamare est iam *βν.*

Let us accept Gertz' supplement and Bonnet's conjecture: there
still remains a certain clumsiness of construction in this passage. After the plural antecedent, *Ciceronem et Calvum*, one expects a plural verb in the relative clause. Instead we find the
singular *distinguit*, with a quotation following it which illustrates *one* man's usage of the term *declamare*. The singular verbs
in the remainder of the sentence: *ait...putat...* forbid us simply
to emend *distinguit* to *distinguunt*. It would be unjust to suggest
that the clumsiness is attributable to lack of care on Seneca's
part in epitomizing his source, for it is clumsiness of a kind
unparalleled in his work, and particularly surprising found in an
otherwise artistically written preface. Perhaps we ought to
transpose *ante Ciceronem et Calvum*, placing them after *inveniri
potest*. Alternatively, as J. B. Hall has recently argued,[47]
either *Ciceronem et* or *et Calvum* may be regarded as an interpolation, most probably the former, as it is much more likely that
the name of Cicero who 'has held the stage since section 11 of
this preface' should have crept in, than that of Calvus; the presence of the words *ante Ciceronem* in a sentence a few lines above
could have precipitated the interpolation of a gratuitous reference to Cicero.[48]*

The other reference to Calvus in Seneca's criticism may seem
at first sight totally to confute any notion that his reading in
Republican oratory could have been very limited. The remarkable
passage *Contr.* VII.4.6-8 presents an estimate of Calvus quite
opposed to that put about by Cicero in his rhetorical works.[49]

Cicero had represented his rival Calvus as a speaker who,
despite many admirable gifts, was less effective than he might

have been owing to his excessive self-criticism and his desire to

be reckoned an orator in the Attic tradition:

sed ad Calvum - is enim nobis erat propositus - revertamur; qui
orator fuit cum litteris eruditior quam Curio tum etiam accuratius
quoddam dicendi et exquisitius adferebat genus; quod quamquam
scienter eleganterque tractabat, nimium tamen inquirens in se
atque ipse sese observans metuensque ne vitiosum colligeret, etiam
verum sanguinem deperdebat. itaque eius oratio nimia religione
attenuata doctis et attente audientibus erat inlustris, <a>
multitudine autem et a foro, cui nata eloquentia est, devorabatur.
   Tum Brutus: Atticum se, inquit, Calvus noster dici oratorem
volebat: inde erat ista exilitas quam ille de industria con-
sequebatur. dicebat, inquam, ita; sed et ipse errabat et alios
etiam errare cogebat. (*Brut.* 82.283f.)

Cicero proceeds to point out to Brutus that there were many var-

ieties of Attic oratory: the style of Lysias so admired by the

modern aspirants to the name of *Attici* was certainly one type, but

Demosthenes was no less Attic, nor was Hyperides, nor, for that

matter, Demetrius of Phalerum. The fundamental mistake of the

Roman Atticists was, according to Cicero, that they assumed that

one only needed *ieiunitatem et siccitatem et inopiam* (82.285) to

emulate the Attic style, and that they failed to recognize that

Demosthenes was the greatest Athenian orator of them all. Therein

lay the reason why, so he says, they failed to hold anyone's at-

tention in court:

ne illud quidem intellegunt, non modo ita memoriae proditum esse
sed ita necesse fuisse, cum Demosthenes dicturus esset, ut concursus audiendi causa ex tota Graecia fierent. at cum isti Attici
dicunt, non modo a corona, quod est ipsum miserabile, sed etiam ab
advocatis relinquuntur. (84.289)

   In *Contr.* VII.4.6-8, on the other hand, Calvus is not only

represented as an orator so totally uninhibited where *actio* was

concerned that he would rush around the court while delivering his

speeches, he is actually said to have imitated Demosthenes in the

rhythmic arrangement of his words:

Calvus, qui diu cum Cicerone iniquissimam litem de principatu
eloquentiae habuit, usque eo violentus actor et concitatus fuit,
ut in media eius actione surgeret Vatinius reus et exclamaret:
rogo vos, iudices: num, si iste disertus est, ideo me damnari
oportet? idem postea, cum videret a clientibus Catonis, rei sui,
Pollionem Asinium circumventum in foro caedi, inponi se supra
cippum iussit - erat enim parvolus statura, propter quod etiam
Catullus in hendecasyllabis vocat illum 'salaputium disertum' - et
iuravit, si quam iniuriam Cato Pollioni Asinio accusatori suo

fecisset, se in eum iuraturum calumniam; nec umquam postea Pollio
a Catone advocatisque eius aut re aut verbo violatus est. solebat
praeterea excedere subsellia sua et inpetu latus usque in
adversariorum partem transcurrere. et carmina quoque eius, quamvis iocosa sint, plena sunt ingentis animi. dicit de Pompeio:
                                digito caput uno
      scalpit. quid credas hunc sibi velle? virum.
conpositio quoque eius in actionibus ad exemplum Demosthenis
viget:[50]* nihil in illa placidum, nihil lene est, omnia excitata
et fluctuantia. hic tamen in epilogo, quem pro Messio tunc tertio
causam dicente habuit, non tantum leniter componit sed
<   >,[51]* cum dicit: 'credite mihi, non est turpe misereri',
et omnia in illo epilogo fere non tantum emollitae compositionis
sunt sed infractae. (*Contr.* VII.4.6-8)

This critique is not the only ancient example of a view of
Calvus radically different from Cicero's. The Catullan hendeca-
syllables cited as an illustration of Calvus' stature are also
evidence of the popular appeal of his oratory:

      risi nescioquem modo e corona
      qui cum mirifice Vatiniana
      meus crimina Calvus explicasset
      admirans ait haec manusque tollens
      'Di magni, salaputium disertum.' (*Carm.* LIII)

Quintilian (X.1.115) tells us that critics in his day were divided
between those who trusted Cicero's judgement on his rival and
those who preferred Calvus to all other writers; his own verdict
lies between the two extremes:

inveni qui Calvum praeferrent omnibus, inveni qui Ciceroni
crederent eum nimia contra se calumnia verum sanguinem perdidisse;
sed est et sancta et gravis oratio et castigata et frequenter
vehemens quoque. imitator autem est Atticorum, fecitque illi
properata mors iniuriam si quid adiecturus sibi, non si quid
detracturus, fuit.[52]

The real reasons for the difference of opinion cannot be un-
covered now that all but the most meagre fragments of Calvus' oratory has been lost. Cicero was to some extent at least sincere in
the opinion of Calvus he expresses in *Brut.* 82.284: it is true
that in a letter to Calvus which embarrassingly got into the wrong
hands he appears to have praised aspects of his writing very ef-
fusively, but even here he seems to have exhorted Calvus to aim at
greater forcefulness. He explains to Trebonius:

ego illas Calvo litteras misi non plus quam has, quas nunc legis,
existimans exituras; aliter enim scribimus quod eos solos quibus
mittimus, aliter quod multos lecturos putamus; deinde ingenium
eius maioribus extuli laudibus quam tu id vere potuisse fieri

putas, primum quod ita iudicabam: acute movebatur, genus quoddam
sequebatur, in quo iudicio lapsus quo valebat, tamen adsequebatur
quod probarat; multae erant et reconditae litterae, *vis non erat;
ad eam igitur adhortabar*; in excitando autem et in acuendo
plurimum valet, si laudes eum quem cohortere. habes de Calvo
iudicium et consilium meum; consilium, quod hortandi causa
laudavi, iudicium, quod de ingenio eius valde existimavi bene.
(*Ad fam.* XV.21.4)[53]

Cicero was obviously being extremely unfair to Calvus in suggesting in *Brut.* 84.289 that he exercised no power over bystanders in
the *corona*, but perhaps the Vatinian orations, to which Catullus'
poem and other favourable estimates of his talent refer, were of a
very much more brilliant style than the rest of his speeches: note
how in Tacitus' *Dialogus* Aper, the arch-disparager of Republican
oratory, has this to say about his contemporaries' reading habits:

quotus enim quisque Calvi in Asicium aut in Drusum legit? at
hercule in omnium studiosorum manibus versantur accusationes quae
in Vatinium inscribuntur, ac praecipue secunda ex his oratio; est
enim verbis ornàta et sententiis, auribus iudicum accommodata, ut
scias ipsum quoque Calvum intellexisse quid melius esset, nec
voluntatem ei, quo <minus> sublimius et cultius diceret, sed
ingenium ac vires defuisse. (*Dial.* 21.2)

Most of Calvus' extant prose fragments come from the *Vatinians*.[54]
Still, Cicero's grudging estimate of his rival's style seems hard
to accept as wholly justified. Perhaps A. D. Leeman has got to
the heart of the matter when he suggests that the character of
Calvus' oratory 'could make Cicero's elaborate pathos look a
little cheap in the eyes of his young contemporaries',[55] and we
should regard *Brut.* 82.283ff. as the product of his discomfort at
realizing this.

   The extant fragments of Calvus' orations[56] certainly provide
evidence of greater rhetorical artistry and forcefulness than one
would expect of an Atticist if one takes seriously Cicero's picture of the would-be *Attici* as men misguidedly aping nothing but
the Lysian plain style. They serve better to support the statements about Calvus' vigorous and agitated *compositio* in *Contr.*
VII.4.8. Study of their *clausulae* yields particularly interesting
results.

De Groot's *clausula* statistics: Cicero's speeches: 'Normal' in percentages[57]		De Groot's *clausula* statistics: Demosthenes: Thucydides in percentages[58]
9.7 : 5.4	Fr. 22 (*In Vat.*) = Quint. VI.1.13 factum esse ambitum scitis omnes et hoc vos scir(e) omnes sciunt.	4.8 : 3.4
25.3:17.2	Fr. 23 (*In Vat.*) = Quint. IX.2.25 perfrica frontem et dic te digniorem qui praetor fieres quam Catonem.	18.9:14.2
Not available	Fr. 25 (*In Vat.*) = Aquila Rom. *RLM* 35.4 cf. Quint. IX.3.56 non ergo pecuniarum magis repetundarum quam maiestatis, neque maiestatis magis quam Plautiae legis, neque Plautiae legis magis quam ambitus, neque ambitus magis quam omnium legum omnia iudicia perierunt.	Not available
2.9 : 1.9	Fr. 26 (*In Vat.*) = Iul. Sever. *RLM* 366.5 hominem nostrae civitatis audacissimum, de factione divitem, sordidum, maledic(um) accuso.	0.8 : 3.1
–◡–◡ 25.3:17.2 –◡––◡–◡ 4.0 : 2.4	Fr. 28 (*In Vat.*) = Charisius *RLM* 296.21 ad ita mihi Iovem deosque inmortales velim bene fecisse, iudices, ut ego pro certo habeo, si parvuli pueri de ambitu iudicarent.	–◡–◡ 18.9:14.2 –◡––◡–◡ 3.0 : 2.3
4.7 : 2.4	Fr. 32 (*Pro Mess.*) = Sen. *Contr.* VII.4.8 credite mihi, non est turpe misereri.	3.5 : 1.2
4.9 : 4.4	Fr. 36 (*incertae sedis*) = Charisius *RLM* 102.20 quorum praedulcem cibum stomachus ferre non potest.	4.8 : 3.7

These are the only fragments of any length extant from Calvus' orations. Fr. 36 may not give us the end of a sentence.

Obviously one might wish for very much fuller evidence. However, fr. 25 in particular shows how unjustifiable it is to trust implicitly Cicero's picture of the Atticists as deliberate seekers of *exilitas*, forever draining the life-blood of their eloquence by excessive purging away of what they regarded as *vitiosum* (*Brut.* 82.283f. cf. *Or.* 9.28ff.), and how unreasonable, despite Cicero, *Or.* 23.75ff., it is to regard as the only Atticist style the plainest of the three types of prose distinguished by Cicero, with its avoidance of rhythmic artifice (*ibid.* 23.77)[59] and brilliant

ornatus (*ibid.* 23.78).[60] There is no doubt that Calvus has to be
classed among the Atticists: indeed he is the one Roman Republican
orator of whom we are explicitly told that he aspired to the epithet *Atticus* (*Brut.* 82.284).[61] Yet the style of fr. 25 is such
that it would have been condemned as an example of Asianic bombast
long ago, had it been ascribed to anyone but Calvus. More to the
point, it can serve as an illustration of the Demosthenic *compositio* alluded to in *Contr.* VII.4.8: compare the famous example
of κλῖμαξ/*gradatio* from the *De corona* (179), cited by Demetrius
(*Eloc.* 270), and in translation by Quintilian (IX.3.55) just
before the Calvan fragment:

οὐκ εἶπον μὲν ταῦτα, οὐκ ἔγραφα δέ, οὐδ᾽ ἔγραφα μέν, οὐκ
ἐπρέσβευσα δέ, οὐδ᾽ ἐπρέσβευσα μέν, οὐκ ἔπεισα δὲ Θηβαίους...[62]

For the *clausula* of fr. 25 we have no statistics to show its relative frequency in rhythmic and virtually non-rhythmic prose, but
as it is a resolution of the much favoured rhythm, cretic +
spondee, there is no reason to suppose that Calvus would have been
thought inartistic in choosing this cadence. Examination of the
clausulae of the other fragments suggests that Calvus' preferences,
at least in the *Vatinians*, were similar to Cicero's, and not too
far from those of Demosthenes. We must be careful, then, not to
attach too much weight to Cicero's allegations (*Or.* 9.28ff.) that
the Atticists invariably avoided rhythm in their prose.[63] Note
also that two sentences out of the seven end with a *dichoreus*,[64]
a rhythm which we should therefore stop regarding as an index of
Asianist tendencies on the strength of Cic. *Or.* 63.212: *insistit
autem ambitus modis pluribus, e quibus unum est secuta Asia maxime,
qui dichoreus vocatur, cum duo extremi chorei sunt, id est e
singulis longis et brevibus.* Bear in mind Shewring's statement
about Demosthenes' rhythms, 'His only well-defined clausula is
‒∪‒∪',[65] and the fact which emerges from Shewring's researches,
that various of the earlier Attic orators, including Lysias, had
shown a decided preference for this rhythm. As for the general
tone of the fragments of Calvus' oratory, all but one of them display the vehemence which Quintilian found in his speeches
frequenter (X.1.115). The exception is fr. 32 which, as we have
seen, was cited expressly to illustrate how Calvus knew how to

employ a 'soft' approach untypical of his style, when this was
appropriate.

The passage describing Calvus in *Contr*. VII.4.6-8 is by any
standards a remarkable piece of criticism. But does its existence
mean that Seneca the Elder was familiar with the works of Atticist
critics now lost? Once more we have to consider whether he may
not be presenting data received at second or third hand. In
Contr. VII.4.6 he has been reporting some observations made by
Latro about the need for a change of style when one wishes to
arouse pity, for example in a peroration:

aiebat...ipsam orationem ad habitum eius quem movere volumus adfectus molliendam. in epilogis nos de industria vocem quoque
infringere et dare operam ne dissimilis orationi sit orator; compositionem quoque illis mitiorem convenire.

The function of the passage about Calvus, which follows immediately after this, is to illustrate the point which Latro was
making: Calvus was normally a *violentus actor et concitatus*, and
normally aimed at vigorous and agitated *compositio*, but if he had
to deliver a pathetic *epilogus*, such as that of the *Pro Messio*, he
would change his style and use far gentler rhythms.[66] Now, given
the fact that Seneca elsewhere has been found to have a tendency
to move from indirect to direct speech while all the time reporting another critic,[67] it is quite likely that the passage about
Calvus originally formed part of Latro's lecture, even though
Seneca gives it in direct speech. And, given the fact that Latro
'despised and was ignorant of the Greeks' (*Contr*. X.4.21), it must
be doubted whether the comparison of Calvus' rhythms with Demosthenes', if this lecture was Seneca's source for it, could have
been the fruit of Latro's own reading. What we have in *Contr*.
VII.4.6-8, perhaps, is Latro displaying his *historiarum omnium
summa notitia* by reeling off a selection of the *acta* of Calvus
(cf. *Contr*. I pr. 18). Lest anyone should suggest that the material in this passage is not the sort of historical data which a
rhetorician was likely to learn as potentially useful for declamations, consider *Contr*. X.1.8 where Latro mentions, in a list of
exempla of the violence of accusations flung around in time of
civil war, the fact that:

in Cn. Pompeium terra marique victorem fuit qui carmen conponeret, uno, ut ait, digito caput scalpentem.

The allusion is to the very poem of Calvus quoted in *Contr.* VII.
4.7.[68]

There is precious little else, either in the critical parts
of Seneca's books or in the declamatory extracts, about Republican
oratory. Seneca tells an anecdote in *Contr.* I pr. 19 about
Hortensius' brilliant memory, but gives us no criticism of his
oratorical manner. Capito, as we have seen, alludes to Hortensius'
late speech *Pro Cn. Pompei bonis*, but tells us nothing about this
speech which could not have been deduced from its title (*Contr.*
VII.5.6). The allusion to Calvus by Latro in *Contr.* X.1.8 is only
one item in quite a long series of illustrations of the prevalence
of invective in the late Republic, which take us into lesser-known
areas of the history of rhetoric:

Macerio qua violentia in absentiam Metelli strepuit! M. Cato
Pulchro obiciente furtorum crimina audivit. quae maior indignitas
illius saeculi esse potuit quam aut Pulcher accusator aut reus
Cato! in Cn. Pompeium terra marique victorem fuit qui carmen conponeret, uno, ut ait, digito caput scalpentem; fuit aliquis qui
licentia carminis tres auratos currus contemneret. M. Bruti
† sacratissimi †[69]* eum eloquentia lacerat, cum quidem eius civili
sanguine non inquinatas solum manus sed infectas ait; atque ille
tamen, cum tres consulatus ac tres triumphos scinderet, adeo non
timuit ne esset reus ut etiam disertus esse curaverit.

But such a display of erudition is extremely unusual. The declaimers have nothing to say about Pompey and Caesar as orators
beyond this reference to Pompey's eloquence in defending himself,
and a quotation by the minor declaimer Tuscus of Caesar's famous
veni, vidi, vici (*Suas.* 2.22). Occasional mention is made in the
suasoriae addressed to Cicero of Antony's inadequacy as a speaker:
Haterius, for example, recalls in *Suas.* 7.3 the eloquence of
Antony's famous grandfather, *M. Antonium illum indignum hoc*
successore generis. Cassius Severus mentions Sallust as an
example of the inability of any one man to excel in more than one
genre: *orationes Sallustii in honorem historiarum leguntur* (*Contr.*
III pr. 8).

There is no way of being sure, then, how much Greek or Republican Roman oratory and literary criticism Seneca the Elder had
read. Nearly all his allusions to such literature could be explained as the outcome of receptiveness to the views of better-

informed critics in and around the schools of declamation or as
derived at second hand from an erudite, but perhaps quite brief,
account of the rise of Roman declamation. On the other hand, the
trouble he takes to assess the value of sources relating to the
last days of Cicero, and his use of the Platonic and Ciceronian
motif of praise for a rising young talent at the end of his series
of ten critical prefaces, serve as reminders that an extreme
scepticism which would deny him any reading beyond that of the
narrowest *scholasticus* cannot be wholly justified.

declamabat autem Cicero non quales nunc controversias dicimus, ne
tales quidem, quales ante Ciceronem dicebantur, quas thesis
vocabant. hoc genus materiae, quo nos exercemur, adeo novum est,
ut nomen quoque eius novum sit. controversias nos dicimus: Cicero
causas vocabat. hoc vero alterum nomen Graecum quidem, sed in
Latinum ita translatum, ut pro Latino sit, scholastica, controversia multo recentius est, sicut ipsa 'declamatio' apud nullum
antiquum auctorem ante Ciceronem et Calvum inveniri potest, qui
declamationem <a dictione> distinguit;[1] ait enim declamare iam se
non mediocriter, dicere bene; alterum putat domesticae exercitationis esse, alterum verae actionis. modo nomen hoc prodiit; nam
et studium ipsum nuper celebrari coepit: ideo facile est mihi ab
incunabulis nosse rem post me natam. (*Contr.* I pr. 12)

The account of the rise of declamation in *Contr.* I pr. 12 is

an excursus prompted by the reference Seneca has just made to

Cicero's late declamations in the company of Hirtius and Pansa.

It is not intended, therefore, to give more than an account of

Roman declamation from around the time of Cicero to his own day.

The indebtedness of the Roman rhetoricians to their Greek counter-

parts, hinted at only in the remarks on the term *scholastica*, is

not given the attention which would be its due in a full account

of ancient rhetorical education. Nevertheless it is essential for

a complete understanding of *Contr.* I pr. 12 to consider what is

known about rhetorical exercises used in Greece before Seneca's

time – the Roman *thesis*, *suasoria* and *controversia* all had Greek

antecedents – and how ancient authorities viewed the history of

Greek education.[2]

The θέσις was an abstract philosophical proposition on which

one could discourse at length from two opposed standpoints. The

question for discussion might be a matter of pure theory

(*cognitionis*), for example: *verine sint sensus*; *sitne ius id quod*

maiori parti sit utile; *ecquisnam perfecte sapiens esse possit*; or

it might be of more practical application (*actionis*), for example:

quibus officiis amicitia colenda sit; *quem ad modum sit res*

publica administranda; *quem ad modum in paupertate vivendum*.[3] The

factor which distinguished the *thesis* from all other exercises was
its total abstraction, the absence from its theme of any reference
to particular people or particular circumstances (see Cic. *Or.*
14.46).

The practice of speaking at length for and against θέσεις
went back to the fifth-century sophists. According to Diogenes
Laertius, Protagoras πρῶτος κατέδειξε τὰς πρὸς τὰς θέσεις ἐπι-
χειρήσεις (Diog. Laert. IX.53). The discourse on the theme, ὡς
χαριστέον μὴ ἐρῶντι μᾶλλον ἢ ἐρῶντι attributed to Lysias in
Plato's *Phaedrus* (227c; 230e-234b) is an early example. According
to Quintilian, Aristotle and Theophrastus were responsible for
initiating the use of the θέσις as an educational exercise (Quint.
XII.2.25). Cicero tells us that Aristotle encouraged his pupils
to treat the themes with rhetorical elaboration:

haec igitur quaestio a propriis personis et temporibus ad universi
generis rationem traducta appellatur θέσις. in hac Aristoteles
adulescentis non ad philosophorum morem tenuiter disserendi, sed
ad copiam rhetorum in utramque partem, ut ornatius et uberius dici
posset, exercuit; idemque locos - sic enim appellat - quasi
argumentorum notas tradidit unde omnis in utramque partem
traheretur oratio. (Cic. *Or.* 14.46)

The catalogue of Aristotle's works includes references to θέσεις
ἐπιχειρηματικαὶ κε′, θέσεις ἐρωτικαὶ δ′ - the tradition represented by the show-speech of Lysias in the *Phaedrus* evidently
continued - θέσεις φιλικαὶ β′, θέσεις περὶ ψυχῆς ἀ′ (Diog. Laert.
V.24); Theophrastus is credited with θέσεις κδ′ (*ibid.* 44) and
θέσεις <ἄλλο> γ′ (*ibid.* 49).[4]

The θέσις appears to have remained in use amongst the later
Peripatetics, and to have gained acceptance by the Academics too,
despite the strong hostility towards rhetoric which persisted long
among members of that school.[5] At any rate, Cicero represents the
use of the θέσις as peculiarly characteristic of both Academics
and Peripatetics: *quae exercitatio nunc propria duarum philosophiarum de quibus ante dixi putatur* (*De or.* III.27.107).[6] These
two philosophical schools did not exercise a complete monopoly
over the θέσις, but were near enough to doing so as to call forth
a lament from one of the speakers in the *De oratore* at the way he
and others whose main care was for rhetoric, had unfairly been
deprived of their patrimony, *de nostra possessione depulsi in parvo*

et eo litigioso praediolo relicti sumus (*ibid.* 108), whereas apud
antiquos - he does not identify them - the discussion of wide abstract issues had been considered the province of people like himself, *a quibus omnis de rebus forensibus dicendi ratio et copia
petebatur* (*ibid.* 107). It is true that Hermagoras, an influential
rhetorician of the second century B.C.,[7] had reasserted the view
that the treatment of abstract issues (θέσεις) was as much a part
of oratory as judicial, deliberative and epideictic rhetoric concerned with particular events (ὑποθέσεις).[8] But it seems that the
Hellenistic rhetoricians devoted very little space in their treatises to the consideration of the ways in which abstract themes
might be treated, and consequently their claim to be concerned
with more than mere pettifoggery did not constitute a serious
challenge to the philosophers. According to a speaker in Cicero's
De oratore the rhetoricians of his time - the dramatic date of the
dialogue is 91 B.C. - exercised an almost complete monopoly over
the teaching of the kind of themes which Hermagoras had classed as
ὑποθέσεις, *illud alterum genus quod est temporibus, locis, reis*[9]*
definitum, despite the interest recently taken by Philo the Academic in this type of subject-matter (see *Tusc. disp.* II.3.9), but
on the other hand they assigned the θέσις to a sadly subordinate
position in their educational scheme: *alterum vero tantum modo in
prima arte tradenda nominant et oratoris esse dicunt; sed neque
vim neque naturam eius nec partis nec genera proponunt, ut praeteriri omnino fuerit satius quam attactum deseri...* (*De or.* III.28.
110).

The history of rhetorical exercises of the ὑπόθεσις type is
harder to trace. Regrettably little relevant information has survived from the Hellenistic schools,[10] so that it is easy to be
misled by the elder Seneca's talk of *rem post me natam* (*Contr.* I
pr. 12) into thinking that *suasoriae* and *controversiae* were indeed
phenomena which sprang up from nowhere in Augustan Rome. It is a
curious fact that, though it is clear that Greek rhetoricians were
declaiming on just the same themes as their Latin-speaking colleagues in the time of Seneca the Elder, the first extant Greek
writings which are generally reckoned to give us treatments of
rhetorical themes equivalent to *suasoriae* and *controversiae* date

from the later Empire.[11] Also, when looking for evidence of the
teaching methods of Hellenistic rhetoricians, one is continually
faced with the difficulty that, while it is unquestionable that
the chief concern of these men was with the types of rhetoric
which Hermagoras classed as ὑποθέσεις, and that it is unlikely
therefore that they set their pupils no exercises more advanced
than those known as *progymnasmata*, it is impossible usually to
prove which, if any, of the numerous examples of fictitious deliberations and law-suits found in works indebted to Hellenistic
theory like Cicero's *De inventione* and the *Rhetorica ad Herennium*,
were actually used as subjects for declamation in their schools.
To be on the safe side we must look for other sources of evidence
for the antecedents of *suasoriae* and *controversiae*.[12]

Philostratus in *Vit. soph.* I.481 divides the history of Greek
school rhetoric into two periods or 'sophistics':

ἡ μὲν δὴ ἀρχαία σοφιστικὴ καὶ τὰ φιλοσοφούμενα ὑποτιθεμένη διῄει
αὐτὰ ἀποτάδην καὶ ἐς μῆκος, διελέγετο μὲν γὰρ περὶ ἀνδρείας,
διαλέγετο δὲ περὶ δικαιότητος, ἡρώων τε περὶ καὶ θεῶν καὶ ὅπη
ἀπεσχημάτισται ἡ ἰδέα τοῦ κόσμου. ἡ δὲ μετ' ἐκείνην, ἣν οὐχὶ
νέαν, ἀρχαία γάρ, δευτέραν δὲ μᾶλλον προσρητέον, τοὺς πένητας
ὑπετυπώσατο καὶ τοὺς πλουσίους καὶ τοὺς ἀριστέας καὶ τοὺς
τυράννους καὶ τὰς ἐς ὄνομα ὑποθέσεις, ἐφ' ἃς ἡ ἱστορία ἄγει. ἦρξε
δὲ τῆς μὲν ἀρχαιοτέρας Γοργίας ὁ Λεοντῖνος ἐν Θετταλοῖς, τῆς δὲ
δευτέρας Αἰσχίνης ὁ 'Ατρομήτου τῶν μὲν 'Αθήνησι πολιτικῶν ἐκπεσών,
Καρίᾳ δὲ ἐνομιλήσας καὶ 'Ρόδῳ, καὶ μετεχειρίζοντο τὰς ὑποθέσεις οἱ
μὲν κατὰ τέχνην, οἱ δὲ ἀπὸ Γοργίου κατὰ τὸ δόξαν.

According to Philostratus, then, the first sophistic, beginning
with Gorgias, was noted for the extended rhetorical treatment of
philosophical themes, for example, questions about courage, justice, cosmology. These, despite Philostratus' loose usage of the
words ὑποτιθεμένη and ὑποθέσεις in connection with them, may be
assumed to have included the exercises called θέσεις whose history
we have been tracing. Philostratus also mentions a rather different type of theme characteristic of the first sophistic 'about
heroes and gods'. Gorgias' *Helen* and *Palamedes*, Alcidamas'
Odysseus, and Antisthenes' *Aias* and *Odysseus* may be taken as
examples of this type. Aeschines is represented as having founded
the second sophistic after his expulsion from Athens (in 330 B.C.).
Characteristic of this new educational movement was the use of
themes peopled by 'poor men, rich men, men renowned for bravery,

and tyrants', and themes derived from history, containing reference to named individuals. Now, the conventional figures *pauper*,
dives, *vir fortis* and *tyrannus* are all familiar from Roman declamation themes, the last two types proclaiming their non-Roman
origins for all to hear, and of course historical subjects find a
place in the Roman collections too, more often among *suasoriae*
than *controversiae*. It seems highly likely, then, that the themes
which Philostratus is describing are Greek forerunners of *controversiae* and *suasoriae*, especially in view of the fact that Quintilian (II.4.41) dates the origins of judicial and deliberative
exercises to approximately the time of Demetrius of Phalerum: *nam
fictas ad imitationem fori consiliorumque materias apud Graecos
dicere circa Demetrium Phalerea institutum fere constat.* Demetrius governed Athens for the ten years before 307, and became li-
brarian at Alexandria in 297, so that Quintilian's dating agrees
with Philostratus'. Quintilian does not seem to have heard the
innovation ascribed to Aeschines; his sources were more inclined
to attribute it to Demetrius, but he questioned whether there was
any external evidence to corroborate this tradition.

The clearest evidence[13] for the use of rhetorical exercises
on deliberative themes in the Hellenistic world is provided by
Polybius in a passage where he criticizes the historical methods
of Timaeus. He attacks, among other things, that historian's manner of presenting τὰς δημηγορίας καὶ τὰς παρακλήσεις, ἔτι δὲ τοὺς
πρεσβευτικοὺς λόγους (XII.25^a.3). Polybius' complaint is that
Timaeus, instead of reporting the speakers' true words in full or
giving the gist of them, puts completely imaginary words into
their mouths, as one might do when holding forth in school on a
set theme:

οὐ γὰρ τὰ ῥηθέντα γέγραφεν, οὐδ᾽ ὡς ἐρρήθη κατ᾽ ἀλήθειαν, ἀλλὰ
προθέμενος ὡς δεῖ ῥηθῆναι, πάντας ἐξαριθμεῖται τοὺς ῥηθέντας
λόγους καὶ τὰ παρεπόμενα τοῖς πράγμασιν οὕτως ὡ ς ἄ ν ε ἴ
τ ι ς ἐ ν δ ι α τ ρ ι β ῇ π ρ ὸ ς ὑ π ό θ ε σ ι ν
ἐ π ι χ ε ι ρ ο ί η...ὥσπερ ἀπόδειξιν τῆς ἑαυτοῦ δυνάμεως
ποιούμενος, ἀλλ᾽ οὐκ ἐξήγησιν τῶν κατ᾽ ἀλήθειαν εἰρημένων.
(XII.25^a.5)

Later (25^k.1ff.) he gives explicit examples of Timaeus' failing:
words which he placed in the mouths of some of Sicily's most sensible rulers were inferior even to the normal products of school

rhetoric (25^k.8). He criticizes Timaeus for attributing to Hermocrates, one such ruler, a speech at a peace conference, which,
consisting as it did largely of a prolonged lecture, full of inept
mythological allusions, on the differences between war and peace,
was an insult to the intelligence of his listeners, the leading
citizens of Gela, who had been in favour of peace from the outset.
He concludes his critique with these words:

θαυμάζω δὴ τίσι ποτ' ἄν ἄλλοις ἐχρήσατο λόγοις ἢ προφοραῖς
μειράκιον ἄρτι γενόμενον περὶ διατριβὰς καὶ <τὰς> ἐκ τῶν ὑπο-
μνημάτων πολυπραγμοσύνας καὶ βουλόμενον παραγγελματικῶς ἐκ τῶν
παρεπομένων τοῖς προσώποις ποιεῖσθαι τὴν ἐπιχείρησιν· δοκεῖ γὰρ
<οὐχ ἑτ>έροις, ἀλλὰ τούτοις οἷς Τίμαιος Ἑρμοκράτην κεχρῆσθαί
φησι. (26.9)

The expression ...παραγγελματικῶς[14] ἐκ τῶν παρεπομένων τοῖς
προσώποις ποιεῖσθαι τὴν ἐπιχείρησιν, taken together with the fact
that Hermocrates' speech comes in the context of negotiations
about peace, and 'war and peace' had been classed by Aristotle
(*Rhet*. I.4.7) as one of the five standard topics of deliberative
rhetoric, must lead us to conclude that the rhetorical exercise
which Polybius has in mind is the deliberative *prosopopoeia*, a
variety of declamation in which the *suasor* actually adopts the
rôle of a historical personage, rather than being merely an
unnamed adviser of some great man, which was the case in some
other *suasoriae* (cf. Quint. III.8.52). The speech in Timaeus'
Histories to which Polybius next turns his attention (26^a.1) is
even more clearly to be compared with this sub-species of *suasoria*:
Timoleon exhorts the Greeks to do battle with the Carthaginians.

Rhetorical exercises in imitation of deliberations were evidently in use, then, in the second century B.C., and nothing makes
it improbable that they were known in the time of Aeschines and
Demetrius of Phalerum. We must call into question, indeed,
whether they originated as late as Aeschines' time. With the
deliberative orations attributed to historical characters by
Timaeus we may compare certain historically dubious speeches in
Herodotus. For example in I.71 Sardanis the Lydian makes a speech
intended to dissuade Croesus from invading Cappadocia. Like Timoleon in Timaeus *ap*. Polyb. XII.26^a.4 Sardanis lays considerable
emphasis on the fact that the enemy were wearers of trousers.

Sen. *Suas.* 4 provides us with an example of a *suasoria* used in
the Roman schools about the advisability of an invasion: *deliberat
Alexander Magnus an Babylona intret, cum denuntiatum esset illi
responso auguris periculum.* Again, in Hdt. III.80ff. the Persians
deliberate in set speeches whether to aim for a democracy, an oli-
garchy or a monarchy. These λόγοι ἄπιστοι...ἐνίοισι 'Ελλήνων, in
which Herodotus nevertheless wants his hearers to believe, may be
compared with the *triplices...suasoriae* known to Quintilian (III.
8.33).[15]

In the case of exercises of the *controversia* type as well,
the question is not whether the dating of their origins given by
Philostratus and Quintilian is too early, but rather whether it
may not be far too late.

Independent evidence for their use in Hellenistic schools
seems to be lacking.[16] A distinction has to be drawn between the
controversia type of judicial declamation (characterized by the
arrangement of conventional figures, *pauper*, *dives*, *vir fortis*,
tyrannus etc. or, more rarely, historical personages, in complex
and purely imaginary legal tangles)[17] and another type of display
speech *ad imitationem fori* in which the declaimer makes a reply to
a speech once delivered in court by a famous orator, or alternatively tackles the case from the same standpoint as the original
orator, but attempts to improve on it. It is an example of this
variety of rhetorical exercise which is preserved in the third-
century B.C. papyrus *Berl. Pap.* P. 9781:[18] the declaimer has
chosen the role of Leptines and defends himself against the
charges levelled against him by Demosthenes in *Or.* XX. The
Apologies of Plato and Xenophon, and Polycrates' *Prosecution of
Socrates* (Diog. Laert. II.38) may be regarded as forerunners of
this type of writing. Similar rhetorical *tours de force* were
occasionally attempted in the elder Seneca's time: such were
Cestius' speech *in Milonem* (*Contr.* III pr. 16), Gallio's re-
scriptum Labieno pro Bathyllo Maecenatis (*Contr.* X pr. 8), and
Latro's most eloquent oration *pro Pythodoro Messalae* (*Contr.* II.
4.8 W).[19]*

The best place to look for the antecedents of *controversiae*
is in the set of *Tetralogies* ascribed to Antiphon, fine examples

of sophistic rhetoric which are generally accepted as dating from the fifth century B.C.,[20] even if maybe not to be attributed to the orator Antiphon. General affinities between these specimen speeches and later judicial declamations have of course long been recognized,[21] but it has not been appreciated just how closely the first and third *Tetralogies* in particular are related, in themes though not in treatment, to the Roman *controversiae*.

In the first *Tetralogy* the given facts of the case appear to have been these. A man has been found murdered one night in an isolated spot, the slave with him having been mortally wounded. Neither has been robbed of his cloak. The man who is charged with the murder is a rich man, who was a known enemy of the murdered man, and had recently been accused by him of embezzling sacred monies. The case was still waiting to be heard at the time of the *Diipoleia* when the murder took place. The wounded slave, when asked to identify the murderer by the people now bringing the charge, presumably the murdered man's relatives, named the rich man, but since then has died.

Nothing more than these sparse facts is taken for granted by the author of the *Tetralogy*[22] and they contain nothing,[23] apart from the specification that the dead men were not robbed of their cloaks, rather than simply not robbed, the assumption that a slave might be worth robbing, and the reference to an explicit date, which a declaimer of the early Roman Empire would not have found very familiar. How similar in kind the theme of the first *Tetralogy* is to those of later *controversiae* will be most simply demonstrated if we translate all the given facts, except these three minor details, into the language of the Roman scholastics, using a pastiche of phrases from themes known to Seneca the Elder and ps.-Quintilian:

qui divitem inimicum peculatus reum detulerat, inter moras iudicii cum servo nocte processit. ille occisus inspoliatus in solitudine inventus est, servus iuxta cadaver vulneratus. placuit propinquis quaeri a servo quem percussorem cognosceret. ille divitem nominavit et decessit. dives caedis reus est.[24]

The affinities of this subject with *Contr.* VII.5 and X.1 are particularly close. The most difficult questions at issue in *Tetralogy* I are these. First, a rich man known to be an enemy of the

murdered man is liable to be suspected of the crime, given that
the murder was not accompanied by robbery, but is probability a
sufficient ground for conviction?[25] Secondly, how far can the
evidence of the slave be relied on, given that slaves are in general an unreliable class, and that this one, being dead, cannot
be subjected to further interrogation? *Contr.* X.1 presents us
with a case in which *quidam, cum haberet filium et divitem
inimicum, occisus inspoliatus inventus est.* The son in this case
does not reckon that the argument from probability alone will
stand up in court, and is looking for further evidence: ...*ait:
'accusabo, cum potero'* (*Contr.* X.1 *thema*). He uses it however
when the *dives* brings a counter-charge, e.g. *Contr.* X.1.3: *quisquis
fuit* [sc. *percussor*]*, quasi dives spolia contempsit* (cf. *Tetr.* I.
1.4). In *Contr* VII.5 the main question at issue is how seriously
one should take the testimony of a witness whose reliability must
be doubted, in this case a five-year-old child:

rumor erat de adulterio procuratoris et matris familiae. quodam
tempore pater familiae in cubiculo occisus inventus est, uxor
volnerata, communis paries perfossus; placuit propinquis quaeri a
filio quinquenni, qui una dormierat, quem percussorem cognosceret;
ille procuratorem digito denotavit.

The prosecutor here, as in *Tetr.* I, has only probabilities from
which to argue, apart from this one dubious piece of testimony.

The second *Tetralogy* concerns involuntary homicide, a crime
which is frequently mentioned in *controversia* themes (e.g. *Contr.*
IV.3 which features a man *imprudentis caedis damnatus*; ps.-Quint.
CCXLVIII, CCCV), though only as an issue subsidiary to the theme
as a whole. The accidental killing in *Tetr.* II takes place in the
gymnasium (*Tetr.* II.1.1): a boy is struck down by a javelin thrown
by an athlete. Athletes do not appear very frequently in Roman
declamation themes, but, for example, in *Contr.* V.3 two brothers
fight each other to the death as *pancratiastae* at Olympia. The
theme on which *Tetr.* II is based is very similar to one which
Pericles is supposed to have debated at great length with Protagoras. According to Plutarch (*Per.* 36.3), Pericles' son Xanth-
ippus maliciously publicized his father's interest in sophistry:

πενταθλου γάρ τινος ἀκοντίῳ πατάξαντος Ἐπίτιμον τὸν Φαρσάλιον
ἀκουσίως καὶ κατακτείναντος, ἡμέραν ὅλην ἀναλῶσαι μετὰ Πρωταγόρου

διαποροῦντα πότερον τὸ ἀκόντιον ἢ τὸν βαλόντα μᾶλλον ἢ τοὺς
ἀγωνοθέτας κατὰ τὸν ὀρθότατον λόγον αἰτίους χρὴ τοῦ παθοῦς
ἡγεῖσθαι.

Note that the reference to ἀγωνοθέτας suggests that the accident
in this case, like the fratricide in *Contr.* V.3, is supposed to
have happened during organized Games, rather than while the javelin thrower was practising as in *Tetr.* II; also that the theme,
like those of the *veteres controversiae* in Suetonius' history of
Roman declamation,[26] is supposed to have been based on a real
occurrence.

The third *Tetralogy* concerns a fight between two drinking
companions (cf. the *luxuriosi* of *controversia* themes e.g. *Contr.*
II.6; IV.1), an old man and a young man. The old man was worsted
in this fight (*Tetr.* III.1.6; 3.2), and, although he received
medical attention, died a few days later (2.4; 3.5; 4.8). The
young man is charged with murder, but the questions arise whether
he was fighting in self-defence when he struck his victim (2.2ff.;
3.2ff.; 4.2ff.), and whether indeed the physician by his incom-
petence may not have been responsible for the old man's death
(2.4; 3.5; 4.8). Once more there are interesting comparisons to
be made with Roman *controversia* themes. In *Tetr.* I we have un-
covered the archetypal 'rich man'; here we have two type figures,
νέος and πρέσβυς, paired, so that the sophist can differentiate
between the two parties with clarity, and incidentally, when it
suits his case, can arouse prejudice against the accused, as for
example in 1.6: ὕβρει δὲ καὶ ἀκολασίᾳ παροινῶν εἰς ἄνδρα πρεσβύτην,
τύπτων τε καὶ πνίγων ἕως τῆς ψυχῆς ἀπεστέρησεν αὐτόν. For an
assault by an inebriated young man on an old man, in this case
pitiable for other reasons, see *Contr.* IV.1:

amissis quidam tribus liberis cum adsideret sepulchro, a luxurioso
adulescente in vicinos hortos abductus est et detonsus coactus
convivio veste mutata interesse. dimissus iniuriarum agit.

The question of the responsibility of a physician in a case where
death is not immediate arises again in Calp. Flacc. *Decl.* XIII,
where the dispute is between two *medici*, both of whom claim to
have poisoned the tyrant:

tyrannus suspicatus sibi venenum datum ab eo medico quem in arce
habebat, torsit eum. ille pernegavit. misit ad medicum civitatis.

dixit datum illi ab illo venenum, sed se remedium daturum. dedit
poculum, quo exhausto statim periit tyrannus. contendunt de
praemio.

The dating given by Quintilian and Philostratus, then, for
the introduction of judicial exercises seems to be far too late.
The sophists of the fifth century B.C. were already composing
speeches on fictitious subjects which, if they were stated in bare
outline, as they surely must have been, would have closely resembled *controversia* themes. Their manner of treating the themes
was different: the *Tetralogies* are sets of four speeches, two for
the prosecution and two for the defence, presented in the sequence
in which they would be delivered in a real trial, whereas it does
not seem to have been normal to declaim *controversiae* alternately
for and against, in imitation of the law-courts.[27] A declaimer of
the Roman Imperial period would not have given a specific date on
which the crime occurred, or offered his slaves to give evidence
under torture as the sophist does in *Tetr.* I.4.8. But the *Tetralogies* have an unquestionable claim to be regarded as the direct
ancestors of *controversiae*, and it seems as if their lineage
stretched some way further back.

Scholars have been puzzled by the fact that the *Tetralogies*
presuppose a legal system akin to, but much more fluid than, that
which obtained in late fifth-century Athens, a system in which,
for example, the participants in *Tetr.* II have to start from the
assumption that any homicide is punishable, whereas under the
Draconian Code, in which it was accepted that φόνος ἀκούσιος was
not a crime of the same order as φόνος ἑκούσιος, it was deemed in
certain circumstances, such as when, as in this case, the accident
took place ἐν ἄθλοις, to be no crime at all.[28] Another notable
feature of the *Tetralogies* is the presence of Ionicisms in their
language. K. J. Dover has suggested as the most probable explanation of them, 'that the *Tetralogies* represent the imitation of
an Ionic genre by an Athenian', pointing out that 'most of the
purely Ionic words - as distinct from those which may as well be
labelled tragic as Ionic - are legal words'.[29] Perhaps, then,
the prototypes of *controversiae* were first contrived by Ionian
sophists for use in cities where laws such as we find associated

with τετραλογιαι and *controversiae*, akin to those of Athens, but
in some ways more backward than them, were in force, all this
in a period when the problems of cities afflicted by insolent
tyrants in their citadels and unreasonably demanding tyrannicides,
so striking an anachronistic feature of the Roman exercises,[31] had
recently become matters of consuming interest.[32]

About the Greek background to the declamatory practices of
his own time Seneca the Elder seems to have had only the vaguest
knowledge. He tells us that declamation was unknown in the time
of Aeschines (*Contr.* I.8.16), misinformation most probably derived
from tirades by critics of the schools, such as Petronius puts
into the mouth of one of his characters in *Sat.* 2, to the effect
that the great figures of classical Greek literature had managed
perfectly well without declamation:

nondum iuvenes declamationibus continebantur, cum Sophocles aut
Euripides invenerunt verba quibus deberent loqui. nondum
umbraticus doctor ingenia deleverat, cum Pindarus novemque lyrici
Homericis versibus canere timuerunt. et ne poetas [quidem] ad
testimonium citem, certe neque Platona neque Demosthenen ad hoc
genus exercitationis accessisse video.[33]

Seneca was acquainted with Greek technical names, *thesis*[34] and
scholastica, for different types of declamation themes (*Contr.* I
pr. 12); he knew that there were a few standard *quaestiones* used
by Greek declaimers in *controversiae*, which the Romans had
'removed' (*submoverunt* - *Contr.* I.7.12 cf. I.8.7); he also dates
(in *Contr.* II pr. 5) the origins of Latin rhetorical education to
the boyhood of Cicero, and yet in *Contr.* I pr. 12 refers to a
stage in scholastic history before Cicero's time. But he nowhere
refers explicitly to the debt owed by Rome to Greek educational
methods or shows any sign of having made a clear assessment of it.

As a history of Roman declamation *Contr.* I pr. 12 can be
criticized on a number of counts. It should first be considered
in relation to Suetonius, *De gramm. et rhet.* 25.8-9 Brugnoli, an
account which, like Seneca's, distinguishes three stages in the
rise of Roman declamation, but describes the first two with a
greater wealth of detail.

1st stage

Seneca
quales ante Ciceronem dicebantur quas thesis vocabant.

Suetonius (25.8)
nam et dicta praeclare per omnes figuras, per casus et apologos
aliter atque aliter exponere et narrationes cum breviter ac presse
tum latius et uberius explicare consueverant, interdum Graecorum
scripta convertere ac viros inlustres laudare vel vituperare,
quaedam etiam ad usum conmunis vitae instituta tum utilia et
necessaria tum perniciosa et supervacanea ostendere, saepe fabulis
fidem firmare aut demere quod genus thesis et anasceuas et cata-
sceuas Graeci vocant: donec sensim haec exoluerunt et ad controversiam ventum est.[35]

(Cf. Quint. II.1.9: an ignoramus antiquis hoc fuisse ad augendam
eloquentiam genus exercitationis, ut thesis dicerent et communes
locos et cetera citra complexum rerum personarumque quibus verae
fictaeque controversiae continentur?)

2nd stage

Seneca
declamabat autem Cicero non quales nunc controversias dicimus...
controversias nos dicimus; Cicero causas vocabat.

Suetonius (25.9)
veteres controversiae aut ex historiis trahebantur sicut sane non-
nullae usque adhuc aut ex veritate ac re, si qua forte recens
accidisset: itaque locorum etiam appellationibus additis proponi
solebant. sic certe conlectae editaeque se habent ex quibus non
alienum fuerit unam et alteram exempli causa ad verbum referre:
aestivo tempore adulescentes urbani cum Ostiam venissent litus
ingressi, piscatores trahentes rete adierunt et pepigerunt bolum
quanti emerent. nummos solverunt. diu expectaverunt dum retia
extraherentur. aliquando extractis piscis nullus infuit sed
sporta auri insuta. tum emptores bolum suum aiunt, piscatores
suum. venalicius cum Brundisi gregem venalium e navi educeret,
formoso et pretioso puero quod portitores verebatur bullam et
praetextam togam inposuit. facile fallaciam celavit. Romam
venitur, res cognita est, petitur puer quod domini voluntate
fuerit liber in libertatem. olim eas †appellationes Graeci syn-
tasis† vocabant...[36]*

3rd stage

Seneca
...quales nunc controversias dicimus...hoc enim genus materiae,
quo nos exercemur, adeo novum est, ut nomen quoque novum sit.
controversias nos dicimus...hoc vero alterum nomen Graecum quidem,
sed in Latinum ita translatum, ut pro Latino sit, scholastica,
controversia multo recentius est, sicut ipsa 'declamatio' etc.

Suetonius (25.9)
...mox controversias quidem [sc. vocabant] sed aut fictas aut
iudiciales.

The exact relationship between the Senecan and Suetonian

accounts is unclear. The main doubtful points are these. First, did Seneca's source give in full the long list of *progymnasmata* alleged by Suetonius to have been dominant in the first stage, or did it just mention the *thesis* (plus perhaps a reference to *communes locos* and *cetera citra complexum rerum personarumque* in general, as in Quint. II.1.9), so that what Suetonius is giving us is post-Senecan elaboration? Secondly, were the verbatim quotations from *veteres controversiae* to be found in Seneca's source? If so, they could explain in what way Seneca might have imagined the first Roman judicial exercises to have differed from the later *controversiae*, but we cannot be sure of this. What the two accounts clearly do have in common is a belief that at first Roman rhetorical education did not deal with themes of the ὑπόθεσις type; that when judicial exercises were first used in Rome they were of a type different from the *controversia*; it was not until a later stage, we are to suppose, that the *controversia* was introduced.

For the pre-Ciceronian period, it is true, there is precious little documentation, and it may seem conceivable that the *progymnasmata* of Greek primary education were introduced to Rome before the more advanced exercises. But it must be doubted whether, once Hellenizing had begun, Roman practicality would have wasted much patience on the *thesis*, the *chria* and the fable, before demanding instruction in techniques of persuasion useful for senatorial debates and the law-courts. Besides, we have seen the evidence of the *De oratore* as to how little attention was normally paid to the *thesis* by rhetoricians in the period immediately before Cicero's time.[37] One might be less sceptical about the Senecan-Suetonian belief in the early dominance of the *thesis* etc. in Roman education, if the later parts of the accounts corresponded closely to the truth, but, as we shall see, they seem wrong in several respects.

First, Seneca's statement that Cicero did not declaim *theses* is erroneous. Secondly, themes of the kind later called *controversiae* were known to Cicero, and one such is explicitly said by him to have been in use at the dramatic date of the *De oratore*. Thirdly, public declamation by adult schoolmasters had been known

in Rome at a period earlier than Seneca's generalization about the
novelty of *declamatio* suggests.

Cicero's attitude towards the *thesis* altered somewhat in the
course of his life, but was always favourable. In his early *De
inventione* he criticized Hermagoras for his suggestion that the
treatment of wide abstract issues was part of the orator's province, but he took this line not out of any disrespect for philosophy, rather for the opposite reason, because he believed that
such matters were too weighty to be treated as a subordinate part
of an orator's work: *nam quibus in rebus summa ingenia philosophorum plurimo cum labore consumpta intellegimus, eas sicut
aliquas parvas res oratori attribuere magna amentia videtur* (*De
inv.* I.6.8). Later he came to regard his *De inventione* as an
immature work (*De or.* I.2.5), having meanwhile arrived at a much
more glowing estimate of the orator's competence and rôle in so-
ciety. In his mature rhetorical works he encourages the orator to
derive all the benefit he can from the schools of philosophy, and
near the beginning of the *Orator* he makes the significant claim:
*fateor me oratorem, si modo sim aut etiam quicumque sim, non ex
rhetorum officinis sed ex Academiae spatiis extitisse...* (*Or.*
3.12). In particular he sees that it is highly beneficial to the
orator if he can penetrate to the basic abstract question (*infinita
quaestio* = θέσις) underlying the complex facts of the case about
which he has to speak:

...orator, non ille vulgaris sed hic excellens, a propriis
personis et temporibus semper, si potest, avocet controversiam;
latius enim de genere quam de parte disceptare licet, ut quod in
universo sit probatum id in parte sit probari necesse; haec igitur
quaestio a propriis personis et temporibus ad universi generis
rationem traducta appellatur θέσις. (*Or.* 14.45f.)

Besides requiring his ideal orator to be something of a philosopher, Cicero had come to demand eloquence of the philosopher
too. He describes at the beginning of the *Tusculan disputations*
(written in 45 B.C.) his own efforts towards the creation of a
Latin philosophical language; in particular he tells us that he
had taken to discoursing in the manner of the Greeks on philosophical subjects, in the company of friends on his Tusculan
estate. Jokingly he refers to the copious and ornate philosophical

discourses produced on these occasions as the declamation of his
old age:

hanc enim perfectam philosophiam semper iudicavi, quae de maximis
quaestionibus copiose posset ornateque dicere, in quam exerci-
tationem ita nos studiose dedimus, ut iam etiam scholas Graecorum
more habere auderemus: ut nuper tuum post discessum in Tusculano,
cum essent complures mecum familiares, temptavi quid in eo genere
possem. ut enim antea declamitabam causas, quod nemo me diutius
fecit, sic haec mihi nunc senilis est declamatio. (*Tusc. disp*. I.
4.7)

One might be tempted to dismiss this account of Cicero's *scholae*
at Tusculum as a fiction, an artificial setting of the scene in
preparation for the ensuing discourses, but it is clear from other
sources that in later life Cicero really had come to believe in
the declamation of θέσεις as an educational method preferable to
those used by the rhetoricians of his time.[38] In a letter to his
brother (*Ad Q. fr*. III.3.4) he explicitly contrasts his own preference for the θέσις with his nephew's liking for the less abstract
types of rhetorical exercise:

Cicero tuus nosterque summo studio est Paeoni sui rhetoris,
hominis, opinor, valde exercitati et boni; sed nostrum instituendi
genus esse paulo eruditius et θετικώτερον non ignoras.

This letter dates from 54; in another written in March 49 he actually lists a number of θέσεις (in Greek) which he was using to
exercise himself at that time. He explains:

...ne me totum aegritudini dedam sumpsi mihi quasdam tamquam
θέσεις quae et πολιτικαί sunt et temporum horum, ut et abducam
animum ab querelis et in ipso de quo agitur exercear. (*Ad Att*. IX.
4.1)

The questions he was setting himself all concerned the problem of
how to act under a tyranny.

     Seneca's flat denial in *Contr*. I pr. 12 that Cicero did not
declaim the kind of exercises called *theses* is therefore one of
his most unfortunate errors. If, on the other hand, he had said
that *theses* were not in common use in the average rhetorical
school of Cicero's time, that would probably have been a true
statement of the facts.

     Seneca was wrong in suggesting that the *controversia* was a
type of exercise as novel as its newly coined name.[39] We have
looked at the evidence for the use of similar themes remarkably
early in the history of Greek education: the introduction to Rome

of judicial themes of the type popular under the Empire has to be
dated at least as early as Cicero's boyhood. In the same letter
to his brother in which he expresses his preference for the θέσις
(*Ad Q. fr.* III.3.4) Cicero makes some interesting remarks about
the type of education which his nephew was receiving at the school
of Paeonius:

...neque ego impediri Ciceronis iter atque illam disciplinam volo
et ipse puer magis illo declamatorio genere duci et delectari
videtur. in quo quoniam ipsi quoque fuimus, patiamur illum ire
nostris itineribus; eodem enim perventurum esse confidimus. (*Ibid.*
5)

Here we learn that Cicero's own education had been along much the
same lines as the training in declamation enjoyed by his nephew,
which dealt with themes less abstract than the θέσις. However
much terminology had changed, the declamations of Cicero's youth,
to which he refers in *Tusc. disp.* I.4.7: *ut antea declamitabam
causas, quod nemo me diutius fecit...* and *Brut.* 90.310: *commentabar declamitans - sic enim nunc loquuntur - saepe cum M.
Pisone et cum Q. Pompeio aut cum aliquo cottidie, idque faciebam
multum etiam Latine, sed Graece saepius...* must have been fundamentally similar to those which Q. Cicero's son, along with most
students and rhetoricians of the very late Republic, preferred to
θέσεις, though probably they were more varied in type and more
rigorously treated than the themes declaimed in the school of
Paeonius.[40] Striking evidence that there was, in fact, a remarkable degree of continuity in educational practice from the early
first century B.C. through to the time of Quintilian, comes in the
De oratore, where Cicero represents M. Antonius, grandfather of
the triumvir, as recommending a training in the techniques of
judicial oratory more rigorous than that provided by the easy
exercises which were generally all the practice which students of
rhetoric were given:

hoc in ludo non praecipitur; faciles enim causae ad pueros
deferuntur; lex peregrinum vetat in murum ascendere; ascendit;
hostis reppulit: accusatur. nihil est negoti eius modi causam
cognoscere; recte igitur nihil de causa discenda praecipiunt;
[haec est enim in ludo causarum formula fere.] at vero in foro
tabulae testimonia. pacta conventa stipulationes, cognationes
affinitates, decreta responsa, vita denique eorum, qui in causa
versantur, tota cognoscenda est. (II.24.100)

Antonius' complaints foreshadow the criticism so often levelled
against the rhetoricians of the Empire,[41] that they were not providing adequate training for the forum; the particular exercise
quoted is also given by Quintilian as an example of a type of
controversia in which one cannot quibble over the interpretation
of the law, but has to consider solely the character and motives
of the individual who has infringed it:

...tale genus controversiarum in quo nullum argumentum est quod ex
lege ipsa peti possit, sed de eo tantum de quo lis est quaerendum
est. 'peregrinus si murum escenderit capite puniatur. cum hostes
murum escendissent, peregrinus eos depulit: petitur ad supplicium.'
(Quint. VII.6.6)

This theme, it should be noted, contains, like the typical
controversiae of the Empire, nothing but a bare statement of the
facts of the case; it includes none of the inessential scene-
setting that distinguishes the *veteres controversiae* which
Suetonius assigns to the second stage of Roman declamation. When
these Italian realist themes, set in Ostia and Brundisium and pur-
porting to be based on real events, were invented, and how
seriously they rivalled the starker type of theme in popularity at
any stage, are intriguing but unanswerable questions. The problem
of the ownership of treasure fished out of the sea, which is at
issue in the first theme, was a legal conundrum known to Plautus,
who exploits its possibilities in the long dispute over the rope
(with trunk attached) from which the *Rudens* takes its name
(938ff.). Note particularly the legalistic quibbling in 975ff.:

GR. mare quidem commune certost omnibus. TR. adsentio:
qui minus hunc communem quaeso mihi esse oportet vidulum?
in mari inventust communi. GR. esne inpudenter inpudens?
nam si istuc ius sit quod memoras, piscatores perierint.

Plautus must have expected his audience to appreciate these soph-
istries to some extent, and this fact might seem to suggest that
the topic disputed was a familiar feature of Roman education even
in Plautus' time. However, as the *Rudens* was an adaptation of a
Greek original by Diphilus (see *Rud.* 31f.), perhaps we should deduce no more than that it was discussed in Hellenistic schools:
Plautus' audience may have been expected to laugh at the scene as
illustrating a typical *ineptum...negotium et Graeculum*.[42] The
origins of Suetonius' *veteres controversiae* must remain a mystery.

They may well be genuine early exercises: the central theme of the
first must have been debated in the Hellenistic world; in the
first *Tetralogy* of Antiphon we have noted the mention of a
specific date (Διιπολείοις 4.8) not essential to the main issue of
the case, like *aestivo tempore* in the first *vetus controversia*.
On the other hand, one also has to consider the possibility that
they were antiquarian fabrications of some quite late *rhetor*, who,
like Quintilian (II.10.4), would have liked to see a greater element of realism in declamation themes.

Whatever the truth of this matter, Seneca is clearly misleading when, referring to the modern *controversia* he says, *hoc
enim genus materiae, quo nos exercemur, adeo novum est, ut nomen
quoque novum sit* (*Contr.* I pr. 12). His denial that Cicero declaimed the sort of exercises now called *controversiae* also seems
to conflict with some other evidence, though it may well be that
Cicero, when declaiming, used a wider variety of ὑποθέσεις than
found favour in the schools of the elder Seneca's time. *De or.*
II.24.100 shows that Cicero knew of at least one school exercise
which Quintilian could class as a *controversia*; it is fairly safe
to infer that he had been set such exercises as a boy, even if
later he came to prefer the tougher training methods which he
makes M. Antonius advocate in the *De oratore*. In addition, Seneca
the Elder himself knew a tradition, conflicting with that set out
in *Contr.* I pr. 12, that Cicero had once declaimed a *controversia*
very like *Contr.* I.4:

color pro adulescente unus ab omnibus, qui declamaverunt, introductus est: 'non potui occidere', ex illa Ciceronis sententia
tractus, quam in simili controversia dixit, cum abdicaretur is,
qui adulteram matrem occidendam acceperat et dimiserat: ter non
<... (*Contr.* I.4.7)

Perhaps we should not lay too much weight on this piece of school
tradition, originating as it may in the realms of Ciceronian
pseudepigrapha, or simply in some rhetorician's fanciful wish to
ascribe a time-honoured *color* to the fount of eloquence himself.
But it is not totally implausible that some memory of the nature
of Cicero's declamations, at least his late ones, should have been
preserved; nor is it inconceivable that, in order to indulge the
tastes of the younger generation, Cicero declaimed *controversiae*

(though not necessarily only *controversiae*) in the company of
Dolabella, Hirtius, and Pansa.

Certainly *controversiae* were not the only sort of judicial
declamations to find favour in the late Republic. Sometimes poli-
ticians would practise all the possible variations of invective
for use against their opponents. Cicero jeers at the way that
Antony '*ipse interea XVII dies de me in Tiburtino Scipionis declamitavit*'... (*Phil.* V.19). Alternatively they might declaim in order
to prepare themselves for rebutting their opponents in an important
speech: *Cn. Pompeium quidam historici tradiderunt sub ipsum civile
bellum quo facilius C. Curioni promptissimo iuveni causam Caesaris
defendenti contradiceret repetiisse declamandi consuetudinem*
(Suet. *De gramm. et rhet.* 25.4 Brugnoli).[43] Cicero's declamations,
in line with M. Antonius' requirements in *De or.* II.24.99f., may
likewise often have been concerned very specifically with contemporary legal issues and politics on which he might be required to
speak. As we shall see, the word *commentari* in Republican usage
can mean 'to prepare one's material (orally) for a forthcoming
speech', as well as 'to declaim' in general, and to Cicero, perhaps, there was not always a clear distinction between these two
activities. Or sometimes he may have harked back to past events
and contrived the ideal speech which he might have delivered in
the circumstances: bear in mind that some of his most famous
speeches were never actually delivered and could therefore in a
sense be described as rhetorical exercises. There may be a hint
that his late ὑποθέσεις included treatments of contemporary problems in *Ad Att.* XIV.22.1 where he sets out the attitudes of
Hirtius and his friends towards Caesar in terms of what he calls
a ὑπόθεσις:

ὑπόθεσιν autem hanc habent eamque prae se ferunt, clarissimum
<virum> interfectum, totam rem publicam illius interitu per-
turbatam, inrita fore quae ille egisset simul ac desisteremus
timere, clementiam illi malo fuisse, qua si usus non esset, nihil
ei tale accidere potuisse.

Just as the θέσεις which he set himself in later life included
some which helped him to thrash out the ethical problems at issue
in the politics of his time (cf. *Ad Att.* IX.4.1), so his ὑποθέσεις
may sometimes have been of a kind which would help him to organize

rigorously his private deliberations about people and events at times of crisis, enabling him, for example, to examine all facets of the question where to place one's allegiance after the death of Caesar.

However, even if the declamations of Cicero and other eminent men of the late Republic were sometimes of a different, and more serious, order than those of the Augustan scholastics, Seneca's history of declamation has to be faulted for obscuring a considerable degree of continuity which must have existed in rhetorical education between Republic and Empire. For there can be no doubt that, whatever Cicero might say or do, throughout this period the pupils of humble rhetoricians continued to debate the legal rights of the foreigner who had scaled the city walls in order to repel the invader.

Similarly, Seneca is misleading when he claims that the practice called *declamatio* was a very recent innovation: *modo nomen hoc prodiit; nam et studium ipsum nuper celebrari coepit: ideo facile est mihi ab incunabulis nosse rem post me natam* (*Contr.* I pr. 12). Leaving aside the question of the Greek background, it seems that the practice of regular declamation by adults in Rome to considerable audiences antedates the use of the word *declamatio* to describe it. Suetonius writes about the rhetorical teaching of M. Antonius Gnipho, a *grammaticus* who taught *primum in Divi Iuli domo pueri adhuc, deinde in sua privata* in the following terms:

docuit autem et rhetoricam ita ut cotidie praecepta eloquentiae traderet, declamaret vero non nisi nundinis. scholam eius claros quoque viros frequentasse aiunt, in his M. Ciceronem, etiam cum praetura fungeretur. (*De gramm. et rhet.* 7.3 Brugnoli)

Cicero was praetor in 66 B.C. It may be that orators, as opposed to rhetoricians, never declaimed in public as early as this, and that rhetoricians did not admit the public to their schools as often as they were later to do, but Seneca is over-simplifying the facts of the matter when he calls declamation '*rem post me natam*'.

Contr. I pr. 12, then, contains several major distortions of the history of Roman declamation. On the other hand the lexicographical data in it about the development of declamatory terminology from Cicero's to Seneca's own time, seem to be sound, as far as can be judged from independent investigation of Cicero's usage.

Causa is the term used by Cicero when referring to the declamations of his early years in *Tusc. disp.* I.4.7: *ut antea
declamitabam causas, quod nemo me diutius fecit, sic haec mihi
nunc senilis est declamatio.* These *causae*, presumably to be
identified with the declamations in both Greek and Latin to which
he refers in *Brut.* 90.310, will often, perhaps most often, have
been judicial exercises, but not always. *Causa* was used by Cicero
and others as a translation of Hermagoras' term ὑπόθεσις: Quintilian makes the equation succinctly in III.5.7: *finitae autem sunt*
[sc. *quaestiones*] *ex complexu rerum personarum temporum ceterorum-
que: hae* ὑποθέσεις *a Graecis dicuntur, causae a nostris.* Now,
according to Hermagorean theory, ὑποθέσεις/*causae* could be of
three different types: judicial, deliberative, or epideictic:
*quales sunt, quae in litibus, quae in deliberationibus versantur,
addat, si quis volet, etiam laudationes* (*De or.* II.16.65). It is
hinted here that in practice the terms were rarely used with reference to epideictic, but later in the *De oratore* Cicero gives an
example of a deliberative *causa: placeatne a Karthaginiensibus
captivos nostros redditis suis recuperari* (*De or.* III.28.109). So
it seems that the exercises which Cicero called *causae* could have
included themes of the *suasoria,* as well as of the *controversia,*
type. The invectives which Antony and others practised could
also, theoretically at least, have been so described.

The word *controversia* is used by Cicero in a variety of technical and non-technical senses,[44] but not, as far as one can make
out, in the precisely limited sense: 'judicial theme for declamation'. The primary meaning of *controversia* is 'quarrel': *nulla
controversia mihi tecum erit,* says Megadorus in Plautus' *Aulularia*
(261); a quarrel of the type customary among shepherds is called a
controversia by Cicero in *Pro Cluentio* 59.161. In technical contexts *controversia* is sometimes used by Cicero as a rendering of
the Greek ἀμφισβήτησις, that is, the fundamental cause for dispute
underlying a θέσις or ὑπόθεσις. Compare Cic. *De inv.* I.6.8 =
Hermagoras fr. 6a Matthes: *Hermagoras...qui causam esse dicat rem,
quae habeat in se controversiam in dicendo positam cum personarum
certarum interpositione,* with Theon, *Prog. Rh. Gr.* II.120.13
Spengel = fr. 6d Matthes: θέσις ἐστὶν ἐπίσκεψις λογικὴ ἀμφισβήτησιν

ἐπιδεχομένη ἄνευ προσώπων ὡρισμένων καὶ πάσης περιστάσεως...
Controversia in such contexts is something underlying, or contained within, a *causa*, but elsewhere Cicero uses it, like *causa*,
as equivalent to ὑπόθεσις. In *De or*. III.28.109 he outlines the
theory of the Academics and Peripatetics about θέσεις and ὑποθέσεις as follows:

omnem civilem orationem in horum alterutro genere versari: aut de
finita controversia certis temporibus ac reis;[45*] hoc modo:
placeatne a Karthaginiensibus captivos nostros redditis suis
recuperari? aut infinite de universo genere quaerentis: quid
omnino de captivo statuendum ac sentiendum sit? atque horum
superius illud genus causam aut controversiam appellant eamque
tribus, lite aut deliberatione aut laudatione, definiunt; haec
autem altera quaestio infinita et quasi proposita consultatio
nominatur.

Causa and *controversia* are explicitly equated in this analysis of
the types of rhetoric. What Cicero does *not* do is to restrict the
use of *controversia* to the judicial type of ὑπόθεσις, still less
to the type of fictitious ὑπόθεσις set for declamation. So it
seems that Seneca was right to regard the usage of *controversia*
accepted in his time as non-Ciceronian. It also seems plausible
that, as Suetonius appears to have suggested (*De gramm. et rhet*.
25.9 Brugnoli), when *controversia* was first used with reference to
judicial declamations, it had to be qualified by the adjectives
ficta or *iudicialis*, if confusion was to be avoided.[46] The word
still retained some of its ambiguity in Quintilian's time: *verae
fictaeque controversiae* are distinguished in II.1.9.

The term *scholastica*, according to Seneca *controversia multo
recentius*, is indeed not to be found in any work earlier than
Seneca's own. It is unmistakably used as a feminine noun in
Contr. II.3.13, III pr. 12 and X.5.12. The dative and ablative
plurals *scholasticis* are found in a number of other contexts,[47]
and as Bonner has pointed out[48] there is no reason to assume, as
lexicographers have generally done, that these are neuter, rather
than feminine, plurals. Bonner surmises that the term was a
Latinization of a Greek word ἡ σχολαστική, formed from σχολαστικός
as ῥητορική developed from ῥητορικός, but evidence is lacking for
this development. It seems relevant to compare the term *suasoria*,
cognate with the adjective *suasorius*.

To turn now to Seneca's statement that *declamatio* itself was not found used by authors earlier than Cicero (?)[49] and Calvus, it should be noted that the quotation he gives to illustrate Calvus' usage, *ait enim declamare iam se non mediocriter, dicere bene*, is evidence for the use of the verb *declamare*, not of the noun *declamatio*. Seneca has sacrificed lexicographical precision for the sake of euphony when he states that *ipsa declamatio*, rather than *declamare*, was not to be found used by early authors.[50] Now, whatever else the quotation may illustrate, it does not, assuming it is by Calvus, represent the first ever use of the verb *declamare*. Calvus was two years old when in 80 B.C. Cicero taunted his opponent in the *Pro Roscio Amerino* (29.82) for making allegations, *quae mihi visus est ex alia oratione declamare quam in alium reum commentaretur*. Here, as in other early contexts, *declamare* probably means simply 'to rant', and *commentari* is best taken to mean 'prepare a speech (for a forthcoming trial)', so that the implication of the whole would be: 'he seemed to me to be ranting on about charges extracted from some other speech, which he was preparing for use against some other defendant'. It is true that *commentari* has sometimes, in Cicero's works, much the same meaning as *declamare* was to have in the Empire, but it was a word with quite a wide range of meanings. It is used with reference to other arts besides rhetoric, even the gladiatorial art, to mean 'remind oneself of one's skills' i.e. 'to practise', e.g. *De or*. III.23.86: *magister hic Samnitium summa iam senectute est et cotidie commentatur*; it can even be used of the self-training by which one prepares for death (*Tusc. disp*. I.31.75). Where rhetoric is concerned it can have two different, though related, meanings. Sometimes it serves as a translation of μελετᾶν, the surprisingly imprecise word used by the Greeks throughout antiquity to mean 'declaim rhetorical exercises': this is how Cicero uses it in *Brut*. 89.305: *...et scribens et legens et commentans oratoriis tantum exercitationibus contentus non eram*; and *ibid*. 90.310: *commentabar declamitans - sic enim nunc loquuntur saepe cum M. Pisone et cum Q. Pompeio*. Elsewhere, however, he uses it to refer to the preparation of real speeches, as for example in *Brut*. 22.87:

unum quasi comperendinatus medium diem fuisse, quem totum Galbam
in consideranda causa componendaque posuisse; et cum cognitionis
dies esset et ipse Rutilius rogatu sociorum domum ad Galbam mane
venisset, ut eum admoneret et ad dicendi tempus adduceret, usque
illum, quoad ei nuntiatum esset consules descendisse, omnibus ex-
clusis commentatum in quadam testudine cum servis litteratis
fuisse, quorum <alii> aliud dictare eodem tempore solitus esset.
interim cum esset ei nuntiatum tempus esse, exisse in aedis eo
colore et eis oculis, ut egisse causam, non commentatum putares.

In *Rosc. Amer.* 29.82 *commentari* is used in association with *oratio*
and *reus*, so it seems best to take it there too as referring to
preparation for a real speech, and not to assume that *declamare*,
used in the same sentence, need have had strong scholastic overtones as early as 80 B.C.[51]

 Declamare is used by Cicero of shouted invective in general,
e.g. *Verr.* II.4.149: *qui pro isto vehementissime contra me
declamasset* (70 B.C.); *Ad fam.* III.11.2: *ne in quemvis inpune
declamari liceret* (50 B.C.); and also of exercises intended to
improve the speaker's vocal powers rather than his skill in argumentation: *De fin.* V.2.5: *quo in loco ad fluctum aiunt declamare
solitum Demosthenem* (45 B.C.). Similarly *declamatio* is sometimes
used by Cicero to mean just 'abusive ranting': *Mur.* 21.44: *non
declamatio potius quam persalutatio* (63 B.C.);[52*] it is used to
mean 'elocution practice' by the *Auctor ad Herennium* (III.12.20).

 Declamare seems to have taken on the absolute sense illustrated by Seneca's quotation from Calvus, 'to declaim rhetorical
exercises (as opposed to true speeches)', only in the last years
of Cicero's life. The advent of the new usage is heralded by the
first appearance of *declamator* in 54 B.C.: *non vobis videtur cum
aliquo declamatore...disputare? (Planc.* 34.83),[53] and disparaging
remarks about *illo declamatorio genere (Ad Q. fr.* III.3.4 - also
54 B.C.), clearly with reference to exercises less abstract than
θέσεις. When, however, in the *Brutus,* composed in 46, Cicero uses
the iterative *declamitare* in conjunction with *commentari,* he still
apologizes for his neologistic expression: *commentabar declamitans
- sic enim nunc loquuntur* (90.310). From these examples it is
evident that Cicero was not responsible for giving *declamare* and
related terms their new absolute sense. (It is interesting that
Seneca should cite Calvus in this connection.) In his latest

letters and treatises Cicero uses *declamare* and *declamatio* in
their new sense, despite his distaste for the new fashion for declaiming when carried to extremes: *haud amo vel hos designatos,
qui etiam declamare me coegerunt, ut ne apud aquas quidem
acquiescere liceret* (*Ad Att*. XIV.12.2 - 44 B.C.). He evidently
recognized that *declamatio* had come to stay, though he would have
been happier if the *instituendi genus...*θετικώτερον which he preferred (*Ad Q. fr*. III.3.4) and which he adopted as his *senilis
declamatio* (*Tusc. disp*. I.4.7), had appealed more to the younger
generation. The statement in *Contr*. I pr. 12 that the usage of
declamatio and *declamare* current in Seneca's day was of recent
origin, seems therefore to have been quite correct, as does the
account of the order in which new Latin names - *causa*, *controversia*, *scholastica* - were given to non-abstract declamatory
exercises.

 Contr. I pr. 12 presents sound lexicographical material, but
this is set within a distorted picture of the whole development of
Roman declamation. In particular we need some explanation why, in
Seneca's account, the *thesis* is represented as exclusively pre-
Ciceronian, in flagrant contradiction to the facts, and the *controversia* as a very recent innovation and as something quite distinct
from the *causa* as Cicero knew it.

 The idea that the dominant pre-Ciceronian exercise had been
the *thesis* could have arisen out of a false inference from *De or*.
III.27.107, where Cicero says of the abstract types of exercise:
*quae exercitatio nunc propria duarum philosophiarum, de quibus
ante dixi, putatur, apud antiquos erat eorum, a quibus omnis de
rebus forensibus dicendi ratio et copia petebatur...*[54] Maybe
Seneca's source affirmed the precedence of θέσεις positively, like
Quintilian in II.1.9: *...antiquis hoc fuisse...genus exercitationis ut thesis dicerent et communes locos et cetera citra complexum rerum personarumque...*, rather than denying, as Seneca
does, that Cicero declaimed them.[55]

 The information (correct) that Cicero called his rhetorical
exercises *causae* could have been gained directly from *Tusc. disp*.
I.4.7,[56] one of Cicero's most explicit references to his prolonged
self-education in early manhood. The denial that Cicero declaimed

controversiae, though possibly based on genuine recollection that
some of Cicero's ὑποθέσεις were different from those of later
schoolmen, may however simply be another inference from Cicero's
use of the term *causa* in *Tusc. disp.* I.4.7, false this time. Note
how, in the problematic opening sentences of *Contr.* I pr. 12,
no clear distinction is drawn between innovation of genre and
innovation of terminology:

declamabat autem non quales nunc controversias dicimus, ne tales
quidem, quales ante Ciceronem dicebantur, quas thesis vocabant.
hoc enim genus materiae, quo nos exercemur, adeo novum est, ut
nomen quoque eius novum sit. controversias nos dicimus: Cicero
causas vocabat.

Perhaps one should detect here a simple inability on Seneca's part
to conceive that Cicero might have given the name *causa* to the
exercise which later generations called *controversia*.

But the lack of any reference to Cicero's late philosophical
declamations cannot be explained as due to false inference. Nor
can it be convincingly argued that Seneca's source cannot have
known the passages in which Cicero refers to his θέσεις. *Tusc.
disp.* I.4.7, which tells us about Cicero's *causae*, also tells us
of his *senilis declamatio* on philosophical themes. The letters
Ad Atticum, although maybe not available when Seneca was writing,[57]
were sufficiently accessible in the 30s B.C. for Nepos to read
them (Nepos, *Att.* 16.2ff.).

To help explain why no reference to Cicero's taste for θέσεις
found a place in any of the ancient accounts of the history of
Roman declamation, it may be relevant to compare Philostratus'
sketch of the rise of the two sophistics. According to Philostratus, the first sophistic dealt exclusively with τὰ φιλοσοφούμενα; themes pertaining to particular men and situations were
the innovation of Aeschines at the beginning of the second. No
mention is made of the *Tetralogies* ascribed to Antiphon, or of the
tradition known to Plutarch (*Per.* 36.3) that Pericles had indulged
in dispute with Protagoras about the accidental death of a named
individual; nor is there any reference to the continued inclusion
of the themes here assigned to the first sophistic, among the *progymnasmata* of later Greek education. Philostratus' account seems
governed by a presupposition that the simple and abstract must

precede the complex and concrete. There is no place in it for
recognition that the two main species of sophistical themes might
exist side by side. So it is with *Contr.* I pr. 12: the abstract
thesis - regarded by most rhetoricians of the time as a simple
preparatory exercise - is assigned to the first stage of Roman
declamation, and we are left to suppose that the more complex
causa and its successors superseded it completely.[58] Thus Roman
education, like Greek, is made to go through a first sophistic
before it can reach its second phase. The uncomfortable evidence
of such passages as *Tusc. disp.* I.4.7, on Cicero's taste for
philosophical declamation, and *De or.* II.24.100, on the early use
of a *controversia* theme, had simply to be ignored, if there was to
be no disruption of a satisfying notion of steady progress along
lines familiar from Greek literary history.

To Seneca the Elder, the time of Cicero seemed the golden age of
Roman eloquence; its glory had lingered on for perhaps one more
generation - he was grateful for the illumination shed on his
studies by the brilliant minds 'born at that time' (Contr. I pr.
7)[1] - but since then rhetoric, in his view, had shown a rapid decline. The causes of this decline were to be the topic of much
discussion throughout the first century A.D.,[2] just as the decay
of Greek eloquence after the downfall of the democracies appears
to have been the subject of earlier scholarly debate.[3] Seneca's
is one of the earliest of the Roman discussions, and it is
interesting to consider which of the explanations for the decline
that were to become more or less standard, he does, or does not,
give.[4]

In Contr. I pr. 7 he offers us three alternative explanations:

in deterius deinde cotidie data res est, sive luxu temporum -
nihil enim tam mortiferum ingeniis quam luxuria est - sive, cum
praemium[5]* pulcherrimae rei cecidisset, translatum est omne
certamen ad turpia multo honore quaestuque vigentia, sive fato
quodam, cuius maligna perpetuaque in rebus omnibus lex est, ut ad
summum perducta rursus ad infimum, velocius quidem quam ascenderant, relabantur.

He then proceeds to give a highly coloured description of contemporary decadence, which owes much to the clichés of declamatory
convicium saeculi (Contr. I pr. 8-10).[6]

Luxus temporum, if we are to judge from this description,
consisted in the dedication of modern youth to bone idleness
(somnus languorque) or else, what was worse, to malarum rerum
industria and the obscena studia of singing and dancing; the
fashion was for effeminate behaviour nisi in libidine, and Seneca
finds it unsurprising that no orators were emerging among the
younger generation: in hos ne dii tantum mali ut cadat eloquentia:
quam non mirarer, nisi animos in quos se conferret eligeret.

The concept that good oratory depended on good morals was an

old one, pin-pointed in the requirement of the elder Cato, which
Seneca quotes in *Contr.* I pr. 9, that an orator should be *vir
bonus* as well as *dicendi peritus.*[7] According to the younger
Seneca (*Ep. mor.* 114.1) the saying *talis hominibus...oratio qualis
vita* originated as a Greek proverb, and was often to be heard on
the lips of his contemporaries; in his view it was unquestionable
that the prevalent style of oratory at any time was a reflection
of the morals of the community at large (*ibid.* 2) so that:
*argumentum est luxuriae publicae orationis lascivia, si modo non
in uno aut in altero fuit, sed adprobata est et recepta.*

Indeed, contemporary luxury was again and again blamed in the
ancient world for the decline of all the arts, not just oratory.
Ps.-Longinus, referring to μεγάλας φύσεις in general, regards their
non-appearance as the result of a combination of φιλοχρηματία and
the φιληδονία which enslaved and submerged the lives of its devotees (*Subl.* 44.6). The debasement of poetry was associated by
satirists with luxury and effeminacy (e.g. Pers. *Sat.* 1.32ff.;
98ff.). A character in Petronius' *Satyricon* attributes the decline of the sculptor's art and all the branches of philosophy, as
well as the decline of oratory, to the low moral standards of his
contemporaries *vino scortisque demersi* (§88). In addition, it was
a commonplace of historians, stated for example in Livy's preface
(9ff.), that political decadence was the consequence of increasing
luxury and avarice.

Luxus temporum is Seneca's first explanation for the decline;
his second: *sive, cum praemium pulcherrimae rei cecidisset, translatum est omne certamen ad turpia multo honore quaestuque
vigentia,*[8*] is expressed in somewhat veiled language, but it seems
certain that the allusion is to changed political conditions.
That the *pulcherrima res* is *eloquentia* is clear enough, but what
did Seneca consider to have been its 'reward', and what were the
turpia multo honore quaestuque vigentia to which men were now
devoting their energies? The rewards of eloquence as Cicero saw
them are conveniently listed in *Pro Caelio* 19.46. Arguing that an
orator's training is very hard work, Cicero asks: *an vos aliam
causam esse ullam putatis cur in tantis praemiis eloquentiae,
tanta voluptate dicendi, tanta laude, tanta gratia, tanto honore,*

tam sint pauci semperque fuerint qui in hoc labore versentur?[9]
The rewards mentioned here surely sum up what the writers have in
mind in discussions of the decline of eloquence where the loss of
praemia/ἔπαθλα is referred to. Besides the elder Seneca, Tacitus
and ps.-Longinus touch on this topic.

    According to ps.-Longinus, there was a popular view sometimes
regarded as hackneyed (πιστευτέον ἐκείνῳ τῷ θρυλουμένῳ; we are
asked in *Subl.* 44.2), that great oratory could not exist outside
free, republican states, indeed that democracy was required for
the fostering of all greatness: ἡ δημοκρατία τῶν μεγάλων ἀγαθὴ
τιθηνός. The idea was an old one: Aristotle had associated the
development of formal rhetoric with the rise of democracies in
Sicily (Cic. *Brut.* 12.46). Cicero, after reporting this in his
Brutus, notes how conspicuously lacking in orators the non-
democratic Greek cities had been, and in *De or.* I.8.30 he again
remarks on the way that eloquence flourished *in omni libero populo*.
Similar observations must have been made in a lost part of Tacitus'
Dialogus, for after a lacuna we find in *Dial.* 36ff. criticism of
the assumption that the conditions which produced great oratory
were necessarily a good thing. It is in summarizing the commonplace political explanation for the decline of rhetoric that ps.-
Longinus refers to 'rewards':

θρέψαι τε γάρ, φησίν, ἱκανὴ τὰ φρονήματα τῶν μεγαλοφρόνων ἡ ἐλευ-
θερία καὶ ἐπελπίσαι, καὶ ἅμα διεγείρειν τὸ πρόθυμον τῆς πρὸς ἀλλή-
λους ἔριδος καὶ τῆς περὶ τὰ πρωτεῖα φιλοτιμίας. ἔτι γε μὴν διὰ τὰ
προκείμενα ἐν ταῖς πολιτείαις ἔ π α θ λ α ἑκάστοτε τὰ ψυχικὰ προ-
τερήματα τῶν ῥητόρων μελετώμενα ἀκονᾶται καὶ οἷον ἐκτρίβεται καὶ
τοῖς πράγμασι κατὰ τὸ εἰκὸς ἐλεύθερα συνεκλάμπει. (*Subl.* 44.2-3)

(πολιτείαις should be taken here in the sense 'republican govern-
ments' for which meaning see LSJ s.v. πολιτεία III.2.) Since the
loss of the 'rewards' available to orators a new era has seen the
rise of servility sanctioned as right behaviour and a genius for
nothing but flattery:

'οἱ δὲ νῦν ἐοίκαμεν' ἔφη 'παιδομαθεῖς εἶναι δ ο υ λ ε ί α ς
δικαίας, τοῖς αὐτοῖς ἔθεσι καὶ ἐπιτηδεύμασιν ἐξ ἁπαλῶν ἔτι
φρονημάτων μόνον οὐκ ἐνεσπαργανωμένοι καὶ ἄγευστοι καλλίστου καὶ
γονιμωτάτου λόγων νάματος, τὴν ἐλευθερίαν' ἔφη 'λέγω· διόπερ οὐδὲν
ὅτι μὴ κ ό λ α κ ε ς ἐκβαίνομεν μεγαλοφυεῖς.' (*Ibid.* 3)

Some sentiments of a related kind are expressed by the elder Pliny
in *NH* XIV.1.5f. Pliny is bewailing the decline of the arts in

general, rather than just oratory, and he holds responsible for
the decline not the loss of republican government, but the sheer
massiveness and material wealth of the Roman Empire, which has en-
gulfed a multitude of small states where the arts, so we are to believe, had flourished thanks to the lack of riches of any other kind,
and to the patronage of rulers desirous of immortality (*NH* XIV.
1.4). But he shares with the philosopher quoted by ps.-Longinus
the conviction that the decline of the arts and the fall of *vitae
pretia* have been accompanied by the rise of an all-pervasive servility. He associates this with the increasing importance which
the possession of wealth had assumed in the Rome of his day:

> postquam senator censu legi coeptus, iudex fieri censu, magistra-
> tum ducemque nihil exornare quam census, postquam coepere orbitas
> in auctoritate summa et potentia esse, captatio in quaestu
> fertilissimo, ac sola gaudia in possidendo, pessum iere vitae
> pretia, omnesque a maximo bono liberales dictae artes in con-
> trarium cecidere, ac servitute sola profici coeptum. hanc alius
> alio modo et in aliis adorare, eodem tamen habendique ad spes
> omnium tendente voto; passim vero etiam egregii aliena vitia quam
> bona sua colere malle. ergo, Hercules, voluptas vivere coepit,
> vita ipsa desiit. (*Ibid*. 5-6)

It must be concluded that the *praemium pulcherrimae rei*, the
loss of which Seneca deplores, was certainly no mere financial
reward, but rather the *laus, gratia* and *honor* which Republican
orators had been able to earn, and that, if pressed to explain
what he meant by *turpia multo honore quaestuque vigentia*, he would
probably have spoken of the varieties of servility and sycophantic
crawling (in particular, perhaps, legacy-hunting) by which influential men of his time had attained their wealth and respected
positions.

Seneca's third explanation: *sive fato quodam, cuius maligna
perpetuaque in rebus omnibus lex est, ut ad summum perducta rursus
ad infimum, velocius quidem quam ascenderant, relabantur*, belongs
to an old-established tradition of theorizing about the rise and
fall of phenomena: 'the famous parabola shape – ascent, highest
point of ἀκμή and inevitable decline – so dear to antiquity'.[10]
As Polybius puts it (VI.51.4): ...παντὸς καὶ σώματος καὶ πολιτείας
καὶ πράξεώς ἐστί τις αὔξησις κατὰ φύσιν, μετὰ δὲ ταύτην ἀκμή,
κἄπειτα φθίσις...[11] Albucius, a declaimer fond of philosophizing,
brought a generalization on these lines somewhat inappositely into

his rendering of *Suas*. 1 (§3): *quidquid ad summum pervenit, incremento non relinquit locum*, and the younger Seneca uses similar language in his *Consolatio ad Marciam* (23.2f.): *quidquid ad summum pervenit, ad exitum prope est...ubi incremento locus non est, vicinus occasus est.*

It is a remarkable fact that Cicero had already, in *Tusc. disp.* II.1.5, prophesied the forthcoming demise of rhetoric from natural causes: *atque oratorum quidem laus ita ducta ab humili venit ad summum, ut iam, quod natura fert in omnibus fere rebus, senescat brevique tempore ad nihilum ventura videatur.* Velleius Paterculus, with whom Seneca may be seen to share other views on literary history,[12] treats the question of the rise and fall of genres, including oratory, in some detail, and his account is the best commentary on Seneca's third explanation for the decline. Velleius is impressed by the way that literary genres, once they have reached perfection, only flourish for a short while, and he subjects literary history to a somewhat procrustean treatment in order to prove his point, making out for example that, just as Greek drama only flourished at its peak for a short time, there was similarly no philosophy of any importance before Socrates or after the death of Plato and Aristotle, no rhetoric of note before Isocrates or after *eius auditores eorumque discipulos* (I.16.3ff.). He takes the view that the classical period of Roman historiography and poetry had been confined to a span of eighty years, now ended; Roman oratory, of course, had reached its peak *sub principe operis sui Tullio*, and there were few orators before him whose work could give the reader any pleasure, no orator whom one could really admire who had not either seen Cicero, or been seen by him (I.17.2f.).[13] Though unable to find a reason which satisfies him completely for the brief efflorescence of genres, he regards the following as the most plausible explanation:

alit aemulatio ingenia, et nunc invidia, nunc admiratio imitationem accendit, naturaque quod summo studio petitum est, ascendit in summum difficilisque in perfecto mora est, naturaliterque quod procedere non potest, recedit. et ut primo ad consequendos quos priores ducimus accendimur, ita ubi aut praeteriri aut aequari eos posse desperavimus, studium cum spe senescit, et quod adsequi non potest, sequi desinit et velut occupatam relinquens materiam quaerit novam, praeteritoque eo, in quo eminere non possumus,

aliquid, in quo nitamur, conquirimus, sequiturque ut frequens ac
mobilis transitus maximum perfecti operis impedimentum sit.
(I.17.6f.)

Such was the type of theorizing current in Seneca's time about a
natural law affecting literature whereby decline was inevitable
after a brief period of perfection. But Seneca has shown himself
in *Contr.* I pr. 6 slightly less gloomy than Velleius about the
apparent impossibility of emulating the achievements of one's predecessors when the genre in which one is working seems to have
reached its ἀκμή already. He sees a possible way out of the
impasse in a less limiting sort of *imitatio* than that envisaged by
Velleius: ...*quo plura exempla inspecta sunt, plus in eloquentiam
proficitur. non est unus, quamvis praecipuus sit, imitandus, quia
numquam par fit imitator auctori*, and the provision of *plura
exempla* is one of the purposes of his collection of declamatory
extracts (*ibid.*).

   It seems misguided to assume that only one of Seneca's
explanations for the decline of oratory can contain any truth.
Modern critics who discuss them tend to find the political explanation by far the most attractive.[14] Bonner, for instance, dismisses *luxus temporum* on the one hand as 'a rhetorical theme' and
the theory about the natural law of rise and fall as an 'easy explanation...hardly satisfactory, and...in any case, probably
little more than a commonplace'. But such a process of elimination only over-simplifies, and perhaps distorts, our picture of
what seemed in antiquity a complex and puzzling phenomenon.

   The first and third explanations should not be dismissed so
lightly. If we look at Seneca's descriptions of individual declaimers, we find in the case of Alfius Flavus a young man whose
considerable natural talents were threatened with extinction by
just the sort of indolence which has been attacked in the tirade
against the morals of the younger generation (*somnus languorque* -
Contr. I pr. 8): *ipse omnia mala faciebat ingenio suo; naturalis
tamen illa vis eminebat, quae per multos annos, iam et desidia
obruta et carminibus enervata, vigorem tamen suum tenuit* (*Contr.*
I.1.22), and in Scaurus an orator who notoriously failed to realize the potential of his gifts owing to what Seneca calls his

perpetua desidia (*Contr.* X pr. 3) and who was, if we are to believe other ancient references to him, a man much given to blatant
impuritas (Tertullian, *De Pallio* 5) and luxurious living (Petr.
Sat. 77). Thus the rhetorical effusions in *Contr.* I pr. 8ff. were
not totally divorced from the realities of the times, though of
course Seneca would have been wrong if he imagined that orators of
earlier generations had all been paragons of virtue. In the case
of Cassius Severus we have a man whose state of mind may be compared to that which Velleius Paterculus attributes to the generation after one which has produced inimitable masterpieces.
Cassius has abandoned Cicero's ideal of an orator perfect in all
departments, arguing that no one can excel in more than òne kind
of writing, and that *in ipsa oratione quamvis una materia sit,
tamen ille, qui optime argumentatur, neglegentius narrat, ille non
tam bene implet quam praeparat* etc. (*Contr.* III pr. 10). By
Tacitus' time Cassius Severus had come to be regarded as the originator of the new phase in Roman rhetoric, and according to Aper
in the *Dialogus* (19.1) he turned the course of rhetoric away from
illa vetere atque directa dicendi via as the result of a conscious
intellectual decision: *non infirmitate ingenii nec inscitia
litterarum transtulisse se ad aliud dicendi genus contendo, sed
iudicio et intellectu*. Though Cassius does not reject the whole
genre of oratory simply because it has reached its ἀκμή, he resembles the typical post-classical generation of Velleius' account,
in deciding that it is hopeless to aspire to the grand ideals of
the past, and (at least according to Aper's interpretation) in
consciously setting out in a completely new direction.

Seneca's theory about the downfall of the *praemium pulcherrimae rei* ought likewise to be considered against the background
of his many casual remarks about early Imperial orators.[15] From
these there emerges quite a varied picture of the state of oratory
in the time of Augustus and Tiberius. The art appears to be far
from dead, or suffering from any total collapse in the esteem ac-
corded to it, even if free speech has been somewhat curtailed; an
optimist might, on the basis of what Seneca says about oratory
outside the first preface, agree with Aper in Tacitus' *Dialogus*
that eloquence in the Empire was still *praesidium simul ac telum,*

quo propugnare pariter et incessere sive in iudicio sive in senatu
sive apud principem possis (*Dial.* 5.6), and might ask as he does:
fama et laus cuius artis cum oratorum gloria comparanda est? (7.3).

The leading orators of the period are named by Cassius
Severus as Pollio, Messala and Passienus (*Contr.* III pr. 14),[16*]
and later tradition, as we have seen, rated Cassius himself as a
highly important figure. Seneca gives a long description of his
oratory in *Contr.* III pr. 2ff. Plenty of other lesser orators receive discriminating attention from Seneca: Mamercus Aemilius
Scaurus (*non novi quemquam, cuius ingenio populus Romanus pertinac-*
ius ignoverit. Contr. X pr. 2-3; cf. *Suas.* 2.22); L. Arruntius
(*Contr.* VII pr. 7); Asilius Sabinus (*Contr.* IX.4.17ff. - *illud non*
probavi, quod multa in re severa temptavit salse dicere); Asinius
Gallus (*Contr.* IV pr. 4: *magnum oratorem, nisi illum, quod semper*
evenit, magnitudo patris non produceret sed obrueret); Fabius
Maximus (*Contr.* II.4.11: ...*nobilissimus vir fuit, qui primus foro*
Romano hunc novicium morbum, quo nunc laborat, intulit); Furius
Saturninus (*Contr.* VII.6.22: *maius nomen in foro quam in declamati-*
onibus habuit); Iunius Otho (*Contr.* II.1.34); T. Labienus (*Contr.*
X pr. 4f.: *magnus orator, qui multa impedimenta eluctatus ad famam*
ingeni confitentibus magis hominibus pervenerat quam volentibus);
Tuscus (*Suas.* 2.22: *homo quam inprobi animi, tam infelicis*
ingenii); Vallius Syriacus (*homo disertus* - *Contr.* IX.4.18; cf.
Contr. II.1.34ff.); Varius Geminus (*Contr.* VI.8 *extra*; cf. *Suas.*
6.11f.); L. Vinicius (*quo nemo civis Romanus in agendis causis*
praesentius habuit ingenium - *Contr.* II.5.19f.); P. Vinicius
(*Contr.* VII.5.11: *exactissimi vir ingeni*); M. Vipsanius Agrippa
(*Contr.* II.4.13); Votienus Montanus (*Contr.* IX.5.15: *homo rarissumi*
etiamsi non emendatissimi ingeni; cf. *Contr.* VII.5.11; IX pr. 1;
6.10, 18).

Orators seem, from Seneca's passing remarks, to have been by
no means short of work.[17] A statement intended to illustrate
Cassius Severus' exceptional carefulness as an orator sheds unexpected light on the frequency with which one might be expected
to deliver speeches:

numquam tamen haec felicitas illi persuasit neglegentiam. uno die
privatas plures <quam duas> non agebat et ita ut alteram ante

meridiem ageret, alteram post meridiem, publicam vero numquam
amplius quam unam uno die. (*Contr.* III pr. 5)

How often, then, would a careless orator speak? Some indication
is found in Seneca's description of the hasty manner in which
Scaurus prepared his speeches: *saepe causam in ipsis subselliis,
saepe dum amicitur discebat* (*Contr.* X pr. 2).

Some limitation of free speech there certainly was. The
libertas which in Augustus' time had allowed one to joke about M.
Vipsanius Agrippa's lowly middle name is referred to as a thing of
the past:

tanta autem sub divo Augusto libertas fuit, ut praepotenti tunc M.
Agrippae non defuerint qui ignobilitatem exprobrarent. Vipsanius
Agrippa fuerat, <at> Vipsani nomen quasi argumentum paternae hum-
ilitatis sustulerat et M. Agrippa dicebatur. cum defenderet reum,
fuit accusator qui diceret: 'Agrippa Marce et quod in medio est' -
volebat Vipsanium intellegi -; fuit qui diceret: 'concurrite!
Agrippa malum habebit. responde sis, Marce uterque.' mihi
videtur admiratione dignus divus Augustus, sub quo tantum licuit...
(*Contr.* II.4.13 W)

Even the reign of Augustus had seen the burning of Labienus'
books,[18] deplored in *Contr.* X pr. 5ff., though Seneca does not
blame the Princeps for it. Now the situation had arisen where one
might have to decide whether it was worthwhile *caput potius quam
dictum perdere*; Seneca advises discretion (*Contr.* II.4.13).

An orator was not necessarily so inhibited by having to conduct a case before the Emperor that he could not produce attractive oratory in the new style, full of pleasing *sententiae*. Of P.
Vinicius' accusation of Votienus Montanus we read in *Contr.* VII.
5.12:

accusaverat illum apud Caesarem, a colonia Narbonensi rogatus. at
Montanus adeo toto animo scholasticus erat, ut eodem die, quo
accusatus est a Vinicio, dic<eret: 'del>ectavit me Vinici actio';
et sententias eius referebat. eleganter illi dixit Surdinus:
rogo: numquid putas illum alteram partem declamasse?

Moreover, to judge from what Seneca says about Sabinus' plea for
an allowance (*Contr.* IX.4.20f.), the Roman Senate still sometimes
heard even late in Tiberius' reign speeches in which both pathos
and humour were to be found:

multa illum diserte dixisse memini, cum introductus esset ex
carcere in senatum postulaturus, ut diaria acciperet. tunc dixit
de fame questus: nihil onerosum a vobis peto, sed ut me aut mori
velitis aut vivere. et illud dixit: nolite, inquam, superbe

audire hominem calamitosum:
     saepe qui misereri potuit misericordiam rogat.
et cum dixisset Seianianos locupletes in carcere esse: homo,
inquit, adhuc indemnatus, ut possim vivere, parricidas panem rogo.
cum movisset homines et flebili oratione et diserta, redit tamen
ad sales: rogavit, ut in lautumias transferretur: non est, inquit,
quod quemquam vestrum decipiat nomen ipsum lautumiae; illa enim
minime lauta res est.

Of course, grovelling flattery towards the Emperor marred
some of the public oratory of this period; *Contr.* VI.8 *extra* pre-
serves an example: *Varius Geminus apud Caesarem dixit: Caesar, qui
apud te audent dicere magnitudinem tuam ignorant, qui non audent,
humanitatem.* (We do not know in what context Seneca quoted this.)
The prosecutors in trials for *maiestas* must have brought eloquence
into some disrepute: note that Tuscus, who prosecuted Scaurus on
this charge, is the one orator in whom Seneca fails to find a redeeming feature (*Suas.* 2.22). And the orator speaking before
Tiberius ran the risk, according to Tacitus, of having his most
carefully contrived flatteries misinterpreted: the calamity of
Iunius Gallio, who in 31 framed a proposal designed to please
Tiberius, only to incur the suspicion of being a two-faced
satelles Seiani (Tac. *Ann.* VI.3),[19] must have saddened his friend,
the elder Seneca, and served to remind him that in a political
career *ipsa quae sperantur timenda sunt* (*Contr.* II pr. 4).

Outside the political sphere, lurid trials still sometimes
provided opportunities for sensational, if not great, oratory.
One such is described in *Contr.* II.1.34ff.:
erat genus iudici tale: speciosum iuvenem dominus suus deprehend-
isse cum uxore in cubiculo testatus est et ob hoc uxorem suam
dimisit. hoc nomine servum adulteri postulatum dominus non
defendebat, mulier, in quam petebatur praeiudicium, tuebatur.
The advocates displayed much ingenuity in dealing with this case,
in particular in finding a *color* to exculpate the woman, *cum in
cubiculo visa esset cum servo et marito*, and the onlookers at the
trial were vastly entertained by witticisms bandied around about
the 'Theodorean' avoidance of narration indulged in by one of the
counsels.[20] Other notable cases recalled by Seneca include the
trial of Moschus the rhetorician for poisoning (*Contr.* II.5.13),
in which Pollio spoke unsuccessfully for the defence, and the
fiasco in the Centumviral Courts which forced Albucius to restrict

his activities from then on to the schools of rhetoric (*Contr.* VII
pr. 6ff.).

Outside Rome eloquence appears to have been in quite a
healthy state. Of course, to an ambitious urban Roman this fact
would seem of little importance: note the dictum of Censorinus,
quoted by Cassius Severus in *Contr.* III pr. 12, that candidates
for public office in the *municipia* were exerting themselves in a
dream world (*in somniis laborare*).[21] Seneca nevertheless had a
high enough regard for his native province to think the leading
orators of Spain worth praising. At the end of the tenth preface
we are told about Gavius Silo, a man of whom Augustus said,
'*numquam audivi patrem familiae disertiorem*' (*Contr.* X pr. 14),
and Clodius Turrinus, the account of whose career shows that at
least in Spain eloquence could still bring enormous prestige, not
to mention financial gain:

causas nemo diligentius proposuit, nemo respondit paratius; et
pecuniam itaque et dignitatem, quam primam in provincia Hispania
habuit, eloquentiae debuit. natus quidem erat patre splendid-
issimo, avo divi Iuli hospite, sed civili bello attenuatas domus
nobilis vires excitavit, et ita ad summam perduxit dignitatem ut,
si quid illi defuerit, scias locum defuisse. (*Contr.* X pr. 16)

There is plenty of evidence, then, even within Seneca's own
work, that the opportunities for eloquence in the early Empire
were abundant. To what extent the prestige - the *laus*, *gratia* and
honor - which could be earned by an orator, was less than it had
been under the Republic is something which it is impossible to
gauge properly now, but the dominant position in Roman education
of the schools which ostensibly trained the orators of the future[22] is some index of the esteem in which oratorical skill continued to be held under the Empire. Thus Seneca's second explanation for the decline of eloquence is not such a resoundingly
complete truth that all other theories should be dismissed as
superficial by comparison. Bear in mind that, like the others, it
was probably taken over from earlier theorizing about the Hellenistic world.

Seneca's threefold theory *de causis corruptae eloquentiae* is
as interesting for what it leaves out as for what it includes.
First, it includes no suggestion that the loss of the *praemium* of

eloquence and the resultant change in people's activities was anything but deplorable, whereas in the discussions of the subject by
Tacitus and ps.-Longinus we find extensive debunking of the view
that the loss of the conditions afforded to the orator by a free
Republic was altogether a bad thing.

In the long summing-up speech which draws Tacitus' *Dialogus*
to its close Maternus makes it clear that he has no regrets about
the demise of the *perturbatio* and *licentia* of the Republic, with
its popularist legislation, its all-night speeches, its pros-
ecutions of the powerful, family feuds, aristocratic factions, and
never-ending enmity between Senate and plebs:

quae singula etsi distrahebant rem publicam, exercebant tamen
illorum temporum eloquentiam et magnis cumulare praemiis vid-
ebantur, quia quanto quisque plus dicendo poterat, tanto facilius
honores adsequebatur, tanto magis in ipsis honoribus collegas suos
anteibat, tanto plus apud principes gratiae, plus auctoritatis
apud patres, plus notitiae ac nominis apud plebem parabat. (*Dial.*
36.4)

If civil strife and the activities of people like Catiline, Milo,
Verres and Antony were the price one had to pay for great oratory,
he for one was not prepared to pay it (37.6ff.). In ps.-Longinus'
treatise doubt is cast on the whole idea that the loss of Republican government was the cause of the disappearance of great literature. The view that an undemocratic constitution enslaves the
intellect is put by ps.-Longinus into the mouth of 'one of the
philosophers' (*Subl.* 44.1); speaking in the first person (44.6) he
proposes that it is ὁ κατέχων ἡμῶν τὰς ἐπιθυμίας ἀπεριόριστος
οὑτοσὶ πόλεμος in particular moral enslavement caused by love of
money and pleasure, rather than ἡ τῆς οἰκουμένης εἰρήνη, which has
stifled literary greatness. It is noteworthy that Seneca the
Elder, whatever reservations he had as to whether free speech
should be left completely untrammelled,[23] did not, in his main
statement on the decline of eloquence, look on an intellectual
desert and call it peace.

But the respect in which Seneca's theorizing in *Contr.* I pr.
7 is most conspicuously different from other discussions of the
decline of eloquence is the lack of any hint in it that the education provided by the schools of rhetoric might in any way be to
blame.

The remoteness from real life of the themes of *controversiae*
and *suasoriae* is again and again jeered at by critics in the first
century A.D.[24] People were for ever pointing out that all the
years spent assiduously in declamation on these fanciful themes
turned out to be of no use at all when the student of rhetoric
finally entered the forum. Encolpius in Petronius' *Satyricon* puts
the matter forcibly when addressing Agamemnon the rhetorician
(*Sat.* 1f.):

nunc et rerum tumore et sententiarum vanissimo strepitu hoc tantum
proficiunt, ut cum in forum venerint, putent se in alium orbem
terrarum delatos. et ideo ego adulescentulos existimo in scholis
stultissimos fieri, quia nihil ex his, quae in usu habemus, aut
audiunt aut vident, sed piratas cum catenis in litore stantes, sed
tyrannos edicta scribentes, quibus imperent filiis ut patrum
suorum capita praecidant, sed responsa in pestilentiam data, ut
virgines tres aut plures immolentur, sed mellitos verborum
globulos et omnia dicta factaque quasi papavere et sesamo sparsa.
qui inter haec nutriuntur, non magis sapere possunt, quam bene
olere, qui in culina habitant. pace vestra liceat dixisse, primi
omnium eloquentiam perdidistis.

It was not hard to find illustrations of the irrelevance of many
controversia themes to modern life: in Tacitus' *Dialogus* we find
singled out for ridicule *tyrannicidarum praemia aut vitiatarum
electiones aut pestilentiae remedia aut incesta matrum*, all subjects common in the schools but rarely or never encountered in the
forum (*Dial.* 35.5).[25] Quintilian saw the justice of such complaints: *nam magos et pestilentiam et responsa et saeviores
tragicis novercas aliaque magis adhuc fabulosa frustra inter
sponsiones et interdicta quaeremus* (II.10.5), and recommended certain reforms: judicial themes of a more realistic type might be
invented, and some of the more pernicious tendencies which had
developed in the schools – the perpetual use of high-flown
language and the total exclusion of humour – could be done away
with:

utinamque adici ad consuetudinem posset ut nominibus uteremur et
perplexae magis et longioris aliquando actus controversiae
fingerentur et verba in usu cotidiano posita minus timeremus et
iocos inserere moris esset: quae nos, quamlibet per alia in
scholis exercitati simus, tirones in foro inveniunt. (*Ibid.* 9)

A type of bombast favoured in declamation had been well parodied
by Petronius:

num alio genere furiarum declamatores inquietantur, qui clamant:

'haec vulnera pro libertate publica excepi; hunc oculum pro vobis
impendi: date mihi ducem, qui me ducat ad liberos meos, nam
succisi poplites membra non sustinent'? (*Sat.* 1)

Evidently drawing on a Greek source,[26] he blames the taste for

such *levibus...atque inanibus sonis* on Asianic influences newly

come to Athens: *nuper ventosa istaec et enormis loquacitas Athenas*

ex Asia commigravit... (§2).

In general the schools were criticized for providing excessively sheltered conditions which gave the students a false sense
of security, later to be rudely shattered as soon as they went out
to speak in the forum. In the *Dialogus* Messala complains:

at nunc adulescentuli nostri deducuntur in scholas istorum, qui
rhetores vocantur...\<in\> quibus non facile dixerim utrumne locus
ipse an condiscipuli an genus studiorum plus mali ingeniis ad-
ferant. nam in loco nihil reverentiae est, in quem nemo nisi
aeque imperitus intrat; in condiscipulis nihil profectus, cum
pueri inter pueros et adulescentuli inter adulescentulos pari
securitate et dicant et audiantur... (35.1ff.)

Quintilian singles out for criticism the frequent applause with
which the students greeted each other's efforts (II.2.9ff.), and
the dangers inherent in the scholastic practice of declaiming only
one side of a *controversia* at a time (XII.6.5, cf. VII.3.20),
which meant that the declaimer could assume that any facts not
made clear in the *thema* were in his own favour (VII.2.54). Such
observations were, as we shall see, already commonplace among hostile critics of the schools in the elder Seneca's time.

Blame for the deep entrenchment of the pernicious practices
customary in the schools of rhetoric was directed variously
towards the *rhetores*, the students, and their parents. Agamemnon,
the rhetorician in the *Satyricon*, concedes the truth of the criticisms levelled against the schools, but points out the difficulties of the teacher's position; he has to give the pupils what they
want:

nihil nimirum in his exercitationibus doctores peccant, qui
necesse habent cum insanientibus furere. nam nisi dixerint quae
adulescentuli probent, ut ait Cicero, 'soli in scholis
relinquentur'. (*Sat.* 3)

He finds that there is no demand from their parents either, for a
strenuous type of education:

parentes obiurgatione digni sunt, qui nolunt liberos suos severa

lege proficere. primum enim sic ut omnia spes quoque suas
ambitioni donant. deinde cum ad vota properant, cruda adhuc
studia in forum pellunt et eloquentiam, qua nihil esse maius con-
fitentur, pueris induunt adhuc nascentibus. (§4)

Quintilian, speaking as a representative of the profession, has
fault to find with the rhetoricians as well: for various reasons
they have a tendency to spend more time than they need in covering
the standard curriculum:

sed culpa est in praeceptoribus prima, qui libenter detinent
<quos> occupaverunt, partim cupiditate diutius exigendi mercedulas,
partim ambitione, quo difficilius <videatur esse> quod pollicentur,
partim etiam inscientia tradendi vel neglegentia: proxima in nobis,
qui morari in eo quod novimus <quam> discere quae nondum scimus
melius putamus. nam ut de nostris potissimum studiis dicam, quid
attinet tam multis annis quam in more est plurimorum, ut de iis a
quibus magna in hoc pars aetatis absumitur taceam, declamitare in
schola et tantum laboris in rebus falsis consumere, cum satis sit
modico tempore imaginem veri discriminis et dicendi leges
comperisse? (XII.11.14f.)

This indictment has the ring of truth.

That there should be no trace of criticism of rhetorical education in *Contr.* I pr. 7 is all the more remarkable seeing that
later in his work the elder Seneca reports two attacks by acquaint-
ances of his on the whole practice of declamation which are even
more devastating and comprehensive than Petronius' anti-scholastic
invective. Cassius Severus is reported in the third preface as
having criticized the schools severely for encouraging in those
who frequented them an exaggerated self-esteem which proved to be
quite unwarranted once they entered public life:

agedum istos declamatores produc in senatum, in forum: cum loco
mutabuntur; velut adsueta clauso et delicatae umbrae corpora sub
divo stare non possunt, non imbrem ferre, non solem sciunt, vix se
inveniunt; adsuerunt enim suo arbitrio diserti esse. non est quod
oratorem in hac puerili exercitatione spectes. quid, si velis
gubernatorem in piscina aestimare? (*Contr.* III pr. 13f.)

In particular he pours scorn on the way that ignorant and tasteless students preferred Cestius and Latro to the leading orators
of their time, Pollio, Messala and Passienus, and only refrained
from expressing a preference for their favourite rhetorician over
Cicero for fear of a stoning (§14f.). In the ninth preface Seneca
reports an even more vehement attack on the schools of declamation.
It opens with an allegation that school practices were having a
damaging effect on the oratory of the forum:

qui declamationem parat, scribit non ut vincat, sed ut placeat.
omnia itaque lenocinia [ita] conquirit; argumentationes, quia
molestae sunt et minimum habent floris, relinquit; sententiis,
explicationibus audientis delinire contentus est. cupit enim se
approbare, non causam. sequitur autem hoc usque in forum declamatores vitium, ut necessaria deserant, dum speciosa sectantur.
(*Contr.* IX pr. 1f.)

The conditions which made for the scholastics' unwarranted over-

confidence are attacked one by one:

accedit etiam illud, quod adversarios quamvis fatuos fingunt:
respondent illis et quae volunt et cum volunt. praeterea nihil
est, quod errorem aliquo damno castiget; stultitia eorum gratuita
est. vix itaque in foro futurus periculosus stupor discuti
potest, qui crevit, dum tutus est. quid, quod laudationibus
crebris sustinentur et memoria illorum adsuevit certis intervallis
quiescere? cum ventum est in forum et desiit illos ad omnem
gestum plausus excipere, aut deficiunt aut labant. adice nunc,
quod <animus> illis nullius interventu excutitur: nemo ridet, nemo
ex industria obloquitur, familiares sunt omnium vultus. in foro,
ut nihil aliud, ipsum illos forum turbat. (§2f. M)

As an illustration we are given an anecdote about Latro, who was

once called upon to speak in a court-case, but was so unaccustomed

to outdoor speaking that he began his speech with a solecism, and

had to get the case moved indoors before he would complete it (§3).

The fundamental failing of declamation as an educational method,

our critic goes on to argue, is that it is so much easier than the

work for which it purports to be a training: gladiators and ath-

letes are trained far more sensibly, required as they are to prac-

tise tests of skill and endurance more arduous than those they

will face in the arena (§4). The schools of rhetoric provide no

such preparation for the adverse conditions to be encountered by

orators in the forum:

in foro partem accipiunt, in schola eligunt; illic iudici blandi-
untur, hic inperant; illic inter fremitum consonantis turbae
intendendus animus est, vox ad aures iudicis perferenda, hic ex
vultu dicentis pendent omnium vultus. (§5)

Trained in such an environment, novices in the forum only mature

into orators after long subjection to ridicule and much hard work

(*ibid.*).

The elder Seneca's own attitude towards declamation seems to

have been much less severe. He was aware that the schools served

sometimes as an escape route for failed orators (*Contr.* VII pr. 6;

IX.4.18), but he was not persuaded by any of his contemporaries'

attacks on the schools to abandon his conviction that rhetorical
education was a useful training even for people who were not
planning to enter public life (*Contr*. II pr. 3). His friendship
with Latro, one must suspect, was a prime cause of his tolerance
towards the declaimers. We must make no mistake about it: this
tolerance was considerable. Modern critics have often suggested
that Seneca thought that declamation ought to return to its proper
place as a mere educational exercise,[27] but there is no evidence
that this was so. Bornecque asserts: '*Il n'ignore pas que la
déclamation n'est qu'un moyen de former les jeunes gens; la preuve
en est que, de tous les professeurs, celui qu'il admire le plus
est Latron, qui, j'aurai l'occasion de le montrer, maintient la
déclamation dans ses justes limites*.' But this will not do as
proof. Certainly Latro did not suffer from gross lapses of taste,
and organized his declamations in a straightforward manner, but it
is important to remember that he was foremost among Latin *rhetores*
in avoiding the chore of actual teaching (*Contr*. IX.2.23) and that
he was alleged to have been a total failure as an orator (*Contr*.
IX pr. 3). By expressing admiration for Latro, Seneca set himself
apart from those who condemned, with *censorium supercilium* raised,
the practice of declaiming for the sake of frivolous ostentation
(*Contr*. X pr. 4). He did not regard declamation as a form of literary activity of the same seriousness as true oratory or the
writing of history: note, in addition to his description of the
declamatory anthology as *non seriam rem* in the somewhat conventional leave-taking of *Contr*. X pr. 1, remarks he makes in *Contr*.
I.8.16: *Diocles Carystius dixit sententiam, quae non in declamatione tantum posset placere sed etiam in solidiore aliquo scripti
genere*, and in *Suas*. 5.8 (referring to Gallio): *hoc loco
disertissimam sententiam dixit <dignam> quae vel in oratione vel
in historia ponatur*... Nevertheless, school rhetoric interested
the elder Seneca sufficiently for him to devote a long work to the
memory of the declaimers he had known, and to present posterity
with minute and sympathetic documentation of the various facets of
their art.

PART III

FIVE ASPECTS OF DECLAMATION: THE ELDER SENECA'S EVIDENCE

Quint. III.3.1: omnis autem orandi ratio, ut plurimi maximique auctores tradiderunt, quinque partibus constat: inventione, dispositione, elocutione, memoria, pronuntiatione sive actione (utroque enim modo dicitur).[1]

The declaimer's first task, as he set about composing a *contro-versia*, was to decide whose part he would take in the imaginary law-suit: *in foro partem accipiunt, in schola eligunt* (*Contr.* IX pr. 5). Some *controversia* themes were so devised that it was possible to make out a fair case both for and against the imagined defendant, but usually one side's case was very much easier to justify than the other's, and few declaimers chose to defend the more obviously villainous characters in the themes, see e.g. *Contr.* X.4.15: *pro illo qui debilitabat expositos pauci admodum dixerunt...* Also perhaps at this stage one might decide whether to speak in the person of the prosecutor or defendant himself, or whether to take the part of an advocate.[2] There were various standard reasons for adopting the latter procedure, never men-tioned by Seneca the Elder, doubtless because he assumed they were common knowledge. Ps.-Quintilian explains the rules as follows:

in plerisque controversiis plerumque hoc quaerere solemus, utrum ipsorum persona utamur ad dicendum, an advocati: vel propter sexum, sicut <in> feminis, vel propter aliquam alioqui vitae vel ipsius, de quo quaeritur, facti deformitatem. (*Decl. Min.* CCLX, 61.12ff. Ritter)

Seneca's declaimers impersonate advocates when speaking on behalf of women (e.g. *Contr.* I.2, IV.6) and slaves (e.g. *Contr.* III.9), and sometimes on account of *facti deformitatem* (*Contr.* X.5.17ff.), but Seneca finds it worthy of note only when a declaimer decides to act as an advocate in order to facilitate a more hard-hitting prosecution, e.g. in a case where a son is prosecuting his father and would be inhibited by *pietas* if he had to speak in person (*Contr.* I.7.13),[3] or in order to allow for a more comprehensive defence involving the use of a variety of *colores* (*Contr.* I.7.17; VII.2.13).

When setting out to declaim a *suasoria* one could choose to give advice either for or against a course of action. Here again,

one side tended to be more popular than the other: faced with the
subject, *deliberat Cicero, an scripta sua conburat promittente
Antonio incolumitatem, si fecisset* (*Suas.* 7), none of the declaimers would advise Cicero to save his skin, and Seneca comments:

huius suasoriae alteram partem neminem scio declamasse; omnes pro
libris Ciceronis solliciti fuerunt, nemo pro ipso, cum adeo illa
pars non sit mala, ut Cicero, si haec condicio lata ei fuisset,
deliberaturus non fuerit. (*Suas.* 7.10)

The choice whether to take the part of the deliberator himself or
of someone advising him seems to have been determined by school
tradition. In *Suas.* 2 and 5 the subject-matter demanded that one
should speak as a participant in a gathering assembled to make a
decision, but only convention can have determined the fact that in
Suas. 3 one took the part of the deliberator, Agamemnon, but in
Suas. 1, 4, 6 and 7 that of an adviser to the man deliberating.[4]

The declaimer next proceeded to that part of his work generally described in Roman rhetorical theory as *inventio*. Seneca the
Elder never uses this term, though he can hardly not have known
what it meant. In his view (and presumably this was the view generally accepted in the schools of his time), the task of 'invention' as it faced someone preparing a *controversia*, consisted of
two parts so distinct that they required separate consideration:[5]
first, *divisio*, the isolating of the basic issues to be disputed,
and secondly, the choice of *colores*, ways of interpreting the
given facts of the case. A *suasoria* involved only *divisio*, no
colores.

Seneca clearly felt that *divisiones* and *colores* were worthy
of as much close attention on the part of the critic as matters of
form and style. Indeed, the bulk of his criticism outside the
prefaces derives more or less directly from a consideration of
these topics.

DIVISIO

Divisio in the elder Seneca's view was the foundation (*Contr.* I
pr. 21: *fundamentum*) on which a declamation was built.[6] In the
completed declamation it would be overlaid with such an elaborate
superstructure (*Contr.* I pr. 21: *superstructis tot et tantis
molibus*) that its existence might hardly be perceptible to the

audience. Indeed, the outpouring of brilliant language would often serve to obscure flaws of *divisio* in a declamation, *ipsa enim actio multas latebras habet, nec facile potest, si quo loco subtilitas defuit, apparere, cum orationis cursus audientis iudicium impediat, dicentis abscondat* (*Contr.* I pr. 21), and it was quite possible for a declaimer to win acclaim without paying much attention to the careful organization of arguments. For instance, Seneca says of the young Ovid, *tunc autem cum studeret, habebatur bonus declamator. hanc certe controversiam ante Arellium Fuscum declamavit, ut mihi videbatur, <illo>*[7]* *longe ingeniosius, excepto eo, quod sine certo ordine per locos discurrebat* (*Contr.* II.2.9), and again, *molesta illi erat omnis argumentatio* (*ibid.* 12). One hostile critic quoted by Seneca went as far as to advance the generalization that the typical declaimer omitted argument altogether, *argumentationes, quia molestae sunt et minimum habent floris, relinquit* (*Contr.* IX pr. 1), but this was probably an overstatement. In Seneca's view, at any rate, a good declaimer was one who paid due attention to the 'virtue of oratory' *subtilitas*, a fine precision in the analysis of the questions at issue. His friend Porcius Latro had laid particular emphasis on the need for a well-ordered *divisio*: it had been his practice, before delivering any declamation in full, to present an unadorned statement of the lines of questioning which he was intending to pursue, a practice which, to Seneca's regret, later rhetoricians had not imitated (*Contr.* I pr. 21).

The *divisiones* of *suasoriae* were usually extremely simple.
When treating *Suas.* 4 (*Deliberat Alexander Magnus an Babylona intret, cum denuntiatum esset illi responso auguris periculum*),
Arellius Fuscus raised the single issue[8] of the validity of prophecy: *in hac suasoria nihil aliud tractare Fuscum scio quam easdem quas supra rettuli quaestiones ad scientiam futuri pertinentis* (*Suas.* 4.4). Occasionally a declaimer would dispense with *divisio* altogether and would simply put on a display of enthusiasm: *Triarius omni dimissa divisione tantum exultavit, quod Xersen audiret venire: adesse ipsis novam victoriam, nova trophaea* (*Suas.* 5.7). Usually, though, one's persuasion would be divided into two or three main sections, called simply *partes* (*Suas.* 2.11; 6.8-9)

or *quaestiones* (*Suas*. 1.8-9; 4.4). Thus Cestius' treatment of
Suas. 1 was divided into two parts:

...quam sic divisit, ut primum diceret, etiamsi navigari posset
Oceanus, navigandum non esse...deinde illam quaestionem subiecit,
ne navigari quidem Oceanum posse. (*Suas*. 1.8)

In the *suasoria* about the three hundred Spartans, Arellius Fuscus
made use of a tripartite plan described by Seneca as *divisione...
illa volgari*:

...non esse honestum fugere, etiamsi tutum esset; deinde: aeque
periculosum esse fugere et pugnare; novissime: periculosius esse
fugere... (*Suas*. 2.11)

Note that the declaimers did not feel at all tied to the classic
plan for persuasion of which Quintilian says in III.8.22, *partes
suadendi quidam putaverunt honestum utile necessarium. ego non
invenio huic tertiae locum.* It was sometimes used, as for example
by Cestius in *Suas*. 6 (§10): ...*mori tibi utile est, honestum est,
necesse est, ut liber et inlibatae dignitatis consummes vitam.*
But it was just one of many alternatives.

Occasionally Seneca presents an analysis of the subsidiary
issues raised by one of the main *quaestiones* in a declaimer's
treatment of a *suasoria*. For example we are told that Fabianus,
having adopted the same two-fold division as Cestius for *Suas*. 1,
dealt with the second part, on the impossibility of crossing
Oceanus, as follows:

ut primum negaret ullas in Oceano aut trans Oceanum esse terras
habitabiles. deinde: si essent, perveniri tamen ad illas non
posse; ...novissime: ut posset perveniri, tanti tamen non esse.
(*Suas*. 1.10)

Seneca also describes in detail how Cestius subdivided a section
in his treatment of *Suas*. 3, where he denied the validity of
prophecy:

...deos rebus humanis non interponere arbitrium suum; ut inter-
ponant, voluntatem eorum ab homine non intellegi; ut intellegatur,
non posse fata revocari. si non sint fata, nesciri futura; si
sint, non posse mutari. (*Suas*. 3.3)

Here is evidence of quite complex argument, encroaching on the
territory of the philosophers. But, on the whole, *suasoriae*
afforded little scope for *subtilitas* in argumentation. Seneca
specifically apologizes for the lack of that quality in the
suasoria on the *trecenti Lacones* (*Suas*. 2.10).

The issues raised by a *controversia* theme and its accompanying laws were usually far more numerous, and it required more
acumen on the part of the declaimer to arrange the questions for
dispute in an appropriate order, duly subordinating the minor
issues to the greater ones.

Seneca distinguishes three types of question which one might
treat in a *controversia*: the *quaestio iuris*,[9] in which one asked
whether the defendant's action was legal, '*an liceat...?*', '*an
possit...?*'; the *quaestio aequitatis*,[10] the treatment of which is
sometimes given the technical name *tractatio*,[11] in which one considered whether his action was morally right, '*an debeat...?*', '*an
oporteat...?*'; and the *quaestio coniecturalis*[12] in which one con-
jectured whether something had, or had not, happened.

Most of the questions found in Seneca's analyses are of the
first two types. Seneca appears perfectly clear in his mind as to
the difference between law and equity. We read, for example, in
Contr. I.1.13, *Latro illas quaestiones fecit: divisit in ius et
aequitatem, an abdicari possit, an debeat*. The distinction was a
very old one, and not peculiar to Roman legal thought.[13] Aristotle
notes in his *Rhetoric* (I.13.2) that the concept of an unwritten
law which can overrule the written one was already recognized by
Sophocles, Empedocles, and Alcidamas. The Latin terminology used
by Seneca is found already in Cicero's works, e.g. *De or.* I.56.240:
pro aequitate contra ius dicere; *Part. or.* 28.100: *in eam formam
causarum, in qua quale sit ambigitur...quae in aequitate et in
iure maxime consistit*.

Generally questions of law were treated first, before any
discussion of equity, e.g. *Contr.* I.8.7: *prima quaestio illa ab
omnibus facta est vulgaris: an filius ob id, quod sui iuris sit,
abdicari possit; deinde: an debeat. haec tota tractationis est*;
Contr. II.5.14: *Latro ex suo more has non quaestiones putabat, sed
membra illius ultimae partis ex aequitatis quaestione pendentis*.
It was obviously best from a psychological point of view to leave
the section which played most on the emotions till last.

Quaestiones iuris

The section of the *divisio* which dealt with points of law was
often quite elaborately constructed. Characteristically there
would be two or three main legal questions at issue, from each of
which a number of lesser questions might spring. Seneca's analyses make the relationship between *quaestiones* quite clear:[14] his
practice is simply to set down the main questions first, and then
to list the subsidiary questions, explaining in a few words how
they were related to the main ones; after that, subdivisions of
the subsidiary questions, if any, might be listed, as for example
in *Contr.* I.2.13f.:

Latro in has quaestiones divisit: an per legem fieri sacerdos non
possit; etiamsi lex illi non obstat, an sacerdotio idonea sit.[15]
an lege prohibeatur, in haec duo divisit: an casta sit, an pura
sit. an casta sit, in haec divisit: utrum castitas tantum ad
virginitatem referatur an ad omnium turpium et obscenarum rerum
abstinentiam...etiamsi ad virginitatem tantum refertur castitas,
an haec virgo sit...an pura sit, in haec divisit: an, etiamsi
merito occiderit hominem, pura tamen non sit homicidio coinquinata;
deinde: an merito occiderit hominem innocentem uti corpore
prostituto volentem.

The complexities set out diagrammatically below (p. 161) are here
described with the minimum of fuss: Seneca found no need for an
elaborate technical terminology in his analyses, no need even to
distinguish by means of adjectives between greater and lesser
questions, as Bardon would like him to have done.[16] Generally he
calls all questions, great and small, simply *quaestiones*. (Once
he uses the diminutive, *quaestiuncula*, but curiously enough with
reference to a *quaestio* which seems to have been of some importance in the *divisio* of at least one declaimer who included it -
Contr. IX.6.15, cf. *ibid*. 10.) As a change from *quaestiones*, he
sometimes substitutes the word *pars*, using it either to mean a
major part of the whole *divisio* (*Contr.* II.5.15; IX.6.15), or a
part of a *quaestio* (*Contr.* IX.4.10). Such lines of speculation as
are not strong enough to stand on their own as *quaestiones* are
variously described as *particulae* (*Contr.* I.3.8: ...*particulas
incurrentes in quaestionem*); *membra* (*Contr.* II.3.15: *haec omnia
quasi membra in aliquam quaestionem incurrentia tractabat, non ut
quaestiones*); or *argumenta* (*Contr.* II.3.16: *Fuscus parum hoc
putabat valens esse tamquam quaestionem, satis valens tamquam*

argumentum).

Quaestiones/tractationes aequitatis

Questions of equity called for more expansive treatment than was appropriate for legal argument. It was presumably for this reason that the term *tractatio* was sometimes preferred to *quaestio* as a word to describe the discussion of *aequitas*:

Contr. I.1.14: adiecit quaestionem [Gallio] alteram: an si abdicari possit etiam adoptatus, <possit> ob id vitium, quod, antequam ad-optaretur, notum fuit adoptanti. haec autem ex aequitatis parte pendet et tractatio magis est quam quaestio.

Contr. I.2.14: an idonea sit, in tractationes quas quisque vult dividit...

Contr. I.4.6: an oportuerit, tractationis quidem est, quam ut quis-que vult variat.

Contr. II.2.5: reliqua, cum ad aequitatem pertineant, tractationis sunt.

Contr. II.5.16: et hoc contra Latronem dicebat [sc. Blandus]: quo-modo istam quaestionem putas in aequitatis tractationem cadere, cum quid liceat quaeratur, non quid oporteat?

Contr. IX.1.9: Latro in has quaestiones divisit...novissume: an si adfectu et indignatione ablatus non fuit in sua potestate, ignoscendum illi sit. hoc non tamquam quaestionem, sed, ut illi mos erat, pro tractatione aut loco.

However, *quaestio* was so much the obvious word to use to denote an enquiry of any sort that it is not surprising that Seneca does not invariably suppress it as the name for a question of equity (as opposed to the treatment of such a question):

Contr. II.5.14: Latro ex suo more has non quaestiones putabat, sed membra illius ultimae partis ex aequitatis quaestione pendentis.

Contr. VII.4.4: Albucius non iuris illam fecit quaestionem sed aequitatis, ita tamen, ut et iuris adiungeret...

Contr. VII.8.8: novissimam quaestionem fecit aequitatis...

On numerous other occasions he applies the term *quaestio* to ques-tions of the type, '*an debeat...?*', or '*an oporteat...?*' (e.g. *Contr.* I.1.13; II.3.12).

With one exception all types of question about moral obli-gation came under the heading of *aequitas*. The exception was the question, often raised in *controversiae*, whether an action consti-tuted a *beneficium* requiring gratitude. This had to be classed as a *quaestio iuris* as it was dealt with under the declamatory *lex ingrati* (see e.g. *Contr.* II.5.10ff.).

Quaestiones coniecturales

The adjective *coniecturalis* is taken from the terminology used by
Latin theorists when translating the στάσις theory of Hermagoras
of Temnos.[17] *Status* (or *constitutio*) *coniecturalis* was the name
given to one of the four basic types of issue distinguished by
Hermagoras, the type in which one raised simple questions of fact,
such as *occideritne Aiacem Ulixes...bonone animo sint erga populum
Romanum Fregellani...si Karthaginem reliquerimus incolumem, num
quid sit incommodi ad rem publicam perventurum?* (Cic. *De inv.*
I.8.11).

Seneca gives the name *controversia coniecturalis* to two of
the declamations in his collection, meaning that they hinge on
questions of fact. These are *Contr.* VII.3, where we have to decide whether a son who has been disowned and then forgiven three
times was preparing poison for his father or himself, *in uno
homine coniectura duplex est* (*Contr.* VII.3.6), and *Contr.* VII.7
where the issue is whether the dying general was referring to his
father when he gave the warning *'cavete proditionem'*. Seneca regards the *divisio* of such *controversiae* as a simple matter: *...con-
iecturalis est et habet quasi certum tritumque iter* (*Contr.* VII.7.
10); *non puto vos exigere divisionem, cum coniecturalis sit controversia* (*Contr.* VII.3.6).

Quaestiones coniecturales were also raised occasionally in
more complex *controversiae* which also involved questions of law
and equity. In *Contr.* II.2.5 we find Latro making a very reason-
able conjecture: had the husband acted with ill intent against his
wife? Seneca approvingly calls it *optimam...quaestionem coniecturalem*, and indeed it is one of the most important questions
raised by the theme. On the other hand in *Contr.* I.5.8-9 we
hear of Cestius trying a conjectural question which is no more
than an innuendo, and is rightly condemned as such by Latro:

Cestius et coniecturalem quaestionem temptavit: an haec cum
raptore conluserit et in hoc rapta sit, ut huic opponeretur.
Latro aiebat non quidquid spargi posset suspiciose, id etiam
indicandum. colorem hunc esse, non quaestionem; eam quaestionem
esse, quae impleri argumentis possit. Cestius aiebat et hanc

posse impleri argumentis. (*Contr*. I.5.8-9 W)

From this we may deduce why *quaestiones coniecturales* are found so rarely in the *divisiones*. Questions of fact had to be more than mere insinuations in order to be classed as *quaestiones* rather than as *colores*. Also, we are told in *Contr*. I.2.14 that the Apollodoreans objected in principle to themes which left a major question of fact in doubt, such as that of *Contr*. I.2, which does not specify whether the would-be priestess is actually a virgin. The Apollodoreans' objections must have helped to make conjectural questions unpopular in the schools of Seneca's time.

In his *divisio* of *Contr*. II.2 Latro included *quaestiones* of all three types, but to do so was rare:

Contr. II.2 *thema*: Vir et uxor iuraverunt, ut, si quid alteri obtigisset, alter moreretur. vir peregre profectus misit nuntium ad uxorem, qui diceret decessisse virum. uxor se praecipitavit. recreata iubetur a patre relinquere virum; non vult. abdicatur.

Latro's *divisio* (*Contr*. II.2.5 M):

ius:	an pater abdicare possit propter matrimonium.
aequitas:	an, etiamsi non malo adversus uxorem animo [fuit] maritus fecit, tamen tam temerarius et inconsultus relinquendus sit...
quaestio coniecturalis:	an etiam malo adversus uxorem animo fecerit.

Latro's plans for *Contr*. I.1 and I.2 exemplify a more normal type of *divisio*, in which *coniectura* is excluded, or allotted only a very minor place in the scheme.

Contr. I.1 *thema*:
Liberi parentes alant aut vinciantur.
Duo fratres inter se dissidebant; alteri filius erat. patruus in egestatem incidit; patre vetante adulescens illum aluit; ob hoc abdicatus tacuit. adoptatus a patruo est. patruus accepta hereditate locuples factus est. egere coepit pater: vetante patruo alit illum. abdicatur.

Latro's *divisio* (*Contr.* I.1.13):

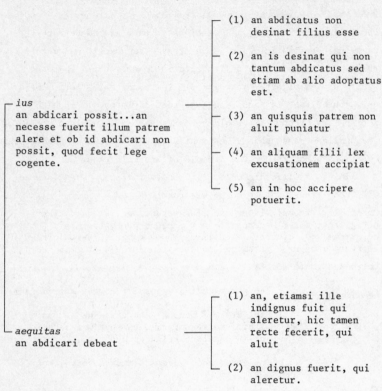

ius
an abdicari possit...an necesse fuerit illum patrem alere et ob id abdicari non possit, quod fecit lege cogente.

(1) an abdicatus non desinat filius esse

(2) an is desinat qui non tantum abdicatus sed etiam ab alio adoptatus est.

(3) an quisquis patrem non aluit puniatur

(4) an aliquam filii lex excusationem accipiat

(5) an in hoc accipere potuerit.

aequitas
an abdicari debeat

(1) an, etiamsi ille indignus fuit qui aleretur, hic tamen recte fecerit, qui aluit

(2) an dignus fuerit, qui aleretur.

Contr. I.2 *thema*:
Sacerdos casta e castis, pura e puris sit.
Quaedam virgo a piratis capta venit; empta a lenone et prostituta est. venientes ad se exorabat stipem. militem, qui ad se venerat, cum exorare non posset, conluctantem et vim inferentem occidit. accusata et absoluta et remissa ad suos est: petit sacerdotium.

Latro's *divisio* (*Contr.* I.2.13f.):

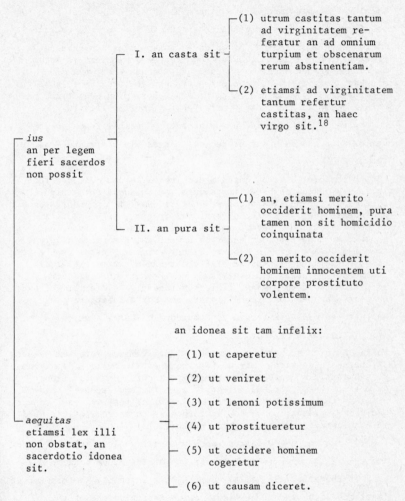

ius
an per legem
fieri sacerdos
non possit

I. an casta sit
(1) utrum castitas tantum ad virginitatem referatur an ad omnium turpium et obscenarum rerum abstinentiam.

(2) etiamsi ad virginitatem tantum refertur castitas, an haec virgo sit.[18]

II. an pura sit
(1) an, etiamsi merito occiderit hominem, pura tamen non sit homicidio coinquinata

(2) an merito occiderit hominem innocentem uti corpore prostituto volentem.

aequitas
etiamsi lex illi non obstat, an sacerdotio idonea sit.

an idonea sit tam infelix:

(1) ut caperetur

(2) ut veniret

(3) ut lenoni potissimum

(4) ut prostitueretur

(5) ut occidere hominem cogeretur

(6) ut causam diceret.

In *Contr.* I.1.13 Seneca tells us that the old type of *divisio*, by which he means primarily the type which had been promoted by Latro, was simpler than that now prevalent: *divisio controversiarum antiqua simplex fuit; recens utrum subtilior an tantum operosior <sit> ipsi aestimabitis*. It will be evident from the samples of his *divisiones* given above that Latro had an eye for the essential issues in a case. It appears from some remarks

Seneca makes that he made conscious efforts to make his *divisiones* simpler than was customary in the schools, and that his intention was to bring scholastic practice closer to that of the courts:

Latro semper contrahebat et quidquid poterat tuto relinquere praeteriebat. itaque et quaestionum numerum minuebat et locos numquam attrahebat; illos quoque, quos occupaverat, non diu dicebat, sed valenter. hoc erat utique praeceptum eius, quaedam declamatorem tamquam praetorem facere debere minuendae litis causa. quod in hac controversia fecit. (*Contr.* VII.7.10)

In *Contr.* II.3.12 we find him elaborating on this teaching and naming some issues which he reckons can safely be regarded as settled:

Latro eleganter dicebat quasdam esse quaestiones, quae deberent inter res iudicatas referri, tamquam, an quidquid optaverit vir fortis aut tyrannicida accipere debeat: quasi iam pronuntiatum sit non debere, nemo iam hanc quaestionem tractat, sicut ne illam quidem, an quidquid pater imperat faciendum sit.[19] inter has putabat et hanc esse, an pater ob dementiam, quae morbo fieret, tantum accusari a filio debeat; aiebat enim manifestum esse e lege et de officio patris quaeri et fingi quasdam controversias, in quibus pater furiosus probari non possit <nec> absolvi tamen propter impietatem nimiam, libidinem foedam. quid ergo? aiebat; numquam utar hac quaestione? utar, cum aliis deficiar.[20]

However, Asinius Pollio was contemptuous of Latro's attempts to imitate forensic methods:

Pollio Asinius aiebat hoc Latronem videri tamquam forensem facere, ut ineptas quaestiones circumcideret, <sed> in nulla magis illum re scholasticum deprehendi. remittit, inquit, eam quaestionem, quae semper pro patribus valentissima est. ego [semper] scio nulli a praetore curatorem dari, quia inicus pater sit aut impius, sed quia furiosus; hoc autem in foro esse curatorem petere, quod in scholastica dementiae agere.[21] (*Ibid.* 13)

Of course, no declaimer worth his salt would simply take over and re-use the *divisio* of Latro or any of the other leading masters of rhetoric. He had to exercise his ingenuity to think of at least one innovation. He might decide to revive one of the *quaestiones* which Latro and others had rejected as *res iudicatas*, or else he might ransack the theme and accompanying laws in search of some previously unnoticed legal or ethical problem. For instance in *Contr.* II.3 (*Raptor raptae patrem exoravit, suum non exorat. accusat dementiae*) Gallio raised the question which Latro passed over: whether a man can be accused *dementiae* for anything other than simple insanity, and then went on to add the ingenious quibble: *an agi cum patre dementiae possit ob id, quod fecerit,*

non ob id quod facturus sit (*Contr.* II.3.14). The declaimer was
encouraged to frame new questions by a scholastic rule that one
should take into consideration every word in the laws accompanying
the *controversia* theme: *praeceptum...quo iubemur ut, quotiens
possumus, de omnibus legis verbis controversiam faciamus* (*Contr.*
I.2.15). A departure by the so-called *novi declamatores*[22] from
Latro's plan, which is mentioned in *Contr.* I.4.6, is based on just
such close reading of a declamatory law:

novi declamatores illam quaestionem temptaverunt ex verbo legis
natam 'adulterum cum adultera qui deprehenderit, dum utrumque
corpus interficiat, sine fraude sit.': an nemo possit occidere
nisi qui deprehenderit...

Another source of new *quaestiones* which the *novi declamatores*
might look to was in the Greek tradition of declamation; see, for
example, *Contr.* I.1.14: *novi declamatores Graecis auctoribus ad-
iecerunt primam illam quaestionem: an adoptatus abdicari possit.*

However, Seneca tells us of certain *quaestiones* which were
popular with Greek declaimers but flatly rejected by their Roman
counterparts. The basic disagreement lay in the fact that the
Greeks assumed that the *tyrannicida* and the *vir fortis* had certain
statutory rights whereas the Romans refused to accept that they
had more than a strong moral claim for privileged treatment:

Contr. I.7.12: Graecorum improbam quaestionem satis erit in eiusmodi controversiis semel aut iterum adnotasse: an in tyrannicidam
uti pater hac lege possit. quasi sacras et publicas manus esse,
in quas ne piratae quidem licere quicquam putent. nostri hoc
genus quaestionis submoverunt.

Contr. I.8.7: Graeci illam quaestionem primam solent temptare,
quam Romanae aures non ferunt: an vir fortis abdicari possit. non
video autem, quid adlaturi sint, quare non possit. nam quod et
vir fortis est et totiens fortiter fecit, non plus iuris illi ad-
fert, sed plus commendationis.

But the declaimers stopped a long way short of really trying to
bring *controversiae* into line with modern Roman legal practice.

So far we have been considering *divisiones* of an orthodox
type, in which *quaestiones iuris* and the issues arising from them
are treated before the *tractatio aequitatis*, and the *quaestio
coniecturalis* if there should be one. Sometimes declaimers broke
away from this type of format and preferred to present the questions at issue in a more artificial, but more striking, way. This

procedure was called *figura dividere*. Here are some examples:

Contr. I.2.16: Albucius figura divisit controversiam; dixit enim: putemus tres sacerdotium petere: unam quae capta est, alteram quae prostitit, tertiam quae hominem occidit: omnibus nego; et sic causam contra singulos egit.

Contr. II.1.23 W: Argentarius omnes priores transit partes, statim ad hoc venit: debueritne patri parere an non debuerit; et in figuram contulit declamationem. 'volo' inquit 'aliquis filium abdicet qui petit a patre paupere ut in adoptionem diviti daretur; quam bonam' inquit 'causam pater habebit! dicet hic...', deinde sic transit, cum declamasset eam controversiam, quae posita non erat: 'si ille filius malam causam habet, ego bonam habeo.' con-tulit suam causam cum illo.

Contr. II.4.9: Cestius bella figura egit: 'dementia' inquit 'res est sanitati contraria. non quaeram extra exemplar sani hominis, ad quod patris mei <mentem exi>gam: ipsum sibi comparabo. fuit aliquando sanus: tunc quid faciebat? oderat luxuriam, vitia castigabat. hunc tam severum senem putabitis sanum, si vobis in lupanari ostendero?' sic declamavit, ut patri accusatorem patrem daret et illum argueret sibi ipsum comparando.

Contr. IX.6.14: Silo a parte patris comparationem fecit inter se matris et filiae <et> totam hac figura declamavit...

The *divisio* of a *controversia* was similar, but not identical, to the organization of arguments for a law-court speech. We have noted the tendency of some declaimers to prune away questions as *res iudicatas*, some of which it would be vitally important to raise in a real court case (*Contr.* II.3.12f.), but the principal difference is that outlined in *Contr.* X.5.12. It appears that one was expected to compress into a single declamation what an orator would take two *actiones* to discuss:

hanc controversiam magna pars declamatorum sic dixit, <vel>ut <non> controversiam divideret, sed accusationem, quomodo solent ordinare actionem suam in foro qui primo loco accusant; in scholastica, quia non duobus dicitur locis, semper non dicendum tantum sed respondendum est. obiciunt, quod hominem torserit, quod Olynthium, quod deorum supplicia imitatus sit, quod tabulam in templo Minervae posuerit. si Parrhasius responsurus non est, satis bene dividunt. nihil est autem turpius quam aut eam contro-versiam declamare, in qua nihil ab altera parte responderi possit, aut non refellere, si responderi potest.

Seneca seems quite content here with the scholastic custom; his rejection of the tactics appropriate to a real-life *actio prima* may be compared with Latro's views on the treatment of the *contro-versia* about Popillius:

Latroni non placebat illum sic accusari, quomodo quidam

accusaverunt: obicio tibi, quod occidisti hominem, quod civem, quod senatorem, quod Ciceronem, quod patronum tuum. hac enim ratione non adgravari indignationem sed fatigari. statim illo veniendum est ad quod properat auditor; nam in reliquis adeo bonam causam habet Popillius ut, detracto eo quod patronum occidit, nihil negoti habiturus sit; patrocinium eius est civilis belli necessitas. itaque nolo per illos reum gradus ducere <per> quos potest tutus evadere. licuit enim in bello et hominem et civem et senatorem et consularem occidere, ne in hoc quidem crimen est, quod Ciceronem, sed quod patronum. naturale est autem ut, quod in nullo patrono fieri oportuit, indignius sit factum in Cicerone patrono. (*Contr.* VII.2.8 M)

That at some stage it had become customary – as it had not been when Antiphon's *Tetralogies* were composed – for the functions of two *actiones* to be covered in one scholastic declamation is curious, just as it seems extremely strange that it was very much the exception rather than the rule among Roman declaimers to arrange any sort of mock trial in which prosecution was pitted against defence. (The only place where Seneca seems to allude to any such arrangement comes in *Contr.* IV pr. 3, where he says of Asinius Pollio,

audivi autem illum et viridem et postea iam senem, cum Marcello Aesernino nepoti suo quasi praeciperet. audiebat illum dicentem et primum disputabat de illa parte, quam Marcellus dixerat: praetermissa ostendebat, tacta leviter implebat, vitiosa co-arguebat. deinde dicebat partem contrariam.)

It is evident from what Seneca and Latro say in *Contr.* X.5.12 and VII.2.8 that in some ways it may well have been easier to organize the *actio prima* of a simple prosecution than a well-balanced *controversia*, but, as critics of the schools were quick to point out, the declaimer's task was much easier than the orator's in one important respect. In the *actio secunda* an orator would have to refute the view of the case presented by his opponent in his first speech. This might be an enormously difficult task. The declaimer met with no such opposition. It was left to him to imagine what objections his opponent might make to his own interpretation of the case, and there was a strong temptation not to credit one's imagined adversary with much intelligence: *adversarios quamvis fatuos fingunt: respondent illis et quae volunt et cum volunt* (*Contr.* IX pr. 2).

COLORES

Seneca used the term *color* in a way which had no precedent in
Cicero's works. To Cicero *color* had meant the distinctive character of a style,[23] or else colourfulness of expression.[24] Χρῶμα is
used similarly by most Greek writers on rhetoric (LSJ s.v. IV 1,2);
it is only in some late examples of theory relating to στάσεις and
modes of defence that we find it used to mean what *color* meant to
Seneca's rhetorician friends, that is, the complexion which a
speaker gave to the actions of the accused in a lawsuit or judicial
declamation (LSJ s.v. IV 4). How it was that the Roman declaimers
came to use *color* in this sense would have to remain a complete
mystery, were it not that D. Matthes, in his Teubner collection of
the fragments of Hermagoras of Temnos, has extracted from obscurity
two significant scholia on the Περὶ στάσεων of Hermogenes of
Tarsus. These show us that the Senecan use of *color* was in line
with Hermagorean usage:

Ἐπειδὴ τὰ ἀπ' ἀρχῆς ἄχρι τέλους σημεῖα ποιούμενος ὁ κατήγορος
δοκεῖ βιάζεσθαι τὸν δικαστὴν καὶ πείθειν ὡς τοῦ ἐγκαλουμένου
ἕνεκεν ταῦτα πεποίηκεν ὁ φεύγων, δεῖ πρὸς τοῦτο ἀγωνίζεσθαι τὸν
φεύγοντα καὶ μὴ τοῦ ἐπιφερομένου ἀδικήματος ἕνεκεν φάσκειν
πεποιηκέναι ἢ εἰρηκέναι ἢ τὸ πάθος συμβεβηκέναι· τοῦτο γάρ ἐστιν ἡ
μετάθεσις τῆς αἰτίας, ὃ χρῶμα προσαγορεύουσιν οἱ Ἑρμαγόρειοι·
ὑπάρχει δὲ τῶν ἀπ' ἀρχῆς ἄχρι τέλους, λύσις δὲ μετὰ ἀντιθέσεως,
καὶ ἔσται ἢ ἀντιστατικὴ ἢ μεταστατικὴ ἢ ἀντεγκληματικὴ ἢ
συγγνωμονική· ἀντιστατικὴ μέν, ἐὰν ὄφελός τι προλαβώμεθα οἷον
'ἀναλαμβάνω τοὺς ἀποκηρύκτους, ἵνα μὴ ἀποροῦντες ἐπὶ κλοπὴν ἢ
ἐπιβουλὴν τράπωνται'. κἀκεῖνα δὲ ὁμοίως ἀντιστατικά, ὅτ' ἂν ὅπλα
ἔχων κρίνηται τυραννίδος ἐπιθέσεως· ἐρεῖ γὰρ ὅτι 'φυλάττω τῇ πόλει
εἰς ἀναγκαῖον ἐπίδοσιν'...καὶ ἀπὸ ἐλέου ἐστὶ μετάθεσις, ὡς ἐπὶ τοῦ
θάπτοντος τὸ νεοσφαγὲς σῶμα, ὅτι 'ἐλεῶν ἔθαπτον'. (Porphyrius *in
Hermog. Stat.*, *Rh. Gr.* IV 397.8 Walz = Hermagoras fr. 14a Matthes)

The scholion given by Matthes as fr. 14b (*Incert. auct. schol.
min. in Hermog. Stat.*, *Rh. Gr.* VII 308 *adn.* Walz) repeats the
statement that the Hermagoreans gave the name χρῶμα to the μετάθεσις τῆς αἰτίας in the course of an explanation of the way in
which a prosecutor may rebut a plea of the type called συγγνώμη.

It may be deduced that the term χρῶμα was used with reference
to pleas in that part of Hermagorean theory, alluded to by Quintilian (VII.4.4ff.), in which types of defence were first distinguished as either κατ' ἀντίλημψιν (*qua ipsum factum, quod
obicitur, dicimus honestum esse*), or κατ' ἀντίθεσιν (*in quo factum*

per se improbabile adsumptis extrinsecus auxiliis tuemur). At any
rate, the adjectives which Porphyrius applies to the μετάθεσις τῆς
αἰτίας, which the Hermagoreans called χρῶμα, are derived from the
names which the Greek theorists gave to the four standard varieties of defence κατ' ἀντίθεσιν, namely: ἀντίστασις (a plea that
an action, though criminal, was justified by some benefit which
ensued); μετάστασις (a plea by which one transferred the blame for
the crime on to some other person or thing); ἀντέγκλημα (a plea
that the criminal act had been committed in response to some prior
injury); and συγγνώμη (a plea that the crime was of a pardonable
nature).[25]

It is curious that Seneca the Elder should use the term *color*
in the sense which the *Hermagorei* gave to χρῶμα, while Cicero and
Quintilian never do so in all their elaborate accounts of the relevant parts of Hermagorean theory.[26] Here, as in a number of
other cases, the schools of rhetoric from which Seneca derived his
terminology appear to have taken over their technical vocabulary
from sources quite outside the Ciceronian tradition.

It is unclear whether Seneca was familiar with a classification of *colores* under the headings: ἀντίστασις (*comparatio, com-
parativum, compensatio*); μετάστασις (*remotio criminis, trans-
latio*); ἀντέγκλημα (*relatio/translatio criminis*); συγγνώμη (*con-
cessio, excusatio, venia*).[27] He certainly shows no inclination to
use any such terms when discussing *colores*, but that could be because he presupposes familiarity with them. He did know of a work
on *colores* in four books - was it laid out according to the four-
fold classification of types of defence? - by Iunius Otho, a rhetorician of his own day, and in the course of describing this work
he refers to a fault in it as having been derived *ab antiquis qui
artem dicendi tradebant* (*Contr.* II.1.33). Otho included so many
dreams among his *colores* that Gallio wittily called his books
Antiphontis libros (the allusion being to the work Περὶ κρίσεως
ὀνείρων by the fifth-century sophist Antiphon);[28] Otho's willingness to approve of *colores* which could not be supported or refuted
by argument[29] was, we are told, a pernicious tendency inherited
from his predecessors in the field. Seneca expresses disapproval
on the ground that a speaker using such *colores* will normally be

suspected of not telling the truth.[30] The reference to *antiquis qui artem dicendi tradebant* is intriguing. It has to be counted among the handful of indications that Seneca the Elder, though more influenced by oral school criticism than by Cicero, cannot have been entirely unread in rhetorical theory - that is, unless we argue that he may be quoting criticisms by Gallio throughout the discussion of Otho's books, or that the *antiqui* in question may have been no earlier than the exponents of the *antiqua divisio* mentioned in *Contr.* I.1.13.

Seneca nowhere defines the term *color*, but he mentions distinctions drawn by Latro between it and the terms *quaestio* and *defensio*. According to Latro (*Contr.* I.5.9), a mere innuendo should not be classed as a *quaestio*, but rather as a *color*, for a *quaestio* has to be capable of being backed up by argumentation: *eam quaestionem esse, quae impleri argumentis possit*. In *Contr.* VII.6.17 we find Latro distinguishing between *color* and *defensio*: *a parte patris magis defensione opus esse dicebat Latro quam colore*; evidently he thought of a *color* as being something flimsier than a full-scale defence. Note that Latro's view that *colores* might include insubstantial suggestions, not necessarily capable of proof, is the view criticized by Seneca - or was it Gallio? - in *Contr.* II.1.33, if my interpretation of that passage is correct, as a *vitium* derived *ab antiquis, qui artem dicendi tradebant*.

According to Seneca one might introduce a *color* right at the beginning of a declamation and use it throughout, e.g. *Contr.* I.1.24: *hoc colore usus est, quem statim a principio induxit...*; *Contr.* I.4.8: *Albucius non narravit, sed hoc colore egit ab initio usque ad finem*. Alternatively one might bring *colores* into play primarily in the *narratio*: *Contr.* VII.1.20: *Latro illum introduxit colorem rectum in narratione, quo per totam actionem usus est*; *Contr.* I.4.8: *Silo hoc colore narravit* (cf. *Contr.* X.2.13, 15, 17). Sometimes people used up all the resources of their *colores* in the *narratio*, but this, at least in the view of Pollio, was not a good idea:

Asinius Pollio dicebat colorem in narratione ostendendum, in argumentis exsequendum. non prudenter facere eos, qui in

narratione omnia instrumenta coloris consumerent; nam et plus
illos ponere quam narratio desiderasset et minus quam probatio.
(*Contr.* IV.3 *extra*)

In *Contr.* VII.1.21 Albucius includes a number of *colores* in his
argumentation: *Albucius in argumentis plura posuit et omnes fere
colores contrectavit.*

Some *colores* are described by Seneca as straightforward,
simple, or openly expressed. *Colores* by Latro are frequently so
described:

Contr. I.1.16 M (on the young man who, though disinherited by
father and uncle in turn, supported them in their hour of need):

Latro colorem simplicem pro adulescente <habuit>: habere non quo
excuset, sed quo glorietur.

Contr. II.6.6 (on the father who followed his son's example in
riotous living):

Cestius <a> parte patris aiebat simulationem luxuriae significandam
magis quam profitendam...Latro aperte putabat simulationem confitendam.

Contr. VII.1.20 (on the young man who would not punish his brother
for parricide in the traditional manner):

Latro illum introduxit colorem rectum in narratione, quo per totam
actionem usus est: non potui occidere.

Contr. VII.2.10 (on Cicero's assassin):

colorem pro Popillio Latro simplicem habuit: necessitate coactum
fecisse.

Simple *colores* are also ascribed to Pollio: *ipse autem hoc colore
usus est, quem aiebat simplicissimum* (*Contr.* IV.6 *extra*); and to
Romanius Hispo: *...simpliciter putavit agendum* (*Contr.* VII.7.14).
Both criticize the over-subtle efforts of other declaimers.
Scaurus was another person critical of unnecessary subtlety: he
described Iunius Otho as a man who would whisper public announce-
ments in one's ear (*acta in aurem legere, Contr.* II.1.39).

In the case of some *controversiae* it was immediately obvious
what sort of *color* one should adopt. It might be that one simply
had to inveigh against one of the characters in the theme, e.g.
Contr. I.2.21: *alterius partis color nihil habet difficultatis...
dicendum est in puellam vehementer, non sordide nec obscene; Contr.*
II.3.17: *omnes infamaverunt raptae patrem quasi cum raptore con-
ludentem; Contr.* IV.8 *extra*: *omnes invecti sunt in libertum.*

Other *controversiae* posed more problems, and the need for a

more subtle approach in such cases was recognized by Seneca. He
commends Otho for his success in dealing with *difficiles contro-*
versias...in quibus inter silentium et detectionem medio
temperamento opus erat (*Contr.* II.1.33), even though he appreci-
ates the wittiness of Scaurus' remark about his whispered announce-
ments. To use Seneca's terminology, difficult themes needed to be
treated *suspiciose* (*Contr.* II.1.34), *per suspiciones et figuras*
(*Contr.* VII.1.20), *schemate* (*Contr.* II.4.10). Otho's treatment of
Contr. II.1 provides one example of an approach of this kind. The
theme was this:

Dives tres filios abdicavit. petit a paupere unicum filium in
adoptionem. pauper dare vult; nolentem ire abdicat.

Otho took the part of the poor father and gave veiled indications
of his motives in a series of *sententiae*:

itaque et hanc controversiam hoc colore dixit, tamquam in
emendationem abdicatorum et reconciliationis causa faceret. hoc
non detegebat, sed omnibus sententiis utebatur ad hoc tendentibus...
(*Contr.* II.1.37)

There were often disagreements as to whether the subtle
approach was better than the straightforward. For example, when
Cestius and Latro considered how to treat *Contr.* II.6 (*Quidam*
luxuriante filio luxuriari coepit. filius accusat patrem
dementiae), they disagreed as to which *color* was best:

Cestius <a> parte patris aiebat simulationem luxuriae significandam
magis quam profitendam. ita, inquit, apparebit illum simulasse si
etiamnunc simulat; si desinit simulare, ostendit iam sibi nihil
opus esse eo consilio, quasi filius emendatus sit; emendatum autem
esse non concessit, et adsidue dixit nihil magis se quam inter-
vallum hoc luxuriae timere; intermissa vitia vehementius surgere.
Latro aperte putabat simulationem confitendam. incipio, inquit,
non tantum honestum senem sed prudentem defendere si, quod vitium
videri poterat, efficio consilium. quare potius significet quam
dicat frugi <se> esse? (*Contr.* II.6.6 W)

Latro, as so often, champions the cause of directness.

With the remarks of Seneca and the declaimers as to where a
controversia called for subtle *colores* and where simpler tactics
were preferable, it is relevant to compare Quintilian's observations on the so-called *controversiae figuratae* (IX.1.14; 2.65ff.)
Seneca, as we have seen, refers to occasions when declaimers proceeded *per suspiciones et figuras* or *schemate*. Quintilian tells
us that one curious usage of the term *schema* which was current in

the common parlance of his day derived from the definition of that
term given by Zoilus (the fourth-century critic better known for
his attacks on Homer). Zoilus defined σχῆμα as a device by which
one gave the impression of saying something other than what one
was actually saying. Quintilian's contemporaries used the term
controversia figurata in a way which presupposed that one accepted
this definition of σχῆμα/*figura* (IX.1.14). According to Quintilian, declaimers gave the name *figuratae* to *controversiae* of three
sorts:

eius triplex usus est: unus si dicere palam parum tutum est, alter
si non decet, tertius qui venustatis modo gratia adhibetur et ipsa
novitate ac varietate magis quam si relatio sit recta delectat.
(IX.2.66)

Quintilian discusses at great length (*ibid.* 65-80) the excessive
subtlety which was often encouraged by the scholastic teaching
about this sort of figuration; he would have agreed with Latro's
statement about figures in general in *Contr.* I pr. 24: *schema
negabat decoris causa inventum, sed subsidii...*

From time to time Seneca describes a *color* as *durus*, *strictus*,
or *asper*. A *color* will be so described if it involves the attribution of hatred or unusual severity to a character in the theme,
sometimes even to the person whom one is defending. Romanius
Hispo and Latro were noted for their readiness to adopt this kind
of *color*:

Contr. IX.3.11: Hispo Romanius erat natura qui asperiorem dicendi
viam sequeretur; itaque hoc colore egit, ut inveheretur tamquam in
malum patrem et diceret crudeliter exponentem, perfide recipientem.

Contr. X pr. 15: Latro...dicebat quosdam esse colores prima facie
duros et asperos: eos non posse nisi actione probari...multa se
non persuadere iudici, sed auferre.

Further examples may be found in:

Contr. I.8.8 (on the war hero who is disinherited by his father
for wishing to enter battle for the fourth time)

colorem a parte patris quidam duriorem fecerunt; voluerunt enim
videri invisum filio patrem: itaque illum malle cum hostibus
vivere quam cum patre;

and *Contr.* VII.1.24 (on the man who casts his brother adrift in an
open boat instead of punishing him for parricide in the traditional
manner)

Hispanus duro colore usus est: hoc, inquit, supplicium tamquam
gravius elegi.

The opposite of *durus* and *asper* as used in such contexts is *tutus*
(*Contr.* X pr. 16), and the verb used to denote the toning down of
harshness in *colores* is *temperare* (*Contr.* I.1.24).

Sometimes the declaimer would explain the defendant's actions
as the result of some more or less irrational impulse.[31] His
defence might be that he was overcome by momentary anger or mad-
ness, or that he had been motivated by portents, a vision, or, as
we have noted, a dream. Declaimers who adopted such *colores* laid
themselves open to criticism and ridicule from some quarters, but
they used them nonetheless, as they had the advantage over more
subtle defences of providing opportunities for emotional out-
pourings in the grand style.

For example, the defence of the father in *Contr.* I.7, who
wrote to the pirates offering them double the ransom demanded if
they cut off the hands of his son (who admittedly had twice committed fratricide, but with just cause), was one of the hardest
tasks the declaimers ever set themselves. Fuscus, Pompeius Silo,
and Sparsus, taking the part of the cruel father, all chose to
hold forth about the anger they had felt at the son's various
actions:

colorem pro patre alius alium introduxit. Fuscus iratum se illi
confessus est fuisse, quod fratrem in conspectu patris occidisset,
et huic loco vehementer institit, quom nemo hoc tyrannus, nemo
pirata fecisset... Silo Pompeius et ipse iram fassus est: aiebat
enim non habiturum fidem si negasset iratum fuisse; sed irae
causam non dixit quam Fuscus; transeundas aiebat eas offensas
quibus ille gloriaretur; hanc causam posuit, quod relictus esset
ab unico filio, quod invito se navigasset, cum videret <se> senem,
orbum, iam paene egentem: iam tum illum fugisse ne aleret; et ad
preces patrem deduxit et rogavit in epilogo filium. et Sparsum
hoc colore declamasse memini, hominem inter scholasticos sanum,
inter sanos scholasticum. (*Contr.* I.7.14f.)

Latro went one step further: the father's action, according to
him, was not the result of mere anger – nor, as Cestius (*Contr.*
I.7.16) had suggested, was it all part of an ingenious plot to
avoid paying the ransom – the balance of his mind had been totally
deranged:

Latro totum se ab istis removit coloribus, et advocavit vires suas
tanto totius actionis impetu ut attonitos homines tenuerit; hoc
enim colore usus est: nescio quid scripserim. olim iam mihi ex-
cussa mens est. ex quo vidi filium unum in arce, alterum in

adulterio, tertium in parricidio, ex quo respersus sum fili
morientis sanguine, ex quo relictus sum solus, orbus, senex, odi
meos. hic color illius viribus adprobandus est; quanta enim vi
opus est ut aliquis accusando se miserabilem faciat! (*Contr.*
I.7.16)

The most notable specialist in portents and visions was
Arellius Fuscus:

Contr. I.1.16: Fuscus illum colorem introduxit, quo frequenter uti
solebat, religionis: movit, inquit, me natura, movit pietas, movit
humanorum casuum tam manifesto approbata exemplo varietas. stare
ante oculos Fortuna videbatur et dicere talia: esuriunt qui suos
non alunt. (Cf. *Contr.* I.8.15; II.1.27)

Iunius Otho was famous for his dreams:

Contr. VII.7.15: erat autem ex somniatoribus Otho: ubicumque illum
defecerat color, somnium narrabat. (Cf. *Contr.* II.1.33)

Sometimes declaimers used more than one *color* in a *contro-*
versia. Arellius Fuscus did not restrict himself to describing
his anger at the fratricidal son in *Contr.* I.7; he went on to explain his cruel letter to the pirates as follows:

illud ad excusandam epistulae crudelitatem adiciebat: scripsi
piratis non eo animo ut manus tibi praeciderentur, sed ut ex-
probrarem tibi cruentatas in conspectu patris fraterno sanguine
manus. tuto autem scribebam; sciebam enim piratas non facturos
nisi pecuniam accepissent, quam non mittebam: denique nec praecid-
erunt. et si sperassent, utique praecidissent: sed apparuit illas
epistulas irascentis esse, non promittentis. (*Contr.* I.7.14 W)

One might have thought this was a rather risky scheme! When a declaimer uses more than one *color* Seneca calls the procedure
miscere colores (*Contr.* I.7.17; IV.6 *extra*), and the complex
colouring itself, *mixtus color* (*Contr.* IV.6 *extra*). As it was
generally best for a defendant speaking on his own behalf to use
one plea consistently, if he were to sound convincing, it was
thought wise for the declaimer to assume the role of an advocate
if he wished to mix many *colores*. For example, Albucius (*Contr.*
I.7.17) impersonated an advocate when attempting to defend by
various means the father who had offered the pirates double the
ransom money if they would cut his son's hands off: *Albucius omnes*
colores miscuit, et, ut hoc liberum sit, patronum patri dedit nec
voluit narrare. When mixing *colores* one had to be very careful
not to appear to 'protest too much'. When explaining in *Contr.*
IV.6 one's refusal to say which of two long-absent sons was the
offspring of one's second wife, it was better, as Pollio pointed

out (*Contr.* 4.6 *extra*), to use the simple *color*, '*scio, sed non
indico, quia pueris hoc utile est*', than to confuse the issue by
mixing two *colores*, '*nescio, sed etiam si scirem, non indicarem.*'

When deciding on *colores* the declaimer had to avoid, above
all, choosing one which ran contrary to his own interests. For
instance, if he were arguing that the condemned priestess who had
survived her fall from the cliff-top ought to be thrown down again,
it would be a mistake to claim that any type of divine inter-
vention had taken place. Cestius points this out in *Contr.* I.3.9:

contra sacerdotem qui<dam> dixerunt: videri deos infestos illi in
hoc eam servasse, ut diutius torqueretur. aiebat Cestius malle se
casu videri factum quam deorum voluntate; nam si semel illos
intervenire huic rei fatemur, manifestius erit <contra> poenam
servatam esse sacerdotem quam in poenam.

Similarly, a declaimer taking the part of the poor father in
Contr. II.1 was liable to lose the sympathy of his hearers if he
expressed a desire for wealth:

color a parte patris aliquid curae desiderat. quidam induxerunt
patrem cupidum divitiarum, quod invidiosum est in hoc visum,[32*]
quia ita divitias filio dare vult ut filiis eripiat. itaque Latro
optimo colore usus est: in hoc, inquit, te in adoptionem volo
dare, ut facilius per te abdicati reconcilientur. (*Contr.* II.1.30)

Severe critics were hard on declaimers who, instead of working out a good *color* consistently, yielded to the temptation of
bringing in *sententiae* which were more elegant than useful to
their case. Thus Messala criticized the sentimental picture con-
jured up by Albucius of an illegitimate child who followed his
grandfather out of the room as if of right (and was consequently
adopted by him):

Albucius ethicos, ut multi putant, dixit - certe laudatum est cum
diceret -: exeuntem <me> puer secutus est. non probabat hanc
Messala sententiam: non habet, inquit, fiduciam si mavult videri
recepisse puerum quam adduxisse; et sine ratione est adoptatum
esse non quia debuerit sed quia secutus est. (*Contr.* II.4.8)

This seems an unnecessarily grudging criticism. Seneca appears to
have been more tolerant. At any rate *aridi declamatores* who keep
too faithfully to the *colores* they have chosen, and refuse to be
led astray by any opportunity for a pleasing *schema* or *sententia*,
are likened by him to plain women, chaste for lack of a seducer
(*Contr.* II.1.24).

It was against the rules of *controversia*-writing to use

colores that introduced elements which were not mentioned in the
thema, or which contradicted in any respect the facts of the case
as set out in it.[33] Take, for example, *Contr.* IX.5, the theme of
which ran as follows:

Quidam duos filios sub noverca amisit: dubia cruditatis et veneni
signa insecuta sunt. tertium filium eius maternus avus rapuit,
qui ad visendos aegros non fuerat admissus. quaerenti patri per
praeconem dixit apud se esse. accusatur de vi.

A declaimer speaking for the prosecution had to think up a very
good excuse for the fact that the grandfather had not been admitted to see the dying boys. Even good declaimers found it hard
not to introduce factors which could not legitimately be deduced
from the theme:

Silonis Pompei color fuit, ut Latroni videbatur, qui controversiae
repugnaret; dixit enim venisse avum ad inbecillum puerum. ad
aegros non semper admitti, utique ad eos qui graviter aegrotent;
saepe et patrem non admissum; sic avo quoque intempestive venienti
dictum: 'nunc non potes'; statim cum convicio abisse. in altero
idem fecisse. Latro aiebat hunc colorem optumum esse si res ita
esset, sed recipi non posse, quia ponatur: 'non est admissus'; sub
hoc themate intellegere nos non hoc illi dictum: 'nunc non potes',
sed 'ex toto non potes'. (*Contr.* IX.5.10)

It was also not thought allowable to make any claim about the
facts of the case which could not be substantiated without a witness. Arellius Fuscus is criticized in *Contr.* VII.2.12 W for
breaking this rule:

Fuscus Arellius hoc colore usus est: Antoni se partem secutum ut,
si quid posset, Ciceroni prodesset; facta proscriptione ad genua
se Antoni procidisse, deprecatum esse pro Cicerone; offensum
Antonium dixisse: 'eo magis occide quem mori non vis.' hic color
displicebat Passieno, quia †ad testem ducit†; nam, si hoc fecit
Popillius, non tantum quod defendat non habet sed habet quod
glorietur.

Whatever Seneca wrote where the manuscripts give us the doubtful
reading *ad testem ducit*, which is obelized by Winterbottom,[34]* it
seems certain that Passienus' objection must have been to the lack
of any witness's evidence to prove that Popillius had acted as
honourably as Fuscus was making out. A *color* contrived on behalf
of Parrhasius, in the *controversia* in which he is charged *laesae
rei publicae* for torturing an aged Olynthian whom he had bought to
serve as his model for a painting of Prometheus, was open to a
similar objection:

†Gallionis† color intolerabilis est; dixit enim <se> senem ex
noxiis Olynthiis emisse; quod si illi licet fingere, non video
quare non eadem opera dicat et conscium proditionis Lastheni
fuisse et se poenae causa torsisse. (*Contr.* X.5.18 W)

The inventor of *colores* had, above all, to aim at verisi-
militude. The more distinguished declaimers regularly attained
this, but the lunatic fringe provided a wide range of far-fetched
and totally unconvincing *colores* to amuse Seneca and his friends:
Contr. I.3.11 (on the priestess thrown from the cliff)

Pastor Aietius hanc controversiam apud Cestium dixit iam senator,
et hunc colorem optimum putavit: sic veneficiis corpus induruit ut
saxa reverberet inultum. Cestius hunc corripuit et dixit: 'hoc
est quare ego auditores meos invitem ad alios audiendos ire?'

Contr. VII.3.8 (on the *ter abdicatus* who was discovered mixing
poison)

Murredius pro cetero suo stupore dixit medicamentum se parasse ad
somnum, quia adsiduae sollicitudines vigiliarum sibi consuetudinem
<fecerint>.

Contr. IX.4.22 (on the young man who beat his father at the command of the tyrant, after his brother had thrown himself from the
citadel to avoid doing so)

Murredius non degeneravit in hac controversia; nam colorem
stultissimum induxit: voluit, inquit, et hic sequi fratris
exemplum: dum retineo, dum luctor, visus est patrem cecidisse.

Convincing characterization was important, especially in certain
controversiae which were described as *ethicae* (*Contr.* II.2.12).
These were the only *controversiae* which Ovid cared to declaim, and
presumably *Contr.* II.2, from which we have an Ovidian extract, is
an example of one. Fabianus found difficulty after his philosophical conversion with the imitating of other people's emotions
that was required of the declaimer: *cum veros conpressisset adfectus et iram doloremque procul expulisset, parum bene imitari
poterat quae effugerat* (*Contr.* II pr. 2). The convincing
portrayal of character could be a delicate matter: the declaimer
had to be careful, when bringing out the merits of the person
whose part he had taken, not to be suspected of some related
fault. Thus Aeschines the declaimer was criticized for the way in
which he portrayed the father who prevented his valiant son from
going into battle for a fourth time:

hoc loco Aeschines ex novis declamatoribus, cum diceret: non me
gloria cupidiorem tui fecit, non omnibus admiranda virtus:

'confitebor' inquit 'adfectus patris, quos ut quisque volet inter-
pretetur: οὕτως ἄν καὶ δειλὸν ἐφίλουν.' videbatur hic, dum
indulgentiam exprimit, non servasse dignitatem patris. (*Contr.*
I.8.11)

The question of the appropriateness of a declaimer's style to the
character he was trying to portray is touched upon by Seneca in
Contr. I.8.16:

Dorion dixit rem paulo quidem elatiorem quam pressa et civilis
oratio recepit, sed qua egregie attonitos patris adfectus
exprimeret.

Latro discusses in *Contr.* VII.4.6 the style to be adopted when
pleading on behalf of someone who seeks pity rather than vengeance:

Latro dixit pro matre summisse et leniter agendum. non enim,
inquit, vindictam sed misericordiam quaerit, et cum eo adulescente
consistit in quo ita exigit pietatem ut impediat. aiebat itaque
verbis quoque horridioribus abstinendum quotiens talis materia
incidisset; ipsam orationem ad habitum eius quem movere volumus
adfectus molliendam.

The declaimer also had to bear in mind which characters
needed to be treated with particular respect. A son must obviously not speak harshly about his father, and, in view of this,
Pompeius Silo put the prosecution of the cruel father in *Contr.*
I.7 into the hands of an advocate:

...descripsit mores hominis impii, cruenti, quia per liberos non
posset per piratas tyrannidem exercentis: quae ut liberius
diceret, patronum filio dedit. (*Contr.* I.7.13)

Similarly, the poor man's son in *Contr.* II.1 could not simply
inveigh against the rich man who wished to adopt him:

de colore magis quaesitum est: an adulescens debeat in divitem
aliquid dicere. quid enim faciet? dicet in eum qui tantum
honoris illi habet, et in amicum paternum, non dicet in eum quem
fugit? (*Contr.* II.1.24)

Fabianus found a way out of this difficulty by attacking riches in
general, rather than the rich man in particular (*Contr.* II.1.25).

There are a few indications that a certain *verecundia* was recommended if one had to inveigh against a woman:

Contr. I.2.21: dicendum est in puellam vehementer, non sordide nec
obscene.

Contr. VII.1.20: fuerunt et qui in novercam inveherentur; fuerunt
et alii, qui non quidem palam dicerent, sed per suspiciones et
figuras, quam rem non probabat Passienus et aiebat minus verecundum
esse aut tolerabile infamare noveram quam accusare.

Slaves, on the other hand, were held to be of no account at

all. One might have thought that the theme of *Contr.* VII.6 would be seen as a golden opportunity for meditations to the effect that misfortune might reduce any man to slavery:

Tyrannus permisit servis dominis interemptis dominas suas rapere. profugerunt principes civitatis; inter eos qui filium et filiam habebat profectus est peregre. cum omnes servi dominas suas vitiassent, servos eius virginem servavit. occiso tyranno reversi sunt principes; in crucem servos sustulerunt; ille manu misit et filiam conlocavit. accusatur a filio dementiae.

Perhaps it is slightly unsafe to draw conclusions from the number of quotations taken by Seneca from each of the two sides of a *controversia*, but it seems striking that he quotes far more declaimers as having prosecuted the father of the bride than as having defended him. Of those who spoke for the defence, only Albucius seems to have adopted the philosophical approach:

Albucius et philosophatus est: dixit neminem natura liberum esse, neminem servum; haec postea nomina singulis inposuisse Fortunam. denique, inquit, scis et nos nuper servos fuisse. rettulit Servium regem. (*Contr.* VII.6.18)

The standard attitude of the declaimers seems to have been that the father's action was exceptionally hard to excuse; as Latro put it: *a parte patris magis defensione opus esse...quam colore* (*Contr.* VII.6.17).

A finished *controversia* normally consisted of four main sections: the *principium* or *prooemium* (e.g. *Contr.* I.1.24f.); the *narratio* (e.g. *Contr.* I.1.21); the *argumenta* or *argumentatio* (e.g. *Contr.* I.6.9; II.2.12) and the *epilogus* (e.g. *Contr.* IV pr. 8).[1] A *suasoria* did not require a *narratio*, and so seems to have consisted simply of a *principium* (e.g. *Suas.* 7.14) followed by various *quaestiones*, and presumably some kind of conclusion (see e.g. *Contr.* VII.7.19, quoted below), though Seneca does not in fact mention any *epilogus* in his extant surveys of *suasoriae*.[2] Seneca assumes a knowledge of the nature and functions of these sections of a declamation, and restricts his attention to details of treatment and departures from the norm.

About the *prooemium* he has little to say. There is an interesting reference, though, in *Contr.* VII.7.19, to the way Cestius criticized his pupils when they used an unsubtle trick which he called *echo*, that is, when they opened a declamation with a quotation which they would bring in once more at the end:

illud et in hac controversia et in omni vitandum aiebat Cestius, quotiens aliqua vox poneretur, ne ad illam quasi ad sententiam decurreremus. sicut in hac apud Cestium quidam auditor eius hoc modo coepit: 'ut verbis ducis vestri, iudices, incipiam, cavete proditionem'; sic finivit declamationem ut diceret: 'finio quibus vitam finit imperator: cavete proditionem.' hoc sententiae genus Cestius echo vocabat et <sic> dicenti discipulo statim exclamabat: ἱμερτὴν ἠχώ: ut in illa suasoria in qua deliberat Alexander an Oceanum naviget cum exaudita vox esset: 'quousque invicte?' ab <hac> ipsa voce quidam coepit declamare et in hac desit; ait illi Cestius desinenti: ἔν σοι μὲν λήξω, σέο δ' ἄρξομαι. et alteri, cum descriptis Alexandri victoriis, gentibus perdomitis, novissime poneret: 'quousque invicte?', exclamavit Cestius: tu autem quousque? (*Contr.* VII.7.19 W)

Arellius Fuscus is said to have composed his *principia*, like his *narrationes* and *argumenta*, in a very arid style quite different from the florid elaboration in which he indulged to excess in descriptive passages (*Contr.* II pr. 1). Fuscus stood in marked

contrast to Passienus, who attracted a large audience for his
principia and *epilogi*, according to Cassius Severus (*Contr*. III
pr. 10), but lost it while he delivered the body of his speech:
*Passienus noster cum coepit dicere, secundum principium statim
fuga fit, ad epilogum omnes revertimur, media tantum quibus
necesse est audiunt.*

Seneca singles out for special approval an ingenious device
for making the transition from *prooemium* to *narratio*:

Hermagoras in hac controversia transit a prooemio in narrationem
eleganter, rarissimo quidem genere, ut <in> eadem re transitus
esset, sententia esset, schema esset, sed, ut Latroni placebat,
schema quod vulnerat, non quod titillat: ...ex altera parte
transit a prooemio in narrationem Gallio et ipse per sententiam
sic: quidni filium mihi nolim cum isto communem esse, cum quo
utinam communem nec patrem habuissem? (*Contr*. I.1.25)

Quintilian was to take a much less favourable view of this
practice:

illa vero frigida et puerilis est in scholis adfectatio, ut ipse
transitus efficiat aliquam utique sententiam et huius velut prae-
stigiae plausum petat, ut Ovidius lascivire in Metamorphosesin
solet; quem tamen excusare necessitas potest, res diversissimas in
speciem unius corporis colligentem: oratori vero quid est necesse
surripere hanc transgressionem, et iudicem fallere qui ut ordini
rerum animum intendat etiam commonendus est? (IV.1.77f.)

Seneca did not need to tell his readers what a normal
narratio was like, but quite often he touched on the question of
whether it was ever appropriate to omit it, a question over which,
as we have seen,[3] the Theodoreans disagreed with the Apollodoreans.
From time to time declaimers did suppress the *narratio*. For
instance, Cestius decided that it would be best not to dwell too
long on the *curriculum vitae* of the would-be priestess in *Contr*.
I.2, when speaking on her behalf:

Cestius timuit se in narrationem demittere; sic illam trans-
cucurrit: haec dixit in sacerdote futura maxime debere aestimari:
pudicitiam, innocentiam, felicitatem. quam pudica sit, miles
ostendit; quam innocens, iudex; quam felix, reditus. etiam
habemus quandam praerogationem sacerdoti ab ipso numine datam,
licet isti obiciant fuisse illam captivam, lenoni postea servisse,
causam novissime dixisse: inter tot pericula non servassent illam
dii nisi sibi. (*Contr*. I.2.19 W)

Votienus Montanus, realizing that the conduct of the proconsul
Flamininus as described in *Contr*. IX.2 *thema* was morally inexcus-
able, decided that a *narratio* would not help his case:

quaedam controversiae sunt in quibus factum defendi potest,
excusari non potest; ex quibus est et haec. non possumus efficere
ut <reus> propter hoc non sit reprehendendus; non speramus ut
illum iudex probet sed ut dimittat; itaque sic agere debemus tamquam pro facto non emendato, non scelerato tamen. itaque negabat
se pro Flaminino narraturum Montanus, sed iis quae obiciuntur
responsurum. (*Contr.* IX.2.18)

On the other hand, Albucius did without a *narratio* in *Contr.* I.4

because he felt he had too *good* a case: *Albucius non narravit, sed*

hoc colore egit ab initio usque ad finem: ego me defendere debeo?

(*Contr.* I.4.8). As a substitute for a full *narratio* one could sum

up in what was called a *propositio* the basic question at issue:

Albucius...patronum patri dedit nec voluit narrare. a propositione

coepit: alimenta pater a filio petit... (*Contr.* I.7.17). Seneca

says nothing against the occasional suppression of the *narratio*,

and we may suspect that he considered the rigidity expected by

people like the Apollodoreans unreasonable,[4] anticipating in this

the view of Quintilian:

plerique semper narrandum putaverunt: quod falsum esse pluribus
coarguitur. sunt enim ante omnia quaedam tam breves causae ut
propositionem potius habeant quam narrationem. (Quint. IV.2.4)

However, some of the instances of omitted *narratio* which Seneca

mentions without adverse comment would have aroused Quintilian's

anger. To shirk the difficulties of a case in the way that

Cestius did in *Contr.* I.2, and Montanus in *Contr.* IX.2, was to ask

for defeat:

sed quatenus etiam forte quadam pervenimus ad difficilius
narrationum genus, iam de iis loquamur in quibus res contra nos
erit: quo loco nonnulli praetereundam narrationem putaverunt. et
sane nihil est facilius nisi prorsus totam causam omnino non
agere. sed si aliqua iusta ratione huiusmodi susceperis litem,
cuius artis est malam esse causam silentio confiteri? nisi forte
tam hebes futurus est iudex ut secundum id pronuntiet quod sciet
narrare te noluisse. (Quint. IV.2.66)

Another declamatory practice which annoyed Quintilian was

that of automatically inserting an ornate digression at the end of

the *narratio*, regardless of relevance:

plerisque moris est, prolato rerum ordine, protinus utique in
aliquem laetum ac plausibilem locum quam maxime possint favorabili-
ter excurrere. quod quidem natum ab ostentatione declamatoria
iam in forum venit, postquam agere causas non ad utilitatem
litigatorum sed ad patronorum iactationem repertum est, ne, si
pressae illi qualis saepius desideratur narrationis gracilitati
coniuncta argumentorum pugnacitas fuerit, dilatis diutius dicendi

voluptatibus oratio refrigescat. (IV.3.lf.)

Descriptive digressions on a wide variety of subjects are quite common in the extracts from the declamations,[5] and, as Bonner[6] has observed, Seneca does sometimes write about *descriptiones* in a way which might suggest that they were already as much an essential, fixed, part of the declamation as were *prooemium*, *narratio*, *argumenta*, and *epilogus*: 'The *descriptio*...became a digression, and that it was regarded as an integral part of the speech is clear from the fact that Seneca says (*Contr.* I.4.8–9) "et *in descriptione* dixit" and "et illud *post descriptionem* adiecit" exactly as he uses *in narratione* and *in argumentis*.' Seneca certainly anticipates Quintilian in objecting when a *descriptio* is inserted without concern for relevance:

in ea descriptione, <quam> primam in hac suasoria posui, Fuscus Arellius Vergilii versus voluit imitari; valde autem longe petit et paene repugnante materie, certe non desiderante, inseruit. (*Suas*. 3.4)

But it does not seem to have been the case that in Seneca's time *descriptiones* were invariably confined to the position between *narratio* and *argumenta* where Quintilian's contemporaries normally placed them. On the rare occasions when Seneca mentions the context of particular *descriptiones*, they come in the course of the *narratio* (*Contr.* VII.1.26, 27 – Artemo, Cestius), or in the *argumenta* (*Suas*. 6.8 – Latro). Arellius Fuscus' long digression describing weather-signs alluded to in *Suas*. 3.4 must have formed part of his treatment of the last item in his *divisio*, the argument that Agamemnon would eventually be able to sail without having sacrificed Iphigenia, as the present calm was due to the blind forces of nature, and the will of the gods could not be known by mortals (*Suas*. 3.3 cf. *ibid*. 1 *init*.).

The *argumentatio* was the section in which the declaimer developed his chosen *quaestiones* and *tractationes*. It is evident from Seneca's discussions of *divisio* that at least some of the leading declaimers took more trouble over this part of their work than critics of the schools would admit (see e.g. *Contr.* IX pr. 1). Seneca takes pains to show that Latro's method of *argumentatio*, sadly underrated by certain contemporary critics, was in fact greatly to be admired. He is critical of declaimers who set out

their arguments in too arid a manner (*Contr.* II pr. 1), and those
whose sole aspiration was to split hairs with clarity; he is all
in favour of logical precision of the finest sort (*subtilitas*),
but only as a foundation on which greater things could be built.
Defending Latro he writes:

nihil est iniquius his, qui nusquam putant esse subtilitatem, nisi
ubi nihil est praeter subtilitatem; et in illo cum omnes oratoriae
virtutes essent, hoc fundamentum superstructis tot et tantis
molibus obruebatur, nec deerat in illo, sed non eminebat; et
nescio an maximum vitium subtilitatis sit nimis se ostendere.
(*Contr.* I pr. 21)

Each *quaestio* or *tractatio* would be developed in the completed
declamation by means of *argumenta*, which might be supported by
moralizing *loci* or historical *exempla* and perhaps ornamented by
descriptiones. Seneca makes it clear at the beginning of his work
that it is no part of his plan to discuss *argumenta* in detail
(*Contr.* I pr. 22), but he does not keep rigidly to his programme,
and quite frequently gives a sketch of the way in which a declaimer elaborated certain of his *quaestiones*, sometimes even
quoting his actual words, as for example in *Contr.* I.5.4 W:

Latro primam fecit quaestionem: non posse raptorem qui ab rapta
mori iussus esset servari. si legatus, inquit, exire debet, peribit; si militare debet, peribit; si ius dicere debet, peribit; si
raptam ducere debet, aeque peribit. si is te ante rapuisset et
nuptias optasses, interposito deinde tempore antequam nuberes hanc
vitiasset, negares illum debere mori rapta iubente? etc.

Loci are distinguished from *quaestiones* in *Contr.* VII.7.10
where Seneca describes with approval Latro's technique of argumentation:

Latro semper contrahebat et quidquid poterat tuto relinquere
praeteriebat. itaque et quaestionum numerum minuebat et locos
numquam attrahebat; illos quoque quos occupaverat non diu dicebat
sed valenter.

But there are one or two instances where a *locus* seems hardly dis-
tinguishable from the treatment of a minor *quaestio*, e.g. in *Suas.*
5.6:

Argentarius his duobus contentus fuit: aut non venturum Xersen aut
non esse metuendum si venerit. his solis institit... locum movit
non inutiliter: iudicare quidem se neque Xersen neque iam quemquam
Persarum ausurum in Graeciam effundi; sed eo magis trophaea ipsis
tuenda, si quis umquam illinc venturus hostis esset, ut conspectu
trophaeorum animi militum accenderentur, hostium frangerentur.

The difference we are supposed to detect perhaps is that a *locus*

introduces only in passing ideas outside the *quaestiones* of the
divisio proper. *Loci* is the term Seneca uses to describe totally
disorganized arguments in *Contr*. II.2.9.

   The word *locus*, as we see, is not restricted in Seneca's
usage to what we would call a commonplace, but that does not prevent it from being used many times with reference to stock moralizing: *philosophumenon locum...quomodo animi magnis calamitatibus
everterentur* (*Contr*. I.7.17); *de fortunae varietate locum* (*Contr*.
I.8.16); *adoptionis locum* (*Contr*. II.4.13); *locum de indulgentia
liberorum in patres* (*Contr*. VII.5.13); *illum locum: quam multa
populus Romanus in suis imperatoribus tulerit* (*Contr*. IX.2.19);
*illum locum: quamvis sceleratos parentes velle tamen innocentes
liberos suos esse* (*Contr*. IX.6.19); *locum contra somnia et deorum
providentiam* (*Suas*. 4.4). Many other obvious commonplaces may be
seen in use in the declamatory extracts.[7] The function of such
loci was to set the issues being disputed in a wider context.
Cicero (see *Or*. 14.45) would have approved of the principle behind their use, but not of the mechanical triteness with which
declaimers usually treated them.

   Historical examples had long been recognized as one of the
most important resources available to a speaker: Aristotle saw
their function as equivalent to that of induction in dialectic
(*Rhet*. I.2.8), just as the function of enthymemes in rhetoric was
parallel to that of syllogisms in philosophy. So it was that some
knowledge of Greek and Roman history was essential to the declaimer and that a noteworthy part of Latro's stock-in-trade was
historiarum omnium summa notitia (*Contr*. I pr. 18). In the declamations of Seneca's day we find historical *exempla* introduced
either singly, to provide a precedent for a particular action, or
several at a time. In *Contr*. VII.1.15 the young man who has set
his parricidal brother adrift in an open boat is made by Musa to
point out that:

centurio Luculli Mithridaten non potuit occidere - dextra simul ac
mens elanguit - pro bone Iuppiter, Mithridaten quam non dubium
parricidam!

In *Contr*. IX.2.19 Votienus Montanus builds up a full-scale *locus*
by assembling instances of the way that the Romans had generally

turned a blind eye to the faults of their generals:

ipse Montanus illum locum pulcherrime tractavit, quam multa
populus Romanus in suis imperatoribus tulerit: in Gurgite
luxuriam, in Manlio inpotentiam, cui non nocuit et filium et
victorem occidere, in Sulla crudelitatem, in Lucullo luxuriam,
in multis avaritiam.[8]*

The declaimer did not need to be a very profound student of history in order to be able to contrive *exempla*. Ready-made collections of *exempla* existed, for instance the work by Nepos mentioned
earlier.[9] Valerius Maximus' *Facta et dicta memorabilia*, published
towards the end of the elder Seneca's life-time, is a good example
of the sort of compilation on which students of rhetoric could
draw;[10] it provides lists of *exempla*, Roman and foreign, suitable
for the treatment of any commonplace from *de religione observata*
(I.1) to *de his, qui per mendacium se in alienas familias in-
seruerunt* (IX.15). There is an important reference in *Contr.* VII.
5.12f. to the mechanical use of memorized *exempla* by scholastics
in places where they were not necessarily appropriate:

gravis scholasticos morbus invasit: exempla cum didicerunt, volunt
illa ad aliquod controversiae thema redigere. hoc quomodo aliquando faciendum est, cum res patitur, ita ineptissimum est
luctari cum materia et longe arcessere, sic quomodo fecit in hac
controversia Musa, qui, cum diceret pro filio locum de indulgentia
liberorum in patres, venit ad filium Croesi et ait: mutus in
periculo patris naturalia vocis impedimenta perrupit, qui plus
quam quinquennio tacuerat. quia quinquennis puer ponitur, putavit
ubicumque nominatum esset quinquennium, sententiam fieri...

The *argumentatio* could be expansive or minimal according to
the declaimer's wishes. The critic who suggested that declaimers
customarily neglected argumentation because it was too troublesome
and undecorative (*Contr.* IX pr. 1: *argumentationes, quia molestae
sunt et minimum habent floris, reliquit*) was overstating the case,
but we do have, in the young Ovid, an example of a declaimer who
avoided argument when possible: *molesta illi erat omnis argumentatio* (*Contr.* II.2.12). According to Seneca, when Ovid declaimed
Contr. II.2, *sine certo ordine per locos discurrebat* (*Contr.* II.
2.9). Haterius was another declaimer incapable of presenting his
arguments in a controlled manner; he suffered from excessive
fluency:

nec verborum illi tantum copia sed etiam rerum erat; quotiens
velles eandem rem et quamdiu velles diceret, aliis totiens

figuris, aliis tractationibus. (*Contr.* IV pr. 7)

If we are to believe Seneca (*Contr.* IV pr. 8), he had to be in-
structed by a freedman when to move on to the next *locus* or to the
epilogus:

iubebat eum ille transire, cum aliquem locum diu dixerat: trans-
ibat; insistere iubebat eidem loco: permanebat; iubebat epilogum
dicere: dicebat.

However, the abandonment of the sequence, *narratio* →
argumentatio, did not necessarily mean total disorganization.
There seems to have been a standard alternative arrangement,
capable of many variations, but sufficiently distinctive for the
practised listener to be able to follow what the declaimer was
doing. Seneca alludes to this arrangement when criticizing a
habit which Albucius had of developing each *quaestio* as if it were
a *controversia*:

erat et illud in argumentatione vitium, quod quaestionem non tamquam partem controversiae sed tamquam controversiam implebat.
omnis quaestio suam propositionem habebat, suam exsecutionem, suos
excessus, suas indignationes, epilogum quoque suum. (*Contr.* VII
pr. 2)

Something like this format: *propositio - exsecutio - excessus -*
indignationes, seems to have been used by Albucius in *Contr.* I.7.
(17):

...nec voluit narrare. a *propositione* coepit: alimenta pater a
filio petit...ad defendendum venit [= *exsecutio*]...philosophumenon
locum introduxit, quomodo animi magnis calamitatibus everterentur
[= *excessus*]...deinde anthypophoran sumpsit: mentiris; ille vero
iratus fuit. cogis, inquit, me dicere iratum tibi merito fuisse
etc. [= *indignatio*].[11]

Seneca refers to the treatment of the *epilogus* in two passages in book VII. The main question at issue in *Contr.* VII.4 was
whether the young man in the theme was right in wanting to go and
ransom his father from the pirates, rather than stay at home to
look after his mother who had gone blind from weeping. Seneca
records how Latro, unlike a certain Greek declaimer, Apollonius,
who was tactlessly vehement in his perorations, recommended that,
even if one were speaking in favour of the young man's decision to
go to his father, one should treat the mother gently in one's concluding words:

in epilogis vehemens fuit Apollonius Graecus: <at periculosum est.>
nihil non; et domi manere et flere.[12]* Latro dixit pro matre

summisse et leniter agendum. non enim, inquit, vindictam sed
misericordiam quaerit, et cum eo adulescente consistit in quo ita
exigit pietatem ut impediat. aiebat itaque verbis quoque
horridioribus abstinendum quotiens talis materia incidisset; ipsam
orationem ad habitum eius quem movere volumus adfectus molliendam.
in epilogis nos de industria vocem quoque infringere et vultum
deicere et dare operam ne dissimilis orationi sit orator; con-
positionem quoque illis mitiorem convenire. (*Contr.* VII.4.5f. W)

Probably still quoting Latro (despite the change to direct
speech), Seneca goes on to cite a precedent for the quelling of
vehemence in the *epilogus* from Calvus' speech *Pro Messio* (*ibid.*
8).[13]

The other passage concerns the best treatment of the *epilogus*
in *controversiae* in which the defendant has both to defend himself
and to inveigh against someone else whom he alleges to be the
guilty party. Three possible courses were open to the declaimer:
to defend himself first and make his accusations second; to mix
defence with accusation; or to make his accusations first and then
defend himself. The discussion, as printed by Müller and Winterbottom, runs as follows, but the text seems unsatisfactory at
several points:

has controversias, quae et accusationem <habent et defensionem>,
non eodem ordine omnes declamaverunt. quidam fuerunt qui ante
defenderent quam accusarent, ex quibus Latro fuit. Fuscus
Arellius: debet, inquit, reus in epilogo desinere. optime autem
epilogum defensioni contexit; et homines magis defendenti quam
accusanti favent. ultima sit pars quae iudicem faventem possit
dimittere. quidam permiscuerunt accusationem ac defensionem, ut
comparationem duorum reorum inirent, et crimen simul reppulissent
statim transferrent; ex quibus fuit Cestius. hoc non semper ex-
pedit. utique ei qui inbecilliorem partem habet non est utile
comminus congredi; facilius latent quae non comparantur. in hac
controversia non sunt duo sed tres rei; noverca enim procuratori
coniungitur. itaque a fili parte utique aiebat prius accusandum,
quia unum deberet crimen defendere, duo obicere, et adulteri et
caedis. (*Contr.* VII.5.7f.)

The subject of the last sentence, as Winterbottom notes *ad loc.*,
can hardly be Arellius Fuscus or Cestius, and a name seems to be
missing: Cestius is ruled out because he mixed accusation with
defence, Fuscus because he asserted that '*debet...reus in epilogo
desinere*', a dictum which I take to mean that the accused should
leave off defence in the *epilogus* (and should turn into a prosecutor).[14] The missing name, I believe, is that of Latro, whose
name also seems out of place where it now stands in the second

sentence of this passage.   Two considerations prompt this suggestion.   First, Latro is recorded in *Contr*. VII.4.5f. to have been
in favour of gentle pathos, rather than vindictiveness, *in epilogis*, so that it seems improbable that in this *controversia*,
given that alternatives were open to him, he was among those who
chose to defend themselves first and to devote the latter part of
their declamation to accusations; rather one would expect him to
leave defence till last.   Secondly, the text of the sentences,
quidam fuerunt...desinere, must be viewed as suspect on internal
grounds: it is contrary to Seneca's practice, when alluding to
something which a declaimer has said, to state his name baldly and
then to follow it immediately with a quotation + *inquit*; Seneca
always prefaces a quotation + *inquit* with some introductory sentence in which a different verb of saying is used, or in which the
declaimer's approach is described in general terms, e.g.:

Contr. VII.2.10: Marcellus Aeserninus *eundem colorem aliter induxit*. cogitabat, *inquit*, secum Antonius: quod Ciceroni ex-
cogitabo supplicium?

Contr. VII.2.13: solus ex declamatoribus *in Ciceronem invectus
est*. quid?   ille, *inquit*, cum Antonium hostem iudicaret et omnis
Antoni milites, non intellegebat se et Popillium proscripsisse?

Contr. VII.4.6: Latro *dixit* pro matre summisse et leniter agendum.
non enim, *inquit*, vindictam, sed misericordiam quaerit...

Contr. VII.5.11 W: Vinicius...*solebat hanc sententiam Saeniani
deridere*... Saenianus in hac eadem controversia dixerat: nihil
puero est teste certius, utique quinquenni...   haec finitio,
inquit, ridicula est...

Contr. VII.5.15: Murredius mimico genere *fatuam sententiam dixit*:
facit, *inquit*, quod solet: pro amatore sanguini suo non parcit.

Contr. VII.6.18: Albucius et *philosophatus est*: *dixit* neminem
liberum esse, neminem servum...denique, *inquit*, scis et nos nuper
servos fuisse.

Read therefore, in *Contr*. VII.5.7:

quidam fuerunt, qui ante defenderent quam accusarent, ex quibus
[Latro] fuit Fuscus Arellius.   debet, inquit, reus in epilogo
desinere.

and in §8:

itaque a fili parte utique <Latro> aiebat prius accusandum, quia
unum deberet crimen defendere, duo obicere, et adulteri et caedis.

It has to be supposed that Latro's name was at some stage omitted,
noted in the margin as missing, and wrongly reinserted by a later

copyist.

Difficulties remain. In the passage, *quidam fuerunt...possit dimittere*, we are presented not with one recommendation as to the treatment of these *controversiae*, but two: first we are told of declaimers who chose to put defence before accusation, and then we are given arguments in favour of the reverse procedure, in which defence comes last. We have to consider where it is that Seneca turns from considering one view and goes on to the other. The *dictum*, *debet...reus in epilogo desinere*, belongs, in my opinion, as in that of Seneca's translators, to the exposition of the first view, and means that the accused should leave off defence in the *epilogus*.[15]* But the opening clause of the next sentence, *optime autem epilogum defensioni contexit*, expressing as it does approval for the practice of weaving together the *epilogus* with the defensive part of a speech, most likely favours the placing of defence *after* accusation.[16]* Now, the subject of this sentence can hardly be Fuscus, if we accept that he preferred the sequence: defence → accusation. More likely *reus* 'the defendant' (in general) is to be regarded as its subject, in which case Bursian's suggestion (which Kiessling printed in his edition) of the prospective future *contexet* for *contexit* has much to recommend it: 'But best of all he will weave his *epilogus* on to the defensive part of his speech.' Whatever the true interpretation is of these words, it needs to be made clear that at least in the following two statements (*et homines...possit dimittere*) Seneca does *not* support those who put defence first and prosecution second. He presents arguments against those *qui ante defenderent quam accusarent*, just as, later in his discussion, he points out the disadvantages of mixing accusation with defence in certain cases. It is only to the third possible procedure, accusation followed by defence, that he gives his full approval.

Omnia ergo habebat [sc. Cassius Severus], quae illum, ut bene
declamaret, instruerent: phrasin non vulgarem nec sordidam, sed
electam, genus dicendi non remissum aut languidum, sed ardens et
concitatum, non lentas nec vacuas explicationes, sed plus sensuum
quam verborum habentes... (*Contr*. III pr. 7)

PHRASIS ELECTA

Tastefulness in the choice of diction, in the elder Seneca's
opinion, was one of the factors which ought to make for a good
declaimer.[1] It emerges from his reports of critical discussions
about declamation that the scholastics of his time hedged themselves around with all manner of prohibitions about diction. It
was not only the use of barbarisms and obscenities that was for-
bidden: any word with mundane associations, any archaism or neologism, was liable to be scrutinized with varying degrees of ped-
antry. Seneca tells us much of interest about these prohibitions,
while himself adopting a fairly tolerant attitude towards all but
the most monstrous breaches of the rules.

Even over the matter of barbarisms we have to distinguish
between Seneca's attitudes and those of the stricter critics of
his time. Seneca did not, of course, positively advocate barbar-
ism, but he had nothing disparaging to say about the diction of
Latro, of whom Messala, *Latini...sermonis observator diligentissi-
mus*, once said on hearing him declaim, *sua lingua disertus est*
(*Contr*. II.4.8). Yet he was evidently not completely deaf to the
strangeness, by metropolitan standards, of Spanish Latin: at any
rate he was reminded by some passages in Sextilius Ena's poetry of
Cicero's reference in the *Pro Archia* to the rich and foreign res-
onances of Corduban poetry (*Suas*. 6.27). As for the vexed question of the admissibility of Grecisms to Latin, we find that in
writing literary criticism he was willing to sacrifice *Latinitas*
in the interests of clarity, showing as he does markedly less

concern than Cicero to find pure Latin equivalents for the technical terminology of the Greek theorists.[2]

Once more, in the case of words with mundane associations
(*verba sordida*) and colloquial language in general, we must be
careful not to confuse Seneca's own opinions with those of the
more rigid critics. The schools of his time, so he tells us,
could not bear the use of 'sordid' words any more than they could
tolerate obscenities: *quaedam enim scholae iam quasi obscena refugiunt nec, si qua sordidiora sunt aut ex cotidiano usu repetita,
possunt pati* (*Contr.* IV pr. 9). The idea, apparently, was that it
was not appropriate to mention humble utensils and undignified
necessities in the highly cultivated realm of artistic prose. In
Contr. VII pr. 3 Seneca gives examples of items which he classes
as *res...omnium sordidissimas*; unfortunately the text of this list
is corrupt, but it seems to have included vinegar, fleabane, lan-
terns and sponges. It is in the schools of rhetoric then (though
one must also bear in mind the possible effects of prolonged study
of epic poetry with the *grammatici*) that we may find one source of
the tendency whereby a Silver Latin orator might choose to refer
to *Hibericas herbas* rather than *spartum* (Quint. VIII.2.2), and
which was to make Tacitus refuse to call a spade a spade and
write, *amissa magna ex parte per quae egeritur humus aut exciditur
caespes* (*Ann.* I.65).

To judge from Seneca's wording in *Contr.* IV pr. 9, *quaedam...
scholae* iam *quasi obscena refugiunt...* the prohibition on mundane
words was a fairly recent development. Some declaimers, in fact,
for various reasons still rejected the restriction. They might be
just old-fashioned, or deliberate archaizers, or might not want to
be classed with the scholastics. There were even people in the
schools who admired the use of 'sordid' diction above all else:
consectari autem solebat [sc. *Bassus Iulius*] *res sordidas et
inveniebat qui illas unice suspicerent* (*Contr.* X.1.13). Bassus
spurned convention to the extent of referring to a dog guarding a
front door: *non mehercules te ferrem, si canem ad ostium
alligasses* (*ibid*).

An important point to notice is that to the declaimers of the
early empire the use of undignified words seemed old-fashioned.

On one occasion Seneca mentions archaizers *qui verba antiqua et sordida consectantur* (*Contr*. IX.2.26). In fact it was not to a very distant past that they were looking back. One result of the scholastic ban on *verba sordida* was that it imposed restrictions on an important means of invective which had been much used by Cicero himself. For example, Seneca remarks, *Rufus Vibius erat, qui antiquo genere diceret; belle cessit illi sententia sordidioris notae: praetor ad occidendum hominem soleas poposcit* (*Contr*. IX.2.25). Now, this *sententia* reminds one of the *Verrines*. Cicero had thought it quite permissible to sneer at praetors for cavorting round in slippers, purple cloaks and ankle-length tunics, supported by their *mulierculae* (*Verr*. II.5.86), but by Seneca's time that sort of thing evidently seemed dated. The use of *verba sordida* like *soleae*, so important in Cicero's techniques of ridicule, was already being rejected by the modernists at the very beginning of the 'Silver' age of Latin prose.

However, the taboo was not yet universally accepted, and was still regarded as peculiar to the schools. Thus a man like Albucius, who did not want to appear a purely scholastic speaker, sprinkled his declamations with the unmentionable words:

splendidissimus erat; idem res dicebat omnium sordidissimas - acetum et puleium et †dammam et philerotem† laternas et spongias: nihil putabat esse quod dici in declamatione non posset. erat autem illa causa: timebat ne scholasticus videretur. dum alterum vitium devitat, incidebat in alterum, nec videbat nimium illum orationis suae splendorem his admixtis sordibus non defendi sed inquinari; et hoc aequale omnium est, ut vitia sua excusare malint quam effugere. (*Contr*. VII pr. 3f. W)

Albucius met with a mixed reception. Seneca notes how one of his expressions, *panem quem cani das, patri non das?*, was admired by some people, but derided by others (*Contr*. I.7.18). This *sententia*, or something very like it, evidently remained well known for a long time. Quintilian tells us that it was admired in his youth but would be quite unacceptable to the scholastics of the time when he was writing:

id tamen in declamatoribus est notabilius, laudarique me puero solebat 'da patri panem', et in eodem 'etiam canem pascis'. res quidem praecipue in scholis anceps et frequenter causa risus, nunc utique cum haec exercitatio procul a veritate seiuncta laboret incredibili verborum fastidio ac sibi magnam partem sermonis absciderit. (VIII.3.22f.)

Quintilian himself could not accept this restrictive canon of diction. He emphasized the value of vulgar words for the heightening
of contempt and for humorous effect, and appreciated Cicero's artistry in this field:

an cum dicit in Pisonem Cicero 'cum tibi tota cognatio serraco ad-
vehatur', incidisse videtur <in> sordidum nomen, non eo contemptum
hominis quem destructum volebat auxisse?

he asks in VIII.3.21. He proposes that the only occasions when
words should be excluded should be when they were beneath the dignity of the subject-matter, or when they were blatantly obscene:

sed ne inornata [quae] sunt quidem, nisi cum sunt infra rei de qua
loquendum est dignitatem, excepto si obscena nudis nominibus
enuntientur. (*Ibid*. 38)

Seneca the Elder does not by any means always accept uncritically the scholastic teaching on *verba sordida*. True, with
reference to the would-be priestess of *Contr*. I.2 he writes,
dicendum est in puellam vehementer, non sordide nec obscene, and
he cites as 'sordid' Iulius Bassus' expressions, *extra portam hanc
virginem* and *ostende istam aeruginosam manum*, and Vibius Rufus'
observation, *redolet adhuc fuliginem fornicis* (*Contr*. I.2.21).
Often, though, he takes a line rather different from that of the
modernist declaimers. He regards the use of colloquialisms as a
positive virtue, but one not far removed from a vice, and hence a
dangerous procedure:

idiotismos est inter oratorias virtutes res quae raro procedit;
magno enim temperamento opus est et occasione quadam. hac virtute
varie usus est [sc. Albucius]: saepe illi bene cessit, saepe
decidit. nec tamen mirum est si difficulter adprehenditur vitio
tam vicina virtus. (*Contr*. VII pr. 5)

He goes on to remark how successful Gallio had been in using this
device, even as a youth, *quod eo magis mirabar*, he adds, *quia
tenera aetas refugit omne, non tantum quod sordidum sed quod
sordido simile est* (*ibid*. 6). This remark on the tastes of the
young hardly seems a universal truth: what it does prove is how
strong a hold the scholastic demands for refined diction exercised
over the younger generation of Seneca's time.

In view of his pronouncement that *idiotismos* was a virtue,
however dangerously close to being a vice, it is not surprising
that we find Seneca elsewhere in his criticism showing tolerance

and sometimes approval for conversational language in declamation.
For example, he considers the effect of a vulgarism (the ethic
dative *mihi*) in a *sententia* by Vibius Rufus 'not bad': *Vibius
Rufus videbatur cotidianis verbis usus non male dixisse: ista
sacerdos quantum mihi abstulit* (*Contr.* I.2.23). It is with defi-
nite approval that he notes a colloquial phrase used by Romanius
Hispo: *Hispo Romanius bello idiotismo usus est: dixerunt, inquit,
amici: eamus ad raptae patrem: hoc curemus, illud domi est* (*Contr.*
II.3.21 W). The reason why Seneca approves is probably that the
slang expression, *illud domi est*, is just the sort of language one
might expect from the friends of the defendant in this particular
controversia. We may compare his remarks on Cornelius Severus'
lines,

> *stratique per herbam*
> *'hic meus est' dixere 'dies'.*

A pernickety grammarian called Porcellus had objected that the
Roman soldiers in Severus' poem were guilty of a solecism when
they said '*hic meus est dies*' rather than '*hic noster*'. Seneca
answers his criticism very effectively:

...in sententia optima id accusabat quod erat optimum. muta enim
ut 'noster' sit: peribit omnis versus elegantia, in quo hoc est
decentissimum, quod ex communi sermone trahitur: nam quasi
proverbii loco est: 'hic dies meus est'; et, cum ad sensum
rettuleris, ne grammaticorum quidem calumnia ab omnibus magnis
ingeniis summovenda habebit locum; dixerunt enim non omnes simul
tamquam in choro manum ducente grammatico, sed singuli ex iis:
'hic meus est dies.' (*Suas.* 2.13)

Once again Seneca is appreciative of the poignant effect of an
every-day phrase. Another example of his approval of *idiotismos*
comes in *Contr.* VII.5.9 where a *sententia* containing the colloquial word *rivalis* is included in a list of *res bellae*: *Brutus
Bruttedius cotidiano verbo significanter usus est: rivalem, inquit,
occidit, amicam sauciavit.* He actually uses the word *rivalis* himself in a passing remark in *Contr.* II.6.12: *Agroitas Massiliensis
longe vividiorem sententiam dixit quam ceteri Graeci declamatores,
qui in hac controversia tamquam rivales rixati sunt.* It is not
always the case, then, that Seneca shared the attitudes of the
modernist scholastics towards the use of everyday language, even
though he considered that it would help one to be a good declaimer

if one used a vocabulary *non vulgarem nec sordidam* (*Contr.* III pr. 7).

In *Contr.* I.2.23 Seneca gives his assent to the principle that obscenity should be avoided: *longe recedendum est ab omni obscenitate et verborum et sensuum: quaedam satius est causae detrimento tacere quam verecundiae dicere.* This veto sounds uncompromising enough, but what it really means is not immediately clear when one considers the unseemly themes of some of the *controversiae*, and the lurid descriptions which were called for when one treated them. Certainly the declaimers do not talk the language of the Petronian gutter, but *Contr.* I.2 is, as Bornecque puts it, '*de tous les ouvrages de l'antiquité celui qui nous fournit le plus de documents sur le recrutement et l'organisation intérieure de certaines maisons que les Romains, sans fausse pudeur, désignent par leur nom*'.[3]

Where did Seneca and the declaimers draw the line? It seems that lesbianism (*Contr.* I.2.23: *controversiam de illo qui tribadas deprehendit et occidit...*), rape (e.g. *Contr.* I.5), and the interior organization of brothels (*Contr.* I.2), were considered subjects perfectly acceptable for treatment in the schools, so long, at any rate, as mention of these subjects was demanded by the theme of the *controversia*. But indecent insinuations unwarranted by the theme, whether relating to perversions or straightforward adultery, were liable to be frowned on when they affected some character - a free-born child, or a woman claiming to be a virgin - whose *verecundia* ought to be respected. Thus Seneca designates as obscene an innuendo by Murredius in *Contr.* I.2.21 about the alleged virginity of the ex-prostitute, *unde scimus an cum venientibus pro virginitate alio libidinis genere deciderit?* and Scaurus silenced, by quoting '*inepta loci*' from a *Priapeion* by Ovid,[4] a certain declaimer who had said in a *controversia* in which a woman sues her husband for failing to consummate the marriage: *novimus istam maritorum abstinentiam, qui etiamsi primam virginibus timidis remisere noctem, vicinis tamen locis ludunt* (*Contr.* I.2.22). Seneca also disapproved of Vibius Gallus' insinuation in *Contr* VII.5.14 that the bailiff who is rumoured to be the lover of the *materfamilias* might also be the father of her

little son, and Cestius made the point that the little boy ought
to be spared such allegations:

Gallus Vibius inprobam dixit sententiam cum caedem describeret:
occidit, inquit, maritum, novercam laesit, puero pepercit: etiamnunc putabat suum. valde enim puero Cestius aiebat parcendum...

Apparently Cestius, and the Greek Hermagoras, treated the boy with
greater delicacy, but in what ways exactly is not clear, given the
brevity of the *sententiae* ascribed to them and the doubtful state
of the text.

Seneca does not make any comments in person on the origins of
the taste for obscenity in the schools. He quotes Scaurus as
having alleged that it originated among the Greek declaimers, *qui
nihil non et permiserint sibi et impetraverint* (*Contr*. I.2.22),
but it is interesting, as an indication of Seneca's attitude
towards the Greeks, that he caps the examples Scaurus gives from
the work of the Greek declaimers Hybreas and Grandaus, with a
Roman example (by Murredius) which he considers no less obscene
(*ibid*. 23).

During the first century A.D. all manner of attitudes towards
propriety of language were current: some people advocated total
avoidance of *verba sordida*, while others maintained that no word
is indecent in itself and that if the subject-matter to be dealt
with is disgusting, no paraphrasing will conceal the fact (Quint.
VIII.3.39). Quintilian ruled that words have no inherent ugli-
ness, giving 'naked' obscenities as the only exception. He ap-
peals to the criterion of 'Roman modesty' (*ibid*). Seneca's view
of the matter seems not unlike Quintilian's, though he had no
illusion that *verecundia* was invariably characteristic of the
Romans.

The next question to consider is how far the use of archaic
expressions on the one hand and neologisms on the other was
thought acceptable in the 'choice diction' of the declaimers. We
have seen how the use of *verba sordida* for denigration had been
rejected by some of the scholastics as old-fashioned. This should
prepare us for the striking fact that, as early as Seneca's time,
some words used by Cicero were already regarded as archaic.
Seneca contrasts Haterius' compliance with the modernists'

prohibition on *verbis calcatis et obsoletis* with his taste for archaisms: *quaedam antiqua et a Cicerone dicta, a ceteris deinde deserta dicebat (Contr.* IV pr. 9). Haterius' rapid delivery could not hide the oddity of his expression: *adeo quidquid insolitum est, etiam in turba notabile est (ibid)*. The clearest evidence for Seneca's attitude towards archaisms comes in his survey of *Contr.* IX.2, a declamation where the subject-matter, the execution of a prisoner at a banquet on the orders of the praetor Flamininus, tempted the declaimer to imitate Ciceronian techniques. Seneca regarded Vibius Rufus' *sententia* about the praetor's slippers, *praetor ad occidendum hominem soleas poposcit*, as successful (*bene cessit*), but he could not share Asinius Pollio's approval for another *sententia*: *at nunc a praetore lege actum est ad lucernam (Contr.* IX.2.25). It was evidently too much to combine in one sentence the ancient formula, *lege actum* with the sordid word, *lucerna*.[5] Seneca goes on to quote a witticism about archaizers which Livy attributed to a rhetorician called Miltiades:

Livius de oratoribus qui verba antiqua et sordida consectantur et orationis obscuritatem severitatem putant aiebat Miltiaden rhetorem eleganter dixisse: ἐπὶ τὸ δεξιὸν μαίνονται. (*Contr.* IX. 2.26)

In his comments on this dictum Seneca disapproves, as he does elsewhere (e.g. *Contr.* II pr. 2), of the kind of austere writing which tends to obscurity, but he does not make any general statement in agreement with Miltiades' distaste for archaisms. The fact seems to be that, while he would not go so far as Pollio in expressing approval for archaic expressions, he considered that the *genus dicendi antiquum* did have some positive merits. At any rate his opinion of Scaurus, who was an exponent of such a style, was that *nihil erat illo venustius, nihil paratius (Contr.* X pr. 2), and he considered Labienus, who combined *color orationis antiquae* with *vigor novae*, a great orator (*ibid.* 5). It was, indeed, usual among ancient critics to express distaste for what they considered to be extreme archaism, while appreciating the aura of gravity which the tasteful deployment of time-honoured words might give to one's style. Thus Cicero likens the imitation of Thucydides to a taste for wines dating from the consulships of Opimius and Anicius, less drinkable than other mature, but rather

more recent vintages (*Brut.* 83.287f.), and Quintilian commends the
artistic use of archaisms as seen in Virgil's poetry, while disapproving of extremes: *adspergunt illam, quae etiam in picturis
est gravissima, vetustatis inimitabilem arti auctoritatem. sed
utendum modo nec ex ultimis tenebris repetenda* (VIII.3.25).

Seneca nowhere in his extant books gives his personal opinion
whether the declaimer should feel free to use newly coined words.
In *Contr.* VII.6.21 he reports the disapproval with which some of
his contemporaries greeted one neologism:

Hispo Romanius dixerat: maritum autem ego istum vocem raptorem
serotinum? verbum hoc quasi apud antiquos non usurpatum quibusdam
displicebat. eiusdem verbi significatione, ut extra reprehensionem
esset, usus est Gavius Sabinus cum diceret nondum esse consummatam
adversus servos publicam vindictam: etiamnunc in domo nostra
residuus raptor est.

But he does not commit himself to this disapproving attitude. The
reason why he considered Marullus to be using language *licenter* in
a *sententia* quoted in *Contr.* II.2.7 may have been that the word
reludere which he used was a new coinage; it is certainly a very
rare word. If so, it is indicative of a certain tolerance towards
neologisms on Seneca's part that, though he thinks it bold to use
such a word, he considers that it expresses the meaning intended
well enough: *licenter verbo usus est satis sensum exprimente...*
But the best evidence for Seneca's attitude towards innovation in
prose diction lies in the way he writes himself. The vocabulary
which he uses for criticism is, as Bardon has shown, not that of
Cicero.[6] It seems hardly likely, then, that he would have agreed
entirely with any scholastic ban on new formations. Once more
Quintilian (VIII.3.31ff.) illustrates a sensible attitude which
one might take if one rejected the rigidity of the schools. Quintilian was familiar with a pedantic prohibition on neologisms: his
own teachers had persisted in forbidding the use of *piratica*,
musica and *fabrica*, and there had been a certain Celsus who banned
the invention of new words by the orator. Quintilian, while regarding Latin as less well adapted to the formation of new words
than Greek, realized that nothing would stop the evolution of
language. He gives examples of several words, now well established, which had once been considered novelties, and argues that,

although men of his day might have lost primitive man's right to
invent new root-words, they were still free to form new compounds.
Seneca trusts in this right to reuse old roots when he employs
words like *pugnacitas* (*Contr.* I.2.16), *efficaciter* (*Contr.* VII pr.
3) and *detractus* (*Suas.* 7.11).

However, he does seem to have conceived of the existence of a
law of diction which writers ought not to infringe. Arellius
Fuscus was one declaimer guilty of breaking it:

in descriptionibus extra legem omnibus verbis, dummodo niterent,
permissa libertas; nihil acre, nihil solidum, nihil horridum;
splendida oratio et magis lasciva quam laeta. (*Contr.* II pr. 1)

Fuscus' offence, as we shall see,[7] lay in his introduction to
prose of whole clusters of markedly poetic words. But poets too
were liable to be upbraided for literary *licentia*. Seneca says of
Ovid: *verbis minime licenter usus est nisi in carminibus, in
quibus non ignoravit vitia sua sed amavit* (*Contr.* II.2.12). The
examples of this 'licence' given by Seneca were the lines *semi-
bovemque virum semivirumque bovem* (*Ars am.* II.24) and *et gelidum
Borean egelidumque Notum* (*Am.* II.11.10), together, almost certainly, with a third example now lost. Here, though, it is Ovid's
way of pairing contrasting words, more than the diction itself,
which seems to be being faulted: *semibos* was probably a neologism,
but none of the other words seems inherently objectionable. Certain declaimers had gone beyond the limits permissible even in
poetry in the use of metaphors. Seneca criticizes one such declaimer, Musa, in *Contr.* X pr. 9:

quis enim ferat hominem de siphonibus dicentem 'caelo repluunt' et
de sparsionibus 'odoratos imbres' et in cultum viridarium
'caelatas silvas' et in †pictura†[8]* 'nemora surgentia'?

Elsewhere he recalls how Maecenas[9] had suggested that a declaimer
could learn how this fault might be avoided by observing Virgil's
discretion in the use of figurative language:

corruptissimam rem omnium, quae umquam dictae sunt, ex quo homines
diserti insanire coeperunt, putabant Dorionis esse in metaphrasi
dictam Homeri, cum excaecatus Cyclops saxum in mare reiecit:
<   >.[10]* haec quo modo ex corruptis eo perveniant, <ut> et
magna et tamen sana sint, aiebat Maecenas apud Vergilium intellegi
posse. tumidum est: ὄρους ὄρος ἀποσπᾶται. Vergilius quid ait?
rapit
        haud partem exiguam montis. (*Aen.* X.128)
ita magnitudini studet, <ut> non inprudenter discedat a fide. est

inflatum: καὶ χειρία βάλλεται νῆσος. Vergilius quid ait [qui] de navibus?

> credas innare revolsas
>   Cycladas.   (*Aen*. VIII.691f.)

non dicit hoc fieri, sed videri. propitiis auribus accipitur, quamvis incredibile sit, quod excusatur, antequam dicitur. (*Suas*. 1.12 M)

Seneca did not think that declaimers should permit themselves *extra legem omnibus verbis...libertas* (*Contr*. II pr. 1), and probably his ideal in declamatory diction was that of Latro, whose admirer Ovid (*Contr*. II.2.8),[11]* is said to have used words *minime licenter* in prose (*ibid*. 12). Nevertheless he is tolerant towards all but the worst offences of the declaimers. At the conclusion of his onslaught on Musa's diction he dissociates himself from those critics who expect everything to conform *ad exactam regulam*, and declares, *multa donanda ingeniis puto; sed donanda vitia, non portenta sunt* (*Contr*. X pr. 10).

GENUS DICENDI ARDENS ET CONCITATUM

The hypothetical good declaimer of *Contr*. III pr. 7 possesses, besides a choice vocabulary, command of a style characterized as *non remissum aut languidum sed ardens et concitatum*, and as containing *non lentas nec vacuas explicationes*,[12] *sed plus sensuum quam verborum habentes*. The pursuit of the fiery and agitated in style was clearly one of the main ideals of the early Imperial rhetoricians and writers under their influence: Quintilian was later to describe Lucan as *ardens et concitatus* (X.1.90). Another word used to distinguish the style of the new rhetoric from that of a previous age was *vigor*: in Labienus' style, we are told in *Contr*. X pr. 5, both the *color antiquae orationis* and the *vigor novae* were in evidence.

The *vigor* of the new style stemmed ultimately from what the theorists called *compositio*,[13] that is, the order of words, the collocation of long and short clauses, and prose-rhythm - *ordo, iunctura, numerus* (Quint. IX.4.22). Arellius Fuscus emerges as the most notable offender against the elder Seneca's taste in *compositio*. We learn that Fabianus, after his philosophical conversion, had found Fuscus' *compositio* no longer acceptable, *mollior quam ut illam tam sanctis fortibusque praeceptis praeparans*

se animus pati posset (*Contr.* II pr. 1). Seneca makes it clear
that in old age he too had come to find Fuscus' *nimius cultus et
fracta compositio* distasteful (*Suas.* 2.23); he suspects nonetheless
that these very faults would appeal to the young (*ibid.*), and recalls how in his own youth, when Fuscus was the acknowledged master of the polished style (*Suas.* 4.5),

...nihil fuisse...tam notum quam has explicationes Fusci, quas
nemo nostrum non alius alia inclinatione vocis velut sua quisque
modulatione cantabat. (*Suas.* 2.10)

Faults of *compositio*, castigated by ancient theorists, which may
frequently be detected in samples of Fuscus' more flowery prose[14]
include the unnatural use of hyperbaton (see Quint. IX.4.28); the
stringing together of too many short words in succession (see
Quint. IX.4.22); and the contrived repetition of the same rhythms
(see Quint. IX.4.55f.). At the other extreme from the *compositio*
of Fuscus' florid descriptions, so we are led to suppose, was that
of Cassius Severus: *compositio aspera et quae vitaret conclusionem*
(*Contr.* III pr. 18).[15] Latro, in so many respects Seneca's ideal
declaimer, appears to have been in general an avoider of *mollis
compositio*, though in *Contr.* VII.4.6 he is said to have recommended
a change of tone and the use of gentler rhythms in pathetic
perorations: *compositionem...illis mitiorem convenire*.[16] A particular instance of poor *compositio* is discussed in *Contr.* IX.2.23f.:

illud, quod tamquam Latronis circumfertur, non esse Latronis pro
testimonio dico et Latronem a sententia inepte tumultuosa vindico;
ipse enim audivi Florum quendam, auditorem Latronis, dicentem non
apud Latronem...: refulsit inter privata pocula publicae securis
acies; inter temulentas ebriorum reliquias humanum everritur
caput. numquam Latro sic composuisset, ut, quia publicam securem
dicturus erat, diceret privata pocula, nec in tam mollem compositionem sententia eius evanuisset; nec tam incredibilis umquam
figuras concipiebat ut in ipso triclinio inter lectos et †loco† et
mensas percussum describeret. (*Contr.* IX.2.23f. W)

The exact implications of Seneca's assertion, *nec...evanuisset*,
are unclear. The reference can hardly be just to what we would
regard as the *clausula* of the sentence in question, *everritur*
caput, for in my sample of Latro's *clausulae* the rhythm $-\cup-\cup\cup$
occurs in 13% of the examples considered;[17] nor is the type of
word-division exemplified by Florus' *clausula* unparalleled in
Latro's usage – compare *trecesimus dies* in *Contr.* II.3.1; nor is

the use at the end of such a *clausula* of a word naturally consisting of two short syllables - compare *Contr.* I.1.1: *alimentā*
non darĕt - despite the view of theorists (see e.g. Quint. IX.4.
106) that pyrrhics at the end of sentences produced instability.
One cannot suggest that what Seneca objected to was the fact that
the whole second part of the *sententia* has a markedly trochaic
rhythm: *inter temulentas ebriorum reliquias human(um) everritur*
caput, for it is possible to find Latronian parallels even for
extended trochaic sequences.[18]   So most likely his objection was
not so much to the rhythm used as to the means by which it was
attained, notably the unnatural ordering of the words *humanum*
everritur caput.

Characteristic of the *genus dicendi ardens et concitatum* was
the brilliance and frequency of its *sententiae*.[19]   The long extract from Latro's version of *Contr.* II.7 (§1ff.), which is generally agreed to consist of continuous prose rather than a collection of excerpts, and which will be analysed in a later chapter,[20]
gives a fair idea of the style of a lover of *sententiae* (*Contr.*
I pr. 22), who abhorred empty passage-work (*Contr.* VII.7.10).

Seneca's description in the first preface of Latro's training
methods and memorized stock-in-trade provides the best guide he
gives us to the main component parts of declamatory prose:

solebat autem et hoc genere exercitationis uti, ut aliquo die
nihil praeter epiphonemata scriberet, aliquo die nihil praeter
enthymemata, aliquo die nihil praeter has translaticias quas
proprie sententias dicimus, quae nihil habent cum ipsa controversia inplicitum, sed satis apte et alio transferuntur, tamquam
quae de fortuna, de crudelitate, de saeculo, de divitiis dicuntur;
hoc genus sententiarum supellectilem vocabat. solebat schemata
quoque per se, quaecumque controversia reciperet, scribere.
(*Contr.* I pr. 23)

It is interesting that Seneca and Latro recognize the grouping,
epiphonemata, *enthymemata*, *sententiae* proper, for in doing so they
anticipate the classification of the main types of *sententiae*
which Quintilian gives us (VIII.5.1ff.). Quintilian's discussion
of these types provides the best available commentary on the
Senecan passage.

Sententiae proper are quasi-proverbial utterances: *antiquiss-*
imae sunt quae proprie, quamvis omnibus idem nomen sit, sententiae

vocantur, quas Graeci gnomas appellant, declares Quintilian (VIII. 5.3). Though of general import, they can have special relevance to the particular case at issue – *ad rem* – or to some particular person – *ad personam* (*ibid.*). Some theorists attempted to define the rôle of the *sententia* within rhetorical syllogisms, either as part of an *enthymema*, or as the conclusion of an *epichirema*,[21] but Quintilian feels that these definitions are not always valid. He prefers to classify gnomic *sententiae* as either single – *simplicem* – or double – *duplicem* (*ibid.* 4). He has given examples of the 'single' type when discussing *sententiae* with relevance *ad rem* and *ad personam* (*ibid.* 3): *nihil est tam populare quam bonitas* and *princeps qui vult omnia scire necesse habet multa ignoscere*. He groups with this type *sententiae* which include an explanation for the truth they are expressing – *ratione subiecta* – for example: *nam in omni certamine qui opulentior est, etiam si accipit iniuriam, tamen quia plus potest facere videtur* (*ibid.* 4). His example of a double *sententia* is *obsequium amicos, veritas odium parit* (*ibid.*). Gnomic *sententiae* did not have to be cast in the form of plain statements, but could be expressed in all manner of indirect and striking ways, *per omnes...figuras* (*ibid.* 5). Some theorists laid down that there were ten possible ways of express- ing them, but Quintilian could not see why there could not be still more; he mentions as possible types *sententiae* expressed *per interrogationem, per comparationem, infitiationem, similitudinem, admirationem...* Such figured *sententiae* could be more forceful than the straightforward sort; he cites the example of Virgil's *usque adeone mori miserum est?* (*Aen.* XII.646), so much more in- cisive than *mors misera non est* (VIII.5.6).

After a few more remarks on the *sententia* proper, in VIII.5.9 Quintilian proceeds to discuss the *enthymema*. Following Cicero (*Top.* 13.55) closely, he observes that though this term could mean 'thought' (*omne quod mente concepimus*) in general, it had acquired the specialized meaning of *sententia ex contrariis* because, so he suggests, this was the greatest of all the varieties of 'thought', *ut Homerus 'poeta', 'urbs' Roma*. Though the *enthymema* was a func- tional part of rhetorical argument and had been treated as such by Quintilian in an earlier book (V.14.1ff.), it is included by him

under items of style as well because it could be used merely *ad
ornatum*, long after one's hearers needed to be convinced of the
point being made (VIII.5.10). It could be used, like the *epiphonema* which he is about to discuss, at the end of a paragraph as
a sort of parting shot. The only example he gives of an *enthymema*
here is a Ciceronian one: *quorum igitur inpunitas, Caesar, tuae
clementiae laus est, eorum te ipsorum ad crudelitatem acuet
oratio? (Lig. 10)*. Closer to the style of declamatory *sententiae*
than this or any of the enthymemes *ex pugnantibus* cited by Quintilian in V.14.2ff. are the examples from drama which Cicero gives
in *Topica* 13.55:

> hoc metuere, alterum in metu non ponere!
> eam quam nihil accusas damnas, bene quam meritam esse autumas
> male merere? id quod scis prodest nihil; id quod nescis obest?

There is a fine Latronian example of a declamatory enthymeme in
Contr. I.1.2: *imitationem alienae culpae innocentiam vocas?* Similar in type and perhaps also to be regarded as *enthymemata* are
such *sententiae* as *eo iam perductus erat, ut omnem spem ultimorum
alimentorum in ea domo poneret in qua habebat <et> abdicatum et
inimicum (ibid.* 1), and *ergo fame morientem videbo per cuius
cineres iuraturus sum? (ibid.* 3).

In giving *enthymema*[22] the restricted technical sense of
sententia ex contrariis Quintilian in VIII.5.9 is following a
tradition related to Aristotle's theory of γνωμολογία rather than
to his theory of argumentation. In his discussion of rhetorical
argument Aristotle had used ἐνθύμημα as a term of very wide application: an enthymeme was nothing less than the rhetorical equivalent of the dialectician's syllogism:

τὸ δὲ τινῶν ὄντων ἕτερόν τι διὰ ταῦτα συμβαίνειν παρὰ ταῦτα τῷ
ταῦτα εἶναι, ἢ καθόλου ἢ ὡς ἐπὶ τὸ πολύ, ἐκεῖ μὲν συλλογισμὸς
ἐνταῦθα δὲ ἐνθύμημα καλεῖται.

(Rhet. I.2.9: 'When certain things being posited, something different results by reason of them, from their being true, either
universally or in most cases, this is called in dialectic a syllogism, in rhetoric an enthymeme.') Usually in an ἐνθύμημα the
orator, out of consideration for his hearers, leaves out some of
the steps of reasoning which a dialectician would give in full in
a συλλογισμός; usually, though not always, because the orator's

subject-matter is human behaviour with all its vagaries, the prem-
isses dealt with in an ἐνθύμημα tend to be probabilities rather
than universal truths (*ibid*. 12ff.). But, in theory at least,
there could be rhetorical enthymemes corresponding to all the
syllogisms of dialectic, and they could include proofs from con-
sequents as well as proofs from contraries. Quintilian comes
closer to this wide conception of an enthymeme in his fifth book,
where he is dealing with argumentation (V.10.1ff.), than in his
passage about *sententiae* in the eighth.

In his discussion of γνωμολογία in *Rhet*. II.21.1ff. Aristotle considers a variety of types of sententious utterance. Some
he looks upon as constituting parts of enthymemes, but γνῶμαι of
one type, which he declares to be the most highly regarded, are
described as ἐνθυμηματικαί:

αἱ δ' ἐνθυμηματικαὶ μέν, οὐκ ἐνθυμήματος δὲ μέρος· αὕπερ καὶ
μάλιστ' εὐδοκιμοῦσιν.²³ εἰσὶ δ' αὗται ἐν ὅσαις ἐμφαίνεται τοῦ
λεγομένου τὸ αἴτιον,²⁴ οἷον ἐν τῷ
   ἀθάνατον ὀργὴν μὴ φύλασσε θνητὸς ὤν·
τὸ μὲν γὰρ φάναι μὴ δεῖν ἀεὶ φυλάττειν τὴν ὀργὴν γνώμη, τὸ δὲ
προσκείμενον 'θνητὸν ὄντα' τὸ διὰ τί λέγει. ὅμοιον δὲ καὶ τὸ
   θνατὰ χρὴ τὸν θνατόν, οὐκ ἀθάνατα τὸν θνατὸν φρονεῖν. (§6)

Aristotle does not actually state that enthymematic γνῶμαι have to
be the equivalent of syllogisms from contraries, but both the
examples he gives could be regarded as such.

The author of the *Rhetorica ad Alexandrum* takes us a step
nearer the Roman equation of *enthymemata* with *sententiae ex contrariis* when he stipulates that ἐνθυμήματα (the fourth of his
types of direct proof) have to do with contraries and are best
expressed in as few words as possible:

ἐνθυμήματα δέ ἐστιν οὐ μόνον τὰ τῷ λόγῳ καὶ τῇ πράξει ἐναντιούμενα,
ἀλλὰ καὶ τοῖς ἄλλοις ἅπασι. λήψῃ δὲ πολλὰ μετιών, ὡς ἐν τῷ
ἐξεταστικῷ εἴδει εἴρηται, καὶ σκοπῶν, εἴ πῃ ὁ λόγος [ἑαυτῷ]
ἐναντιοῦται ἢ τὰ πεπραγμένα τοῖς δικαίοις ἢ τῷ νόμῳ ἢ τῷ συμ-
φέροντι ἢ τῷ καλῷ ἢ τῷ δυνατῷ ἢ τῷ ῥαδίῳ ἢ τῷ εἰκότι ἢ τῷ ἤθει τοῦ
λέγοντος ἢ τῷ ἔθει τῶν πραγμάτων. τὰ μὲν οὖν τοιαῦτα τῶν ἐνθυμη-
μάτων κατὰ τῶν ἐναντίων ἐκληπτέον. τὰ δ' ἐναντία τούτοις ὑπὲρ
ἡμῶν αὐτῶν δεῖ λέγειν ἀποφαίνοντας τὰς πράξεις τὰς ἡμετέρας καὶ
τοὺς λόγους ἐναντιουμένους τοῖς ἀδίκοις καὶ τοῖς ἀνόμοις καὶ τοῖς
ἀσυμφόροις καὶ τοῖς τῶν ἀνθρώπων τῶν πονηρῶν ἤθεσι, καὶ συλλήβδην
τοῖς μοχθηροῖς νομιζομένοις εἶναι. δεῖ δὲ τούτων ἕκαστα συνάγειν
ὡς εἰς βραχύτατα καὶ φράζειν ὅτι μάλιστα ἐν ὀλίγοις τοῖς ὀνόμασι.
τὰ μὲν οὖν ἐνθυμήματα τοῦτον τὸν τρόπον πολλὰ ποιήσομεν, καὶ οὕτως
αὐτοῖς ἄριστα χρησόμεθα. (*Rhet. Alex*. 1430a)

It is to this sort of theory, not to the elaborate precepts about
argument in Aristotle's *Rhetoric* and logical treatises, that
Cicero is referring when in *Topica* 13.55 he notes that what the
rhetoricians call an ἐνθύμημα is equivalent to the dialecticians'
third mode of *conclusio*:

cum autem aliqua coniuncta negaris et ex eis unum aut plura
sumpseris, ut quod relinquitur tollendum sit, is tertius appellatur
conclusionis modus. ex hoc illa rhetorum ex contrariis conclusa,
quae ipsi ἐνθυμήματα appellant...[25]

The author of the *Rhetorica ad Herennium* uses the Latin term *contrarium* in the same sense (IV.18.25).[26]

It is almost certain that when Seneca the Elder and Latro
referred to *enthymemata* they meant *sententiae ex contrariis*,
though just conceivably they were among those, with whom Quintilian disagrees (VIII.5.4), who classed all *sententiae cum ratione*
as enthymemes (see V.10.2). At any rate, it is totally unlikely
that they would have used the term to refer to rhetorical syllogisms in general, as Aristotle does in *Rhet.* I.2.9. For though
Quintilian knew of definitions of *enthymema* much wider than
sententia ex contrariis, he only discussed them in the part of his
work concerned with *argumentatio* (V.10.1ff.). When he turned to
consider *enthymemata* as items of *elocutio* it was the definition
sententiae ex contrariis that alone sprang to his mind (VIII.5.9).
And as Seneca, when writing about Latro's practice methods in
Contr. I pr. 23, mentions *enthymemata* in conjunction with *epiphonemata* and *sententiae* proper, it is clear that he is thinking
of them as stylistic rather than argumentative devices.

Quintilian (VIII.5.11) defines *epiphonema* as *rei narratae vel
probatae summa adclamatio*, and as examples cites Virgil's *tantae
molis erat Romanam condere gentem* (*Aen.* I.33), and Cicero's *facere
enim probus adulescens periculose quam perpeti turpiter maluit*
(*Mil.* 9).[27] This is a type of *sententia* of which Silver Latin
authors were extremely fond. Quintilian considered that it had
been used to excess:

sed nunc aliud volunt, ut omnis locus, omnis sensus in fine
sermonis feriat aurem. turpe autem ac prope nefas ducunt respirare
ullo loco qui adclamationem non petierit. inde minuti corruptique
sensiculi et extra rem petiti: neque enim possunt tam multae bonae
sententiae esse quam necesse est multae sint clausulae. (VIII.5.

13f.)

Sententiae proper, *enthymemata* and *epiphonemata*, the types of
sententiae practised regularly by Latro, are the types which
Quintilian discusses first and in most detail, but he observes
that certain additional new varieties had come to be favoured by
orators and rhetoricians in recent years. We must therefore not
necessarily expect to be able to classify all the *sententiae* used
by Latro and his colleagues under the three main headings. Some
of the new varieties, including *sententiae ex inopinato*, *alio
relatae*, *aliunde petitae*, *sententiae* playing on simple *geminatio*;
and *sententiae...a verbo* (these last usually in the worst of
taste), are listed and illustrated by Quintilian in VIII.5.15-25.
Quintilian's *sententiae...a verbo* are of the type which the elder
Seneca and his contemporaries sometimes called *sententiae Publi-
lianae*, after Publilius Syrus, the writer of mimes - which was
unfair to Publilius, according to Cassius Severus:

Cassius Severus, summus Publili amator, aiebat non illius hoc
vitium esse, sed eorum, qui illum ex parte qua transire deberent
imitarentur, <non imitarentur> quae apud eum melius essent dicta
quam apud quemquam comicum tragicumque aut Romanum aut Graecum...
(*Contr*. VII.3.8)

We find examples of the so-called Publilian *sententiae* in *Contr*.
VII.3.8:

Murredius...Publilianam sententiam dedit: abdicationes, inquit,
suas veneno diluit; et iterum: mortem, inquit, meam effudit;

again in VII.4.8:

in hac controversia Publilianam sententiam dedit Festus quidam
rhetor...fuit autem Festi sententia: 'captus est, inquit, pater.'
si te capti movent, et haec capta est. et quasi non intellexisse-
mus, ait: nescitis dici 'captos luminibus'?

(the blind mother of the theme refused to let her son go to ransom
her husband from the pirates); and also in VII.2.14, where the
text unfortunately is corrupt.

Besides devoting days to the practice of each of the main
types of *sententiae*, Latro, we are told, would write out in full
any *schemata* required in his declamations (*Contr*. I pr. 23). We
may look to Quintilian's ninth book (IX.1.1-3.102) for a detailed
- though confessedly not exhaustive[28] - survey of the *figurae* or
schemata recognized in his day. Quintilian's definition of a

figura is: *conformatio quaedam orationis remota a communi et primum se offerente ratione* (IX.1.4). Latro's opinion of the proper use of figures is given in *Contr.* I pr. 24:

schema negabat decoris causa inventum, sed subsidii, ut quod [palam] aures offensurum esset si palam diceretur, id oblique et furtim subreperet. summam quidem esse dementiam detorquere orationem cui esse rectam liceret.

With this view of the matter Quintilian was in full agreement: figures were an aid to persuasiveness, not merely decorative,

nam etsi minime videtur pertinere ad probationem qua figura quidque dicatur, facit tamen credibilia quae dicimus, et in animos iudicum qua non observatur inrepit. (IX.1.19)

Like Latro, he considered that one should not use figures all the time:

et oratio habet rectam quandam velut faciem, quae ut stupere inmobili rigore non debebit, ita saepius in ea quam natura dedit specie continenda est. (IX.3.101)

Seneca mentions surprisingly few *figurae* by name, considering the large number of types known to Quintilian.[29] It is usually only the grander types of figure which he finds worthy of note, and more often those which theorists would have classed as figures of thought than those classed as figures of speech, on which distinction see Quint. IX.1.17:

inter plurimos enim, quod sciam, consensus est duas eius esse partes, διανοίας, id est mentis vel sensus vel sententiarum (nam his omnibus modis dictum est), et λέξεως, id est verborum vel dictionis vel elocutionis vel sermonis vel orationis: nam et variatur et nihil refert.

The only figures of the latter class which he mentions by name are the *tricolum*[30] (*Contr.* II.4.12, IX.2.27) and the *tetracolon* (*Contr.* IX.2.27). These come to his attention because they were being seriously misused by inferior speakers:

hanc controversiam cum declamaret, Maximus dixit [quasi] tricolum tale qualia sunt quae basilicani sectantur. dicebat autem a parte patris: omnes aliquid ad vos inbecilli, alter alterius onera, detulimus: accusatur pater in ultimis annis, nepos in primis †abdicatur nullus†. haec autem subinde refero quod aeque vitandarum rerum exempla ponenda sunt quam sequendarum. (*Contr.* II.4.12 W)

(Müller reconstructs the end of the *tricolon* as follows: *nepos in primis <adoptatur, in mediis> abdicatur filius.*)

sed ne hoc genus furoris protegere videar, in Flaminino tumidissime dixit Murredius: praetorem nostrum in illa ferali cena saginatum meretricis sinu excitavit ictus securis. et illud tetracolon:

serviebat forum cubiculo, praetor meretrici, carcer convivio, dies
nocti. novissima pars sine sensu dicta est, ut impleretur numerus;
quem enim sensum habet: 'serviebat dies nocti'? hanc ideo sententiam rettuli quia et in tricolis et in omnibus huius generis
sententiis curamus ut numerus constet, non curamus an sensus.
omnia autem genera corruptarum quoque sententiarum de industria
pono, quia facilius et quid imitandum et quid vitandum sit docemur
exemplo. (*Contr.* IX.2.27)

Figures of thought to which Seneca refers are the *testamenti*

figura:

Contr. IX.3.14: Gallio autem elegantissime dixit a parte patris
cum ultima per testamenti figuram tractaret: quandoque ego mortuus
ero, tunc mihi heres sit: vis interrogem, uter?

(cf. Pollio's parody of a will, Quint. IX.2.34f.);

the *iusiurandum*:

Contr. VII pr. 6f. (on Albucius): haec illum sollicitudo fugavit a
foro et tantum unius figurae crudelis eventus. nam in quodam
iudicio centumvirali, cum diceretur iurisiurandi condicio aliquando delata ab adversario, induxit eiusmodi figuram, qua illi
omnia crimina regereret. placet, inquit, tibi rem iure iurando
transigi? iura, sed ego iusiurandum mandabo: iura per patris
cineres, qui inconditi sunt, iura per patris memoriam; et executus
est locum. quo perfecto surrexit L. Arruntius ex diverso et ait:
accipimus condicionem; iurabit. clamabat Albucius: non detuli
condicionem; schema dixi. Arruntius instabat. centumviri rebus
iam ultimis properabant. Albucius clamabat: ista ratione schemata
de rerum natura tolluntur. Arruntius aiebat: tollantur; poterimus
sine illis vivere.

(cf. *Suas.* 2.14; 7.14; Quint. IX.2.62f., 95);

ironia:

Contr. I.7.13: et cum diu pressisset [sc. Silo Pompeius] illum
tyranni patrem esse, adiecit: aude postulare ut illud tibi prosit,
quod tyrannicidae pater es. Blandus hunc sensum, cum postero die
declamaret, in ironiam vertit, et, cum obiecisset quod tyranni
pater esset, adiecit: nolite illum aversari; habet quod adponat:
et adulteri pater est.

(cf. Quint. IX.2.44);

anthypophora or *contradictio*:

Contr. I.7.17: deinde anthypophoran sumpsit [sc. Albucius]:
mentiris; ille vero iratus fuit. cogis, inquit, me dicere iratum
tibi merito fuisse;

Suas. 2.18: [sc. Statorius Victor] sumpsit contradictionem: 'at'
inquit 'trecenti sumus'; et ita respondit: trecenti, sed viri, sed
armati, sed Lacones, sed ad Thermopylas; numquam vidi plures
trecentos.

(cf. Quint. IX.2.106; 3.87).

Finally, though Seneca never uses the term *praesumptio* (on which see Quint. IX.2.16ff.), he mentions two sub-species of this important figure, *praeparatio* and *confessio*:

Contr. VII pr. 3: itaque moderatio est adhibenda, ut sit illa praeparatio, non confessio.

As we have seen,[31] Seneca also mentions a class of *figurae* distinct from any recognized by Quintilian, figures of *divisio*, whereby the whole of a declaimer's argumentation was arranged in an abnormal fashion.

It has been observed earlier[32] that the term *locus* is not restricted in the elder Seneca's criticism to the meaning 'moralizing commonplace', and some types of *loci* may suitably be considered under the heading of *elocutio*. The development of an elaborate *figura*, Albucius' ill-fated *iusiurandum*, is classed as a *locus* in *Contr.* VII pr. 7. In *Contr.* X.5.23 we read how all the declaimers taunted Parrhasius for torturing his model for a painting of Prometheus, and once more Seneca uses the term *locus*: *illum locum omnes temptaverunt: quid, si volueris bellum pingere? quid si incendium? quid, si parricidium?* The word is also used with reference to passages of description[33] in *Contr.* II.1.26:

solebat autem [sc. Vibius Gallus] sic ad locos pervenire, ut amorem descripturus paene cantantis modo diceret: 'amorem describere volo' sic tamquam 'bacchari volo.' deinde describebat et <ut> totiens coepturus repetebat: 'amorem describere volo.'

As to the proper length and style for *loci*, Seneca probably shared the views of Latro who, on the rare occasions when he introduced such passages, spoke *non diu...sed valenter* (*Contr.* VII.7.10).

Numerous descriptive passages are to be found in Seneca's declamatory extracts, for example: *Contr.* II.1.10ff. - battle-field, extravagant building and resultant evils, beauties of simple life (Fabianus); II.5.6 - torture (Fabianus); VII.1.4, 26 - storm at sea (Haterius, Artemo); IX.2.4 - drunken orgy (Iulius Bassus); X.4.2 - mangled beggars (Cassius Severus); *Suas.* 1.1, 2, 4, 11-13 - *Oceanus*; 2.1 - treacherous straits (Arellius Fuscus); 3.1 - variation of weather, phases of the moon (Fuscus); 5.1 - the broken spirit of Xerxes (Fuscus). *Descriptiones* could be extended set-pieces, like most of these, but it must not be imagined that Seneca always has such long digressions in mind when he uses the terms, *descriptio*, *describere*: in *Contr.* VII.5.10 there is a

reference to a description of the step-mother's wound, a subject
on which even Musa could hardly have expatiated for very long; a
descriptio mentioned in *Contr.* I.4.8 appears merely to have been
an extra-vivid piece of narrative:

et in descriptione dixit: cum me vocavit pater, 'hoc' inquam
'putavit supplicium futurum morte gravius, si adulteram filio
ostenderit.' et illud dixit: exierunt adulteri inter patrem
debilem et filium stupentem.

Other critics would have classed such descriptions as this and the
one mentioned in the analysis of Latro's *divisio* for *Suas.* 6 (§8)
in which Cicero was invited to envisage *acerbitatem servitutis
futurae*, as examples of the figure *sub oculos subiectio*/ὑποτύπωσις
(see e.g. Quint. IX.2.40f.).

The term *explicatio*, which Seneca uses in the stylistic re-
commendations of *Contr.* III pr. 7, seems to serve in his usage as a
synonym for *descriptio*. At least, the one thing which the passages with reference to which he uses this term have in common is
an element of description. That an *explicatio* does not have to be
long is proved by a passage in *Contr.* VII.1.27:

soleo dicere vobis Cestium Latinorum verborum inopia <ut> hominem
Graecum laborasse, sensibus abundasse; itaque, quotiens latius
aliquid describere ausus est, totiens substitit, utique cum se ad
imitationem magni alicuius ingeni derexerat, sicut in hac controversia fecit. nam in narratione, cum fratrem traditum sibi describeret, placuit sibi in hac explicatione una et infelici: nox
erat concubia, et omnia, iudices, canentia <sub> sideribus muta
erant.

Consequently no translation of *explicatio* suggestive of prolonged
unfolding seems wholly appropriate. Now, particular *explicationes*
of Arellius Fuscus are referred to in *Suas.* 2.10, 2.23 and 4.5:

huius suasoriae feci mentionem, non quia in ea subtilitatis erat
aliquid, quod vos excitare posset, sed ut sciretis, quam nitide
Fuscus dixisset vel quam licenter; ipse sententiam <non> feram;
vestri arbitrii erit, utrum explicationes eius luxuriosas putetis
an vegetas. Pollio Asinius aiebat hoc non esse suadere, sed
ludere. recolo nihil fuisse me iuvene tam notum quam has explicationes Fusci, quas nemo nostrum non alius alia inclinatione vocis
velut sua quisque modulatione cantabat. at quia semel in mentionem
incidi Fusci, ex omnibus suasoriis celebres descriptiunculas subtexam, etiamsi nihil occurrerit, quod quisquam alius nisi suasor
dilexerit. (*Suas.* 2.10)

sed ne vos diutius infatuem, quia dixeram me Fusci Arelli explicationes subiecturum, hic finem suasoriae faciam. quarum nimius cultus et fracta compositio poterit vos offendere, cum ad meam aetatem

veneritis; interim <non> dubito, quin nunc vos ipsa, quae offensura sunt, vitia delectent. (*Suas*. 2.23)

et quia soletis mihi molesti esse de Fusco, quid fuerit, quare
nemo videretur dixisse cultius, ingeram vobis Fuscinas explicationes. (*Suas*. 4.5)

The passages which are referred to here as presenting *explicationes* are *Suas*. 2.1f., 3.1 and 5.1ff.; all of which, though not
wholly descriptive, *contain* descriptions.[34] That it is quite
possible that when the elder Seneca uses *explicatio* he is referring
to the descriptive elements within the extracts, rather than to
the extracts themselves, is evident from the way in which, to vary
his terminology, he uses *descriptio* in a parallel passage, when
referring forward to another, not wholly descriptive, Fuscine
extract (*Suas*. 4.1ff.):

iam, <si> vultis, ad Fuscum revertar et descriptionibus eius vos
statim satiabo, ac potissimum eis quas in simili huius tractatione
posuit, cum diceret omnino non concessam futurorum scientiam.
(*Suas*. 3.7 W)

If this reasoning is correct, the slow-moving, empty *explicationes*
which the imagined good declaimer of *Contr*. III pr. 7 avoids, are
verbose descriptive passages. It was not only in descriptions,
however, that Seneca disliked verbosity.

Seneca's preference for fiery agitation did not prevent him
completely from appreciating richness and fluency of language.
Rather he deplored the inability of those declaimers whose style
was notable for *copia* and *facultas* to exercise control over their
material. Thus he does not object to Albucius' copious use of
language, which left one with no complaint about the deficiencies
of Latin: *non posses de inopia sermonis Latini queri, cum illum
audires*[35] (*Contr*. VII pr. 3); but he does complain about the over-
discursive philosophizing to which he was prone in his private
declamations (*ibid*. 1) and his habit of developing each *quaestio*
as if it were a *controversia* in itself (*ibid*. 2). Similarly,
after acknowledging Haterius' remarkable services to the Latin
language: *solus omnium Romanorum, quos modo ipse cognovi, in
Latinam linguam transtulit Graecam facultatem* (*Contr*. IV pr. 7),
he finds much to censure in this declaimer, who warranted comparison with a muddy torrent (*ibid*. 11),[36] being both excessively
rapid in his delivery (*ibid*. 7) and totally unable to gauge when

he had said enough about any topic (*ibid.* 8). A type of repetitiveness particularly associated with the declaimer Votienus
Montanus[37] is castigated as a *vitium* in *Contr.* IX.5.17.

Seneca disapproved of extreme sparseness and brevity as well
as excesses of loquaciousness. Latro as a schoolboy had so taken
exception to the *exilitas* of his teacher Marullus' style that he
went as far as to interpolate *sententiae* into his argumentation
while he was declaiming to the class (*Contr.* I pr. 22). Seneca,
likewise a pupil of Marullus, calls this master *hominem satis
aridum* (*ibid.*), and he can be scornful of *aridi declamatores* in
general (*Contr.* II.1.24). We have seen how he observed that the
inopia of Cestius' Latin prevented him from imitating poetic
models successfully (*Contr.* VII.1.27). He is critical too of the
obscureness which results from extreme brevity, a fault which
marred the declamations of Fabianus, and was still occasionally
to be found in his philosophical works, in which *quaedam tam
subito desinunt, ut non brevia sint, sed abrupta* (*Contr.* II pr.
2).

Inaequalitas is mentioned as a fault of style in *Contr.* II
pr. 1. It emerges from Seneca's criticism elsewhere that he did
realize that the declaimer needed to vary his tone to some extent;
what he was averse to was the juxtaposition of totally opposed
styles within a declamation. When considering Seneca's views on
colores we have seen how he occasionally displays a concern that
the declaimer should not adopt a tone inappropriate to the characters involved in the case at issue;[38] he ponders whether some
words quoted in *Contr.* I.8.16 were not too high-flown for *pressa
et civilis oratio*, and, like Latro (*Contr.* VII.4.6), is in favour
of a certain restraint in the use of language when women are concerned (*Contr.* I.2.21). We have noted also[39] how Latro recommended
a change of *compositio* when one's *epilogus* was given over to a
plea for mercy (*Contr.* VII.4.6). But Seneca seems to have believed quite strongly that a man should basically have one style
and keep to it. He is critical of the way in which Albucius, inconsistent through lack of self-confidence, ranged through all the
genera dicendi known to him, and ended up a worse declaimer than
he had originally been:

nulla erat fiducia ingenii sui et ideo adsidua mutatio; itaque dum genera dicendi transfert et modo exilis esse volt nudisque rebus haerere, modo horridus et valens potius quam cultus, modo brevis et concinnus, modo nimis se attollit, modo nimis se deprimit, ingenio suo inlusit et longe deterius senex dixit quam iuvenis dixerat. (*Contr.* VII pr. 5)

In particular he finds fault with the uncomfortable combination in Albucius' declamations of the *supervacuus strepitus* characteristic of the schools, with the *verba sordida* of old-fashioned forensic oratory. It is not clear, though, that Albucius actually juxtaposed passages in completely different styles within the same declamation. This was a practice particularly characteristic of Fuscus, whose habit of delivering his *principia*, *argumenta* and *narrationes* in a dry style, but of indulging in all manner of syntactical complication and audacity of diction in his *descriptiones*, is so vividly recalled in *Contr.* II pr. 1.[40]

The Fuscine manner was perhaps the most important rival to the *genus dicendi ardens et concitatum*. It seems to have supplanted the Latronian ideal in the favour of the scholastics in the later first century A.D., and even to have come to influence oratory outside the schools. At least, when Quintilian refers in IV.3.1ff.[41] to the practice of separating the plain style of the *narratio* from the pugnacity of the argumentation by means of a flowery digression, he declares that this custom was followed by most people (*plerisque*), and, though it was in origin a product of declamatory ostentation, it had now entered the forum. Seneca realized the importance of Fuscus as a declaimer, awarding him, together with Albucius, a place in his *primum tetradeum*. But predictably, it is to Latro, along with Gallio, another master of consistent sententiousness[42] - of whom, unfortunately, we have no full critical appraisal in Seneca's extant books - that he assigns the highest honours: *hi quotiens conflixissent, penes Latronem gloria fuisset, penes Gallionem palma* (*Contr.* X pr. 13).

VITIOSA: SOME GENERAL TERMS DENOTING BAD TASTE

Frequently in his surveys of the declamations Seneca pauses to give his verdict whether or not a particular *sententia* is in good taste. In criticizing the bad he often uses the words *corruptus*,

corrupte, *corrumpere*, and occasionally also *cacozelia*, *cacozelōs*.
It seems worth demonstrating to what extent his judgements fall
into line with the criteria for distinguishing *corrupti generis
oratio* set out by his son in *Ep. mor.* 114.1, and the account of
cacozelon given by Quintilian in VIII.3.56-8.

In *Ep. mor.* 114.1 the younger Seneca undertakes to answer a
query of Lucilius as to the cause of the popularity at certain
times of various types of corrupt style:

Quare quibusdam temporibus provenerit corrupti generis oratio
quaeris et quomodo in quaedam vitia inclinatio ingeniorum facta
sit, ut aliquando inflata explicatio vigeret, aliquando infracta
et in morem cantici ducta; quare alias sensus audaces et fidem
egressi placuerint, alias abruptae sententiae et suspiciosae, in
quibus plus intellegendum esset quam audiendum; quare aliqua aetas
fuerit quae translationis iure uteretur inverecunde.

Describing the vice *cacozelon* in VIII.3.56-8 Quintilian appears to
equate it with *corrupta oratio*: both comprise a wide range of
stylistic faults, but do not include *rerum vitia*.

cacozelon, <id> est mala adfectatio, per omne dicendi genus
peccat; nam et tumida et pusilla et praedulcia et abundantia et
arcessita et exultantia sub idem nomen cadunt. denique cacozelon
vocatur quidquid est ultra virtutem, quotiens ingenium iudicio
caret et specie boni fallitur, omnium in eloquentia vitiorum
pessimum: nam cetera parum vitantur, hoc petitur. est autem totum
in elocutione. nam rerum vitia sunt stultum commune contrarium
supervacuum: corrupta oratio in verbis maxime inpropriis, redund-
antibus, compressione obscura, compositione fracta, vocum similium
aut ambiguarum puerili captatione consistit. est autem omne cacozelon utique falsum, etiam si non omne falsum cacozelon: †et†
dicitur aliter quam se natura habet et quam oportet et quam sat
est. totidem autem generibus corrumpitur oratio quot ornatur.

But the faults of content, *stultum*, *commune*, *contrarium* and *supervacuum*,[43] are not the only *vitia* Quintilian distinguishes from
cacozelon, which is only one item in a long list he gives of
possible departures from appropriate *ornatus*, the others being:
cacemphaton/*deformitas* (VIII.3.44ff.); ταπείνωσις/*humilitas* (48f.);
ἔλλειψις - *cum sermoni deest aliquid, quo minus plenus sit* (50f.);
ὁμοείδεια - *quae nulla varietatis gratia levat taedium* (52);
macrologia and *pleonasmos* (53f.); *periergia* (55); *male dispositum*/
ἀνοικονόμητον (59); *male figuratum*/ἀσχημάτιστον (*ibid.*); *male
conlocatum*/κακοσύνθετον (*ibid.*); Σαρδισμός (*ibid.*) and the related
vice in Latin of mixing different types of diction, *sublimia
humilibus, vetera novis, poetica vulgaribus* (60). Just why

Quintilian should have distinguished some of these faults from
cacozelon is not self-evident: it seems inconsistent to distinguish
macrologia, *pleonasmos* and *periergia* from *cacozelon* and then to
list *abundantia* among the species of this last-named fault; to
mention *compositio fracta* as a form of *corrupta oratio*, and then
to include κακοσύνθετον as a distinct item in the continuation of
his list of *inornata*.[44] It looks very much as though Quintilian
is presenting in this section on departures from *ornatus* a con-
flation of two traditions, in one of which *cacozelon* was used to
cover all aspects of stylistic bad taste, *quidquid est ultra
virtutem*, and another in which it was given some more restricted
meaning, and so could be named as one item in a long list of
faults of style.[45]

Seneca and Quintilian agree in classing as species of
corrupta oratio or *cacozelon* the following faults: tumidity
(Seneca: *inflata*; Quintilian: *tumida*, *abundantia*, *verbis...redund-
antibus*); the abuse of metaphors (Seneca: *translationis iure
uteretur inverecunde*; Quintilian: *verbis...inpropriis*); effeminacy
in the rhythmic arrangement of words (Seneca: *explicatio...in-
fracta et in morem cantici ducta*; Quintilian: *compositione fracta*);
the expression of far-fetched ideas (Seneca: *sensus audaces et
fidem egressi*; Quintilian: *arcessita*); obscurity arising from excessive concision (Seneca: *abruptae sententiae et suspiciosae, in
quibus plus intellegendum esset quam audiendum*; Quintilian: *compressione obscura*). Quintilian mentions some other species in
addition.

Similarly in the elder Seneca's criticism *corruptus* and its
cognates are used with reference to a wide range of faults.
Corrupte is used as the opposite of *bene* in *Contr.* IX.2.21, *ex
altera parte multa bene dicta sunt, multa corrupte...*, and of
pulchre in *Contr.* X.4.18, *multa ab illis pulchre dicta sunt...
multa corrupte*. Cassius Severus uses *corruptius* as virtually
equivalent to *peius* in *Contr.* III pr. 15: *non illi peius dicunt,
sed hi corruptius iudicant*. In *Contr.* IX.2.27 Seneca affirms his
intention to show *quid vitandum sit* by recording *omnia...genera
corruptarum...sententiarum*. The use of the verb *corrumpere* may
be illustrated by *Contr.* IX.5.17: *habet hoc Montanus vitium:*

*sententias suas repetendo corrumpit; dum non est contentus unam
rem semel bene dicere, efficit ne bene dixerit.*

The term *sanus* is sometimes used as the opposite of *corruptus*,
and *insanire* to denote the activity of writing in a 'corrupt'
manner: *et volebam vos experiri non adiciendo iudicium meum nec
separando a corruptis sana; potuisset* [*et*] *enim fieri ut vos magis
illa laudaretis quae insaniunt* (*Suas.* 1.16); *corruptissimam rem
omnium quae umquam dictae sunt ex quo homines diserti insanire
coeperunt* (*ibid.* 12). In *Contr.* IX.2.27f. the synonymous terms
insania and *furor* are used with reference to corrupt style; this
passage also serves to illustrate the close connection in the
elder Seneca's mind between the concepts of *corruptum* and *cacozelia*:

sed ne hoc genus furoris protegere videar, in Flaminino tumidissime dixit Murredius[46]...omnia autem genera corruptarum quoque
sententiarum de industria pono, quia facilius et quid imitandum et
quid vitandum sit docemur exemplo. ecce et illud genus cacozeliae
est quod amaritudinem verborum quasi adgravaturam res petit...et
illud quod Saenianus dixit habet sui generis insaniam... (*Contr.*
IX.2.27f. W)

Criticisms in which the elder Seneca uses the terms *corruptus*,
corrupte, *corrumpere*; *insania*, *insanus*, *insanire*; *furor*, *furiose*;
and *cacozelia*, *cacozelōs*,[47] can be used to illustrate all the main
points in the analyses of corrupt style given by Seneca the
Younger and Quintilian.

To consider first tumidity, the use of the synonyms *tumidus*
and *inflatus* in connection with *corruptus* is well exemplified by
Maecenas' remarks on Dorion's paraphrase of Homer in *Suas.* 1.12.[48]
It seems that two types of faulty expression were considered tumid
by Seneca the Elder: not just redundance, but also the bombastic
use of tropes and *verba impropia*.[49] In *Contr.* IX.2.27 one of the
examples of tumidity, the *genus furoris* represented by Murredius
in his treatment of this *controversia* (*tumidissime dixit*) is a
tetracolon with a last member which Seneca considered redundant:[50]
*serviebat forum cubiculo, praetor meretrici, carcer convivio, dies
nocti.* One of several things wrong with the last[51] of the utterances by Musa which are described in *Contr.* X pr. 9 as *ad
ultimum tumorem perducta, ut non extra sanitatem sed extra naturam
essent*, is the redundant use of circumlocutions: *quidquid avium*

volitat, quidquid piscium natat, quidquid ferarum discurrit,
nostris sepelitur ventribus. quaere nunc cur subito moriamur:
mortibus vivimus. But other quotations which Seneca considers
tumid seem objectionable not so much because of redundance – they
may even be quite concise – as on account of the perverse avoidance of plain language and the abuse of various tropes. Maecenas'
reason for describing as *tumidum* and *inflatum* Dorion's Homeric
paraphrase, ὄρους ὄρος ἀποσπᾶται...καὶ χειρία βάλλεται νῆσος, was
that his use of hyperbolic language lacked the restraint which was
so admirable in Virgil's poetry:[52] *haec quo modo ex corruptis eo*
perveniant ut et magna et tamen sana sint aiebat Maecenas apud
Vergilium intellegi posse; he quoted to illustrate his point
Virgil's *haud partem exiguam montis* (*Aen.* X.128) and *credas innare*
revolsas|Cycladas (*Aen.* VIII.691f.).[53] In *Contr.* X pr. 9 Seneca
cites as illustrations of Musa's *tumor* a series of far-fetched
metaphors: *caelo repluunt, odoratos imbres, caelatas silvas,*
nemora surgentia,[54] as well as the invective against meat-eating
quoted above, which contains, besides a certain amount of redundance, a far-fetched funerary metaphor, *nostris sepelitur*
ventribus, and a grotesque use of metonymy,[55] *mortibus* (rather
than *mortuis*) *vivimus.* Another sentence by Murredius, *praetorem*
nostrum in illa ferali cena saginatum meretricis sinu excitavit
ictus securis, deemed very tumid by Seneca in *Contr.* IX.2.27,
includes another bold use of funerary language in an unexpected
context (*ferali cena*, with reference to a banquet at which an
execution took place); the application of the term *saginatum*
(fattened up) to a human being offends against classical standards
of restraint in metaphor; Murredius' notion that the praetor was
only roused by the fall of the executioner's axe made heavy demands on his listeners' credulity.[56] In regarding both redundance
and misuse of tropes as species of tumidity Seneca the Elder appears to differ from his son who distinguishes the improper use of
metaphor (his fifth species of *corrupti generis oratio*) from
inflata explicatio which is listed first in *Ep. mor.* 114.1.[57]

    Next in the younger Seneca's list comes *explicatio...infracta*
et in morem cantici ducta (cf. Quint. VIII.3.57 *compositione*
fracta). As we have seen, the elder Seneca in his youth had

enjoyed chanting the *explicationes* of Arellius Fuscus to various
melodies (*Suas.* 2.10), but he makes it clear in *Suas.* 2.23 that he
no longer admired the *fracta conpositio* of the passages which inspired such chanting:

quarum nimius cultus et fracta conpositio poterit vos offendere
cum ad meam aetatem veneritis; interim <non> dubito quin nunc vos
ipsa quae offensura sunt vitia delectent.

Vibius Gallus, who opened his descriptions *paene cantantis modo* by
proclaiming '*amorem*', or whatever, '*describere volo*', earns criticism in *Contr.* II.1.25 for deliberately imitating insane stylists
(*insanos*), as if *insania* and *furor* were desirable. Perhaps it was
the affected rhythm which Seneca deemed corrupt when Glycon began
an evocation of the discordant music of beggars' cries with the
words, ἄγε, σὺ δὲ κλαῖε, σὺ δὲ θρήνει. (*Contr.* X.4.22)

   There is no shortage of *sensus audaces et fidem egressi*, to
use the younger Seneca's terms, among the *sententiae* which his
father and the critics quoted by him consider corrupt or insane.
Maecenas finds it admirable that, unlike Dorion, the author of the
corrupt and tumid paraphrase of Homer quoted in *Suas.* 1.12,
Virgil, when treating similar subject-matter, *ita magnitudini
studet <ut> non inprudenter discedat a fide.* In *Contr.* X.5[58]
Seneca designates two *sententiae* as corrupt or insane expressly
because they are based on incredible or impossible presuppositions:

Sparsi sententia in descriptione picturae habet aliquid corrupti:
'et, ubicumque sanguine opus est, humano utitur'; dixit enim quod
fieri non potest. (*Contr.* X.5.23)

Spyridion honeste <dixisse> Romanos fecit; multo enim vehementius
insanit quam nostri phrenetici. voluit videri volturios ad
tabulam Parrhasi advolare...aeque familiariter in templum
volturios subire putavit quam passeres aut columbas; dixit enim:
σαρκοφάγα σοῦ γ' ἡ γραφὴ ἥπατα ζῷα. (*Ibid.* 27-8)

The theme of *Suas.* 2[59] inspired both *audaces sensus* about writing
in blood and impossible claims about the victory of dead Spartans;
insanire and *cacozelos* are among the terms used to criticize them:

insanierunt in hac suasoria multi circa Othryadem: Murredius, qui
dixit: fugerunt Athenienses; non enim Othryadis nostri litteras
didicerant. Gargonius dixit, Othryades, qui perit ut falleret,
revixit ut vinceret. Licinius Nepos: cum exemplo vobis etiam
mortuis vincendum fuit. Antonius Atticus inter has puerilis
sententias videtur palmam meruisse; dixit enim: Othryades paene a
sepulchro victor digitis vulnera pressit ut trophaeo †Laconem†
inscriberet. o dignum Spartano atramentum! o virum, cuius ne

litterae quidem fuere sine sanguine! Catius Crispus, municipalis
<rhetor>, cacozelos dixit post relatum exemplum Othryadis: aliud
ceteros, aliud Laconas decet; nos sine deliciis educamur, sine
muris vivimus, sine vita vincimus. (*Suas*. 2.16 W)

The term *arcessita*, used by Quintilian in his analysis of *cacozelon* to denote far-fetched expressions, is not paralleled in the
elder Seneca's criticisms of the style and content of *sententiae*,
but he uses the expression *longe arcessito colore* in *Contr*. I.6.9,
and *longe arcessere* with reference to *exempla* in *Contr*. VII.5.13.

The elder Seneca's view of allusive brevity seems to have
been that *explicationes...plus sensuum quam verborum habentes*
(*Contr*. III pr. 7) were commendable in declamation (in this respect his critical position differs from that of his son in *Ep.
mor*. 114.1), but that obscurity was a fault which well deserved
the name of *furor*. In *Contr*. II pr. 2 he observes how Fabianus'
style long after his philosophical conversion was still marred by
the obscurity and abruptness he had learnt to cultivate in the
school of Fuscus; in his view these qualities were *vitia*:

...luxuriam quidem cum voluit abiecit, obscuritatem non potuit
evadere; haec illum usque in philosophiam prosecuta est. saepe
minus quam audienti satis est eloquitur, et in summa eius ac
simplicissima facultate dicendi antiquorum tamen vitiorum remanent
vestigia. quaedam tam subito desinunt, ut non brevia sint, sed
abrupta. (*Contr*. II pr. 2)

In *Contr*. IX.2.26f. he does not hesitate to follow Livy and the
rhetorician Miltiades in regarding the obscurity sought after by
archaizers as just as much a variety of *furor* as the opposite vice
of redundance:

Livius de oratoribus qui verba antiqua et sordida consectantur et
orationis obscuritatem severitatem putant aiebat Miltiaden
rhetorem eleganter dixisse: ἐπὶ τὸ δεξιὸν μαίνονται. tamen in his
etiamsi minus est insaniae minus spei est; illi qui tument, illi
qui abundantia laborant, plus habent furoris, sed plus et corporis;
semper autem ad sanitatem proclivius est quod potest detractione
curari; illi succurri non potest qui simul et insanit et deficit.
sed ne hoc genus furoris protegere videar, in Flaminino tumidissime dixit Murredius...

The views expressed by Livy and Miltiades should be compared with
the reference to the Attic fever of the archaizer Annius Cimber in
ps.-Verg. *Catal*. 2.[60] It may be appropriate to note at this point
that another feature of style which the elder Seneca rather surprisingly described as a kind of *cacozelia* was that mainstay of

the old-fashioned prosecutor, the use of harsh diction for vilification:[61]

ecce et illud genus cacozeliae est, quod amaritudinem verborum quasi adgravaturam res petit; ut in hac controversia Licinius Nepos dixit: reus damnatus est legi, perit fornici. (*Contr.* IX. 2.28)

Puerile word-play was regarded as a form of corrupt style by the elder Seneca as well as Quintilian, who complains of *vocum similium aut ambiguarum puerili captatione* in VIII.3.57 along with the other vices which we have been considering. In *Suas.* 7.11 we are told that a certain declaimer, whose name has accidentally dropped out of the text,

dixit...sententiam cacozeliae genere humillimo et sordidissimo, quod detractu aut adiectione syllabae facit sensum: 'pro facinus indignum! peribit ergo quod Cicero scripsit, manebit quod Antonius proscripsit?'

The craze for 'Publilian' *sententiae* is described as an *insania* by Moschus in *Contr.* VII.3.8.

The theory of *corrupti generis oratio* was closely bound up, as we see from Sen. *Ep. mor.* 114, with the discussion of the causes of the decline of Roman eloquence, which seems to have been an echo of earlier Greek theorizing about the corruption of oratory after Athens, along with the other city-states, lost her independence. For this reason, if for no other, it might seem safe enough to conjecture that the theory of corrupt eloquence in all its details had been imported into Latin criticism by the Atticists of Cicero's time, concerned as we know them to have been with the imitation of Greek orators belonging to the time before this decline set in. Besides, the interesting point emerges from a consideration of the elder Seneca's use of the terms *corruptus*, *corrumpere* in connection with *cacozelia* and *insania* and their cognates, that in his time *corruptum* was regarded as the opposite of *sanum* and *sanitas*. One remembers that the words *sanitas* and *insania* figure in Cicero's critique of the Atticists in the *Brutus* (82.284) and are commonly believed to have been favourite slogans of these anti-Ciceronians.[62]

Actually the truth of the matter may be much more complicated. If the reports of Tacitus and Quintilian on Cicero's *obtrectatores* are based on genuine correspondence,[63] Cicero certainly was

accused by contemporary critics, including Calvus and Brutus, of a
number of the faults which later critics considered species of
cacozelon or *corruptum*:

satis constat ne Ciceroni quidem obtrectatores defuisse, quibus
inflatus et tumens nec satis pressus sed supra modum exultans et
superfluens et parum Atticus videretur. legistis utique et Calvi
et Bruti ad Ciceronem missas epistulas, ex quibus facile est
deprehendere Calvum quidem Ciceroni visum exsanguem et attritum,
Brutum autem otiosum atque diiunctum, rursusque Ciceronem a Calvo
quidem male audisse tamquam solutum et enervem, a Bruto autem, ut
ipsius verbis utar, tamquam fractum atque elumbem. (Tac. *Dial.*
18.4ff.)

at M. Tullium...habemus...in omnibus quae in quoque laudantur
eminentissimum. quem tamen et suorum homines temporum incessere
audebant ut tumidiorem et Asianum et redundantem et in repetitio-
nibus nimium et in salibus aliquando frigidum et in compositione
fractum, exultantem ac paene, quod procul absit, viro molliorem...
(Quint. XII.10.12)

But nowhere is it made clear that these critics who considered
Cicero *parum Atticus* grouped the faults of which they accused him
together in a comprehensive theory of *cacozelon* or *corrupta oratio*.
And, probable though it is that *sanitas* and *insania* were used in
Latin Atticist criticism of the late Republic, the only thing
proved about the use of these words in Cic. *Brut.* 82.284 is that
they were terms acceptable to Cicero. For in this passage, far
from rejecting *sanitas* as an ideal, Cicero uses the term in a
description of a hypothetical type of Atticism to which he himself
would not be averse:

nam si quis eos qui nec inepte dicunt nec odiose nec putide Attice
putat dicere, is recte nisi Atticum probat neminem. insulsitatem
enim et insolentiam tamquam insaniam quandam orationis odit,
sanitatem autem et integritatem quasi religionem et verecundiam
oratoris probat.[64]

Cicero also recognizes in *Brut.* 55.202 that *inflatum et corruptum*
were faults to be avoided by any orator who favoured a copious
style. The fact may be that the notions of *sanitas* and *corruptum*
had already been established in Latin literary criticism so long
that, no matter what ideals of style a critic might believe in, he
would find it difficult to avoid using these terms completely, but
was free to reinterpret them according to his taste, and might
place as much or as little emphasis on them as he pleased.[65]

Cicero uses such terms very sparingly,[66] usually without

strong technical overtones,[67] and never presents us with a fully
worked out theory of *corrupti generis oratio* or *cacozelia*. This
may be because the critics who attacked him were in his view over-
fond of these concepts, though we cannot be sure. He actually
seems to have succeeded in never using in all his *Rhetorica* one
type of abusive term they used against him, *tumens*, *tumidus*, *tumor*;
he also seems to have avoided using *inflatus* in a derogatory sense,
and only to have lapsed from his resolve in *Brut.* 55.202, where it
is used in conjuction with *corruptus*.

Cicero's position seems to have been that, though *sanitas* was
an admirable ideal and *corruptum* was to be avoided in diction and
style, his tastes in *sanitas* and *incorruptum* were less narrowly
restricted than those of some of his contemporaries. It is well
known that after *Brut.* 82.284 Cicero moves on from expressing
general assent to the principle that Attic *sanitas* was admirable,
into a tirade in which he points out the diversity of styles
within Attic oratory, and in particular argues the case for preferring Demosthenes to Lysias. His usage of the term *incorruptum*
provides interesting further testimony of the catholicity of
Cicero's tastes: he finds this quality in the language, unaffected
by modern developments, sometimes preserved by women (*De or.* III.
12.45); in the critical taste of Athenians (*Or.* 8.25); in philosophical writing (*ibid.* 19.64); in the style of Attic orators as
late as Hyperides, Aeschines, Lycurgus, Dinarchus and Demades
(*Brut.* 9.36); in the diction of Q. Catulus (*ibid.* 35.132).

Quintilian maintains in VIII.3.57 that *cacozelon* and *corrupta
oratio* comprise only faults of *elocutio*, not the *rerum vitia*:
stultum, *commune*, *contrarium*, *supervacuum*.[68] This distinction, if
known to Seneca the Elder, was not observed by him with total
rigidity. Indeed, it is a somewhat unreal distinction, for
arcessita and *sensus audaces et fidem egressi* are objectionable
for their content more than for their style and yet are regarded
as species of *cacozelon* and *corrupti generis oratio*. And *stultus*
was a term with such wide connotations in non-literary contexts
that it would be unrealistic to expect its usage to be confined
within narrow bounds in literary criticism. Together with such

terms as *fatuus* and *ineptus* and the nouns *stupor* and *ineptiae*,[69]
it was obviously handy for the criticism of such varieties of
cacozelia as the trivial word-play of 'Publilian' *sententiae*.
Nevertheless there seem to be certain contexts in which the elder
Seneca always uses such terms as *stultus*, *fatuus*, *ineptus* in preference to *corruptus*, *insanus*, *cacozelia*, namely with reference to
incredible *colores*, futile legal quibbling, *contrarium*, and the
related fault of anachronism, all faults of *inventio* rather than
elocutio, or, to use Quintilian's terms, *rerum vitia*.[70]

That the terms *stultus* and *ineptus* were applied to much the
same range of failings is best illustrated by *Contr.* VII.5.8-11 W:

circa vulnus novercae[71] quidam bellas res dixerunt, quidam ineptas...
prius illa quae belle dicta sunt referam...(10) ex illis qui res
ineptas dixerant primus ibi ante omnis Musa voster, qui cum vulnus
novercae descripsisset adiecit: at, hercules, pater meus tamquam
paries perfossus est. Murredius: patrocinium putat esse causae
suae quod sanguinem misit. Nepos Licinius ait: non est istud
vulnus, sed ludentis adulteri morsus. Saenianus ex illa stultorum
nota sententiam protulit: non vulneravit, inquit, novercam sed
viri sui sanguine aspersit; cum illa vulnerata ponatur. Vinicius,
exactissimi vir ingeni, qui nec dicere res ineptas nec ferre
poterat, solebat hanc sententiam Saeniani deridere...: nihil puero
est teste certius, utique quinquenni; nam et ad eos pervenit annos
ut intellegat, et nondum ad eos quibus fingat. haec finitio,
inquit, ridicula est: 'nihil est puero teste certius, utique quinquenni'; puta nec si quadrimus puer testis est nec si sex annorum.
illud venustissime adiciebat: putes, inquit, aliquid agi: omnia in
hac sententia circumspecti hominis sunt, finitio, exceptio; nihil
est autem amabilius quam diligens stultitia.

An equation between *fatuus* and *ineptus* is to be found in *Contr.*
VII.4.3:

Buteo fatuam quaestionem moverat primam: an lex quae de alendis
parentibus lata esset ad patres tantum pertineret. illis omnia
privilegia data et ipsam poenam non alentium signum esse non
muliebris potestatis. res est ineptior quam ut coarguenda sit...

The overlapping of his usage of *stultus*, *ineptus*, *fatuus* and
their cognates, with that of such words as *corrumpere* and *insania*
can be seen in *Contr.* IX.6.11:

Triarius multo rem magis ineptam, quia non invenit illam sed
conrupit...

and *Contr.* X.5.24f.:

sed si vultis audire supra quod non possit procedere insania,
Licinius Nepos ait: si vultis digne punire Parrhasium, ipse se
pingat. non minus stulte Aemilianus quidam Graecus rhetor, quod

genus stultorum amabilissimum est, ex arido fatuus dixit: ἀπο-
κτείνατε Παρράσιον, μὴ θελήσας γράφειν ἐξ ὑμῶν ἀρχέτυπον εὕρῃ.

Cases where the terms *stupor*, *fatuus*, and *stultus* are applied
to *sententiae* of the 'Publilian' sort are to be found in:

Contr. VII.2.14: et Murredius non est passus hanc controversiam
transire sine aliqua stuporis sui nota. descripsit enim ferentem
caput et manum Ciceronis Popillium et Publilianum dedit: Popilli,
quanto aliter reus Ciceronis <tangebas caput> et tenebas manum
eius!

Contr. VII.5.15: Murredius mimico genere fatuam sententiam dixit,
cum dixisset novercam disputare contra filii sui testimonium:
facit, inquit, quod solet: pro amatore sanguini suo non parcit.

Suas. 7.14: Gargonius, <fatuorum>[72]* amabilissimus, in hac suasoria dixit duas res quibus stultiores ne ipse quidem umquam
dixerat; unam in principio: nam, cum coepisset scholasticorum
frequentissimo iam more a iureiurando et dixisset multa †ita quam
primum tantum timeat†[73]* quantum potest, 'ita aut totus vivat
Cicero aut totus moriatur ut ego quae hodie pro Ciceronis ingenio
dixero nulla pactione delebo.' alteram rem dixit, cum exempla
referret eorum qui fortiter perierant: 'Iuba et Petreius mutuis
vulneribus concucurrerunt et mortes faeneraverunt.'

The second of the quotations in this last passage may be compared
with the 'Publilian' *sententiae* of Murredius quoted in *Contr.* VII.
3.8: *abdicationes, inquit, suas veneno diluit; et iterum: mortem,
inquit, meam effudit.* The other one is not so easily classified;
it comes closest to the type of writing criticized elsewhere for
tumidity. Hence Shackleton Bailey's ingenious conjecture, *ait, ut
quam primum tantum tumeat, quantum potest,*[74]* seems to point in
the right direction; note that the *sententia* in question came near
the beginning of Gargonius' declamation.

Unreasonable questioning of the established interpretation of
a law is criticized in a passage (*Contr.* VII.4.3) which has already
been quoted to illustrate the use of *fatuus* and *ineptus* in close
conjunction.[75] It seems relevant to compare Quintilian's dictum
in V.12.8: *in rebus vero apertis argumentari tam sit stultum quam
in clarissimum solem mortale lumen inferre.*

Unconvincing ingenuity in the invention of *colores* is castigated with words denoting stupidity on a number of occasions. Two
passages concerning Murredius' habitual foolishness in the choice
of *colores* (*Contr.* VII.3.8: *Murredius pro cetero suo stupore...;*
Contr. IX.4.22: *Murredius non degeneravit in hac controversia; nam
colorem stultissimum induxit*) have already been quoted in another

connection.[76]   Other good examples of stupid and inept *colores* are
found in:

Contr. I.3.11 (on the priestess thrown from the cliff)

Othonem Iunium patrem memini colorem stultum inducere, quod eo
minus ferendum est quod libros colorum edidit. 'fortasse' inquit
'poenae se praeparavit, et ex quo peccare coepit cadere condidi-
cit.'

Contr. IX.2.20 (on the execution at Flamininus' banquet)

Triarius ineptum introduxit colorem: sermo erat, inquit, in convivio contemni nimiam praetoris lenitatem; alios fuisse pro-
consules, qui cotidie animadverterent, huius anno nullum esse
occisum. dixit aliquis ex convivis: 'ego numquam [iratus] <vidi
hominem occidi>.' dixit et mulier: 'et ego numquam.' iratus quod
clementia sua contemptui esset, 'curabo' inquit 'sciant non deesse
mihi <severitatem.' adducitur> sceleratus, quem videre lucem
ultra non oportet.

(Cf. also *Contr.* I.4.7; VII.7.14.)

Seneca never seems to use *corruptus*, *insania*, *cacozelia* and their
cognates with reference to *colores*.

The fault of *contrarium*, the making of statements contrary to
the given facts of the case, or to one's own interests,[77] could be
committed in a *sententia* which was also 'corrupt' (tumid and far-
fetched):

illud Sparsus dixit quod non corruptum tantum sed contrarium
dicebat esse Montanus: 'solus plura habes membra quam tot hominibus
reliquisti.' ita enim hic potest videri laesisse rem publicam[78]
si multi sunt debilitati; apparet autem non esse multos si plura
habet membra quam debilitatis reliquit. et illud aeque aiebat ab
illo corrupte dictum: 'prodierunt plures mendici quam membra.'
(*Contr.* X.4.23)

But *inepte* and *stultus* are the words used to criticize errors of
this type in *Contr.* I.6.11 and VII.5.10:

Contr. I.6.10f. W (on the young man who swore to marry the pirate
chief's daughter, but is now ordered by his father to divorce her
and marry a rich orphan)

<Iulius Bassus>...adiecit iurasse se per patrem. Triarius dum
sententiam puerilem[79]* captat, inepte dixit iurasse se et per
orbam. aiebat enim Cestius male deseri hanc orbam <si per eam>
etiam iurasset. Latro aiebat <alterum> quoque iusiurandum ineptum
esse; nihil enim minus convenire quam aliquem per patrem iurare
patrem relicturae.

Contr. VII.5.10 W[80]

Saenianus ex illa stultorum nota sententiam protulit: non vulneravit, inquit, novercam sed viri sui sanguine aspersit; cum illa
vulnerata ponatur.

Triarius also laid himself open to a charge of *contrarium* when, in
his *ineptus color* about the banquet of Flamininus (*Contr.* IX.2.20),
he referred to the *meretrix* of the theme merely as a *mulier*, and
made her out to have been just a seconder of proposals for greater
proconsular severity.

The clearest case of the use of terms denoting stupidity in
the criticism of notions which conflict with the true sequence of
historical events comes in *Suas.* 2.22:

sed, si vultis, historicum quoque vobis fatuum dabo. Tuscus...cum
hanc suasoriam declamaret, dixit: 'expectemus, si nihil aliud hoc
effecturi, ne insolens barbarus dicat: veni, vidi, vici', cum hoc
post multos annos divus Iulius victo Pharnace dixerit.

The *suasoria* in question was the one about the Spartans at Thermopylae. Another declaimer tried to make a rhetorical point out of
the glorious name of Thermopylae - as if it had been possible to
do so *before* the Spartans' stand against Xerxes - and, probably
for this reason among others, was criticized for stupidity:

decentissimi[81]* generis stultam sententiam referam Victoris
Statori, municipis mei...sumpsit contradictionem: 'at' inquit
'trecenti sumus'; et ita respondit: trecenti, sed viri, sed armati,
sed Lacones, sed ad Thermopylas; numquam vidi plures trecentos.
(*Suas.* 2.18 M)

The elder Seneca's usage of the word *ineptus* in connection
with stupidity provides interesting corroboration of the statement
in Cic. *De or.* II.4.17f. that it was a word with no Greek equivalent:

quem enim nos ineptum vocamus, is mihi videtur ab hoc nomen habere
ductum, quod non sit aptus, idque in sermonis nostri consuetudine
perlate patet; nam qui aut tempus quid postulet non videt aut
plura loquitur aut se ostentat aut eorum, quibuscum est, vel
dignitatis vel commodi rationem non habet aut denique in aliquo
genere aut inconcinnus aut multus est, is ineptus esse dicitur.
hoc vitio cumulata est eruditissima illa Graecorum natio; itaque
quod vim huius mali Graeci non vident, ne nomen quidem ei vitio
imposuerunt; ut enim quaeras omnia, quomodo Graeci ineptum
appellent, non reperies. omnium autem ineptiarum, quae sunt in-
numerabiles, haud sciam an nulla sit maior quam, ut illi solent,
quocumque in loco, quoscumque inter homines visum est, de rebus
aut difficillimis aut non necessariis argutissime disputare.

Seneca the Elder makes it clear that he did not consider *ineptiae*
a monopoly of the Greeks, but he confirms the fact, implied in
these remarks in the *De oratore*, that *ineptus*, despite appearances,
was not equivalent to the Greek ἀπρεπής.

According to Quintilian (III.3.4), Albucius had advanced the her-
etical view that the art of oratory consisted of only three, not
five, parts: *memoria* and *actio* were to be excluded as being
natural gifts. Quintilian disagreed with Albucius, though he had
to concede that the opinion that *actio* was the product of natural
endowments was nothing new, but even had the support of the sophist Thrasymachus. Seneca the Elder says nothing about this theory
of Albucius, but his own position with regard to one side of the
issue is clear enough. He was convinced that memory could be
assisted by art: Latro's memory, for example, was *natura quidem
felix, plurimum tamen arte adiuta* (*Contr.* I pr. 17).

As we have seen,[1] Seneca claims in *Contr.* I pr. 2 to have
been the proud possessor in youth of a memory which verged on the
miraculous: he had been capable of remembering two thousand random
names and reproducing them in the correct sequence, and of memorizing more than two hundred assorted lines of poetry and then
reeling them back to his amazed school-fellows in reverse order.
About Latro's memory too he makes claims calculated to astound his
readers:

in illo non tantum naturalis memoriae felicitas erat, sed ars
summa et ad conprehendenda quae tenere debebat et ad custodienda,
adeo ut omnes declamationes suas, quascumque dixerat, teneret
etiam. itaque supervacuos sibi fecerat codices; aiebat se in
animo scribere. cogitata dicebat ita ut in nullo umquam verbo eum
memoria deceperit. historiarum omnium summa notitia: iubebat aliquem nominari ducem et statim eius acta cursu reddebat; adeo,
quaecumque semel in animum eius descenderant, in promptu erant.
(*Contr.* I pr. 18)

He goes on to assure his sons that there is nothing to prevent
them from achieving similar feats:

video vos, iuvenes mei, plus iusto ad hanc eius virtutem obstup-
escere; alia vos mirari in illo volo: hoc quod tantum vobis
videtur, non operosa arte tradi potest. intra exiguum paucissim-
orum dierum tempus poterit quilibet facere illud, quod Cineas
fecit, qui missus a Pyrrho legatus ad Romanos postero die novus

homo et senatum et omnem urbanam circumfusam senatui plebem
nominibus suis persalutavit; aut quod ille fecit, qui recitatum a
poeta novum carmen dixit suum esse et protinus <ex> memoria
recitavit, cum hoc ille cuius carmen erat facere non posset; aut
quod fecit Hortensius, qui a Sisenna provocatus in auctione per-
sedit per diem totum et omnes res et pretia et emptores ordine suo
argentariis recognoscentibus ita ut in nulla re falleretur,
recensuit. cupitis statim discere? suspendam cupiditatem vestram
et faciam alteri beneficio locum; interim hoc vobis in quo iam
obligatus sum persolvam. (*Contr.* I pr. 19 W)

Thus he leaves the topic of memory without giving us any infor-

mation about the mnemonic technique in the efficacy of which he so

firmly believed.

It is to Cicero (*De or.* II.86.350ff.), the *Rhetorica ad*

Herennium (III.16.28ff.) and Quintilian (XI.2.1ff.) that we must

look for descriptions of the chief classical system of mnemonics.[2]

The assumption fundamental to this system was that visual images

were more easily remembered than the written word: *acerrimum...ex*

omnibus nostris sensibus esse sensum videndi (Cic. *De or.* II.87.

357). It was also noticed that the sight of places revisited had

the power to bring back to one's mind all manner of details about

the previous occasions when one had been there:

nam cum in loca aliqua post tempus reversi sumus, non ipsa
agnoscimus tantum sed etiam quae in iis fecerimus reminiscimur,
personaeque subeunt, nonnumquam tacitae quoque cogitationes in
mentem revertuntur. (Quint. XI.2.17)

The memorizer was therefore recommended to fix in his mind an

image of some complex piece of architecture:

loca discunt quam maxime spatiosa, multa varietate signata, domum
forte magnam et in multos diductam recessus. in ea quidquid
notabile est animo diligenter adfigunt, ut sine cunctatione ac
mora partis eius omnis cogitatio posset percurrere. (Quint. XI.2.
18; cf. Cic. *De or.* II.86.354; *Rhet. Her.* III.16.29ff.)

Against the background of the various parts of the imagined

building - its rooms, for example, or the spaces between its

columns - he was told to set mental pictures designed to remind

him of the various items to be memorized:

imagines sunt formae quaedam et notae et simulacra eius rei quam
meminisse volumus; quod genus equi, leonis, aquilae memoriam si
volemus habere, imagines eorum locis certis conlocare oportebit.
(*Rhet. Her.* III.16.30; cf. Cic. *De or.* II.86.354; Quint. XI.2.
19ff.)

Their arrangement in relation to the architectural background was

intended, of course, to remind him of the correct order in which
they were to be recalled (Cic. *De or*. II.86.354: *ut ordinem rerum
locorum ordo conservaret*). The items to be memorized might be
words (single words or whole lines of poetry), or events, for
example the circumstances of a crime alleged to have been committed:

duplices igitur similitudines esse debent, unae rerum, alterae
verborum. rerum similitudines exprimuntur cum summatim ipsorum
negotiorum imagines conparamus; verborum similitudines constitu-
untur cum unius cuiusque nominis et vocabuli memoria imagine
notatur. (*Rhet. Her*. III.20.33; cf. Cic. *De or*. II.86.354; Quint.
XI.2.19)

If the items to be memorized were names of concrete objects
there was no difficulty about conceiving *imagines* of them. Quintilian, though sceptical about some of the claims of the mnemonists
(XI.2.22, 24ff.), recognizes the usefulness of the visual mnemonic
system for such feats as the one which Hortensius was said to have
performed at an auction:

equidem haec ad quaedam prodesse non negaverim, ut si rerum nomina
multa per ordinem audita reddenda sint. namque in iis quae didicerunt locis ponunt res illas: mensam, ut hoc utar, in vestibulo et
pulpitum in atrio et sic cetera, deinde relegentes inveniunt ubi
posuerunt. et forsitan hoc sunt adiuti qui auctione dimissa quid
cuique vendidissent testibus argentariorum tabulis reddiderunt,
quod praestitisse Q. Hortensium dicunt. (*Ibid*. 23f.)

Rather heavier demands were made on one's imagination when abstrac-
tions had to be remembered, though for the commoner ones standard
imagines, whether invented by the memorizer himself or derived from
some theorist, could be used over and over again.[3] Quintilian
suggests two simple images to denote abstract concepts: *sit autem
signum navigationis ut ancora, militiae ut aliquid ex armis* (XI.
2.19). There were two main ways in which the memorizer could remind himself of names. The first was to conceive a picture of
some namesake of the man he wished to remember, either a famous
historical figure or one of his own friends who happened to share
the same name: *si Fabius forte sit tenendus, referamus ad illum
Cunctatorem, qui excidere non potest, aut ad aliquem amicum qui
idem vocetur* (Quint. XI.2.30). The other method was to derive an
image from the etymology of the man's name: *quod est facilius in
Apris et in Ursis et Nasone aut Crispo, ut id memoriae adfigatur*

unde sunt nomina. origo quoque aliquando declinatorum tenendi
magis causa est, ut in Cicerone, Verrio, Aurelio (ibid. 31). To
memorize a line of poetry one was required to go through some very
odd mental contortions:

cum verborum similitudines imaginibus exprimere volemus, plus
negotii suscipiemus et magis ingenium nostrum exercebimus. id nos
hoc modo facere oportebit:
    iam domum itionem reges Atridae parant.
<hunc versum meminisse si volemus, conveniet primo> in loco con-
stituere manus ad caelum tollentem Domitium cum a Regibus Marciis
loris caedatur – hoc erit 'iam domum itionem reges'; in altero
loco Aesopum et Cimbrum subornari ut ad Iphigeniam in Agamemnonem
et Menelaum – hoc erit 'Atridae parant'. hoc modo omnia verba
erunt expressa. (*Rhet. Her.* III.21.34)[4]

Some of the visual punning recommended as an aid to the memorizing
of facts in a lawsuit is equally bizarre:

rei totius memoriam saepe una nota et imagine simplici conprehend-
imus; hoc modo, ut si accusator dixerit ab reo hominem veneno
necatum et hereditatis causa factum arguerit et eius rei multos
dixerit testes et conscios esse. si hoc primum, ut ad defendendum
nobis expeditum sit, meminisse volemus, in primo loco rei totius
imaginem conformabimus; aegrotum in lecto cubantem faciemus ipsum
illum de quo agetur, si formam eius detinebimus; si eum non
agnoverimus, at aliquem aegrotum non de minimo loco sumemus, ut
cito in mentem venire possit. et reum ad lectum eius adstituemus,
dextera poculum, sinistra tabulas, medico testiculos arietinos
tendentem. hoc modo et testium et hereditatis et veneno necati
memoriam habere poterimus. (*Ibid.* 20.33)

The memorizer was supposed to form images in the same way to express the other counts against the accused, and to set each in
sequence against its architectural background (*ibid.* 16.29).

     Rival mnemonic systems existed, notably the astrological
method of Metrodorus, with its provision of three hundred and
sixty distinct *loci*, to which Quintilian refers contemptuously in
XI.2.22. But the principle that images of the items to be remembered should be set against a background was the same even here.
The detailed discussions of memory in the *Rhetorica ad Herennium*
and Quintilian's eleventh book can be relied upon as providing a
rough guide at least to the principles on which the elder Seneca's
mnemonic system must have worked, and probably more than that,
seeing that the feat of Hortensius which is mentioned in *Contr.* I
pr. 10 is associated by Quintilian with the architectural method
(XI.2.23f.). The secret behind the elder Seneca's ability in

youth to reproduce countless names or lines of poetry in sequence
is laid bare. What is not made clear is how such a mnemonic system could have been of much assistance to him in the word-for-word
memorizing of thousands of declamatory excerpts, many dealing with
the same faceless characters and stock situations. He would have
needed to go through life envisaging hieroglyphs for every brick
in Corduba. That is not to deny, however, that reports of seemingly miraculous feats of memory, however achieved, are widespread
throughout human history.[5]

There is no doubt that the memorizing of declamatory models
for imitation was encouraged in the schools of rhetoric, along
with the kind of rote-learning which provided Latro with a ready
supply of *exempla*.[6] Pupils of a traditionally-minded rhetorician
might perhaps be recommended to look to Cicero's speeches for
their models, though there was a growing tendency, deplored by
Cassius Severus, for students to learn by heart the declamations
of their teacher to the exclusion of classical exemplars; this was
the practice in the school of Cestius, where the students read no
Cicero except the speeches to which their master had composed
answers, and did not memorize even these (*Contr.* III pr. 15).
Poetic extracts were also sometimes recommended as rhetorical
models worth remembering:

P. Vinicius, summus amator Ovidi, hunc aiebat sensum disertissime
apud Nasonem Ovidium esse positum, quem ad fingendas similes
sententias aiebat memoria tenendum. occiso Achille hoc epiphonema
poni:
    quod Priamus gaudere senex post Hectora posset,
    hoc fuit.
(*Contr.* X.4.25; Ov. *Met.* XII.607f.)

Twice, however, Seneca complains that there had been during
his life-time a marked decline in the amount of memorizing customary among students of rhetoric; one result of this had been an
increase in undetected plagiarism:

quis est, qui memoriae studeat? quis est, qui non dico magnis
virtutibus, sed suis placeat? sententias a disertissimis viris
iactas facile in tanta hominum desidia pro suis dicunt et sic
sacerrimam eloquentiam, quam praestare non possunt, violare non
desinunt. (*Contr.* I pr. 10)

...memini auditorem Latronis Abronium Silonem...recitare carmen
in quo agnovimus sensum Latronis...tam diligentes tunc auditores
erant, ne dicam tam maligni, ut unum verbum surripi non posset;

at nunc cuilibet orationes in Verrem[7] tuto licet pro suis <dicere>.
(*Suas.* 2.19 W)

Orators and declaimers of Seneca's time did not always write
out their speeches and declamations in full before committing them
to memory. Extemporization was known in both fields, though total
reliance on it was not normal, and even some of the most competent
speakers suffered from a curious lack of confidence which prevented them as a rule from improvising. Haterius declaimed *admisso populo ex tempore* (*Contr.* IV pr. 7), but Albucius, that
other master of declamatory fluency, did not trust his powers of
improvisation sufficiently to use them in public: *dicebat enim
citato et effuso cursu, sed praeparatus. extemporalis illi
facultas, ut adfirmabant qui propius norant, non deerat, sed
putabat ipse sibi deesse* (*Contr.* VII pr. 2). Cassius Severus
always wrote very full notes before speaking in the courts, though
it was a remarkable fact that when forced to make an impromptu
reply to anyone he would excel himself:

sine commentario numquam dixit nec hoc commentario contentus erat,
in quo nudae res ponuntur, sed ex maxima parte perscribebatur
actio; illa quoque, quae salse dici poterant, adnotabantur; sed
cum procedere nollet nisi instructus, libenter ab instrumentis
recedebat. ex tempore coactus dicere infinito se antecedebat.
numquam non utilius erat illi deprehendi quam praeparari; sed
magis illum suspiceres, quod diligentiam non relinquebat, cum illi
tam bene temeritas cederet. (*Contr.* III pr. 6)

Some declaimers, especially beginners, must similarly have felt
the need to write out very full *commentarii* before venturing to
declaim, but there was an alternative practice which came part way
between declamation completely prepared in writing and total improvisation. Latro devoted days on end to writing (*Contr.* I pr.
14: *cum se ad scribendum concitaverat, iungebantur noctibus dies
et sine intervallo gravius sibi instabat nec desinebat, nisi defecerat*), but he does not seem to have written out full versions
of his declamations. He wrote out in full the *schemata* required
in a declamation (*Contr.* I pr. 23); he may also have written down
the *sententiae* to which he devoted whole days of practice (*ibid.*),[8]
and in the case of *enthymemata* and *epiphonemata* these must generally have been contrived with particular declamations in mind.
Latro's carefully worked-out *divisiones* also look like the product

of written preparation,[9] though we are told nothing about the way in which they were composed. Nevertheless to some extent he evidently relied on mental, unwritten, preparation: *cogitata dicebat ita, ut in nullo umquam verbo eum memoria deceperit* (*Contr.* I pr. 18). Quintilian, when weighing up the arguments for and against the written word as an aid to memory, was to reflect on the way that *quae per plures dies scribimus ediscenda sint, cogitatio se ipsa contineat* (XI.2.10). What Seneca says about the tenaciousness of Latro's memory for *cogitata* bears out the truth, at least where a gifted man was concerned, of the latter half of Quintilian's observation; Latro was also fortunate in not needing, unlike most people, to spend days memorizing what he had written, despite the fact that he was not a slow or anxious writer:

numquam ille quae dicturus erat ediscendi causa relegebat: edidicerat illa, cum scripserat. id eo magis in illo mirabile videri potest, quod non lente et anxie, sed eodem paene quod dicebat impetu scribebat. illi, qui scripta sua torquent, qui de singulis verbis in consilium eunt, necesse est quae totiens animo suo admovent novissime adfigant; at quorumcumque stilus velox est, tardior memoria est. (*Contr.* I pr. 17f.)

His memory was not only good in the short term: he could remember all his past declamations (*ibid.* 18).

It would probably be fair to surmise that declaimers varied in the extent to which they prepared their work in writing as widely as orators, whose ranks included in this period the negligent Scaurus, who used to learn the essentials of a forthcoming lawsuit while getting dressed or actually after arrival in court (*Contr.* X pr. 2), as well as the painstaking Cassius Severus, whose preparations are described in *Contr.* III pr. 6.

Pronuntiatio a plerisque actio dicitur, sed prius nomen a voce,
sequens a gestu videtur accipere. namque actionem Cicero alias
'quasi sermonem', alias 'eloquentiam quandam corporis' dicit.
idem tamen duas eius partis facit, quae sunt eaedem pronuntiati-
onis, vocem atque motum: quapropter utraque appellatione in-
differenter uti licet. (Quint. XI.3.1)

The standard view of rhetorical theorists was that *actio*,[1]
like *memoria*, was not wholly the product of the speaker's natural
gifts (e.g. Quint. III.3.1), though in the elder Seneca's day
Albucius, not without some support from earlier tradition, rejected the normal inclusion of *actio* among the five parts of
orandi ratio (*ibid.* 4). The attitudes of Seneca and Latro towards
this question seem closely comparable with those of Cicero and
Quintilian. Seneca does not deny that prior *exercitatio* of a kind
could be beneficial to the speaker's *actio*, but, in common with
the theorists, he does not wish orators to sound like actors, and
Porcius Latro is said to have rejected certain forms of vocal and
physical exercise which we know from Cicero and Quintilian to have
formed part of the training of actors and singers.

It was recognized to be an advantage for the declaimer to
have, as Latro had, a naturally strong voice (*robusta - Contr.* I
pr. 16), best of all one which combined strength with sweetness,
such as Cassius Severus possessed, *suavitas valentissimae vocis -
quamvis haec inter se raro coeant, ut eadem vox et dulcis sit et
solida* (*Contr.* III pr. 3), but it was possible to be a successful
declaimer without a perfect voice. As one critic pointed out, it
was easier to keep the attention of an audience in the schools
than to project one's voice and personality in the forum: *illic
inter fremitum consonantis turbae intendendus animus est, vox ad
aures iudicis perferenda, hic ex vultu dicentis pendent omnium
vultus...* (*Contr.* IX pr. 5).[2] Latro's success was not impeded by
the fact that his voice was not as clear as it should have been,

as a result of his contempt for training in *actio* and a tendency
to overwork, *vox robusta sed surda, lucubrationibus et neglegentia,*
non natura infuscata (*Contr.* I pr. 16). One might have thought
that Gargonius' vocal qualities would have ruled out any prospects
for him of a career in rhetoric, and yet he succeeded in becoming
master of a school: *Gargonius fuit Buteonis auditor, postea scholae*
quoque successor, vocis obtusae sed pugnacissimae, cui Barrus
scurra rem venustissimam dixit: centum raucorum vocem habes (*Contr.*
I.7.18).

A strong rib-cage was reckoned important for effective voice-
production: Latro coped with the heavy demands made on his voice
beneficio...laterum (*Contr.* I pr. 16). One way of exercising the
latera was to go for healthy walks, *latus ambulatione reparare*
(*ibid.*). This Latro neglected to do, but fortunately at various
times he had led a sufficiently active life for Seneca to be able
to say *corpus illi erat et natura solidum et multa exercitatione*
duratum... (*Contr.* I pr. 16).[3] Another exercise recommended for
the voice and similarly neglected by Latro because, according to
.Seneca, he could not unlearn *illum fortem et agrestem et Hispanae*
consuetudinis morem...: utcumque res tulerat, ita vivere (*ibid.*),
was intended to give the speaker command over all the gradations
of tone which he might require: *per gradus paulatim ab imo ad*
summum perducere...a summa contentione paribus intervallis
descendere (*ibid.*).

In order to deliver a declamation in the fiery and agitated
style one needed to muster all one's strength – *Contr.* VII pr. 1:
omnes vires advocabat [sc. Albucius] – so as to gather sufficient
impetus to carry one through. Latro found no difficulty in sum-
moning up the necessary energy, *numquam impetus ardentis animi*
deseruit (*Contr.* I pr. 16), and so, in spite of his lack of care
for his voice and physique, he was able to amaze his audiences
with sustained forcefulness – *Contr.* I.7.16: *advocavit vires suas*
tanto totius actionis impetu, ut attonitos homines tenuerit – and
to deliver the high points of his declamations *summis clamoribus*
(*Contr.* I.1.21; VII.2.9).

For violent delivery, as for agitated *compositio*, we are told
in *Contr.* VII.4.7 that Calvus provided a precedent: we are informed

that he was a *violentus actor et concitatus*, who had been known to
leave his place in court and, *impetu latus*, to run right over to
the benches of his opponents. It is also implied (*Contr.* VII.4.8)
that the *epilogus* of his *Pro Messio* could serve as an illustration
of Latro's teaching that one should desist from agitated delivery
for special effects of pathos (*Contr.* VII.4.6: *in epilogis nos de
industria vocem quoque infringere et vultum deicere et dare
operam, ne dissimilis orationi sit orator*). Cicero would have
been surprised to find his rival credited with that controlled
variability of *actio* which he had recommended for his ideal orator:
volet igitur ille qui eloquentiae principatum petet[4] *et contenta
voce atrociter dicere et summissa leniter et inclinata videri
gravis et inflexa miserabilis...* (*Or.* 17.56).

Seneca does not tell us much about the gestures which accompanied declamation beyond his reference to Latro's teaching
that the speaker's facial expression, like his voice, should accord with his subject-matter (*Contr.* VII.4.6). He mentions how
the declaimer Seneca Grandio at one juncture stood on tip-toe and
raised his hands in the air before uttering the portentous words,
gaudeo, gaudeo: totus Xerses meus erit! (*Suas.* 2.17), but as this
attempt to increase his height was but one manifestation of the
megalomania for which this individual was noted,[5] it cannot be
supposed typical of declamatory *gestus*. Much use must however
have been made in the schools of what Cicero had described as
quasi sermo corporis (*De or.* III.59.222); at any rate the gestures
of declaimers were evidently often applauded: *cum ventum est in
forum et desiit illos ad omnem gestum plausus excipere, aut deficiunt aut labant* (*Contr.* IX pr. 2). Seneca's remarks on Cassius
Severus in *Contr.* III pr. 3 show that he was well aware that impressive physical appearance (*corporis magnitudo conspicua*) could
contribute greatly to any speaker's success.

It appears that it was normal to declaim standing up (see
e.g. *Suas.* 2.17), but Albucius in his private declamations began
sitting, and only stood up when he started to feel inspired (*Contr.*
VII pr. 1). Latro's custom was to sit while giving his preliminary
plain statement of the *divisio*, before he began to declaim (*Contr.*
I pr. 21). We learn from *Contr.* IX.3.13 that some declaimers at

least changed their dress to suit the language in which they were going to declaim: *non...contenti unius linguae eloquentia, cum Latine declamaverant, toga posita sumpto pallio quasi persona mutata rediebant et Graece declamabant.*

Faults of *actio* mentioned by Seneca the Elder include, besides the raucousness of Gargonius and the exaggerated gestures of Seneca Grandio, excessive rapidity of speaking, inability to project violent emotions, and sing-song delivery. The *velocitas orationis* of Haterius provoked Augustus to quip, *Haterius noster sufflaminandus est* (*Contr.* IV pr. 7). Fabianus, having endeavoured to overcome his own emotions in accordance with his philosophical beliefs, became too tranquil to enact effectively the highly-wrought emotions of the characters whose part he had to take in declamations (*Contr.* II pr. 2). When Arellius Fuscus abandoned the dry style of his *principia*, *narrationes* and *argumenta* in favour of his more luxuriant manner (*ibid.* 1), the *compositio* of his elaborate sentences was such that they almost demanded to be sung (*Suas.* 2.10). Vibius Gallus is reported to have introduced his descriptions *paene cantantis modo* (*Contr.* II.1.25).[6] One recalls how Cicero (*Or.* 17.57) refers to the *epilogus paene canticum* characteristic of Phrygian and Carian rhetoricians. Quintilian was to complain that in the years since Cicero had written the habit of chanting had become more and more widespread among orators until in his day he might well ask: *quisquamne, non dico de homicidio sacrilegio parricidio, sed de calculis certe atque rationibus, quisquam denique, ut semel finiam, in lite cantat?* (XI.3.58). It is not, however, warrantable to assume that this habit was as generally prevalent in the elder Seneca's time as in Quintilian's.

In the third preface Seneca distinguishes between the *pronuntiatio* of Cassius Severus and the type which one would expect from an actor: *pronuntiatio quae histrionem posset producere, <nec> tamen quae histrionis posset videri* (*Contr.* III pr. 3 W). This distinction was one which it was customary for critics to draw when discussing *actio*: Cicero, before Porcius Latro, had questioned the need for importing into oratorical training such practice methods, evolved by Greek tragic actors, as the exercise in which *vocem cubantes sensim excitant eandemque, cum egerunt, sedentes ab acutissimo sono usque ad gravissimum sonum recipiunt et quasi quodam modo conligunt* (*De or.* I.59.251). Quintilian (XI. 3.19ff.) contrasts the moderate amount of attention which the orator should pay to *actio* with the training methods of *phonasci*. Interestingly, he considers it unreasonable to expect the orator to find time even for those healthy walks spurned by Latro, let alone for elaborate vocal exercises, *nam neque certa tempora ad spatiandum dari possunt tot civilibus officiis occupato, nec praeparare ab imis sonis vocem ad summos nec semper a contentione condere licet, cum pluribus iudiciis saepe dicendum sit* (*ibid.* 22).

Much less in line with the teaching of the classical theorists is a remark made by Seneca in *Contr.* X pr. 12. Referring to Iulius Bassus he comments: ...*demptam velles quam consectabatur amaritudinem et simulationem actionis oratoriae. nihil est indecentius quam ubi scholasticus forum quod non novit imitatur.* That Seneca the Elder should have affirmed, even if half in jest, the belief that it was not desirable for scholastics to imitate forensic *actio*, sets him apart both from the uncompromising enemies of the declamatory schools, and from Quintilian who, though fairly tolerant of the use of *suasoriae* and *controversiae* in rhetorical training, would never have lost sight of the idea that their function was to train future orators.

PART IV

THE PLACE OF EARLY IMPERIAL DECLAMATION IN LITERARY HISTORY:
THE ELDER SENECA'S EVIDENCE

Eduard Norden, who in his *Antike Kunstprosa* viewed the whole history of Hellenistic and Latin prose style as a centuries-long
battle[1] between the rival tendencies of Atticism and Asianism, was
confident that what he called the new style (*der neue Stil*) characteristic of early Imperial declaimers, could in its entirety be
regarded as a manifestation of Asianism.[2] Various points emerge,
however, from the elder Seneca's criticism of the declaimers which
suggest that Norden's diagnosis was an over-simplification. First,
it is evident that, however uniform in style declamatory *sententiae*
as excerpted by the elder Seneca may seem to readers today, the
sensitive ears of the anthologist himself detected many distinct
genera dicendi in use among the declaimers of his time, not just
one all-embracing type of modernity.[3] Secondly, though the elder
Seneca does use the term *Asianus* in his criticism, it is noteworthy that he does so very sparingly, applying this epithet only
to four Greek declaimers and probably, though the text of the
passage in question is doubtful, to one Latin declaimer, namely
Fuscus, whose style, as we have seen,[4] had certain characteristics
which set it apart from that of Latro and the *genus dicendi ardens
et concitatum* which was Seneca's ideal.

Norden based his contention that the new Latin style of the
early Empire was a species of Asianism on four passages from
ancient authorities.[5] He cites first Suetonius, *Aug.* 86, a description of the efforts of Augustus to steer a middle course in
style. Augustus, we are told here, was contemptuous of two distinct kinds of extremists, *cacozelos et antiquarios, ut diverso
genere vitiosos*, laughing on the one hand at Maecenas for his
'*myrobrechis...cincinnos*', and on the other at Tiberius for his
predilection for *exoletas...et reconditas voces*; he also found
fault with Mark Antony for the eccentric wavering of his style
between archaism fit to rival that of Annius Cimber, Veranius

Flaccus and Sallust, and imitation of the *Asiaticorum oratorum inanis sententiis verborum volubilitas*. From this passage Norden infers that the dominant trends in the prose style of the Augustan age must have been towards archaism on the one hand and, on the other, towards a modern style, whose exponents were criticized for *cacozelia* and considered imitators of Asiatic orators. He acknowledges that some stylists avoided both extremes, but names only Augustus in this connection among prose writers of the elder Seneca's period. The second passage which Norden cites is Plutarch, *Ant.* 2.5, where it is said of Antony: ἐχρῆτο δὲ τῷ καλουμένῳ μὲν Ἀσιανῷ ζήλῳ τῶν λόγων ἀνθοῦντι μάλιστα κατ' ἐκεῖνον τὸν χρόνον... He fails to point out that the time of Antony's activity as an orator was rather too early for evidence about his style and that of his contemporaries κατ' ἐκεῖνον τὸν χρόνον, necessarily to have any relevance to a consideration of early Silver Latin. He also omits to observe that Suetonius' analysis of Antony's rhetorical manner is more complex than Plutarch's. For further evidence that the modernism of early Imperial Latin rhetoric should be considered a form of Asianism, Norden then turns to Petronius' *Satyricon*, the extant remains of which open with an attack on the style of declamation represented by the *rhetor* Agamemnon, whose school Encolpius has been visiting. After a fine parody of a melodramatic type of declamation, '*haec vulnera pro libertate publica excepi, hunc oculum pro vobis impendi: date mihi ducem qui me ducat ad liberos meos, nam succisi poplites membra non sustinent*', and various strictures on the empty racket of *sententiae*, on unrealistic declamation themes, and on *mellitos verborum globulos et omnia dicta factaque quasi papavere et sesamo sparsa*, Encolpius alleges that:

nuper ventosa istaec et enormis loquacitas Athenas ex Asia commigravit animosque iuvenum ad magna surgentis veluti pestilenti quodam sidere afflavit, semelque corrupta regula eloquentia stetit et obmutuit. (*Sat.* 1-2)

Norden's last piece of evidence is Quintilian's remark on *actio* in XI.3.58: *Cicero illos ex Lycia et Caria rhetoras paene cantare in epilogis dixit: nos etiam cantandi severiorem paulo modum excessimus.* The modern development referred to,[6] as we have noted, need not be assumed to have become general as early as the elder

Seneca's time.

Full consideration of Norden's equation of the early Imperial 'New Style' with Asianism must be postponed until all the main varieties of declamatory prose recognized by the elder Seneca have been considered in turn.[7] Meanwhile let us look at Seneca's explicit references to *Asiani*. They are very few in number.

Contr. I.2.23 W (Seneca is quoting Scaurus on the subject of obscenity)
Hybreas, inquit, cum diceret controversiam de illo qui tribadas deprehendit et occidit, describere coepit mariti adfectum, in quo non deberet exigi inhonesta inquisitio: ἐγὼ δ' ἐσκόπησα πρότερον τὸν ἄνδρα, <εἰ> ἐγγεγένηταί τις ἢ προσέρραπται. Grandaus, Asianus aeque declamator, cum diceret in eadem controversia: 'non ideo occidi adulteros [non] paterentur', dixit: εἰ δὲ φηλάρρενα μοιχὸν ἔλαβον.

Contr. IX.1.12f.: Latro dixit: filiam tuam dimittam? quid adultero faciam? pro una rogas, duos eripis. hanc Hybreas aliter dixit sententiam: σοὶ δέ, μοιχέ, τί ποιήσω; μὴ καὶ σοῦ Καλλίας πατήρ ἐστιν; haec tota diversa sententia est a priore, etiamsi ex eadem est petita materia. illa non est similis sed eadem quam dixit prior Adaeus, rhetor ex Asianis non proiecti nominis, deinde Arellius Fuscus: ἀχάριστός σοι δοκῶ, Καλλία; οὐκ οἶδας ποῦ μοι τὴν χάριν ἔδωκας; hanc sic mutavit Arellius Fuscus: non dices me, Callia, ingratum: unde redemeris cogita. memini deinde Fuscum, cum haec Adaei sententia obiceretur, non infitiari transtulisse se eam in Latinum; et aiebat non commendationis id se aut furti, sed exercitationis causa facere.

(After this, Fuscus defends himself by citing an imitation by Sallust of a *sententia* allegedly by Thucydides.)

Contr. IX.6.16 (Seneca is quoting Pompeius Silo)
dixit, inquit, Hybreas: τί οὖν; ἐφεύσατο κατὰ τῆς ἰδίας θυγατρός; οὖκ· ἀλλὰ κατὰ τῆς ἐμῆς. hanc sententiam Fuscus Arellius, cum esset ex Asia<nis>, non casu dixit, sed transtulit ad verbum quidem: quid ergo? inquit, mentita est de filia sua? immo de mea.
    Asianis *Schultingh*: asia *MSS*[8]*

Contr. X.5.21: hic est Craton, venustissimus homo et professus Asianus, qui bellum cum omnibus Atticis gerebat. cum donaret illi Caesar talentum, in quo viginti quattuor sestertia sunt Atheniensium more: ἢ πρόσθες, φησίν, ἢ ἄφελ', ἵνα μὴ 'Αττικὸν ᾖ.

This last passage contains the only reference in the whole of the elder Seneca's writing to the Attic side of the polemic.[9] It is a frivolous reference, but the words *professus Asianus*[10]* used in the description of Craton's animosity are significant in showing that *Asianus* cannot simply be regarded as a geographical designation when it occurs in the elder Seneca's criticism.

As we see, all Seneca's explicit references to the rhetoric

of *Asiani* have to do with minutiae, that is, imitations of particular *sententiae* in particular *controversiae*. However, it is
notable that the style of Arellius Fuscus differs strikingly from
that of most of his contemporaries in the Latin schools, and it
may well be that it is only accidental that no passage is extant
in which Seneca designates his *genus dicendi*, or one of his *genera
dicendi*, as Asianic.

The chief peculiarity of Fuscus' style was his habit of di-
versifying an otherwise dry declamatory manner with extraordinarily florid descriptive passages, unmanly in *compositio* and out-
rageously bold in diction. In excerpts from his drier passages
his style does not seem fundamentally different from that of
Latro. Compare for example Latro in *Contr.* I.2.1:

o egregium pudicitiae patrocinium: 'militem occidi'! at hercule
lenonem non occidisti. deducta es in lupanar, accepisti locum,
pretium constitutum est, titulus inscriptus est: hactenus in te
inquiri potest; cetera nescio,

with Fuscus in *Contr.* I.2.5:

ne metue puella: pudica es; sed sic te viro lauda, non templo.
meretrix vocata es, in communi loco stetisti, superpositus est
cellae tuae titulus, venientem recepisti: cetera, etiamsi in
communi loco essem, tamen potius silerem.

But there is nothing in the fragments of Latro's declamations to
compare, for example, with the *explicatio* quoted from Fuscus'
treatment of the theme, *Agamemnon deliberat an Iphigeniam immolet
negante Calchante aliter navigari fas esse:*

non in aliam condicionem deus fudit aequora, quam ne omnis ex voto
iret dies; nec ea sors mari tantum est: caelum specta, non sub
eadem condicione sidera sunt? alias negatis imbribus exurunt
solum, et miseri cremata agricolae lugent[11*] semina, et haec
interdum anno lex est; alias serena clauduntur, et omnis dies
caelum nubilo gravat: subsidit solum, et creditum sibi terra non
retinet; alias incertus sideribus cursus est, et variantur tempora,
neque soles nimis urguent neque ultra debitum imbres cadunt: quidquid asperatum aestu est, quidquid nimio diffluxit imbre, invicem
temperatur altero; sive ista natura disposuit, sive, ut ferunt,
luna cursu gerit - quae, sive plena lucis suae est splendensque
pariter adsurgit in cornua, imbres prohibet, sive occurrente
nubilo sordidiorem ostendit orbem suum, non ante finit quam lucem
reddit -, sive ne lunae quidem ista potentia est, sed flatus, qui
occupavere, annum tenent: quidquid horum est, extra iussum dei
tutum fuit adultero mare. (*Suas.* 3.1 M)

There could be no better illustration than this sentence of
Seneca's criticism, *erat explicatio Fusci Arelli splendida quidem*

sed operosa et implicata (Contr. II pr. 1).[12] Sentence construction of this exceptional complexity must have seemed most abnormal
to an audience accustomed to the tersely paratactic *genus dicendi*
ardens et concitatum. Balancing words serve to mark the limits of
the various sections of the elaborate, not to say top-heavy,
structure:

> alias ...   alias ... · alias ...
>   quidquid ...   quidquid ...
>   sive ...   sive ...
>   sive ...   sive ...
>   sive ...
>   quidquid ...

Within this framework Fuscus works out such small-scale effects of
rhetorical symmetry as the *isocolon,*

          alias negatis imbribus exurunt sol(um) et   14 syllables
          miseri cremat(a) agricolae lugent semina   14 syllables

and may well have made conscious efforts to ensure that the opening long parallel sections,

          alias...lex est   35 syllables
          alias...retinet   37 syllables
          alias...cadunt   39 syllables

were of comparable, but progressively increasing, length. He
certainly seems to have aimed at conformity of rhythm at the openings of certain successive clauses, for example,

          alias negatis imbribus...
          miseri cremat(a) agricolae...
          alias serena clauduntur...

and again,

          siv(e) ista natura disposuit...
          siv(e) ut ferunt luna cursu gerit...

a rhythm on which he then produces a slight variation at the opening of the next clause,

          quae sive plena lucis suae (e)st...

which is resolved in the next into

          splendensque pariter adsurgit...

Yet the effect of the whole is not one of discipline, but of that
wandering effusiveness of which Seneca complains in *Contr.* II pr.
1 (*nimia licentia vaga et effusa*).

All through the *explicatio* of *Suas.* 3.1 over-poetic snatches of rhythm catch the attention, minor Ionics here, *nĕquĕ sōlēs nimĭs urgŭēnt...*, anapaests there, *ălĭās īncērtūs sīdĕrĭbūs...* We have, in fact, in this passage, a fine object lesson in the reasons why we find classical theorists recommending that rhetorical prose should be rhythmical, but not strictly metrical,[13] and we need no further explanation why Seneca and his friends when young had been tempted to set Fuscus' *explicationes* to music (*Suas.* 2.10). But Fuscus' style in *Suas.* 3.1 somehow has none of the grace of poetry; in particular the flow is broken by the occasional intrusion of jerky successions of short and prosaic words: *et haec interdum anno lex est*[14]*...; non ante finit quam lucem reddit...*

It is interesting that the *clausula* with which the sentence ends, *adultero mare*, is comparable, both in rhythm and in the contrived placement of a pyrrhic in the final position, with the type, *everritur caput*, criticized in *Contr.* IX.2.24 as *mollis* and not in Latro's manner.[15]

Suas. 3.1 will also serve to illustrate Seneca's criticism of Fuscus' diction: *in descriptionibus extra legem omnibus verbis, dummodo niterent, permissa libertas* (*Contr.* II pr. 1). One cannot fail to notice the highly poetic colour of the expression. Again and again Fuscus chooses words and usages which in the Augustan age - and it has to be remembered that he was already famous in the elder Seneca's youth (*Suas.* 2.10) - one would not have expected to encounter in prose: *aequora* and *serena*; *gravare* transitive, meaning 'to weigh down' (*ThLL* s.v. *gravo* IA 1b); *subsidere* with reference to an inanimate substance (cf. Lucr. V.493); *credere terrae* (cf. Virg. *Geor.* I.224); *variare* (cf. Ov. *Fast.* III.449) and *urgere* (cf. Hor. *Carm.* I.22.20) with reference to the weather; *asperare* used of the effects of heat (cf. Val. Flacc. V. 368); *splendere* used literally to mean 'to shine'; *sordidus* used metaphorically of the dark side of the moon; *flatus* in the sense 'winds' (*ThLL* s.v. *flatus* IB);[16] *occupare* referring to winds which 'invade' a year.

It comes as no surprise to learn that Fuscus was known to make conscious efforts to imitate Virgil in his prose - efforts of which Seneca is suitably scornful (*Suas.* 3.4-5 W):

in ea descriptione <quam> primam in hac suasoria posui Fuscus
Arellius Vergilii versus voluit imitari; valde autem longe petit
et paene repugnante materia, certe non desiderante, inseruit. ait
enim de luna: 'quae, sive plena lucis suae est splendensque
pariter assurgit in cornua, imbres prohibet, sive occupata nubilo
sordidiorem ostendit orbem suum, non ante finit quam lucem reddit.'
at Vergilius haec quanto et simplicius et beatius dixit:
  luna, revertentes cum primum colligit ignes,
  si nigrum obscuro comprenderit aera cornu,
  maximus agricolis pelagoque parabitur imber. (*Georg*. I.427-9)
et rursus:
  sin...
  pura nec obtunsis per caelum cornibus ibit. (*Ibid*. 432-3)

We are told furthermore that one of his reasons for aspiring to
imitate Virgil was a desire to please Maecenas:

solebat autem Fuscus ex Vergilio multa trahere, ut Maecenati
imputaret; totiens enim pro beneficio narrabat in aliqua se Vergi-
liana descriptione placuisse; sicut in hac ipsa suasoria dixit:
'cur iste <in> interpretis ministerium placuit? cur hoc os deus
elegit? cur hoc sortitur potissimum pectus quod tanto numine
impleat?' aiebat se imitatum esse Vergilianum 'plena deo'. (*Ibid*.
5)

  This link with Maecenas is most interesting, for it is in the
fragments of Maecenas' prose, which Suetonius mentions as exemp-
lifying *cacozelia* in the time of Augustus, that we find writing
most closely comparable with the Fuscine manner. The younger
Seneca, who in *Ep. mor*. 114.4 describes Maecenas' style as *eloquentiam ebrii hominis involutam et errantem et licentiae plenam*,
quotes several examples to illustrate his point:

quid turpius 'amne silvisque ripa comantibus'? vide ut 'alveum
lyntribus arent versoque vado remittant hortos'. quid? si quis
'feminae cinno crispat et labris columbatur incipitque suspirans,
ut cervice lassa fanantur nemoris tyranni.' 'inremediabilis
factio rimantur epulis lagonaque temptant domos et spe mortem
exigunt.' 'genium festo vix suo testem.' 'tenuisve cerei fila et
crepacem molam.' 'focum mater aut uxor investiunt.' (*Ibid*. 5 =
Maecenas fr. 11 Lunderstedt)[17*]

Another example, *ipsa enim altitudo attonat summa* (fr. 10 Lunderstedt), is recorded in *Ep. mor*. 19.9. Seneca wonders why Maecenas
did not simply say of the mountain in question, '*attonita habet
summa*'. Quintilian complains in particular about Maecenas' use of
unnatural hyperbaton and deliberate seeking out of 'lascivious'
rhythms:

quaedam vero transgressiones et longae sunt nimis...et interim
etiam compositione vitiosae, quae in hoc ipsum petuntur, ut

exultent atque lasciviant, quales illae Maecenatis: 'sole et
aurora rubent plurima'; 'inter sacra movit aqua fraxinos'; 'ne
exequias quidem unus inter miserrimos viderem meas' (quod inter
haec pessimum est, quia in re tristi ludit compositio).
(IX.4.28 = fr. 16 Lunderstedt)

Arellius Fuscus' *explicatio* in *Suas*. 3.1 is open to criticisms similar to these levelled against Maecenas' style: there
were simpler ways of expressing in Latin the concept, 'it is
cloudy', than Fuscus' *serena clauduntur, et omnis dies caelum
nubilo gravat*;[18] hyperbaton of the type represented by *miseri
cremata agricolae lugent semina* is abnormal in prose; Fuscus
shared with Maecenas a fondness for affectation in rhythm and unusual vocabulary. It is not surprising then that the wording of
parts of the elder Seneca's critique of Fuscus in *Contr*. II pr. 1,
explicatio...implicata...[sc. *oratio*] *nimia licentia vaga et
effusa*, should resemble the terms in which his son condemns
Maecenas' style in *Ep. mor*. 114.4.

The eccentricities of Fuscus' descriptive manner also have
close parallels in the fragments (*FGrHist* 142) of Hegesias, one of
the chief founding fathers of Asianism.[19] Norden's criticisms of
this stylist in *Die antike Kunstprosa*[20] could be taken over almost
point by point and applied to the Fuscine extract in *Suas*. 3.1.
Hegesias' *compositio*, samples of which are analysed by Norden,
features efforts at *isocolon*:

βασιλικῆι μανίαι προσπταίσασα πόλις   13 syllables
τραγωδίας ἐλεεινοτέρα γέγονε (F 10)   13 syllables

There is an abundance of audacious metaphors, for example a funerary image in F 16: αἱ δὲ γυναῖκες μετήχθησαν εἰς Μακεδονίαν, τὴν
πόλιν θάψασαί τινα τρόπον. Hegesias had a fondness for making abstract nouns the subjects of sentences, for example: ἡ μὲν οὖν
ἐλπὶς αὔτη συνέδραμεν εἰς τὸ τολμᾶν (F 5.10f.); τοὺς δ' ἄλλους
ὀργὴ πρόσφατος ἐπίμπρατο (F 5.18), a tendency which Fuscus was
to share, as we see not only in *Suas*. 3.1 where we read, *et omnis
dies caelum nubilo gravat*, but elsewhere, for example in *Suas*. 5.1:
suis ira ardet ignibus et in pacta non solvitur. The use of peri-
phrasis[21] was recognized in antiquity as particularly characteristic of the Asiatic style (Quint. XII.10.16: *circumitu...
enuntiare*). Thus, when Hegesias means ἐκ τοῦ οὐρανοῦ he writes

ἐκ τῆς κατ' οὐρανὸν μερίδος (F 12). Similarly Fuscus, wishing to describe sunny intervals and scattered showers, relates that *quidquid asperatum aestu est, quidquid nimio diffluxit imbre, invicem temperatur altero.*

The justifications for giving the name Asianist to the descriptive manner of Arellius Fuscus are many. The question we now have to ask is whether there are any such grounds for attaching the same label to the *genus dicendi ardens et concitatum*, the type of style favoured pre-eminently by Latro. This style differed from the Fuscine, as we have seen, in that *explicationes* were kept brief (*Contr.* III pr. 7), and a fiery intensity was consistently aimed at; Latro, for instance, would never dwell on *loci* at any great length (*Contr.* VII.7.10). Yet the fault of aridity was avoided by the best exponents of this style. Latro even as a schoolboy had seen scope for *sententiae* where his more cautious master had not (*Contr.* I pr. 22), and the effect of a Latronian declamation was one of considerable richness while, at least in the elder Seneca's view, a certain *subtilitas* of structure always provided a sound foundation for the elaborate whole (*ibid.* 20f.).

The most extended example we have of Latro's style is the extract from his treatment of *Contr.* II.7, the theme of which was as follows:

quidam, cum haberet formonsam uxorem, peregre profectus est. in viciniam mulieris peregrinus mercator commigravit; ter illam appellavit de stupro adiectis pretiis; negavit illa. decessit mercator, testamento heredem omnibus bonis reliquit formonsam et adiecit elogium: 'pudicam repperi.' adit hereditatem. redit maritus, accusat adulteri ex suspicione.

It seems that, contrary to his usual practice, the elder Seneca may actually have recorded the whole of this declamation of Latro's, but the last part of it (though perhaps not very much) is now lost. The extant part of the declamation seems to consist of the *prooemium* (§1); a vestigial *narratio* leading up to the *propositio*,[22] '*poteram ego salvo pudore meo nihil de hereditate suspicari, in qua etiam nomen auctoris ab uxore doctus sum?*' (§2 W); the rest (§3ff.) is given over to argumentation. The *controversia* was of the type which Seneca called *coniecturalis* and, unless we have lost a great deal of Latro's argumentation, it would appear that his *divisio* was of the uncomplicated sort customary in the treatment of such themes.[23] Throughout the extant argumentation Latro seems to be treating just one *quaestio coniecturalis* about the wife's character, *utrum adultera sit an pudica*. He diversifies his arguments by means of *excessus* and *indignationes*.

At the opening, and just before the end of §1 we find carefully constructed periods involving more subordination of clauses than was usual in the fiery and agitated style.

Quamquam eo prolapsi iam mores civitatis sunt ut nemo ad suspicanda adulteria nimium credulus possit videri, tamen ego adeo longe ab eo vitio afui ut magis timeam ne quis in me aut nimiam patientiam aut nimium stuporem arguat quod tam seram querellam detuli.

illud, iudices, mihi tormentum est, quod notata iudicio vestro, ut multiplicatam dotem perdat, plus tamen ex quaestu habitura est quam quantum damnatae perdendum est...

But these are the only concessions Latro makes to the tradition of prefatorial rotundity. For the rest, one *sententia* follows another throughout §1 in brilliant succession: *non accuso adulteram nisi divitem factam; ex ea domo ream protraho in qua iam nihil meum est*, and so on. The *prooemium* ends with the indignant exclamation: *tantum in istam dives amator effudit ut post poenam quoque expediat fuisse adulteram.*

Latro abstains from providing a full-length *narratio* for the good reason that the husband, whose part he is taking, was absent abroad at the time of his wife's alleged adultery. He contents himself with drawing the jurors' attention to the rumours which were supposedly circulating about his wife and her benefactor, before putting it to them, in the brief *propositio* quoted above, that it was inevitable that he should be suspicious (§2).

He next (§3) begins the argumentation with an *anthypophora* designed to anticipate the argument that a beautiful woman such as his wife could not be blamed for not remaining chaste, and that it was inevitable, at any rate, that she should attract lovers. Latro's counter-argument is that any married woman, if she so wishes, can thwart the hopes of potential admirers by dressing sombrely and behaving with sufficient modesty:

matrona, quae <tuta> esse adversus sollicitatoris lasciviam volet, prodeat in tantum ornata quantum ne inmunda sit; habeat comites eius aetatis quae inpudicum, si nihil aliud, in verecundiam

annorum movere possit; ferat iacentis in terram oculos; adversus
officiosum salutatorem inhumana potius quam inverecunda sit; etiam
in necessaria resalutandi vice multo rubore confusa <sit>. sic se
in verecundiam pigneret <ut> longe ante inpudicitiam suam ore quam
verbo neget. in has servandae integritatis custodias nulla libido
inrumpet.

Latro next (§4) launches into an *indignatio* in two parts, first an
imaginative description of women in seductive clothes behaving
shamelessly, and then a further *imago*[24] in which the would-be
seducer's go-between is imagined (likely story!) to have been
flogged and tortured:

prodite mihi fronte in omne lenocinium composita, paulo obscurius
quam posita veste nudae, exquisito in omnes facetias sermone,
tantum non ultro blandientes ut quisquis viderit non metuat ac-
cedere: deinde miramini si, cum tot argumentis inpudicitiam prae-
scripseritis, cultu, incessu, sermone, facie, aliquis repertus est
qui incurrenti adulterae se non subduceret. internuntium, puto,
illa sollicitatoris arripi et denudari iussit, flagella et verbera
et omne genus cruciatus poposcit, in plagas deterrimi mancipi vix
inbecillitatem muliebris manus continuit. nemo sic negantem iterum
rogat.

Note that both cases of *sub oculos subiectio* are kept brief. The
sententia which closes this section[25][*] is an obvious applause-
winner.

    In his next argument Latro makes all the capital he can out
of the words in the theme, *ter illam appellavit de stupro adiectis
pretiis*. From the fact that three approaches were made he deduces
(at the risk of being accused of *contrarium*)[26] that her refusals
took the form of silence: *quod proximum est a promittente, rogata
stuprum tacet* (§6). He assumes that the gifts were accepted and
magnifies them to vast proportions, skirting the difficulty of
describing them by means of the useful device of *praeteritio*:

inspicite adulterae censum; ex eo inpune sit quod adulter isti
dedit si est aliquid quod non dederit. quid singillatim omnia
percenseo? quid ego non emi in mundo tibi? <me> miserum: maritus
cum omni censu meo inter munera adulteri lateo. (*Ibid.*)

    There follows in the next section (§7) another *indignatio*
opening with the heavily ironic exclamation, *o nos nimium felici
et aureo, quod aiunt, saeculo natos!* Latro sums up in a resounding *enthymema* the fundamental contradiction in the wife's pleas as
viewed by the suspicious husband: *sic etiam qui inpudicas quaerunt
pudicas honorant?*

Most of the rest of the extract is given over to detailed
consideration of the will. First Latro reads out a passage from
the imagined will and reflects how much it sounds like the will of
a husband bequeathing his property to his wife; suppose he were to
believe that his wife was chaste and wished to add a final codicil
to his own will, he would have to look to the will of this *adulter*
for suitable wording (§7). Then (§8), after reading again from
the will he muses on the implausibility of the notion that the
family of his wife's admirer included no chaste women and that nowhere on his travels had he met any women but prostitutes, that
everywhere he went he had been looking for a chaste woman to be
his heiress. After a plain statement of his allegation of adultery
and a few more pointed remarks on the decadence of the age, Latro
concludes his examination of the will with a *figura testamenti*,[27]
inviting the jurors to consider, along with the will of his wife's
admirer, a proposal for his own will, the better to decide which
contains the more accurate description of his wife's character
(§9 W):

atque ego, si hunc morem scribendi recipitis, in conspectu vestro
ita scribam: 'uxor mea heres <ne> esto, quod peregrinante me
adamata est, quod heres ab adulescente alieno ac libidinoso
relicta est, quod tam infamem hereditatem adit.' a duobus vos
testamentis in consilium mitto: utrum secuturi estis? quo ab
adultero absolvitur, an quo damnatur a viro?

The extract of Latro's declamation as preserved in the 'full
text' manuscripts ends with *sententiae* on the theme that true
chastity provokes nobody to comment upon it. It is quite possible
that remarks on this theme marked the end of Latro's argumentation,
but it does seem that we lack at least his *epilogus*, and it is
doubtful whether any *sententiae* from it have been preserved in the
Excerpta.[28]

Contr. II.7.1-9 illustrates well Latro's virtuoso command
over the various types of *sententiae* and *figurae* and his terseness
in the treatment of *loci*. Illustrations of his compendious grasp
of the *acta* of historical personages (*Contr.* I pr. 18) are lacking
in this *controversia* but are available elsewhere, for example in
Contr. X.1.8. More significant is the absence from *Contr.* II.7.1-9
of any protracted *descriptiones*; one searches in vain for these in

Latro's other fragments too. Also lacking, surely, are instances
of the kinds of bad taste which Seneca castigates in the work of
less distinguished declaimers with such words as *corruptum* and
ineptum.[29]

That Latro's declamatory style was not identical with that of
Fuscus would be apparent even if Seneca had not alluded specifically to the difference as he does in the words *diversum...dicendi*
genus in *Contr.* II.2.8.[30] It does not seem an unreasonable hypothesis that the elder Seneca regarded Latro's style as distinct
from that of the *Asiani*. Note how in *Contr.* IX.1.12[31] he takes
pains to point out that a *sententia* of Latro's was quite different
from one, concerned with similar subject-matter, by the *Asianus*
Hybreas, whereas Fuscus in the same *controversia* had copied Adaeus,
another *Asianus*, exactly. On another occasion Seneca goes as far
as to say that it was out of the question that Latro could have
imitated any Greek:

Artemon dixit: τὰ μὲν τῶν ἄλλων εὔρωστα· πλεῖ, γεωργεῖ. τὰ δ'
ἡμέτερα ἀνάπηρα· τρέφει ἄρα τὸν ὁλόκληρον. hanc sententiam Latro
Porcius virilius dixit, qui non potest <de> furto suspectus esse;
Graecos enim et contemnebat et ignorabat. (*Contr.* X.4.20f.)

No other statement made by Seneca the Elder proclaims as
emphatically as this one, about Latro's lack of indebtedness to
Greek models, the fact that a new age of Latin prose-writing had
dawned, very different from the one which had preceded it. Latro,
educated perhaps entirely in far-off Corduba,[32] seems to have been
cut off in his formative years even more completely than his
school friend Seneca from the Greek-based literary culture which
Cicero and his *familiares* had taken for granted. Was it that
Latro's family - much less well off, perhaps, than the Annaei
Senecae, for it was exceptional for an *eques* to become a rhetorician in their time (*Contr.* II pr. 5) - did not possess any Greek-
speaking slaves, so that he was deprived of the chance of becoming
bilingual at home in the way that was customary (see Quint. I.1.
12-14) among the Roman upper classes?[33] In the circumstances it
is not self-evident that there need be any justification for describing the style of Latro in terms taken over from the late
Republican controversy between Atticists and Asianists, implying
as they do imitation of Greek models, whether Attic or Asiatic.

That is not to deny, however, that Greek influences of either sort could have reached Latro in his boyhood by an indirect route and without his recognizing them for what they were.

Let us consider some possible formative influences on Latro as a stylist. First there was the idiom of his native Spain: Messala's jibe, *sua lingua disertus est* (*Contr.* II.4.8), serves to show that this was a factor to be reckoned with. Secondly there was the poetry which he studied with the *grammaticus* which presumably, in those days before the poems of Virgil and Horace had become the standard school texts, comprised the Latin drama and epics of the Republic. Insofar as these poems were modelled on Greek originals, a certain amount of Hellenic literary technique would have been absorbed by Latro through the study of them. The terse rhetoric of the speeches contained in them should not be ignored as a possible source of inspiration for Latro's sententiousness. The acquaintance with drama of a schoolboy from Corduba need not, by the way, have been confined to his grammatical studies: a performance of a *praetexta* at Gades during the Civil Wars is attested by Pollio in *Ad fam.* X.32.3.

After his years with the *grammaticus* Latro moved on to study rhetoric in the school of Marullus. The question we must now ask is whether the rhetorical manner he learnt to cultivate there was (even if he and his friends did not realize it) in any real sense Asianic. In other words, was the sententious manner customary in the treatment of *controversiae* and *suasoriae* in the time of Seneca the Elder a direct descendant of a style originating in the Greek schools of Asia Minor some time in the previous three centuries?

Several factors make this hypothesis seem quite attractive. First, the popularity of sententiousness seems to have been universal among the declaimers of the time: Cestius Pius from Smyrna[34] declaimed in a style not fundamentally different from that of Latro the Corduban, and it is clear from Seneca's quotations that brief *sententiae* were sought after by Greek-speaking, as well as Latin, rhetoricians. Secondly, it is a well known fact that the ponderous conservatism of the Hellenistic rhetorical school tradition was such that even arguments by a critic of Cicero's stature in favour of change made no lasting impact upon it. For

instance, Cicero's desire for the *thesis* to be given an important
place in the rhetorical curriculum[35] does not seem to have had the
slightest effect on the subsequent development of Greco-Roman
education. Also, as we have seen, the Hegesian brand of Asianism,
despite everything which its detractors said against it, survived
the centuries, presumably fostered by a continuous tradition in
certain Hellenistic schools, to re-emerge in the Latin *explicationes* of Arellius Fuscus.[36] Is it not highly plausible, then,
that the more arid style of Fuscus - not so different from that of
Latro, and presumably quite similar to that of Marullus, whom
Seneca describes as *hominem satis aridum* (*Contr*. I pr. 22) - had
its origins in the schools of Asia Minor? We have seen that the
Hellenistic age saw a movement towards brevity in the treatment of
judicial declamations as a whole, in that it became customary to
declaim only one speech on a given theme rather than four;[37]
furthermore, brevity in the composition of all *enthymemata* was
already encouraged by the author of the *Rhetorica ad Alexandrum*.[38]

  Yet there are objections which may fairly be levelled against
the supposition that a prototype of the *genus dicendi ardens et
concitatum* had been developed in the schools of Hellenistic Asia
several centuries earlier. A passage in Cicero's *Brutus* might be
cited in support of the notion that the 'pointed' style of the
early Roman Empire had a precedent in an early Asiatic type of
rhetoric:

genera autem Asiaticae dictionis duo sunt: unum sententiosum et
argutum, sententiis non tam gravibus et severis quam concinnis et
venustis, qualis in historia Timaeus, in dicendo autem pueris
nobis Hierocles Alabandeus, magis etiam Menecles frater eius fuit,
quorum utriusque orationes sunt in primis ut Asiatico in genere
laudabiles. aliud autem genus est non tam sententiis frequentatum
quam verbis volucre atque incitatum, quale est nunc Asia tota, nec
flumine solum orationis, sed etiam exornato et faceto genere
verborum, in quo fuit Aeschylus Cnidius et meus aequalis Milesius
Aeschines. in his erat admirabilis orationis cursus, ornata
sententiarum concinnitas non erat. (*Brut*. 95.325)

It is to the first of Cicero's two types of Asianism that we must
direct our attention. Fortunately, though the speeches of Hierocles and Menecles of Alabanda are hopelessly lost, there do survive a number of fragments of the *Histories* of Timaeus, which
according to Cicero were representative of this style.[39] But one

searches in vain in these fragments (*FGrHist* 566) for anticipations of the style we find in the declamations of Porcius Latro.
Polybius, who criticizes Timaeus for imitating the techniques of
school rhetoric when putting speeches into the mouths of historical characters, actually quotes from one such speech, in which
Timoleon exhorts the Greeks to enter battle with a numerically
superior Carthaginian army (XII.26a = Timaeus F 31). Here if anywhere, seeing that the speech was of the *suasoria* type, one would
expect to find any anticipations there were in Timaeus' style of
Latronian sententiousness. Timoleon is made to encourage the
Greeks not to consider the numerical strength but the unmanliness
of the enemy:

καὶ γὰρ τῆς Λιβύης ἁπάσης συνεχῶς οἰκουμένης καὶ πληθούσης
ἀνθρώπων, ὅμως ἐν ταῖς παροιμίαις, ὅταν περὶ ἐρημίας ἔμφασιν
βουλώμεθα ποιῆσαι, λέγειν ἡμᾶς "ἐρημότερα τῆς Λιβύης", οὐκ ἐπὶ τὴν
ἐρημίαν φέροντας τὸν λόγον, ἀλλ᾽ ἐπὶ τὴν ἀνανδρίαν τῶν κατοικ-
ούντων.⁴⁰ καθόλου δέ, φησί, τίς ἂν φοβηθείη τοὺς ἄνδρας, οὕτινες
τῆς φύσεως τοῦτο τοῖς ἀνθρώποις δεδωκυίας ἴδιον παρὰ τὰ λοιπὰ τῶν
ζῴων, λέγω δὲ τὰς χεῖρας, ταύτας παρ᾽ ὅλον τὸν βίον ἐντὸς τῶν
χιτώνων ἔχοντες ἀπράκτους περιφέρουσι; τὸ δὲ μέγιστον ὅτι καὶ ὑπὸ
τοῖς χιτωνίσκοις, φησί, περιζώματα φοροῦσιν, ἵνα μηδ᾽ ὅταν ἀπο-
θάνωσιν ἐν ταῖς μάχαις φανεροὶ γένωνται τοῖς ὑπεναντίοις...

Nothing in this speech, surely, or in any other of Timaeus' fragments, bears any noticeable resemblance to the *genus dicendi
ardens et concitatum*. Rather the naïve techniques of persuasion
in this fragment seem to hark back to the speeches in Herodotus,
notably the speech of Sardanis in I.71. Only the very feeble
argument about the proverbial expression, ἐρημότερα τῆς Λιβύης,
marks it out as the product of a more pedantic age than that of
Herodotus; compare the point made by Hegesias in *FGrHist* 142 F 14:
δεινὸν τὴν χώραν ἄσπορον εἶναι τὴν τοὺς Σπαρτοὺς τεκοῦσαν.

From Cicero's remarks in *Brut*. 95.325 it appears that the
Timaean variety of Asiatic style, characterized as *sententiosum et
argutum*, had been popular with certain orators when he was a boy,
but that since then it had been superseded throughout Asia by a
more voluble style, *non tam sententiis frequentatum quam verbis
volucre atque incitatum, quale est nunc Asia tota*... It may well
be that this second style had already largely ousted the first by
the time when Cicero came to study with Asian and other Greek
rhetoricians. This supposition would account for the fact that it

is volubility rather than sententiousness that we think of as the
dominant characteristic of his early oratory. It would accord
well also with the fact that, as far as we can judge from the
fragmentary evidence available, a flowing periodic style seems to
have been the one generally favoured by Roman orators throughout
the first half of the first century B.C.[41]

To sum up, the more sententious of the two Asiatic styles
distinguished by Cicero went out of fashion at the beginning of
the first century B.C. Traces of it remained in the later
speeches of Hortensius, though these were not much admired (*Brut.*
95.327), and perhaps it was never ousted from the Asian schools
completely, but continued to be favoured in a few circles, together
with the Hegesian elements which may have been inseparably linked
to this *genus dicendi*. But this possibility is of no relevance to
our present enquiry, as there is no evidence that the Timaean type
of Asianism in any way resembled the kind of style which Latro
learnt to cultivate in the school of Marullus.

Why there should have been a general move towards greater
terseness in rhetorical style in the latter half of the first century B.C. is mysterious. M. Aper in Tacitus' *Dialogus* attributes
the change to the need for speakers to appeal to an increasingly
sophisticated audience and, with the advent of the Empire, to take
account of certain changes in the nature of jurisdiction:

at hercule pervulgatis iam omnibus, cum vix in cortina adsistat
quin elementis studiorum, etsi non instructus, at certe inbutus
sit, novis et exquisitis eloquentiae itineribus opus est, per quae
orator fastidium aurium effugiat, utique apud eos iudices qui vi
et potestate, non iure et legibus cognoscunt, nec accipiunt
tempora sed constituunt, nec expectandum habent oratorem dum illi
libeat de ipso negotio dicere, sed saepe ultro admonent atque alio
transgredientem revocant et festinare se testantur. (19.5)

There may well be much truth in this analysis, though it does not
explain everything.[42]

It might be suggested that the newly introduced practice of
declaiming *controversiae* and *suasoriae* in the Latin schools could
have been a major factor in the rise of the fashion for sententiousness: the stock characters in *controversia* themes in particular are placed in the sorts of situation which might seem expressly designed to prompt the composition of pointed ironic

sententiae; besides, the subject-matter to be treated by declaimers of these themes was much sparser than the circumstantial data available to orators in even the simplest of court cases, and so they could not indulge in otiose repetition without inviting adverse criticism from their hearers (*Contr.* IX.5.15).

However, it would be wrong to assume that *controversia* themes were bound to be treated in a pithy style: the arguments in Antiphon's *Tetralogies* are expressed in language more diffuse than Latronian Latin; the *Declamationes maiores* of ps.-Quintilian, though far from deficient in brief and striking *sententiae*, contain a rather larger proportion of complex periods in their composition than does, for example, Latro's version of *Contr.* II.7. We may take as an illustration a passage from *Decl. mai.* XVII which is a treatment of the theme which appears in Seneca's collection as *Contr.* VII.3. It concerns a young man whose father has tried unsuccessfully to disown him three times and who now, having been discovered mixing poison, is accused of intended parricide.

o pertinacissimum accusatorum genus victi parentes! dum auctoritatem nominis vestri fortius imperiosis adseritis adfectibus et, ne pudorem paenitentiam fateamini, contumacia vindicatis errorem, calamitatibus meis accessit, ut ter absolverer. namque ut erat in supervacuo odio mei senex prima lite[43]* deprensus, ferre non potuit quod reddebar invito, et quia a iudicibus non inpetraverat ut abdicaret, apud se tenuit, ne desineret hoc velle. credidit tandem[44]* aliquid profecturum querelarum errore repetito et speravit iuxta contentionem suam, ut lassesceret pro me iusta miseratio. quid facerem igitur? quo verterem iam fatigatam innocentiam? nec exire me decebat ex domo, ne viderer quidquid vos non credideratis, agnoscere, nec expectare poteram, cum mihi rursus aliam seriem malorum minaretur, quod me iam coeperat pater contentione qua vobis irascebatur, odisse. (*Decl. mai.* XVII.3)

There is no reason to suppose, then, that *controversia* themes could not have been treated in the orotund style prevalent towards the end of the Republic. Still less is it self-evident that the style used in *suasoriae* had to be pithy: there is no reason why a declaimer, if he cared to do sufficient research into the mythological or historical background of his chosen subject, should not have treated deliberative themes with great elaboration, and in a correspondingly copious style.

More to the point, perhaps, we have noted in passing that the speeches in epic and drama which Latro must have studied with the

grammaticus could have been a formative influence on his style.
It is worth considering whether the style of rhetoric to be found
in poetry might not have appealed very widely to the educated
youth of Latro's generation throughout the Greek and Roman world,
impatient, for whatever reason, with the long-windedness which had
been acceptable when Cicero had started out on his oratorical
career. The conventions of epic and drama had always demanded a
terser style of rhetoric than had been customary in the law-courts
or assemblies of either Athens or Rome. We have seen how the
examples of *enthymemata* taken from drama by Cicero in his *Topica*
seem stylistically akin to Silver Latin rhetoric. The same may be
said of Cicero's own verse translations of tragedy included in the
Tusculan disputations. Take, for example, part of his version
of a speech of Hercules in torment from the Greek of Sophocles'
Trachiniae:

> non Graia vis, non barbara ulla immanitas,
> non saeva terris gens relegata ultimis,
> quas peragrans undique omnem ecferitatem expuli:
> sed feminae vir, feminea interemor manu.
> o nate, vere hoc nomen usurpa patri
> neve occidentem matris superet caritas.
> huc adripe ad me manibus abstractam piis.
> iam cernam mene an illam potiorem putes.
> perge, aude, nate, illacrima patris pestibus,
> miserere! gentes nostras flebunt miserias.
> heu! virginalem me ore ploratum edere,
> quem vidit nemo ulli ingemescentem malo!
> accede, nate, adsiste, miserandum aspice
> eviscerati corpus laceratum patris![45]

Here surely – and observe that this is a rendering of an impeccably
Attic original – is rhetoric not so very far removed from the
melodramatic declamatory style later to be parodied by Petronius.

But it is not only in the poetry of the Republic and its
classical Greek models that we find precedents for the sententiousness favoured by Latro and his contemporaries. Cicero's late
speeches contain passages which were surely a major source of
inspiration to the early Imperial declaimers. Consider the peroration of the second Philippic, in particular the following
resounding words:

defendi rem publicam adulescens, non deseram senex: contempsi
Catilinae gladios, non pertimescam tuos. quin etiam corpus

libenter obtulerim, si repraesentari morte mea libertas civitatis
potest, ut aliquando dolor populi Romani pariat quod iam diu
parturit! etenim si abhinc annos prope viginti hoc ipso in templo
negavi posse mortem immaturam esse consulari, quanto verius nunc
negabo seni? (*Phil*. II.118f.)

What better example could there be of the *genus dicendi ardens et
concitatum* at its most elevated? For once Cicero confutes the
famous criticism of 'Longinus' that whereas his was a fire which
burnt widely and steadily, that of Demosthenes was the fire of
thunderbolts (*Subl*. 12.4).

Cicero, of course, recommended Demosthenes above all other
Attic orators as the model for his contemporaries to imitate (*Brut*.
84.288ff.). They perhaps hardly needed the advice. There is a
statement in *Opt. gen. or.*[46] 2.6 to the effect that *nemo est
orator qui Demostheni <se> similem nolit esse*, and some people at
least seem to have considered that Calvus had succeeded in attain-
ing to the Demosthenic ideal, for Seneca's excursus on Calvus in
Contr. VII.4.6-8 clearly derived at least in part from the criticism of people who held this view. Now, in this passage Seneca
is quite probably quoting Latro.[47] And, significantly, the
stylistic virtues supposedly shared by Calvus and Demosthenes
which are singled out for praise, vigour and agitation (*compositio
quoque eius ad exemplum Demosthenis viget: nihil in illa placidum,
nihil lene est, omnia excitata et fluctuantia*), are very much the
same as those which he reckons in *Contr*. III pr. 7 to be the mark
of a good declaimer.

It looks, then, as though the rhetoricians of the early
Empire who favoured consistent fiery agitation saw themselves as
the successors of the late Republican admirers of Demosthenes'
style and preserved at least a few memories of Atticist, non-
Ciceronian, theory on the subject. But, as we have seen,[48] the
information about Calvus in *Contr*. VII.4.6-8 may well have been
taken from a collection of *exempla*, and among the men who exercised most influence in promoting the agitated style were some,
including Latro, who were ignorant of Greek. It is not surprising
that the attempts of such narrowly educated westerners to emulate
the Demosthenic ideal produced results which do not strike the
modern reader forcibly with their resemblance to the thunderbolts

of the great Athenian.

   Certain tendencies in Republican rhetoric, the rhetoric of
the stage as well as that of the forum, can be seen, then, to
foreshadow the extreme sententiousness universally favoured in the
early Imperial schools. But let us admit that the difference between late Cicero and the pointed style evidently sought after to
some extent by every schoolman from Latro of Corduba to Cestius of
Smyrna is too great to be accounted for as the outcome of gradual
literary evolution. (The declaimers from the eastern provinces
had no such excuse as Latro not to have approached closer than
they did to the style of Demosthenes.) Let us also admit that the
difference is not wholly accounted for in the sociological speculations of Aper in the *Dialogus*.[49] Possibly one of the main
reasons for it lies in certain emphases which had become standard
in the curricula of rhetorical schools throughout the Greco-Roman
world, notably the restriction of the philosophical and historical
education of future orators to the rote-learning of ready-made
loci and *exempla*, and the limiting of their training in *inventio*
to practice in the contrivance of *divisiones* and *colores*, and
their training in *elocutio* to practice in the composition of
sententiae, this last element in the curriculum being, if any safe
deduction may be drawn from the elder Seneca's low estimate of his
sons' tastes expressed in *Contr.* I pr. 22, the only aspect of
declamation which interested the non-analytical mind of the average student of rhetoric.

   Where and when this drastic narrowing of the rhetorical
curriculum originated is unknown. The encouragement of wide
learning in history and philosophy had probably never been considered by any but the most exceptional of Hellenistic rhetoricians
as part of their duties.[50] However, the restriction of training
in *inventio* and *elocutio* to instruction in the contriving of *sententiae*, *divisiones* and *colores* may well have been quite a recent
development, owing its universal acceptance throughout the Empire
of the elder Seneca's day to the widespread use of one or two
influential text-books, now lost. Note that the term *color*, as
used by Imperial rhetoricians, does not seem to have been of any
great antiquity.[51] It is indeed by no means out of the question

that the inventor of the system, and hence one of the main promoters of sententiousness, was a *Latinus rhetor* of the late
Republic, or a Greek teacher of the same period, prompted to
simplify the rhetorical curriculum by Roman parents who wanted
rapid results if they were to supply him with pupils.

It may still be, though, that the first impulse towards agitated sententiousness was purely Greek, and had a root cause quite
different from curricular reorganization - disgust at the redundant style fostered in certain earlier Hellenistic schools, maybe,
or even a hankering after Laconic brevity.[52] But any Greeks responsible for innovation in this direction are unlikely to have
been Asianists: volubility seems still to have been the main
characteristic of Asian orators and their Roman imitators in the
40s B.C.[53] It may be relevant to note in this connection that a
tantalizingly fragmentary passage of Philodemus (*Rhet.* II.218f.
Sudhaus) seems to discuss Athenian rejection of periodic structure
in relation to school rhetoric. Seneca the Elder certainly does
not seem to have considered the style he most admired to be
Asiatic: he finds nothing inconsistent about including in *Contr.*
VII.4.6-8 expressions of approval for Demosthenes, Calvus and
Porcius Latro, and, when he refers to *Asiani*, he gives us no
warrant for supposing that he considered himself, or the declaimers
he most admired, to be among their ranks.

Of the two declamatory *genera dicendi* so far discussed, the
Fuscine and the Latronian, it was probably Latro's which had the
greater influence on the development of early Silver Latin. At any
rate, neither of Fuscus' two most distinguished pupils, Ovid and
Fabianus, were whole-hearted in their admiration for their master.

In *Contr.* II.2.8f. we are given an intriguing account of
Ovid's relations with Fuscus and Latro. Unfortunately, at an important juncture in this passage the received text seems suspect:

hanc controversiam memini ab Ovidio Nasone declamari apud rhetorem
Arellium Fuscum, cuius auditor fuit; nam Latronis admirator erat,
cum diversum sequeretur dicendi genus. habebat ille comptum et
decens et amabile ingenium. oratio eius iam tum nihil aliud
poterat videri quam solutum carmen. adeo autem studiose Latronem
audit ut multas illius sententias in versus suos transtulerit. in
armorum iudicio dixerat Latro: mittamus arma in hostis et petamus.
Naso dixit:

> arma viri fortis medios mittantur in hostis;
> inde iubete peti. (*Met.* XIII.121f.)
> et alium ex illa suasoria sensum aeque a Latrone mutuatus est.
> memini Latronem in praefatione quadam dicere quod scholastici
> quasi carmen didicerunt: non vides ut immota fax torpeat, ut ex-
> agitata reddat ignes? mollit viros otium, ferrum situ carpitur et
> rubiginem ducit, desidia dedocet. Naso dixit:
>   vidi ego iactatas mota face crescere flammas
>   et rursus nullo concutiente mori. (*Am.* I.2.11f.)
> tunc autem cum studeret habebatur bonus declamator. hanc certe
> controversiam ante Arellium Fuscum declamavit, ut mihi videbatur,
> <illo> longe ingeniosius, excepto eo quod sine certo ordine per
> locos discurrebat.

The problem lies in the meaning of *nam* in the opening sentence.[54]*

A clear contrast needs to be pointed between the fact that Ovid
was a pupil of Fuscus and the fact that he was an admirer of
Latro, for, given that the two rhetoricians favoured different
genera dicendi, the latter fact does not explain the former. Such
was the reasoning which must have led Gertz[55]* to propose the conjecture, *tamen Latronis admirator erat.* But an alternative way of
emending the passage might be by transposition, as follows:

hanc controversiam memini ab Ovidio Nasone declamari apud rhetorem
Arellium Fuscum, cuius auditor fuit, cum diversum sequeretur
dicendi genus; nam Latronis admirator erat.[56]*

'I remember this *controversia* being declaimed by Ovidius Naso at
the school of the rhetor Arellius Fuscus, whose pupil he was (at
that time - therefore perf.), although he favoured a different
style of speaking (from his master's); for he was (always -
therefore imperf.) an admirer of Latro.'

This transposition, if correct, would be of some importance, for
we would have to abandon any notion that the *dicendi genus* which
Ovid preferred as a student of rhetoric was that of his master
Fuscus, and take it that Latro was the more important influence
on him.

Various arguments might be used against this suggestion and
in favour of preferring an interpretation which made Ovid an ad-
herent of the Fuscine *dicendi genus*. First, it is said of Ovid's
prose later in *Contr.* II.2.8, *oratio eius iam tum nihil aliud
poterat videri quam solutum carmen.* Might the same not truly be
said of Fuscus' style in his *explicationes*? It might indeed be
suggested that the words, *habebat ille...transtulerit*, look like
a commentary on an assertion that Ovid was an admirer of Latro in
spite of favouring Fuscus' style. Again, Ovid is said not to have

organized his argumentation systematically in *Contr.* II.2; in this
respect he was no true follower of Latro. He preferred *suasoriae*
to *controversiae* (*Contr.* II.2.12); Fuscus is said to have declaimed
suasoriae '*libentissime*' (*Suas.* 4.5).[57]

Yet there is much to be said in favour of the supposition
that Latro had more influence on Ovid's style than Fuscus. Wandering and over-elaborate descriptive digressions are distinctly not a
typical feature of Ovid's poetry. Would one not expect to find
numerous examples of them, especially in the *Heroides* where Ovid
comes closest in his poetry to indulging his taste for *suasoriae*,
if he had been a true devotee of the Fuscine manner? Given that
he was a poet, it would be ludicrous to view his habit of imitating
Virgilian phrases as evidence of a predilection for the prose-
poetry of contemporary Asianists. He had in any case better taste
than they, as may readily be seen from a comparison between two
phrases concerning a river and its banks, one by Maecenas and one
from Ovid's *Amores*. Seneca the Younger in *Ep. mor.* 114.5 attributes to Maecenas the words, *amne silvisque ripa comantibus* (fr. 11
Lunderstedt), and Ovid opens *Am.* III.6 with the line, *amnis
harundinibus limosas obsite ripas* (cf. Virg. *Ecl.* 7.12f., *hic
virides tenera praetexit harundine ripas|Mincius*). Note how
Ovid's invocatory description of the river contains none of the
ambiguity of case endings which renders Maecenas' words obscure;
note too that it is confined to one line of poetry. Ovid's view
of the best length for descriptions is summed up in his criticism,
reported in *Contr.* VII.1.27, of some lines by Varro of Atax (fr. 8
Morel):

> desierant latrare canes urbesque silebant;
> omnia noctis erant placida composta quiete.
solebat Ovidius de his versibus dicere potuisse fieri longe
meliores si secundi versus ultima pars abscideretur et sic
desineret:
> omnia noctis erant.

And it is a view which we find reflected in his poetic practice;
as T. F. Higham has observed, 'Nature's operations on the grandest
scale are more than once depicted by Ovid with equal concise-
ness.'[58] It seems relevant to recall that Latro preferred *loci* of
all kinds to be kept short (*Contr.* VII.7.10) and how the fiery and

agitated style as described by Seneca contained *non lentas nec vacuas explicationes, sed plus sensuum quam verborum habentes* (*Contr.* III pr. 7). In the important matter of description, then, Ovid in his poetry is more Latronian than Fuscine, and there is no reason to suppose it was otherwise in his prose. That there is no extended *descriptio* in the sample of his declamation in *Contr.* II. 2.9ff. would prove nothing if considered in isolation, but we happen to be informed in *Contr.* II.2.12 that Ovid *verbis minime licenter usus est nisi in carminibus*... In his prose, therefore, he can hardly have been a very faithful follower of his master Fuscus, whose *licentia* of style in parts of his declamations is described by Seneca in *Contr.* II pr. 1 and elsewhere.

Having dismissed the hypothesis that poetic diction in the Fuscine manner was a feature of Ovid's prose, one next has to consider whether there are rhythmical qualities in it which mark it out as *nihil aliud...quam solutum carmen*, and whether in this respect Ovid has to be regarded as a follower of Fuscus rather than Latro. Here we move on to dangerous ground. For one thing, it is not only resemblances to dactylic verse in Ovid's prose which could be of significance in this enquiry for, although we only know Ovid as a composer of hexameters and pentameters, he was celebrated in antiquity also for his tragedy, the *Medea*, which was presumably written in a diversity of metres but principally in iambics. Further, in the analysis of prose-rhythm the simple truth has always to be remembered that all Latin sentences consist of collections of long and short syllables:[59] hence it is impossible to write prose in which sequences of iambs, trochees, cretics, dactyls, spondees and so on, will never occur.[60] So the mere fact that it is possible to analyse snatches of the Ovidian declamatory extract (*Contr.* II.2.9-11) as quasi-metrical, for example: *quĭd est quŏd ĭll(am) ăb ĭndulgentĭā sŭ(a) ăvocĕt* (§9) as iambic; *fer socer felicitatem* and *exciderat iurantibus* (§11) as trochaic; *sic amant. paucă nostĭ, pater, criminā* (§10) as cretic; *tŭ nōbīs religiōsum* (§9) as dactylic; *ecc(e) obiurgator nostri qu(am) effrenato* (*ibid.*) as heavily spondaic; *queritur pericul(um) eius* (§10) as anacreontic; and *sĭ solus moriturus essem* (§11) as hipponactean, need not by itself account for the elder Seneca's statement that Ovid's youthful prose style resembled *solutum carmen*, unless it proves to be the case that there is a much more pervasive metrical element in his prose than in that of other declaimers, in particular that of Latro.

This does not seem to be so, as can be demonstrated (to take a passage at random) from *Contr.* II.7.3, where Latro admits such quasi-metrical sequences as: *tempus est iudices* (cretic); *sollicitaretur potuit* and *quam faciem quamvis* (dactylic); *habeat comites* (anapaestic); *nequ(e) est quod dicat* (iambic); *-sum salutator(em) inhumana potius qu(am) inverecunda <sit>* (trochaic). It is true that similar rhythmic sequences can be extracted from samples of the 'dry' style of Arellius Fuscus as well as from his descriptions, for example from *Contr.* II.1.4: *iuvenum sine patre* (dactylic); *navigabo, militabo* and *pauperes sumus qu(i) habemus* (trochaic). The fact remains that the study of sentence rhythm gives us no grounds for supposing that a declaimer whose prose could be described as resembling *solutum carmen* could not have been a follower of Latro, rather than Fuscus, in his *dicendi genus*.[61]

Even more dangerous territory is entered if it is suggested that it was not so much the *actual* rhythms of Ovid's declamatory prose that justified the description *solutum carmen*, as rhythms *implied* in his various *sententiae*, that the *disiecti membra poetae* could be rearranged and with a certain amount of patching up could be turned into acceptable verses in the Ovidian manner. It can be pointed out, certainly, that it takes little remoulding to convert *quid ad patrem pertinet quod amantes iurant?* (*Contr.* II.2.10) into *pertinet ad patrem quod vos iuratis, amantes?*[62] But clearly such observations are unlikely to help us to decide which *dicendi genus* Ovid preferred, for surely a sufficiently determined versifier could achieve similar results by tampering with many a declamatory *sententia*, Fuscine or Latronian.

Perhaps in any case, despite the terms in which Ovid himself refers to his early attempts at writing (*Trist.* IV.10.25f.),

> sponte sua carmen numeros veniebat ad aptos,
>   et quod temptabam dicere versus erat,

it is wrong to suppose that Seneca had rhythmical qualities

primarily in mind when he wrote, *oratio eius iam tum nihil aliud poterat videri quam solutum carmen*. Maybe it was rather in Ovid's taste for *amatoriis...sententiis* (cf. *Contr*. III.7 *extra*), certainly apparent in *Contr*. II.2.9-11, that Seneca chiefly saw the characteristics of the poet foreshadowed in his declamatory prose. Affinities may certainly be found between the extract from Ovid's declamation and the elegiac tradition. It is not just that the theme of *Contr*. II.2 posed the question of how much weight should be attached to lovers' vows, a topic also treated in elegy, for example .in Tib. *El*. I.4.21ff. Most strikingly a sentence in §9, in which the word *pater* is used during an address to a father-in-law, *parce pater: non peieravimus*, is surely an imitation of Tibullus' protestation of his innocence before Jupiter in *El*. I. 3.51f.:

> parce, Pater. timidum non me peiuria terrent,
> non dicta in sanctos impia verba deos.

Tibullus' first book appeared in 27 or 26 B.C., when Ovid was about sixteen years old. Here is evidence that the younger man, presumably before briefly entering public life at about the age of nineteen (*Trist*. IV.10.29ff.), was given to imitating at least one poet in his declamations, thus producing something which could fairly be called *solutum carmen*.

To return to the hypothesis that Ovid preferred the *dicendi genus* of Latro to that of Fuscus, there is nothing in Seneca's criticism that makes it impossible to accept. Obviously in some respects Ovid differed in his tastes from both his official and his unofficial mentor. The repetitiousness which was to mar some of his verse had a counterpart in the speeches and declamations of Votienus Montanus (*Contr*. IX.5.15ff.), but not, as far as one can tell, in the style of either Fuscus or Latro. His manner of arranging arguments was probably in general less rigorous than that of Latro, but this was a respect in which he differed from Fuscus too, as we learn from *Contr*. II.2.9. In other ways he resembled both Fuscus and Latro. His liking for *suasoriae* was certainly a taste which he shared with Fuscus, but we must not be misled by the fact that Fuscus happens to figure more prominently than Latro in the extant surveys of *suasoriae* into thinking that

Latro despised this type of declamation: remember that in *Contr.*
II.4.8 he is reported to have declaimed a certain *suasoria* about
Theodotus for three days on end. Latro was just as inclined as
Fuscus to declaim *controversiae ethicae*, the other type of declamation favoured by Ovid (see *Contr.* II.2.12): like Fuscus and Ovid
he declaimed *Contr.* II.2 (see §1); as we have seen,[63] Seneca gives
us a very long extract from Latro's treatment of *Contr.* II.7,
which is certainly another example of this type of *controversia*.
Incidentally, there are no grounds for being surprised that Ovid,
if he was an admirer of Latro's *genus dicendi*, should have remained
a pupil of Fuscus, seeing that Latro refused to listen to his
pupils' declamations or correct their work (*Contr.* IX.2.23).

One more point of interpretation needs to be settled before
we leave the question of Ovid's preference in rhetorical style.
If we accept the transposition of the words *nam Latronis admirator
erat* to the end of the first sentence of *Contr.* II.2.8, we have to
abandon any notion that the words in the third sentence likening
Ovid's *oratio* to *solutum carmen* allude to a debt which he owed to
the Fuscine style. Consequently *autem* in the fourth sentence can
no longer be taken as pointing a contrast between adherence to
Fuscus' *dicendi genus* and admiration for Latro. If it does point
an antithesis it is between the fact that Ovid's poetic gifts were
apparent in his declamations and the fact that his declamatory
tastes left their mark on his poetry. But perhaps this is to read
a more rigorous logic into Seneca's reminiscences than was intended. *Autem* in his usage sometimes serves as a very vague connective with no particular antithetical force.[64]

That Fabianus, Fuscus' other most distinguished pupil, re-
acted against his master's style is clearly stated in *Contr.* II
pr. 1ff.

Cum repeterem, quos umquam bene declamantes audissem, occurrit
mihi inter alios Fabianus philosophus qui adulescens admodum
tantae opinionis in declamando, quantae postea in disputando fuit.
exercebatur apud Arellium Fuscum, cuius genus dicendi imitatus
plus deinde laboris impendit, ut similitudinem eius effugeret,
quam impenderat, ut exprimeret.

(There follows the description of Fuscus' style quoted above,
pp. 77f.)

ab hac cito se Fabianus separavit et luxuriam quidem cum voluit
abiecit, obscuritatem non potuit evadere; haec illum usque in
philosophiam prosecuta est. saepe minus quam audienti satis est
eloquitur, et in summa eius ac simplicissima facultate dicendi
antiquorum tamen vitiorum remanent vestigia. quaedam tam subito
desinunt, ut non brevia sint, sed abrupta. dicebat autem Fabianus
fere dulces sententias et, quotiens inciderat aliqua materia, quae
convicium saeculi reciperet, inspirabat magno magis quam acri
animo. deerat illi oratorium robur et ille pugnatorius mucro,
splendor vero velut voluntarius non elaboratae orationi aderat.
vultus dicentis lenis et pro tranquillitate morum remissus; vocis
nulla contentio, nulla corporis adseveratio, cum verba velut in-
iussa fluerent. iam videlicet conpositus et pacatus animus; cum
veros compressisset adfectus et iram doloremque procul expulisset,
parum bene imitari poterat quae effugerat. suasoriis aptior erat;
locorum habitus fluminumque decursus nemo descripsit abundantius.
numquam inopia verbi substitit, sed velocissimo ac facillimo cursu
omnes res beata circumfluebat oratio.

Not surprisingly we can find among the fragments of Fabianus'
declamations some which typify the standard sententious style of
the early Imperial schools, an arid version of which was to be
found in Fuscus' *prooemia*, *narrationes* and *argumenta*, others in
the Fuscine sing-song descriptive manner, and still others in a
rather different style, which we may suspect to belong to the
period after his conversion to philosophy.

Contr. II.2.4 will serve to show that Fabianus was fully
capable of hammering out clever *sententiae* and contriving the
sorts of figures of speech and thought which most delighted the
scholastic audiences:[65]

'non possum' inquit 'relinquere virum.' quicquam non potes, quae
mori potes? paene qui falsae mortis nuntium miserat verae recepit.
vir, dum nimis amat uxorem, paene causa periculi fuit; uxor, dum
nimis amat virum, paene causa luctus fuit; pater, dum nimis amat
filiam, abdicat. servate, <di>, totam domum amore mutuo labor-
antem. 'moriar' inquit: hoc patri minaris, viro promittis. potes
sine viro pati; peregrinationem eius tulisti. facilius potest
carere eo, cui spiritum debet, quam eo, cui inpendit.[66]

His description of Ocean in *Suas.* I.4 shows him to have been a
competent imitator of the more eccentric side of Fuscus' art:

quid? ista toto pelago infusa caligo navigantem tibi videtur ad-
mittere, quae prospicientem quoque excludit? non haec India est
nec ferarum terribilis ille conventus. inmanes propone beluas,
aspice quibus procellis fluctibusque saeviat, quas ad litora undas
agat. tantus ventorum concursus, tanta convulsi funditus maris
insania est; nulla praesens navigantibus statio est, nihil
salutare, nihil notum; rudis et inperfecta natura penitus recessit.
ista maria ne illi quidem petierunt qui fugiebant Alexandrum.

sacrum quiddam terris natura circumfudit Oceanum. illi qui iam
siderum collegerunt meatus et annuas hiemis atque aestatis vices
ad certam legem redegerunt, quibus nulla pars ignota mundi est, de
Oceano tamen dubitant, utrumne terras velut vinculum cludat an in
suum colligatur orbem et in hos per quos navigatur sinus quasi
spiramenta quaedam magnitudinis <suae> exaestuet; ignem post se,
cuius augmentum ipse sit, habeat an spiritum. quid agitis, con-
militones? domitoremne generis humani, magnum Alexandrum, eo
dimittitis quod adhuc quid sit disputatur? memento, Alexander:
matrem in orbe victo adhuc magis quam pacato relinquis.

Notice in particular the highly poetic quality of, for example,
the words in the opening sentence, *ista toto pelago infusa caligo*,
and his usages of *statio*, *meatus* and *spiramenta*; also the elaborate construction of the sentence (*illi qui...an spiritum*) in which
he describes the bafflement of learned men as to the nature and
extent of Oceanus; note too the occasional repetition of rhythmic
patterns at the beginning of phrases:

$$\text{ī}\breve{\text{s}}\text{tā tōtō pēlago...}$$
nāvīgāntēm tĭbi...

tāntă cŏnvulsī...
nūllā praēsēns navigantibus...[67]

One can also appreciate that if he continued to use such language
as we find in the passage, *an in suum colligatur orbem...habeat an
spiritum*, when he came to deal with questions of natural science
in his philosophical works, he might justly have been accused of
obscurity.

For a passage which may well belong to the period after
Fabianus' break with Fuscus we may look to the long extract, *Contr.*
II.1.10-13. The subject-matter, *convicium saeculi*, is of a type
which, so we have been told in *Contr.* II pr. 2, the future philosopher found particularly inspiring. The quest of riches is seen
as the cause of civil wars:

ecce instructi exercitus saepe civium cognatorumque conserturi
[praelium] manus constiterunt et colles equis utrimque complentur
et subinde omnis regio trucidatorum corporibus consternitur; illa
tum in multitudine cadaverum vel spoliantium sic quaesierit aliquis: quae causa hominem adversus hominem in facinus coegit? - nam
neque feris inter se bella sunt nec, si forent, eadem hominem
deceant, placidum proximumque divino genus; quae tanta vos pestis,
cum una stirps idemque sanguis sitis, quaeve furiae in mutuum
sanguinem egere? quod tantum malum <huic> uni generi vel fato vel
forte iniunctum? an, ut convivia populis instruantur et tecta
auro fulgeant, parricidium tanti fuit? magna enim vero et lauta
sunt propter quae mensam et lacunaria sua <nocentes> potius quam

lucem innocentes intueri maluerint. an, ne quid ventri negetur
libidinique, orbis servitium expetendum est? in quid tandem sic
pestiferae istae divitiae expetuntur si ne in hoc quidem, ut
liberis relinquantur? (*Contr.* II.1.10f. W)

As an instance of the general corruption brought about by riches,

modern extravagance in building is berated:

quid tandem est quod non divitiae corruperint? primum, si inde
incipere velis, aedes ipsas, quas in tantum extruxere ut, cum
domus ad usum ac munimentum paratae sint, nunc periculo, non
praesidio <sint>: tanta altitudo aedificiorum est tantaeque viarum
angustiae ut neque adversus ignem praesidium nec ex ruinis ullam
[villam] in partem effugium sit. (§11)

After enlarging on the topics of the use of expensive building

materials and the consequent anxiety of the rich about possible

accidental fires, arson and looting (all themes, like so much else

in Fabianus' declamation, paralleled in Senecan philosophy and

Imperial satire),[68] he goes on to reflect that the rich act as if

they had never seen the true beauties of nature:

o paupertas, quam ignotum bonum es! quin etiam montes silvasque
in domibus marcidis et in umbra fumoque viridia aut maria amnesque
imitantur. vix possum credere quemquam eorum vidisse silvas
virentisque gramine campos, quos rapidus amnis ex praecipitio vel,
cum per plana infusus est, placidus interfluit; non maria umquam
ex colle vidisse lenta, aut hiberna cum ventis penitus agitata
sunt: quis enim tam pravis oblectare animum imitamentis possit si
vera cognoverit? videlicet <haec illis placent> ut infantibus
quae tangi comprehendique manibus aut sinu possunt; nam magna non
capit exigua mens. ex hoc litoribus quoque moles iniungunt con-
gestisque in alto terris exaggerant sinus; alii fossis inducunt
mare: adeo nullis gaudere veris sciunt, sed adversum naturam
alieno loco aut terra aut mare mentita aegris oblectamenta sunt.
et miraris <si> fastidio rerum naturae laborantibus iam ne liberi
quidem nisi alieni placent? (§13)

Fabianus' fluency, and his particular aptitude for topographical

description are well illustrated in this last extract.

It is easy to imagine these sentiments being expressed by a

young man imbued with a newly found moral earnestness, but none-

theless one must be careful not to overstate any claim that

Fabianus in this passage departs from the style of Fuscine rhet-

oric. If faced, for instance, with the first sentence of *Contr.*

II.1.10 out of context, who would dare to state categorically that

it could not have been by Fuscus? But examination of Fabianus'

clausulae in the extract *Contr.* II.1.10-13 (25 in all, discounting

those where textual restoration has been necessary) perhaps

confirms one's subjective impression that it must have been composed after the break with Fuscus.[69] Of the 16 *clausula* types
found only 5 occur more than once. Three of these certainly are
types favoured by Fuscus: −∪−≚ (Fuscus: 18%) and −∪−−≚ (Fuscus:
12%) occur 3 times each; −∪−∪≚ (Fuscus: 13%) occurs twice. But
Fabianus departs from Fuscine practice in tolerating the hexameter
ending −∪∪−≚ twice[70] in this small sample (Fuscus 4%), and, most
strikingly, in using the rarely favoured rhythm ∪−−−∪≚ 4 times[71]
(Fuscus 1%). One of Fuscus' favourite *clausulae* −∪−−∪≚ (15%) is
used only once in this passage by Fabianus. How far he is depart-
ing from the usage of Fuscus and other rhetoricians in sentence
rhythm as a whole and in diction might be an interesting subject
for further investigation, but until much more research has been
done on the styles of the declaimers it would be dangerous to
assert that there is anything remarkable about, for example, the
frequency of elision (or hiatus) in the sentence, *tanta altitudo
aedificiorum est, tantaeque viarum angustiae ut neque adversus
ignem praesidium nec ex ruinis ullam in partem effugium sit,* or
the presence of such long and unsubtle alliterative sequences as,
*civium cognatorumque conserturi manus constiterunt et colles equis
virisque complentur et subinde omnis regio trucidatorum corporibus
consternitur.* The presence of such series of long syllables as
aedes ipsas quas in tant(um) extruxere, might similarly strike an
unwary analyst new to the field as an indication that Fabianus was
reacting against conventional rhetorical technique, but, as it
turns out, parallels for them can be found in the usage of both
Fuscus (e.g. *Suas.* 3.1: *haec interd(um) anno lex est*) and Latro
(e.g. *Contr.* II.7.3: *irritamentum spem corrumpendi; si tant(um) in
formonsa sperari posset, quantum...*). Such are the hazards of
close stylistic analysis when applied to the elder Seneca's declamatory collection.

   Fabianus was to be one of the philosophers most admired by
the younger Seneca. In *De brev. vit.* 10.1 he is described as *non
ex his cathedrariis philosophis sed ex veris et antiquis* and in
Ep. mor. 40.12 as *vir egregius et vita et scientia et, quod post
ista est, eloquentia.* *Ep. mor.* 100 consists of a long defence of
Fabianus against various strictures which Lucilius, Seneca's

correspondent, is said to have made on his style.   In a number of
respects the younger Seneca shares the opinions expressed by his
father in *Contr*. II pr. 1ff.[72]   All through the letter he is insistent that it is inappropriate to require a philosopher to aim
at the rhetorical standards which one expects from other types of
prose writer.   Lucilius had criticized Fabianus' *compositio* adversely (*Ep. mor*. 100.1), but Seneca has nothing but praise for
the untroubled flow of his language, so suitable for the conveying
of moral precepts,

Fabianus mihi non effundere videtur orationem sed fundere; adeo
larga est et sine perturbatione, non sine cursu tamen veniens.
illud plane fatetur et praefert, non esse tractatam nec diu tortam.
sed ita, ut vis, esse credamus: mores ille, non verba composuit et
animis scripsit ista, non auribus. (§2)

his disregard for modern fashions in the choice and arrangement of
words,

Fabianus non erat neglegens in oratione sed securus. itaque nihil
invenies sordidum: electa verba sunt, non captata, nec huius
saeculi more contra naturam suam posita et inversa, splendida
tamen quamvis sumantur e medio. (§5)

and his rejection of sententious brevity in favour of greater
breadth of expression,

sensus honestos et magnificos habes, non coactos in sententiam sed
latius dictos. (*Ibid.*)

To read these criticisms reinforces one's suspicions that the
declamatory excerpt, *Contr*. II.1.10-13, is not far removed stylistically from Fabianus' mature philosophical writings: certainly
there is a scarcity of ingeniously contrived *sententiae* in it, and
the diction and style, though not without parallels in the poetry
of his day,[73] do not offend the ear by any outlandish artifici-
ality; one can imagine Fabianus' audience already sensing that, as
Seneca was to put it in *Ep. mor*. 100.11, *ad profectum omnia tendunt,
ad bonam mentem: non quaeritur plausus.*

The younger Seneca's appreciation for Fabianus' unosten-
tatious mode of expression did not, of course, deter him from
using in his own philosophical works a style rather more in accordance with the taste of his rhetorically educated contemporaries.
In particular his fondness for sententiousness is well known.
However, like Fabianus, he seems to have rejected the excesses of

the Fuscine *explicatio*. Contrast, for example, with Fuscus' digression on weather signs in *Suas.* 3.1, Seneca's expression when
he describes the human mind contemplating the heavenly bodies
(*Quaest. nat.* I pr. 12),

secure spectat occasus siderum atque ortus et tam diversas con-
cordantium vias; observat ubi quaeque stella primum terris lumen
ostendat, ubi columen eius summumque cursus sit, quousque
descendat; curiosus spectator excutit singula et quaerit. quidni
quaerat? scit illa ad se pertinere,

or windless cloudy weather (*ibid.* V.3.1),

hoc falsum esse vel ex eo colligas licet quod tunc minime ventus
est cum aer nubilo gravis est; atqui tunc plurima corpora se in
angustum contulerunt et inde est spissarum nubium gravitas.

In both passages the sentence structure is clear and simple, ob-
scurities such as he criticizes elsewhere in Maecenas' descriptions
are absent, and there is none of the *licentia* of vocabulary for
which Fuscus, in common with Maecenas, was notorious. Seneca's
usages of *concordare, columen* and *in angustum* all have precedents
in extant Republican prose,[74] and it may well be accidental (due,
perhaps, merely to the fact that Cicero preferred ethics to phys-
ics) that we appear not to have a non-poetic precedent for the use
of *spissus* with reference to the density of matter. Seneca's
philosophical style might perhaps be described as a novel blend
between the discursiveness and *verba non captata* of Fabianus and
the *genus dicendi ardens et concitatum* favoured in the schools of
rhetoric.

Once we have recognized that Seneca the Younger, though a
modernist, shows himself, both by his admiration for Fabianus and
by his rejection of the style of descriptive writing characteristic of Fuscus, an opponent of the phenomenon which his age regarded as Asianism, it becomes easier to understand how it was
that he not only felt capable of preaching to his readers in *Ep.
mor.* 114 on the diverse types of corrupt style, but could also
join in a debate on the causes of the corruption which was in all
probability[75] an echo of earlier speculations of Greek theorists
who deplored the decline of oratory in the Hellenistic world.

To return to the early Imperial declaimers, none of them
seemed to the elder Seneca's sensitive ears to have sounded
exactly like Fuscus or exactly like Latro. Nearest to Fuscus,

perhaps, of the declaimers criticized in his prefaces,[76] was Musa,
a rhetorician whose *floruit* must have been much later than that of
Fuscus, seeing that the elder Seneca's sons were able to attend
his declamations (*Contr.* X pr. 9). That Musa is recorded to have
used such far-fetched metaphors as *caelo repluunt, odoratos imbres,
caelatas silvas* and *nemora surgentia*[77] (*ibid.*) seems clear enough
evidence as to the type of description which he favoured. Some
other egregious examples of his descriptive technique are quoted
in *Suas.* 1.13 where, after quoting a *sententia* (now lost) by one
Menestratus, Seneca remarks:

efficit haec sententia ut ignoscam Musae, qui dixit ipsis Charybdi
et Scylla maius portentum: 'Charybdis ipsius maris naufragium' et,
ne in una re semel insaniret: 'quid ibi potest esse salvi ubi
ipsum mare perit?'

Elsewhere we are told of another declaimer, Vibius Gallus, who was
unique in making positive efforts to attain *insania* and in particular was notorious for his manner of introducing descriptions:

Gallus Vibius fuit tam magnae olim eloquentiae quam postea
insaniae, cui hoc accidisse uni scio, ut in insaniam non casu in-
cideret, sed iudicio perveniret; nam dum insanos imitatur, dum
lenocinium ingeni furorem putat, quod cotidie simulabat ad verum
redegit...solebat autem sic ad locos pervenire, ut amorem descripturus paene cantantis modo diceret: 'amorem describere volo'
sic tamquam 'bacchari volo.' deinde describebat et <ut> totiens
coepturus repetebat: 'amorem describere volo.' (*Contr.* II.1.25f.)

Vibius Gallus evidently had some redeeming features, for Seneca
says of his description of riches in *Contr.* II.1, *multa facunde
explicuit, corruptius quam Fabianus sed dulcius* (§26), but for
sheer bombast it would be difficult to beat a portentous utterance,
ad mortis auctorem per vulnera sua ruunt, in his description of
concitatissuma...in morte rabies in *Contr.* IX.6.2. Clearly he and
Musa were kindred spirits, and there may have been affinities between his manner of delivery and that of Fuscus.[78]

   Latro's closest rival, in the elder Seneca's view (*Contr.* X
pr. 13), and probably the declaimer who most resembled him, was
Iunius Gallio. There must surely have been some sort of tribute
to him in one of the prefaces now lost, even though Gallio was
still alive when Seneca was writing and was evidently a great
friend of his three sons,[79] who therefore did not need to be told
about his gifts as an orator and declaimer. It is most unfortunate

that only a few of Seneca's passing remarks about his declamations
are extant.

Gallio's style was to be adversely criticized, though distinguished from that of Maecenas, by Vipstanus Messala in Tacitus'
Dialogus,

ceterum si omisso optimo illo et perfectissimo genere eloquentiae
eligenda sit forma dicendi, malim hercule C. Gracchi impetum aut
L. Crassi maturitatem quam calamistros Maecenatis aut tinnitus
Gallionis... (*Dial.* 26.1)

and almost any extract from Gallio's declamations will serve to
show why a critic surveying the whole development of Roman eloquence should have dismissed his style as *tinnitus*. Take, for
example, *Contr.* II.3.6:[80]

'rogo' inquit. nunc? hic? sic? si volebas rogare, admovisses
propinquos, amicos, maiorum imagines, lacrimas, repetitos alte
gemitus. testor deos, sic rogaturus fui puellae patrem. 'quando'
inquit <'misereberis?' cum> vultum in supplicis habitum summiseris,
cum dixeris: 'paenitet quod rapui, quod te priorem non rogavi',
cum dixeris te dementem fuisse, deliberabo cum amicis, deliberabo
cum propinquis, deliberabo cum tua matre. me miserum, quam paene
promisi! <dura>, anime, dura; here fortior eras. et multum habeo
quod deliberem: diversi me adfectus distringunt, inter reum et
patrem distrahor; hinc iniuria est, hinc natura.

Fortunately, we are not left completely in the dark as to why
Seneca the Elder, by contrast, had a high opinion of Gallio. We
are told that he displayed remarkably good taste in the use of
colloquial language (*idiotismos*): *iam adulescentulus cum declamaret
apte et convenienter et decenter hoc genere utebatur; quod eo magis
mirabar quia tenera aetas refugit omne non tantum quod sordidum
sed quod sordido simile est* (*Contr.* VII pr. 6). In this respect
Seneca evidently regarded him as superior to Albucius, another
member of the *primum tetradeum* (*Contr.* VII pr. 3; cf. X pr. 13).
That Gallio was appreciative of the power of others to sway the
emotions of their hearers is evident from his praise of Cassius
Severus in *Contr.* III pr. 2, and presumably he tried to emulate
what he admired. Certainly we see from his *testamenti figura* in
Contr. IX.3.14 that he was a virtuoso in the treatment of figures,
than which, in Quintilian's view (IX.1.21), *adfectus nihil magis
ducit*. On certain occasions we find him contriving *sententiae* of
the types most admired by his friend: in *Contr.* I.1.25 he effects
a transition from *prooemium* to *narratio* by means of a *sententia*

and, just before, Seneca has praised Hermagoras' use of this very
device; in *Suas.* 5.8 Seneca singles out one of Gallio's *sententiae*
for some of the highest praise he ever gives, *hoc loco disertissimam sententiam dixit, <dignam> quae in oratione vel in historia
ponatur: diutius illi perire possunt quam nos vincere.* To us, as
to Gerth, who in his Pauly-Wissowa article comments *'sehr
sophistisch'*,[81] it may not seem worthy of such high commendation,
but it should be borne in mind that this *sententia* was uttered in
the course of a very unusual treatment of the *suasoria* in question.
Gallio was the only declaimer whom Seneca remembered taking the
part of a representative of the peace party at Athens when faced
with renewed threats of invasion from Xerxes (*Suas.* 5.8), and
Seneca is elsewhere found to be appreciative when a declaimer presents *vivum consilium* rather than merely reeling off stock arguments (*Suas.* 6.11). When choosing lines of argument Gallio was
unafraid of *quaestiones durae* (*Contr.* IX.1.10), a characteristic
he shared with Latro (*Contr.* X pr. 15). In the matter of *colores*
Gallio agreed with Seneca that excuses about dreams were a poor
substitute for more rational pleas (*Contr.* II.1.33). To some
limited extent, then, we are able to form an impression of Gallio's
talent, and to appreciate how near it came to the elder Seneca's
declamatory ideal.

All the other declaimers fell short of it, but for a wide
variety of reasons. Cassius Severus, though he possessed all the
qualities which ought to have made him a good declaimer (*Contr.*
III pr. 7), was one of those men who, though highly successful in
the forum, were deserted by their talent when they turned to
declamation: *non tantum infra se, cum declamaret, sed infra multos
erat* (*Contr.* III pr. 7 cf. *ibid.* 1). His declamations struck
Seneca as uneven: *declamationes eius inaequales erant, sed ea,
quae eminebant, in quacumque declamatione posuisses, inaequalem
eam fecissent* (*ibid.* 18); other notable characteristics of his
style included *compositio aspera et quae vitaret conclusionem,
sententiae vivae* (*ibid.*). Seneca apologizes for not being able to
give an adequately representative sample of Severus' declamatory
manner: *iniquom tamen erit ex his eum aestimari, quae statim subtexam; non enim haec ille optime dixit, sed haec ego optime teneo*

(*ibid.*).   Now that the full text of *Contr.* III-VI and VIII is lost
the sampling available to us is all the more inadequate: only two
extracts of any length and a few isolated *sententiae* are extant.
The report of his harangue against the pretensions of the schools
(*Contr.* III pr. 8-18) may perhaps be looked to for evidence of the
gift for forceful impromptu speaking to which Seneca refers in
Contr. III pr. 6, *ex tempore coactus dicere infinito se ante-*
cedebat. numquam non utilius erat illi deprehendi quam prae-
parari.   But it is impossible for us now to assess the full range
of Severus' style.

The longest of the declamatory extracts reveals an unexpected
gift on Cassius Severus' part for gruesome description:

hinc caeci innitentes baculis vagantur, hinc trunca bracchia
circumferunt, huic convulsi pedum articuli sunt et <ex>torti tali,
huic elisa crura, illius inviolatis pedibus cruribusque femina
contudit: aliter in quemque saeviens ossifragus iste alterius
bracchia amputat, alterius enervat, alium distorquet, alium de-
lumbat, alterius diminutas scapulas in deforme tuber extundit et
risum <e> crudelitate captat. produc, agedum, familiam semivivam,
tremulam, debilem, caecam, mancam, famelicam; ostende nobis
captivos tuos. volo mehercules nosse illum specum tuum, illam
humanarum calamitatium officinam, illud infantium spoliarium. sua
quoique calamitas tamquam ars adsignatur: huic recta membra sunt,
et, si nemo moratur, proceritas emicabit: ita frangantur, ut humo
se adlevare non possit, sed pedum crurumque resolutis vertebris
reptet. huic <eximii oculi sunt>: extirpentur radicitus. huic
[non] speciosa facies est: potest formonsus mendicus esse; reliqua
membra inutilia sint, ut Fortunae iniquitas in beneficia sua
saevientis magis hominum animos percellat. <sic> sine satellitibus
tyrannus calamitates humanas dispensat. (*Contr.* X.4.2 M)

A number of the words used by Severus in this passage seem to be
either neologisms or new to prose: *extundere*, *spoliarium*, *reptare*,
extirpare, *speciosus*.   Other expressions, however, contribute
something of an archaic flavour to the passage: *famelicus*, a
favourite word of the ante-classical comic poets, appears not to
have been used at all by Cicero; the long string of adjectives in
the sentence, *produc, agedum, familiam semivivam, tremulam,*
debilem, caecam, mancam, famelicam, may be compared with Plaut.
Merc. 630, *ad mandata claudus, caecus, mutus, mancus, debilis.*
Interestingly, it emerges from *Contr.* VII.3.8f. that Severus had
an interest in Republican drama - he refers to Pomponius and
Laberius as early Latin punsters - and that he did not eschew even

the mimes of Publilius as a source of expressions worth imitating.
In the other main extant fragment from his declamations (*Contr.*
IX.2.12) we find him echoing another sort of archaic expression,
the language of Roman law:

ne de servo quidem aut captivo omni loco aut omni genere aut per
quos libebit aut cum libebit supplicium sumi fas est, adhibeturque
ad ea magistratus ob custodiam, non ob laetitiam.

In both these declamatory extracts we detect something of the
censoriousness which, according to Seneca, characterized his oratory so long as he refrained from joking: *quamdiu citra iocos se
continebat, censoria oratio erat* (*Contr.* III pr. 4). Less clear
is what Seneca meant when he described his *compositio* as *aspera et
quae vitaret conclusionem* (*ibid.* 18). This last word, Thomas'
emendation of the MSS reading *compositionem*, probably refers to
artistic *clausula*-rhythm[82] rather than to 'periodic structure',[83]
the avoidance of which was so general in his time that Seneca would
hardly have thought it worthy of comment. Too few of Severus'
declamatory *sententiae* are extant to allow systematic investigation of his rhythmical practice. One which may be singled out
as jerkily constructed is the *anthypophora* in *Contr.* VII.3.10,
quare ergo nunc non moreris? dicet aliquis.[84] For almost invariably declaimers, when imagining possible retorts of an adversary, would say *dicet aliquis* or the like *first*, before voicing
the hypothetical objection.

Severus' harangue against the rhetoricians in *Contr.* III pr.
8ff. is illustrative of his wit, for which however there can have
been little scope in his declamations; funniest of all is his
story about Cestius Pius in §16:

memini me intrare scholam eius cum recitaturus esset in Milonem;
Cestius ex consuetudine sua miratus dicebat: si Thraex essem,
Fusius essem; si pantomimus essem, Bathyllus essem, si equus,
Melissio. non continui bilem et exclamavi: si cloaca esses,
maxima esses. risus omnium ingens; scholastici intueri me, quis
essem qui tam crassas cervices haberem. Cestius Ciceroni responsurus mihi quod responderet non invenit, sed negavit se
executurum nisi exissem de domo. ego negavi me de balneo publico
exiturum nisi lotus essem.

Other passages in the harangue serve to show how unsubtle he might
be when speaking impromptu - hence perhaps his effectiveness on
such occasions.[85] We have to take it on trust from the elder

Seneca that Severus normally composed speeches with the utmost
care, always expunging anything redundant or irrelevant to his
case: *nemo minus passus est aliquid in actione sua otiosi esse;*
nulla pars erat, quae non sua virtute staret, nihil in quo auditor
sine damno aliud ageret (Contr. III pr. 2). No one would have
guessed this from the style of the opening of the explanation he
gives why he was not so successful in declamation as in oratory,
where he hammers home the point that specialization was a common
phenomenon with quite unnecessary verbosity, showing by means of
example after example that poets, historians, philosophers, strong
men, dogs, horses, actors and gladiators as well as orators tended
to be successful in only one, sometimes very limited, sphere of
activity (*Contr.* III pr. 8-11).

Cassius Severus was later to be considered a very important
figure in the transition from the old to the new style of Latin
oratory at the beginning of the Empire - the first of the moderns
in the view of Aper in Tacitus' *Dialogus,*

...quem primum adfirmant flexisse ab illa vetere atque derecta
dicendi via, non infirmitate ingenii nec inscitia litterarum
transtulisse se ad illud dicendi genus contendo, sed iudicio et
intellectu. vidit namque, ut paulo ante dicebam, cum condicione
temporum et diversitate aurium formam quoque ac speciem orationis
esse mutandam. (19.1f.)

Vipstanus Messala later in the dialogue does not dispute Severus'
primacy in the new style, though he takes a less glowing view of
his achievement:

equidem non negaverim Cassium Severum, quem solum Aper noster
nominare ausus est, si iis comparetur qui postea fuerunt, posse
oratorem vocari, quamquam in magna parte librorum suorum plus
bilis habeat quam sanguinis. primus enim contempto ordine rerum,
omissa modestia ac pudore verborum, ipsis etiam quibus utitur
armis incompositus et studio feriendi plerumque deiectus, non
pugnat sed rixatur. ceterum, ut dixi, sequentibus comparatus et
varietate eruditionis et lepore urbanitatis et ipsarum virium
robore multum ceteros superat. (26.4)

The elder Seneca nowhere in his extant books singles out
Severus as the originator of the new oratory, though it is apparent from his descriptions of Scaurus and Labienus in the tenth
preface[86] that he recognized a distinction between an old and a
new style of oratory. Seneca only gives us Severus' own opinion
as to who were the leading orators of his day, and he had the

modesty to exclude himself, naming instead *Pollionem Asinium et Messalam Corvinum et Passienum, qui nunc primo loco stat* (*Contr.* III pr. 14). Something of the bile and brawling criticized by Vipstanus Messala in the *Dialogus* can be detected in Severus' onslaught on the rhetoricians, and there is perhaps a good example of contempt for any predictable *ordo rerum* in the way he moves from human to animal examples of specialization and back again in *Contr.* III pr. 8-11. Seneca does anticipate the critics of the *Dialogus* in thinking highly of Severus as an orator, considering him to be underrated by people who had not heard and seen him in action:

non est quod illum ex his quae edidit aestimetis; sunt quidem et hic quibus eloquentia eius <agnoscatur; tamen auditus> longe maior erat quam lectus. non hoc ea portione illi accidit qua omnibus fere, quibus maiori commendationi est audiri quam legi, sed in illo longe maius discrimen est. (*Contr.* III pr. 3 W)

It is a great pity that we have lost so many of the fragments of his declamations which Seneca must originally have provided, even though they would have given us no adequate notion of the strengths of his oratorical manner.

Cestius Pius, singled out by Cassius Severus as typifying the lunacy of the rhetorical schools, was an interesting character. A. D. Leeman has described him as 'venomous',[87] but this seems rather a hard verdict on a man who, though he compromised his own talent by his willingness to play to the gallery, and may have discouraged certain of the younger generation from the pursuit of any high literary ideals they might otherwise have had, can hardly be reckoned more noxious than the average *poseur*.

Cestius was a Greek (from Smyrna according to St Jerome),[88] but overturned the normal order of things by choosing to work as a Latin rhetorician (see *Contr.* IX.3.13). The most notable fact about Cestius as a stylist would seem to be that his command of Latin was somewhat limited and that for this reason, if for no other, his *explicationes* were not of the same order as those of Arellius Fuscus:

soleo dicere vobis Cestium Latinorum verborum inopia <ut> hominem Graecum laborasse, sensibus abundasse; itaque, quotiens latius aliquid describere ausus est, totiens substitit, utique cum se ad imitationem magni alicuius ingeni derexerat, sicut in hac

controversia fecit. nam in narratione, cum fratrem traditum sibi
describeret, placuit sibi in hac explicatione una et infelici: nox
erat concubia, et omnia, iudices, canentia <sub> sideribus muta
erant. (*Contr.* VII.1.27)

Despite his inadequacies, however, his self-esteem knew no bounds,
and one of his chief poses was to belittle Cicero, encouraging his
pupils to learn by heart his own declamations, but only to read
those speeches of Cicero to which he, Cestius, had composed
answers (*Contr.* III pr. 15). He was once pointed out to Cicero's
drunken son at a banquet as *Cestius, qui patrem tuum negabat
litteras scisse*, and duly received a horse-whipping (*Suas.* 7.14).

For all this, Cestius was an influential teacher, preferred,
along with Latro, by the younger generation, to the leading orators of his time (*Contr.* III pr. 14f.). He numbered among his
pupils, besides Argentarius, so thorough-going a plagiarist of his
master's *sententiae* that Cestius called him *Cesti simius* or ὁ
πίθηκός μου (*Contr.* IX.3.12), Alfius Flavus, a remarkable child
prodigy (*Contr.* I.1.22), and Surdinus, a gifted youth, *a quo
Graecae fabulae eleganter in sermonem Latinum conversae sunt* (*Suas.*
7.12). Mature men also sometimes declaimed in his school, for
example the senator Aietius Pastor (*Contr.* I.3.11).

It appears from the quite numerous criticisms by Cestius
quoted by Seneca the Elder that he was by no means lacking in
natural good taste and discrimination. His remarks in *Suas.* 1.
5ff.,[89] on the need to vary one's tactics in *suasoriae* to suit the
character of the person one is addressing, are perfectly sensible.
Elsewhere we often find Cestius intolerant of lapses of taste or
inconsistencies, whether committed by his pupils or by rival rhetoricians: unfortunate *doubles entendres* (*Contr.* I.3.10; *Suas.* 7.
12); breaches of propriety (*Contr.* I.5.3; 6.11); statements damaging to the declaimer's own case (*Contr.* I.3.9; II.3.22; 6.8);
incredibility (*Contr.* I.3.11); the discussion of scarcely relevant
philosophical quibbles (*Contr.* VII pr. 8f.); naïve use of the device of *echo* (*Contr.* VII.7.19); fanciful metaphorical expression
(*Contr.* VII pr. 9); even incorrect Latin usage (*Contr.* I.3.9) -
all these faults call forth scorn from Cestius. Yet it was a
curious fact that Cestius did not eliminate from his own work the
faults which he criticized in others':

tantus autem error est in omnibus quidem studiis, <sed> maxime in
eloquentia, cuius regula incerta est, ut vitia quidam sua et
intellegant et ament. Cestius pueriliter se dixisse intellegebat:
'mater, quid est venenum?'; deridebat enim Murredium qui hanc
sententiam imitatus in epilogo, cum adloqui coepisset puellam et
diceret: 'compone te in periclitantium habitum, profunde lacrimas,
manus ad genua dimitte, rea es', fecerat respondentem puellam:
pater, quid est rea? et aiebat Cestius: quod si ad deridendum me
dixit, homo venustus fuit, et ego nunc scio me ineptam sententiam
dicere; multa autem dico non quia mihi placent sed quia audientibus
placitura sunt. (*Contr.* IX.6.11f.)

Asinius Pollio, introduced by Seneca in the fourth preface,
was obviously a much greater man than Cestius, and differed from
him enormously in his attitude towards declamation, regarding it,
so Seneca believed (*Contr.* IV pr. 2), as an exercise too far
beneath his intellectual dignity for him to perform in public.
Yet he resembled Cestius in not demanding of himself, when declaiming, the high standards of which he was capable, and which
he demanded of others. In his declamations he adopted a style
different from that of his speeches, and was less rigorously self-
critical than usual:

floridior[90] erat aliquanto in declamando quam in agendo: illud
strictum eius et asperum et nimis iratum ingenio suo iudicium adeo
cessabat, ut in multis illi venia opus esset, quae ab ipso vix inpetrabatur. (*Contr.* IV pr. 3)

Insufficient fragments are extant from which to form an adequate impression of Pollio's oratory, but there is certainly a
marked contrast between the style of the quotation from his *Pro
Lamia* in *Suas.* 6.15 (= Pollio fr. 19, *ORF*[3] 519):

itaque numquam per Ciceronem mora fuit quin eiuraret suas [esse]
quas cupidissime effuderat orationes in Antonium; multiplicesque
numero et accuratius scriptas illis contrarias edere ac vel ipse
palam pro contione recitare pollicebatur

and the declamatory extract in *Contr.* VII.1.4 W:

aequas mihi praebete aures: dabo vobis etiam damnatum absolvendum.
'vivit' inquit 'frater'; non credo. 'servavit' inquit 'me';
fecisti ut crederem. haec est summa rerum gestarum: in ea domo in
qua facile parricidium creditum est, ego fratrem occidere non potui,
frater patrem. 'quid mihi cum ista tabula? semel mori volo.'

Note particularly the extraordinary number of disyllabic words in
the latter example and the resulting jerkiness of effect.[91]
Another declamatory extract begins with a sentence cast in a form
which seems to have been a favourite among the least austere of

the declaimers, *inter nuptiales fescenninas in crucem generi
nostri iocabantur* (*Contr.* VII.6.12), with which we may compare,
for example, *Contr.* I.1.6: *inter funestas acies armatae manus in
foedus porriguntur* (Fuscus); *Contr.* IX.2.24: *inter temulentas
ebriorum reliquias humanum everritur caput* (Florus). Without
Seneca's testimony one would never have believed it possible that
Asinius Pollio, with his reputation for rugged *compositio* (Sen.
Ep. mor. 100.7) and archaizing tendencies (Quint. X.1.113), could
have declaimed in this manner. It is not as if Pollio's *strictum
...et asperum...iudicium* (*Contr.* IV pr. 3) was not provoked by the
efforts of other declaimers. He was hard on Latro, who prided
himself on the quasi-forensic simplicity of his *divisiones*, for
leaving out, when he declaimed *Contr.* II.3, a *quaestio* on which
the whole case would have hinged if it were being heard in the
courts (*Contr.* II.3.13). He condemned the famous *explicationes* in
Fuscus' *suasoriae* as not being aimed at persuasion (*Suas.* 2.10).
His archaizing tastes are reflected in his approval of Vibius
Rufus' *sententia* in *Contr.* IX.2.25, *at nunc a praetore lege actum
est ad lucernam*,[92] and also perhaps in his revival of the ancient
practice of alternating declamations for the prosecution and the
defence when teaching his grandson Marcellus Aeserninus (*Contr.*
IV pr. 3).

Q. Haterius, introduced along with Pollio in the fourth preface, fell short of Seneca's ideal in declamation mainly because of
his excessive verbosity (*Contr.* IV pr. 7ff.), a trait which was
evidently also a feature of his oratory (Sen. *Ep. mor.* 40.10f.;
Tac. *Ann.* 4.61). He was noted for declaiming impromptu and at
great speed:

declamabat autem Haterius admisso populo ex tempore: solus omnium
Romanorum, quos modo ipse cognovi, in Latinam linguam transtulit
Graecam facultatem. tanta erat illi velocitas orationis ut vitium
fieret. itaque divus Augustus optime dixit: 'Haterius noster
sufflaminandus est'; adeo non currere sed decurrere videbatur.
nec verborum illi tantum copia sed etiam rerum erat: quotiens
velles eandem rem et quamdiu velles diceret, aliis totiens figuris,
aliis tractationibus, ita ut regi posset nec consumi. (*Contr.* IV
pr. 7)

He was evidently a highly-strung individual, having been moved to
tears by the pathos of his own declamation on one memorable

occasion, and it was at times like this, when his emotions were
aroused, that he was at his most powerful (*Contr*. IV pr. 6,11).
His worst fault seems to have been the lack of clear structure in
his declamations. We are told that he had to employ a freedman to
tell him when he had treated any given topic sufficiently and
needed to move on to the next (*ibid*. 8). His argumentation did
not give the impression of being at all well organized, *dividere
controversiam putabat ad rem pertinere, si illum interrogares, non
putabat, si audires* (*ibid*. 9); Seneca never refers to him in his
analyses of *divisiones*.

Some idea of Haterius' technique of amplification may be
gained from an examination of the extract from his treatment of
Suas. 6, *deliberat Cicero an Antonium deprecetur*:

sciant posteri potuisse Antonio servire rem publicam, non potuisse
Ciceronem. laudandus erit tibi Antonius; in hac causa etiam
Ciceronem verba deficient. crede mihi, cum diligenter te custodi-
eris, faciet tamen Antonius quod Cicero tacere non possit. si
intellegis, Cicero, non dicit 'roga ut vivas', sed 'roga ut
servias.' quemadmodum autem hunc senatum intrare poteris, ex-
haustum crudeliter, repletum turpiter? intrare autem tu senatum
voles in quo non Cn. Pompeium visurus \<es\>, non M. Catonem, non
Lucullos, non Hortensium, non Lentulum atque Marcellum, non \<tuos\>,
tuos, inquam, consules Hirtium ac Pansam? Cicero, quid in alieno
saeculo tibi? iam nostra peracta sunt. M. Cato, solus maximum
vivendi moriendique exemplum, mori maluit quam rogare – nec erat
Antonium rogaturus – et illas usque ad ultimum diem puras a civili
sanguine manus in pectus sacerrimum armavit. Scipio, cum gladium
\<in\> pectus abdidisset, quaerentibus qui in navem transierant
militibus imperatorem 'imperator' inquit 'bene se habet.' victus
vocem victoris emisit. 'vetat' inquis '\<me\> Milo rogare iudices';
i nunc et Antonium roga. (*Suas*. 6.1f. W)

As early Imperial rhetoric goes, this passage has quite a flowing
quality, *canorum illud et profluens*, to use Tacitus' expression
(*Ann*. IV.61). Haterius allows himself plenty of time to dwell on
each point. The first four sentences, for example, form a group,
in that the first and the fourth relate to the proposition that
Cicero cannot be a slave, and the middle two to the related notion
that he will not be able to remain silent. Haterius is indulging
in ring-composition, one of the oldest devices in the impromptu
speaker's technique. The list of missing members of the Senate
(*quemadmodum...Pansam*) does not lack amplitude; two examples of
noble suicides are given where one might have sufficed.

C. Albucius Silus was another declaimer lacking in a due
sense of proportion and given to over-developing the various sections of his declamations (*Contr.* VII pr. 1f.),[93*] but the elder
Seneca evidently preferred his efforts to those of Haterius. On
Haterius his verdict had been that despite the muddy flow of his
rhetoric (*cum turbidus flueret*) there was more to praise in it
than to pardon (*Contr.* IV pr. 11); he is even more generous to
Albucius, going as far as to include him in his *primum tetradeum*
(*Contr.* X pr. 13).

The chief features which recommended his work were the
splendor which generally characterized his style (*Contr.* VII pr.
2); his straightforward, unambiguous *sententiae* (*ibid.*); his skill
at arousing the right reactions in his audience (*ibid.* 3: *adfectus
efficaciter movit, figurabat egregie, praeparabat suspiciose*),[94]
and his apparently effortless command of inexhaustibly rich
supplies of Latin expression (*ibid.*).

The long extract from Albucius' treatment of *Contr.* VII.1
which follows immediately after his introduction in the seventh
preface may be taken to illustrate some of the best features of
his style. It certainly contains some noteworthy figures of
speech and thought. Take, for example, a passage from near the
beginning of §2, where the young man who cast his brother, con-
victed of *parricidium*, adrift in an open boat, rather than punishing him in the traditional manner, defends his action:

a me frater ut viveret non impetravit, ut fugeret non impetravit:
nihil aliud impetravit quam ut aliter quam in culleo moreretur.
malam causam habeo, ut inter fratres. ubi spes? in gubernaculo?
nulla est. in remigio? ne in hoc quidem est. in comite? nemo
repertus est naufragi comes. in velo? in antemna? omnia [paene]
instrumenta circumcisa sunt, adminiculum spei nullum est.

The first sentence provides examples of ἰσόκωλον (Quint. IX.3.80),
repetitio - repetition of like openings - and *conversio* -
repetition of like endings (*Rhet. Her.* IV.13.19):

        ut viveret non impetravit
        ut fugeret non impetravit
        nihil aliud impetravit...

The section beginning with *in gubernaculo*, by way of a change,
takes the form of a *tetracolon* with members of progressively
increasing length:

```
in gubernaculo?  nulla est.
in remigio?  ne in hoc quidem est.
in comite?  nemo repertus est naufragi comes.
in velo?  in antemna?  omnia instrumenta circumcisa sunt,
   adminiculum spei nullum est.
```

Each member begins with the same word, as had the first two members of the preceding sentence, but Albucius avoids the jingling
effect which would have resulted if each had ended similarly, by
varying the close of the third one. There are other clever
touches. Notice the calculated decrease in the number of syllables in the second word of each member: *gubernaculo* 5, *remigio*
4, *comite* 3, *velo* 2. Notice also how, to avoid excessive styl-
ization, Albucius asks in the last member not one but two rhetorical questions. The sentence, *malam causam habeo, ut inter fratres*,
may be taken as an instance of one of those simple *sententiae,*
quas optime Pollio Asinius albas vocabat (*Contr*. VII pr. 2); it
can also be regarded as an example of the figure *confessio nihil*
nocitura (Quint. IX.2.51). This was classed as a figure of
thought, whereas *isocolon*, *tetracolon*, *repetitio* and *conversio*
count as figures of speech. But Albucius' distinguished performance in the use of these two main classes of *figurae* was probably
not all that Seneca had in mind when he wrote of him in *Contr*. VII
pr. 3, *figurabat egregie*, for, as we have seen,[95] he occasionally
refers to a procedure *figura dividere*, and one instance of it is
credited to Albucius in *Contr*. I.2.16.

For all its merits, however, Albucius' declamatory manner
lacked the *aequalitas* which Seneca could have wished for (*Contr*.
VII pr. 3). In particular he had the habit of flouting declamatory convention by using *verba sordida* which sounded to Seneca's
ears most incongruous amidst his otherwise resplendent diction
(*ibid*. 4).[96*] Examples of his taste for sordid words may be found
in *Contr*. I.5.9; 7.18; X.1.14. Furthermore Albucius' style de-
teriorated as he grew older, owing to his inability to settle down
and use any one style consistently. He was for ever imitating the
last stylist to whom he happened to have been listening. Seneca
could remember him listening to Fabianus the philosopher with
codices at the ready, oblivious to all else, and similarly listening, stupified, to the eloquence of Hermagoras, filled with an

ardent desire to imitate him (*Contr.* VII pr. 4f.). Subject as he
was to such overwhelming enthusiasms, he ranged from time to time
through all the available *genera dicendi*, and never fulfilled the
great promise of his youth by developing a distinctive style of
his own: sometimes he would be *exilis* and expound only bare facts,
sometimes he would be *horridus et valens potius quam cultus*, sometimes *brevis et concinnus*, sometimes too elevated, at other times
not elevated enough (*ibid.* 5).[97]

The nature of Seneca's declamatory extracts is such that we
are prevented from illustrating all the variations of Albucius'
style. Terseness in the extracts may, for example, on many occasions perhaps be attributable to Senecan excerpting rather than
to Albucius' aping of an arid declaimer. It is however possible
to point out a few parallels between his *sententiae* and others by
Fabianus and Hermagoras.

ALBUCI SILI. Terrae quoque suum finem habent, et ipsius mundi
aliquis occasus est; nihil infinitum est; modum <tu> magnitudini
facere debes, quoniam Fortuna non facit. *magni pectoris est inter
secunda moderatio*. *eundem Fortuna victoriae tuae quem naturae
finem facit*: imperium tuum cludit Oceanus. *o quantum magnitudo
tua rerum quoque naturam supergressa est*! Alexander orbi magnus
est, Alexandro orbis angustus est...non procedit ultra spatia sua
caelum, maria intra terminos suos agitantur. quidquid ad summum
pervenit, incremento non relinquit locum. non magis quicquam
ultra Alexandrum novimus quam ultra Oceanum. (*Suas*. 1.3)

Fabianus philosophus primam fecit quaestionem eandem: etiamsi
navigari posset Oceanus, navigandum non esse. at rationem aliam
primam fecit: *modum inponendum esse rebus secundis*. hic dixit
sententiam: illa demum est magna felicitas quae arbitrio suo con-
stitit. dixit deinde locum de varietate fortunae et, cum descripsisset nihil esse stabile, omnia fluitare et incertis motibus
modo attolli, modo deprimi, absorberi terras et maria siccari,
montes subsidere, deinde exempla regum ex fastigio suo devolutorum,
adiecit: '*sine potius rerum naturam quam fortunam tuam deficere.*'
secundam quoque quaestionem aliter tractavit; divisit enim illam
sic ut primum negaret ullas in Oceano aut trans Oceanum esse
terras habitabiles. deinde...novissime: ut posset perveniri,
tanti tamen non esse. hic dixit incerta peti, certa deseri;
descituras gentes si *Alexandrum rerum naturae terminos super-
gressum* enotuisset... (*Ibid*. 9f.)

The sentiments italicized, commonplace though they may appear, do
not seem to have any particularly close parallels in the extracts
from other declaimers' treatments of this *suasoria* quoted by
Seneca. Very few *sententiae* by the declaimer Hermagoras are

extant, but there is a clear parallel between one of them in
Contr. X.1.15, εἶχεν ἐχθροὺς φύσει παρρησιαστὴς κακηγορεῖν
δυνάμενος, and another by Albucius, *dum libere loquitur multos
offendit* (*ibid.* 1). Albucius' tendency to use on occasion too
high-flown a style (*Contr.* VII pr. 5: *modo nimis se attollit*) had
evidently already begun before he devoted himself entirely to
school rhetoric: the fateful *figura iurisiurandi* which precipitated his retirement from the law-courts (*ibid.* 6ff.) was a fine
instance of it. His liking for *verba sordida* is sufficient explanation for Seneca's criticism (*ibid.* 5), *modo nimis se deprimit.*

Votienus Montanus is described in *Contr.* IX.5.15 as *homo
rarissumi etiamsi non emendatissimi ingeni.* As to the rareness of
his intellect, we have to take Seneca's word for it, but we are
given a fair indication of the nature of its flaws in the several
references to him outside the problematic ninth preface.[98*] Like
Albucius he had a regrettable tendency to forget when he was engaged in a real lawsuit and to act as if he were back in the
schoolroom (*Contr.* VII.5.12). Like Cestius he is reported to have
jeered at the *ineptiae* of others (*Contr.* IX.6.10), but did not exclude them entirely from his own declamations (*Contr.* VII.5.11f.).
However, his most distinctive and interesting failing was his
habit of composing strings of *sententiae* all making the same point,
a failing which, it was recognized, he shared with Ovid:[99]

habet hoc Montanus vitium: sententias suas repetendo corrumpit;
dum non est contentus unam rem semel bene dicere, efficit ne bene
dixerit. et propter hoc et propter alia quibus orator potest
poetae similis videri solebat Scaurus Montanum inter oratores
Ovidium vocare; nam et Ovidius nescit quod bene cessit relinquere.
(*Contr.* IX.5.17)

Seneca records two examples of Montanus' repetitiveness, the first
from his speech for one Galla Numisia, accused of poisoning her
father, one twelfth of whose property she stood to inherit.

uncia nec filiae debetur nec veneficae.
in paternis tabulis filiae locus aut suus debetur aut nullus.
relinquis nocenti nimium, innocenti parum.
non potest filia tam anguste paternis tabulis adhaerere, quas aut
totas possidere debet aut totas perdere. (*Ibid.* 15f.)

Apparently, though Seneca could not recall it all, he said much
more to the same effect. Seneca comments: *nihil non ex eis bellum
est, si solum sit; nihil non rursus ex eis alteri obstat.* His

other example comes from Montanus' treatment of *Contr.* IX.5, which
concerns a boy who, after the death of his brothers in suspicious
circumstances, was seized by his grandfather from the care of his
stepmother.

erras, pater, et vehementer erras: quos perdidisti non quaeris,
quem quaeris non perdidisti.
puer iste <si> invenitur perit.
quisquis puero favet ne inveniatur optet.
puer, nisi avum sequitur, fratres secuturus est; desine quaerere
quem si inveneris sic perdes ut invenire non possis.
rapuit istum avos ne raperet noverca.
unum tantum pater ex liberis suis quaerit qui salvus est. (*Ibid*.
16)

Probably the *sententiae* quoted followed immediately upon one
another, as do the three which he cites for the sake of comparison
from Ovid, *Met.* XIII.503-5:

ne multa referam quae Montaniana Scaurus vocabat, uno hoc contentus ero: cum Polyxene esset abducta ut ad tumulum Achillis
immolaretur, Hecuba dicit:

                              cinis ipse sepulti
     in genus hoc pugnat.
poterat hoc contentus esse; adiecit:

                              tumulo quoque sensimus hostem.
nec hoc contentus est: adiecit:
     Aeacidae fecunda fui.
aiebat autem Scaurus rem veram: non minus magnam virtutem esse
scire desinere quam scire dicere. (*Contr.* IX.5.17)[100]*

Among the declaimers introduced in Seneca's tenth preface,
none of them consistently first-rate, several appear to have had
styles distinct from any we have so far encountered.

By Seneca's standards Scaurus and Labienus were more or less
old-fashioned stylists. In *Contr.* X pr. 2 he classes Scaurus'
oratorical style unequivocally as *antiquum*, praising his *verborum
...non vulgarium gravitas* and the authority lent to his utterances
by his distinguished appearance. His only regret is that Scaurus
had ruined his chances of becoming a great orator through negli-
gence (*ibid.* 3). Labienus affected the contempt for public declamation still evidently customary among orators of his generation
(*ibid.* 4), but he appears to have made more concessions than
Scaurus to modern tastes in style: *color orationis antiquae, vigor
novae, cultus inter nostrum ac prius saeculum medius ut illum
posset utraque pars sibi vindicare* (*ibid.* 5). We are more adequately provided with samples of Labienus' style than of Scaurus'.

A celebrated attack of his on the unpunished vices of the upper
classes - a subject doubtless congenial to this writer, whose
books were burnt as a consequence of his belief in free speech
(*ibid.*) - is quoted in *Contr.* X.4.17f. W:

> Labienus tam diserte declamavit partem eius qui debilitabat ex-
> positos quam nemo alteram partem, cum illam omnes disertissimi
> viri velut ad experimentum suarum virium dixerint. illum autem
> locum vehementissime dixit: vacare homines huic cogitationi, ut
> curent quid homo mendicus inter mendicos faciat! principes,
> inquit, viri contra naturam divitias suas exercent: castratorum
> greges habent, exoletos suos ut ad longiorem patientiam inpudic-
> itiae idonei sint amputant, et, quia ipsos pudet viros esse, id
> agunt ut quam paucissimi sint. his nemo succurrit delicatis et
> formosis debilibus. curare vobis in mentem venit quis ex soli-
> tudine infantes auferat perituros nisi auferantur; non curatis
> quod solitudines suas isti beati ingenuorum ergastulis excolunt,
> non curatis quod iuvenum miserorum simplicitatem circumeunt et
> speciosissimum quemque ac maxime idoneum castris in ludum con-
> iciunt. in mentem vobis venit misereri horum quod membra non
> habeant. quidni illorum quod habent? et hoc genere insectatus
> saeculi vitia egregia figura inquinatum et infamem reum maiorum
> criminum inpunitate defendit.

Nobody would be tempted to date Labienus' invective earlier than
the Augustan age: such turns of phrase as *contra naturam divitias
suas exercent* and *quia ipsos pudet viros esse, id agunt, ut quam
paucissimi sint* bear the unmistakable stamp of their period. Yet
the rhythms favoured in an earlier age reverberate in Labienus'
sequences of polysyllabic words, for example: *longiorem patientiam
inpudicitiae* and *iuvenum miserorum simplicitatem circumeunt*, even
though the use of *iuvenum...simplicitatem* to denote *iuvenes* belongs to the new era. Such circumlocutions as *curare vobis in
mentem venit* instead of *curatis*, and *in mentem vobis venit misereri*
instead of *miseremini*, also distinguish him from the modernist
devotees of fiery agitation.

We have already considered the style of Musa, described in
Contr. X pr. 9.[101] The chief distinguishing feature of Moschus,
who is introduced next (*ibid.* 10f.) seems to have been excess in
the employment of *figurae*:

> Moschus non incommode dixit, sed ipse sibi nocuit; nam dum nihil
> non schemate dicere cupit, oratio eius non figurata erat sed prava.
> itaque non inurbane Pacatus rhetor, cum illi Massiliae mane oc-
> currisset, schemate illum salutavit: 'poteram' inquit 'dicere: ave
> Mosche.'

Such cautious qualifying of terms was a variety of the figure *praesumptio* to which Quintilian refers in IX.2.18: *verborum quoque vis ac proprietas confirmatur...reprehensione: 'cives, inquam, si hoc eos nomine appellari fas est'*, and it is indeed to be found in Moschus' fragments in *Contr.* X.1.3: *mortuo patre meo - timeo enim ne quis sibi iniuriam fieri putet si dixero 'occiso'*. and in *Contr.* X.3.1: *inquinasti filiae sanguine penates. quamquam quid ego dico penates, tamquam in domo perierit?*

Study of the fragments suggests that there was more that could have been said about Moschus' style than Seneca cares to mention in the tenth preface. It is clear that he was a declaimer, much like Fuscus, with two styles: a dry style for narrative and argumentation (e.g. *Contr.* II.3.4; X.1.3; 2.17; 6.1) and the quasi-poetic descriptive manner which we find in *Suas.* 1.2:

inmensum et humanae intemptatum experientiae pelagus, totius orbis vinculum terrarumque custodia, inagitata remigio vastitas, litora modo saeviente fluctu inquieta, modo fugiente deserta; taetra caligo fluctus premit, et nescio qui, quod humanis natura subduxit oculis, aeterna nox obruit.[102]

According to Porphyrion,[103] Moschus hailed from Pergamum; it was only after conviction on a charge of poisoning that he went west to teach at Massilia (*Contr.* II.5.13).

Fulvius Sparsus and Iulius Bassus, introduced in *Contr.* X pr. 11f., are both criticized for harshness. Sparsus attempted to imitate Latro, but lacked the originality to seem more than a mimic:

Sparsus autem dicebat valenter[104]* sed dure. ad imitationem se Latronis derexerat nec tamen umquam similis illi erat, nisi cum eadem diceret. utebatur suis verbis, Latronis sententiis.

Parallels between Sparsus and Latro do not actually seem to be very common in the fragments, though quite large samples exist of both men's writing. In *Contr.* VII.6, however, two *sententiae* by Sparsus: *eligitur maritus quem sanus pater dotalem dedisset*, and *gener tuus ipsis nuptiis crucem meruit* (§3), may be compared with two by Latro: *cum infelici face ad dotalem suum nova nupta deduceretur...exhorrui...* and *vocat servum et, quia crucem non meruerat, mereri iubet* (§9).

Iulius Bassus was the declaimer whose *amaritudo* and imitation of forensic *actio* provoked Seneca to make the remark, *nihil est indecentius quam ubi scholasticus forum, quod non novit, imitatur*

(*Contr.* X pr. 12).[105] One means by which Bassus attempted to
dissociate himself from scholastic convention and to acquire
amaritudo was evidently by the use of *verba sordida* (e.g. *Contr.*
I.2.21; 3.11; X.1.13);[106] in the first two of these passages he
also defies the declaimers' ruling that women were to be respect-
fully treated.[107] We have to take Seneca at his word that Bassus
aped the practice of the forum in his delivery, but one can well
imagine one particular passage from his treatment of *Contr.* I.7[108]
being accompanied by a wide variety of gestures:

nolo me tam bene alas quam ego te alui; nolo ignoscas mihi: quidquid passus es, quidquid timuisti, patiar: posce flagella, scinde
rugas. ustus es? subice ignes, semimortuam hanc faciem, quae
tantum in contumeliam suam spirat, quia extingui non potest,
exure. si parum est, fac quod ais ne piratas quidem fecisse,
manus praecide. exhibeo tibi. hae sunt illae quae quidlibet
scribunt. ubi est gladius tuus? stringe. (*Contr.* I.7.9)

The very fact that Capito, introduced next (in *Contr.* X pr.
12), was, by contrast with Bassus, a *bona fide scholasticus* made
Seneca look upon him with a certain whimsical indulgence. He even
goes as far as to say that Capito was *in his declamationibus, quae
bene illi cesserunt, nulli non post primum tetradeum praeferendus*.
Nevertheless he still considered it regrettable that Capito's
declamation about Popillius was commonly attributed to 'poor
Latro' (*ibid.*). Reading the extract (*Contr.* VII.2.5ff.) which
Seneca gives from this declamation, we can discover one of the
reasons why it might have been damaging to Latro's reputation:
Capito appears to have been suffering, when he wrote it, from that
disease by which, according to Seneca in *Contr.* VII.5.12, *scholastici* in general were afflicted, a lack of moderation in the use
of *exempla*:

Ciceronem quisquam potuit occidere qui audiit? Minturnensis palus
exulem Marium non hausit; Cimber etiam in capto vidit imperantem;
praetor iter a conspectu exulis flexit; qui in crepidine viderat
Marium in sella figuravit. non possumus de Popillio queri: eodem
loco patronum habuit quo patrem. Cn. Pompeius terrarum marisque
domitor Hortensio se clientem libenter professus est; et Hortensius
bona Pompei, non Pompeium defenderat. Romulus, horum moenium
conditor et sacratus caelo parens, non tantam urbem fecit quantam
Cicero servavit. Metellus Vestae extinxit incendium, Cicero Romae.
glorietur devicto Hannibale Scipio, Pyrrho Fabricius, Antiocho
alter Scipio, Perse Paulus, Spartaco Crassus, Sertorio et Mithri-
date Pompeius; nemo hostis Catilina propius accessit. (*Contr.* VII.
2.6f. W)

None of the three Spanish declaimers, Gavius Silo and the Clodii Turrini, father and son, praised at the end of the tenth preface (§14ff.), appears, either from Seneca's critical remarks or from the extracts attributed to them, to have been a very distinctive stylist. True, we may find *sententias...excitatas, insidiosas, aliquid petentis* (*Contr.* X pr. 15) in the elder Turrinus' fragments, but the same could be said of almost any extract in Seneca's anthology. It remains an important fact that such men lived, cultivating in such remote cities as Tarraco (*ibid.* 14) and 'eloquent' Corduba (Martial I.61.7) standards, both in declamation and oratory proper, which seemed to Seneca the Elder comparable with those of the metropolis (*Contr.* X pr. 13), thus helping to ensure that the economic prosperity of early Imperial Spain was matched by a good measure of cultural prosperity.

Among the declaimers introduced in Seneca's prefaces there are, as we see, exponents of all the *genera dicendi* mentioned in the account of influences on Albucius in *Contr.* VII pr. 5[109] (except perhaps anyone who could be described as consistently *brevis et concinnus*), and representatives of a few more styles besides. And nowhere does Seneca give us any warrant for supposing that all these diverse stylists were considered either by themselves or by their contemporaries as belonging to a single united Asianist movement. He uses the term *Asianus* just enough to show that the battle of the books between Atticists and Asianists was not a dead issue, but he uses it in a way that makes it implausible that he regarded himself or Latro, his favourite declaimer, as belonging to the Asianist camp, and so sparingly that it might not seem unreasonable to deduce that in his time it was very much the exception, rather than the rule, for a rhetorician to be classifiable as *ex Asianis*.[110]

However, Asianist rhetoricians were probably rather more numerous and influential than examination of Seneca's extant criticism alone might lead us to believe. True, surprisingly few declaimers are mentioned by Seneca as having imitated or inspired *sententiae* by the five explicitly named *Asiani*. Among Greek declaimers, Dionysius the Younger seems to have composed a *sententia* along the same lines as one by Hybreas which Seneca quoted in

Contr. I.4.11, though now that both fragments are lost we cannot
know if he imitated him closely, and one Glaucippus Cappadox
possibly inspired a *sententia* by Adaeus in *Contr.* IX.2.29. In
Contr. X.4.20 M certain Latin declaimers are reported to have
copied another of Adaeus' *sententiae*, '*sed sic*', Seneca is at pains
to assure us, '*ut putem illos non mutuatos esse aperte hanc sententiam, sed imitatos.*' Rather surprisingly, one of them was Blandus,
Fabianus' second teacher (cf. *Contr.* II pr. 5); the others were
Moschus and Fuscus. We cannot now tell how close Vibius Rufus'
sententia in *Contr.* I.4.11 came to Hybreas' treatment of the same
idea. It is perhaps remarkable, in view of the obvious importance
of Arellius Fuscus in the scholastic circles of his day, how seldom Seneca tells us of straightforward imitations of his *sententiae*, *divisiones* and *colores*, or of precedents for them, in the
work of other declaimers. There is a certain affinity between a
sententia of his in *Contr.* I.4.10 and one of Latro's (*ibid.*), but
Fuscus' version is condemned as *illius sententiae frigidius...
contrarium.* In *Contr.* VII.3.7 Fuscus uses the same *color* as
Albucius, *sed aliter.* In *Contr.* I.1.15 Cestius is found force-
fully elaborating the concluding *quaestio* of Fuscus' *divisio*, and
correspondingly in *Contr.* X.4.21 Fuscus is found rendering a
sentiment of Cestius', taken from the Greek of one Damas Scombros,
aliter, that is, as it happens, with greater elaboration and force.
But, for a reason already explained,[111] Cestius was incapable of
being a successful imitator of Fuscus in all respects, and in any
case, as we see from *Contr.* II.3.22, he was not an uncritical admirer of him. An interesting possible candidate for inclusion
among the *Asiani* is Haterius, who in *Contr.* IX.6.16 is named as
the author of a *sententia* very similar to one which Fuscus translated word for word from Adaeus:[112] *modestius hanc sententiam
vertit Haterius: quid ergo? mentita est? quidni illa mentiretur
de accusatoris sui filia?* Perhaps his verbosity should be regarded as an imitation of what Augustus, criticizing Antony,
called *Asiaticorum oratorum inanis sententiis verborum volubilitas*
(Suet. *Aug.* 86.3), even though Seneca says nothing more precise
about the sources of inspiration for his fluency than that they
were Greek (*Contr.* IV pr. 7).

Probably some, if not all, of the *enfants terribles* castigated frequently by Seneca for *corruptum*, *insania* and *cacozelia*,
should also be grouped with the *Asiani*. That is not to accept the
presumption[113] that the use of these terms in antiquity was necessarily confined to criticism directed against professed Asianists,
any more than their use was confined exclusively to the remarks of
critics of the extreme Atticist persuasion, which, as we have
seen,[114] was not the case in Cicero's time, and certainly was not
in the early Empire, when we find even Maecenas extolling the virtues of 'sane' expression and condemning tumidity (*Suas*. 1.12).
It should be noted that Seneca the Elder did not consider that
insania was a stylistic tendency which anyone, apart from Vibius
Gallus, the great exception, cultivated deliberately; rather
people were liable to lapse into it *casu*, by accident (*Contr*. II.
1.25). But, unquestionably, many of the faults which he criticizes as insane or corrupt[115] are the same which marred the style
of Hegesias, Maecenas and Arellius Fuscus. And it has to be remembered that even the declaimers whom Seneca liked least, Murredius, Gargonius and the rest, each had their regular gatherings of
pupils, and doubtless exercised more influence on the impression-
able young than he would have wished. It seems quite likely too
that in the period immediately following the elder Seneca's death,
men of their stamp came to dominate the scholastic world as they
had not in the days when Latro flourished, hence Quintilian's
strictures in XI.3.58 on the universal prevalence of sing-song
delivery.

However, even if we assume that *Asiani* were more numerous in
the schools of the elder Seneca's time than the scarcity of explicit references to them might suggest, it still seems unjustifiable to follow Norden in his supposition that all the varieties
of the 'new style' of the early Empire were manifestations of
Asianism.[116] Of the passages cited by him in this connection,
Suet. *Aug*. 86.3 and Plut. *Ant*. 2.5, concerned as they are with
Mark Antony's style, relate to a period too early for them to demand discussion here, and Quint. XI.3.58 refers to a period too
late. So, indeed, does Petr. *Sat*. 1ff., but this passage, being
closer in date to Seneca the Elder, and containing as it does a

reference to Asianism in the course of an attack on modern declaimers in general, cannot be so lightly dismissed as without
relevance to our present investigations.

In *Sat.* 1f. Petronius' versatile hero Encolpius is declaiming,
on his own admission (§3), against declamation, and in particular
that of the rhetorician Agamemnon to whom he has just been listening. It is in the course of this tirade that he makes the allegation that this windy and monstrous loquaciousness of his was a
recent immigrant to Athens from Asia: *nuper ventosa istaec et
enormis loquacitas Athenas ex Asia commigravit...* (§2). He argues
that style of this kind had been a pernicious influence on young
talent, and points out that the great lyric poets and tragedians
had not needed to declaim and nor, moreover, had Plato and Demosthenes. It should be noted that, with the exception of the opening
parody of declamatory style which, like all the dialogue in the
Satyricon, is in Latin, the whole of Encolpius' harangue has to do
with Greek literary history. It sounds suspiciously like the
parroting of stock arguments which had been in circulation ever
since scholars had started to object to the way that pernicious
oriental influences had 'recently' begun to pollute Athenian oratory. Encolpius' use of *nuper* may be compared with the use of
πρώην by Dionysius of Halicarnassus in *De rhet. vet.* 1:

ἡ μὲν Ἀττικὴ μοῦσα καὶ ἀρχαία καὶ αὐτόχθων ἄτιμον εἰλήφει σχῆμα,
τῶν ἑαυτῆς ἐκπεσοῦσα ἀγαθῶν, ἡ δὲ ἔκ τινων βαράθρων τῆς Ἀσίας
ἐχθὲς καὶ πρώην ἀφικομένη, Μυσὴ ἢ Φρυγία τις ἢ Καρικόν τι κακόν,
Ἑλληνίδας ἠξίου διοικεῖν πόλεις ἀπελάσασα τῶν κοινῶν τὴν ἑτέραν,
ἡ ἀμαθὴς τὴν φιλόσοφον καὶ ἡ μαινομένη τὴν σώφρονα.

The fact remains that the dispute between Encolpius and Agamemnon
is supposed to be taken as referring to the Roman schools of Petronius' time: Encolpius has been attacking *declamatores* in general
(§1) just before he makes his reference to Asiatic *loquacitas*, and
it emerges from §5, where Agamemnon describes his educational
ideals, that the *declamatores* in question are rhetoricians en-
trusted with the education of Roman youths in the post-Ciceronian
era.

But how seriously ought we to take this passage in the *Satyricon* as an analysis of Imperial declamatory style? How are we to
weigh Encolpius' generalization that the bombast of the declaimers

was of Asiatic origin against the view discernible in the elder
Seneca's criticism that, while some declaimers were *Asiani*, others
were not?

Perhaps one might argue that we need see no conflict between
the two views: *Asiani* could have been so much more in the ascend-
ant in Petronius' day than in the elder Seneca's that to say that
by then they had come to dominate the schools totally might not
have been much of an over-statement. One could also argue that
Seneca, no less than Encolpius, would have found fault with the
type of style parodied in *Sat*. I.[117]

But maybe this would be to pay more respect to Encolpius'
criticism than is its due. It is surely to be doubted whether the
type of critic portrayed by Petronius in the person of Encolpius
is likely to have been a very reliable authority on the question
of the origins of early Imperial *sententiarum strepitus*, seeing
how he is prepared to regurgitate anti-Asianist criticisms which
had obviously long been out of date, without making even so much
of an attempt to adapt them to a modern Roman context as to substitute *Romam ex Asia* for *Athenas ex Asia*. One can fairly expect
such a critic to have known that *suasoriae* and *controversiae* had
Hellenistic precedents, for this fact had been pointed out by
scholars prior to Quintilian (see II.4.41); he would also be
likely to know that Asiatic orators had been known for their verbosity before the rise of the Roman Imperial schools of rhetoric,
for Cicero (*Brut*. 95.325) was among the authorities for this information. But it does not seem at all likely that such a man
would have thought very deeply about the possible origins of the
particular variety of *loquacitas* represented by rhetoricians like
Agamemnon, or that any Roman scholar of the early Empire would
have been disposed to do the necessary research in the archives of
the Hellenistic schools to discover whether the *genus dicendi
ardens et concitatum* came into favour first in Asia, or elsewhere.

If we have to choose between the evidence of Seneca the Elder
and Petronius' Encolpius on this issue, it is surely more sensible
to take seriously the objective reporting of the older authority
than to accept without question the partisan and hackneyed generalizations in Petr. *Sat*. 2. And the elder Seneca gives us no

warrant for supposing that the whole of early Imperial school
rhetoric ought to be labelled as Asiatic. His criticism rather
serves to undermine that supposition. Asianism there was in some
of the schools of his day, but in the van of the Augustan declamatory movement we find Latro, a man ignorant of Greek rhetoric
(*Contr*. X.4.21), who, if not himself responsible for expressing
the highest praise for Calvus the Atticist which has survived from
antiquity (*Contr*. VII.4.6ff.), was the closest friend of our
authority for it,[118] and whose novelties of expression were open
to criticism from purists (*Contr*. II.4.8) probably as occidental
rather than oriental.

A fact which makes it all the more implausible that all the
declaimers of the elder Seneca's time, Greek and Latin, could have
been regarded by any contemporary critic as all representatives of
a united Asianist movement is that Dionysius of Halicarnassus, who
lived in Rome from 30 B.C. until his death some time after 8 B.C.,
and thus all through the period when Latro was the leading Latin
rhetorician,[119] took the view that Asianism was no longer an important force in the schools of his day. When Dionysius wrote
disparagingly about the meretricious style of expression recently
arrived from out of the hell-holes of Asia, and referred to it in
De rhet. vet. 2 as 'the new rhetoric', τῇ δε νέᾳ...[sc. ῥητορικῇ]
- thereby suggesting to Norden the term '*der neue Stil*' which he
uses as a synonym for '*Asianismus*'[120] - he was referring not to
the rhetoric of his own time, but to a type of style favoured in
the recent past but now almost universally rejected, thanks to the
good taste of the Romans (§3), in favour of a return to the so-
briety of the old (i.e. classical Attic) style (§2). He has this
to say about the Greek rhetoric of his time:

ἔξω γὰρ ὀλίγων τινῶν 'Ασιανῶν πόλεων, αἷς δι' ἀμαθίαν βραδεῖά
ἐστιν ἡ τῶν καλῶν μάθησις, αἱ λοιπαὶ πέπαυνται τοὺς φορτικοὺς καὶ
ψυχροὺς καὶ ἀναισθήτους ἀγαπῶσαι λόγους, τῶν μὲν πρότερον μέγα ἐπ'
αὑτοῖς φρονούντων αἰδουμένων ἤδη καὶ κατὰ μικρὸν ἀπαυτομολούντων
πρὸς τοὺς ἑτέρους, εἰ μή τινες παντάπασιν ἀνιάτως ἔχουσι, τῶν δὲ
νεωστὶ τοῦ μαθήματος ἁπτομένων εἰς καταφρονήσιν ἀγόντων τοὺς
λόγους καὶ γέλωτα ποιουμένων τὴν ἐπ' αὑτοῖς σπουδήν. (*Ibid.*)

Here we have a reference to a phase in the history of Greek rhetoric of which there is no mention in Encolpius' tirade in Petronius, *Sat.* 1f. It is interesting to compare Dionysius' optimism

about the tastes of Greek students of rhetoric at the time of his
sojourn in Rome,[121] with the elder Seneca's pleasure at recalling
the standards of declamation customary in those 'better years'
(*Contr.* I pr. 1), when men born within Cicero's life-time had
still been the shining lights of the literary world (*ibid.* 7).

Suetonius in *Aug.* 86.2 refers to *cacozelos et antiquarios* as
standing at the two opposite poles of this literary world.
Maecenas, who, as we have agreed, deserved the epithet *Asianus* as
much as Arellius Fuscus deserved it, is named by Suetonius as a
representative of the *cacozeli*, while Tiberius and Annius Cimber
are classed as *antiquarii*. What Suetonius does *not* say is that
all prose writers of the Principate were deemed by Augustus, or
anyone else, to have adhered without exception to one or other of
the alternative types of extremism. Augustus himself, we are
given to understand (*ibid.*), tried to find a golden mean somewhere
between them. And this, surely, is what most of the declaimers
quoted by the elder Seneca would have claimed to have been doing,
whatever we may think of their efforts now. Within the range of
styles to be heard in the *auditoria* of the declaimers contemporary
critics detected good taste as well as bad. Amateurs visiting the
schools and professional rhetoricians alike considered they had
every right to criticize inferior declaimers for lapses of taste,
without issuing any general condemnation of the sententiousness so
widely - we may think excessively - cultivated in the rhetorical
prose of their day. The modern critic of Silver Latin literature
therefore needs to exercise great caution if he wishes to use such
terms as *corruptum*, *cacozelia*, *tumor* and *cultus* in contexts where
no ancient critic has anticipated him. Still more, he should use
the term 'Asianist' only with the utmost circumspection, bearing
in mind that this epithet may certainly be applied to the type of
style favoured by Fuscus in his *explicationes*, but not, it seems,
despite the fact that *Asiani* were undoubtedly among those who in
the elder Seneca's day participated in the general fashion for
sententiousness, to the consistently fiery agitation of Latro, or,
to put the matter in Tacitean terms (see *Dial.* 26.1), it may
safely be used with reference to the *calamistros Maecenatis*, but
not, however much distaste we may feel for this kind of writing,

as a term with which to issue general condemnation of the *tinnitus Gallionis.*

In the early years of the elder Seneca's life-time it appears that
literary Latin had undergone a profound and rapid change. A
startling indication of the rapidity with which it had come about
is that he found it remarkable (*Contr.* IV pr. 9) that Haterius
used words which were *antiqua et a Cicerone dicta, a ceteris
deinde deserta.* Consequently, though he does occasionally distinguish between an old style and a new, for example in his descriptions of Scaurus and Labienus in the tenth preface,[1] it is
not to be imagined that men described as *antiqui* in his criticism,
for example the declaimer named Crispus whom he calls an *antiquum
rhetorem* in *Contr.* VII.4.9, were the kind of stylists whom Augustus
would have referred to as *antiquarii* (Suet. *Aug.* 86.2). It is
evident from his remarks on the old and new types of *divisio* in
Contr. I.1.13 that to the elder Seneca *veteres* meant the generation of Porcius Latro. For he promises, '*ego exponam quae aut
veteres invenerunt aut sequentes*[2] *adstruxerunt*', and yet he never
gives examples of the simple *divisio controversiarum antiqua*
earlier than those of Latro and the rhetoricians active at the
time when he rose to fame. Extreme archaism does not appear, from
anything the elder Seneca says, to have been a strong force in
early Imperial declamation. Even such a stylist as Pollio, of
whom Quintilian was to write, *a nitore et iucunditate Ciceronis
ita longe abest ut videri possit saeculo prior* (X.1.113), became
extraordinarily self-indulgent when he declaimed.[3]

Seneca the Elder, as we have seen, pays lip-service in *Contr.*
I pr. 9 to the elder Cato and in *Contr.* VII.4.8, quoting Latro
maybe, to Demosthenes, but otherwise shows remarkably little
interest in pre-Ciceronian oratory.[4] And it was not only in the
case of rhetoric that he seems to have turned his back on the past
and directed practically his whole attention towards modern literature: in historiography, philosophy and poetry too his interest

seems to have been confined almost exclusively to the writings of
the last generation of the Republic and his own contemporaries.

That his neglect of the older Latin literature was the result
of distaste for it, rather than mere ignorance, is evident from
his disagreement with Pollio over the acceptability of a *sententia*
in *Contr.* IX.2.25, and most strikingly in his agreement with
Livy's remarks to the effect that the pursuit of *verba antiqua et
sordida* and a *severitas* which resulted in obscurity was as much a
form of *insania* as the opposite vice of tumidity (*ibid.* 26f.).[5]
By agreeing with Livy over this matter Seneca the Elder falls into
line with the attitude expressed by Cicero towards the Thucydideans
(*Or.* 9.30ff.).

In the field of historiography it is clear that the elder
Seneca's chief interest was in the writings of modern Romans from
Sallust onwards, though he does mention both the greatest Greek
historians (Quint. X.1.73: *longe duos ceteris praeferendos*),
Herodotus and Thucydides. He was mistaken in believing (*Suas.* 2.
11) that a famous dictum of Leonidas, in which he urged his men to
eat their morning meal, destined as they were to dine in Hades,
was to be found in Herodotus,[6] but one at least of his references
to Thucydides seems the fruit of better scholarship. In one of
his rare displays of erudition (*Suas.* 6.21), he notes that Thucydides had once or twice employed the device of ἐπιτάφιον, in which
the historian, having narrated the death of a great man, assesses
his achievements in a *consummatio totius vitae et quasi funebris
laudatio*; this device, he goes on to observe, was used occasionally by Sallust, more frequently by Livy, and even more profusely
by Livy's successors. As D. R. Stuart has pointed out, such
ἐπιτάφια do indeed occur very occasionally in Thucydides.[7]
Whether the research which sought out this honourable precedent
for the practice of Sallust and his successors was the elder
Seneca's own may be doubted. Sallust's debt to Thucydides was not
a subject in which only dedicated historians were interested.[8] It
was even discussed by Arellius Fuscus, of all people, in an argument aimed to confute someone (an Atticist?) who disapproved of
his close imitation of the Asian rhetorician Adaeus:
do, inquit, operam ut cum optimis sententiis certem, nec illas

corrumpere conor sed vincere. multa oratores, historici, poetae
Romani a Graecis dicta non subripuerunt sed provocaverunt.
tunc deinde rettulit aliquam Thucydidis sententiam: δειναὶ γὰρ αἱ
εὐπραξίαι συγκρύψαι καὶ συσκιάσαι τὰ ἑκάστων ἁμαρτήματα. deinde
Sallustianam: res secundae mire sunt vitiis obtentui. cum sit
praecipua in Thucydide virtus brevitas, hac eum Sallustius vicit
et in suis illum castris cecidit; nam in sententia Graeca tam
brevi habes quae salvo sensu detrahas: deme vel συγκρύψαι vel
συσκιάσαι, deme ἑκάστων: constabit sensus, etiamsi non aeque
comptus, aeque tamen integer. at ex Sallusti sententia nihil demi
sine detrimento sensus potest. (*Contr.* IX.1.13 W)

The Greek *sententia* quoted actually came from ps.-Demosthenes (*In
ep. Phil.* 13), not Thucydides, but the fact that Seneca did not
notice the error in such a point of detail tells us nothing about
the extent of his Greek reading, for Livy, too, was deceived:

T. autem Livius tam iniquus Sallustio fuit ut hanc ipsam sententiam et tamquam translatam et tamquam corruptam dum transfertur
obiceret Sallustio. nec hoc amore Thucydidis facit, ut illum
praeferat, sed laudat quem non timet et facilius putat posse a se
Sallustium vinci si ante a Thucydide vincatur. (*Contr.* IX.1.14)

Was Livy, one wonders, present in Fuscus' audience, or was this
example of Sallust's art a famous one which he discussed on
another occasion?

None of the Latin historians prior to Sallust receives any
mention in Seneca's criticism. As we have seen, there is a parallel for the elder Seneca's apparent neglect of pre-Ciceronian
oratory in the views expressly stated by Velleius Paterculus in
a digression (I.16-17) where he reflects on the brief efflorescence
of the various literary genres. There is a similar parallel for
Seneca's apparent lack of interest in the pre-Sallustian Roman
historians in Velleius' remarks on historiography:

historicos etiam, ut Livium quoque priorum aetati adstruas,
praeter Catonem et quosdam veteres et obscuros minus octoginta
annis circumdatum aevum tulit... (I.17.2)

Seneca's interest in historiography extended to writers who survived Livy, whose death in A.D. 17 presumably marked the end of
Velleius' 'less than eighty years' of great history writing, for
Cremutius Cordus, quoted in *Suas.* 6.19, 23, did not die until A.D.
25, Bruttedius Niger, quoted in *Suas.* 6.20, survived to be impli-
cated in the fall of Sejanus in 31, and he himself continued
writing history almost right up to his death well on in the 30s.[9]
That is not to say that he would necessarily have disputed

Velleius' contention that Livy was the last of the great historians. In the remarkable passage, *Suas.* 6.14–27, where he compares and contrasts various writers' narratives of the death, and
estimates of the achievements, of Cicero, it is Livy who, among
the historians, receives the highest praise. Seneca approved of
the way that Livy was generous (*benignus*) in the distribution of
ἐπιτάφια to the great men of history (§21), and admired in particular his tribute to Cicero: *ut est natura candidissimus omnium
magnorum ingeniorum aestimator T. Livius, plenissimum Ciceroni
testimonium reddidit* (§22). He also found much to admire in the
ἐπιτάφιον on Cicero by Asinius Pollio, another historian whose
literary activity was confined to Velleius' 'less than eighty
years' (§25: *adfirmare vobis possum nihil esse in historiis eius
hoc quem rettuli loco disertius, ut mihi tunc non laudasse
Ciceronem sed certasse cum Cicerone videatur*), even though he disapproved of the anti-Ciceronianism in Pollio's writings, as exemplified by his outrageous allegation in the speech *Pro Lamia* (so
baseless that he dared not include it in his *Histories*) that
Cicero had promised to recant and write as many speeches *for*
Antony as he had previously written against him (§14f.), and by
the narrative in which he made out that Verres, when proscribed,
had faced his death with great courage (§24). By contrast, Seneca
does not single out any of the other historians whom he quotes in
Suas. 6.14ff. for particular praise, and he is highly critical of
Cremutius Cordus' tribute to Cicero: *Cordi Cremuti non est operae
pretium referre redditam Ciceroni laudationem; nihil enim in ea
Cicerone dignum est, ac ne hoc quidem, quod [paene] maxime tolerabile est* (§23). However, he must have had the eloquence of these
three historians in mind as well as that of Livy and Pollio when
he referred in §25 to *tot disertissimis viris*. Quintilian, re-
viewing Roman historiography in X.1.101ff., was to take the line
that though Sallust and Livy, equal in his view to Thucydides and
Herodotus respectively, were Rome's greatest historians, Aufidius
Bassus and Cremutius Cordus had much to recommend them.

The only philosophers to whom Seneca the Elder, as opposed to
the critics quoted by him, refers are all modern ones. The reference to Plato in *Contr.* III pr. 8 occurs in the course of Cassius

Severus' remarks on specialization; the passing allusion to Aristotle in *Suas.* 1.5 comes within a quotation from Cestius. Among
modern Roman philosophers, Seneca the Elder mentions Fabianus
(*Contr.* II pr. *passim*), Sextius, Fabianus' mentor (*Contr.* II pr.
4), and Attalus, a Stoic who suffered banishment at the instigation
of Sejanus and was, so he tells his sons, *magnae vir eloquentiae,
ex his philosophis, quos vestra aetas vidit, longe et subtilissimus
et facundissumus* (*Suas.* 2.12).

All these three were philosophers admired by the younger
Seneca. In *Quaest. nat.* VII.32.2, for example, there is an approving reference to the *Sextiorum nova et Romani roboris secta*,[10]
and extended praise for the elder Sextius in *Ep. mor.* 64.2ff.
Fabianus, whose lectures the younger Seneca had attended (*Ep. mor.*
52.11), is praised for the sincerity of his teaching in *Brev. vit.*
10.1, for the excellence of his way of life, his learning and his
eloquence in *Ep. mor.* 40.12, and is defended in *Ep. mor.* 100 from
criticisms which had been levelled against his style. As for
Attalus, we have in *Ep. mor.* 108.3 a lively account of the younger
Seneca's enthusiasm for his teaching: *haec nobis praecipere Attalum
memini, cum scholam eius obsideremus et primi veniremus et nov-
issimi exiremus, ambulantem quoque illum ad aliquas disputationes
evocaremus, non tantum paratum discentibus sed obvium.*

There is not a trace of disapproval in the elder Seneca's
references to these men, in spite of his son's statement in *Ep.
mor.* 108.22 that the reason why his father had made him give up
vegetarianism in his youth was that he abhorred philosophy:

in primum Tiberii Caesaris principatum iuventae tempus inciderat:
alienigena tum sacra movebantur et inter argumenta superstitionis
ponebatur quorundam animalium abstinentia. patre itaque meo
rogante, qui non calumniam timebat sed philosophiam oderat, ad
pristinam consuetudinem redii; nec difficulter mihi ut inciperem
melius cenare persuasit.

Why he interpreted his father's motives in this way is mysterious.
Perhaps it was because the elder Seneca's view that discretion was
sometimes the better part of valour (expressed, for example, in
Contr. II.4.13) seemed out of keeping with the *antiquus rigor* he
is credited with in *Cons. Helv.* 17.3,[11] that the younger Seneca is
so insistent that his father did not act out of fear. What we can

be sure of is that it was none of the three philosophers praised
by father and son alike who persuaded Seneca the Younger to adopt
his vegetarian diet, but one Sotion, a philosopher never mentioned
by his father in the extant books, who differed from Sextius in
using the Pythagorean doctrine of the transmigration of souls as
an argument against meat-eating, in addition to the usual medical
and moral arguments (*Ep. mor.* 108.17ff.).

Insofar as the elder Seneca can be said to have had a philosophical position, it appears to have anticipated in certain respects the views later to be expounded by his second son, which is
hardly surprising in view of their shared admiration for the
Sextians and Attalus.

In *Contr.* IV pr. 4ff. and *Suas.* 2.15 he tells two pairs of
anecdotes describing the contrasting reactions of fathers to the
death of their sons; the first pair concerns two Romans, Pollio
and Haterius, the second, two Greeks, Lesbocles and Potamon.
These anecdotes are accompanied by reflections which may be compared with similar sentiments in the younger Seneca's *Ep. mor.* 63.
In *Contr.* IV pr. 6, recalling Pollio's fortitude in not withdraw-
ing from his normal social life even on the day of his son's
death, he marvels: *o magnos viros, qui fortunae succumbere ne-
sciunt et adversas res suae virtutis experimenta faciunt!* With a
similar ideal in mind the younger Seneca remarks in *Ep. mor.* 63.1:
*illud, ut non doleas, vix audebo exigere; et esse melius scio.
sed cui ista firmitas animi continget nisi iam multum supra
fortunam elato?* We see from the elder Seneca's recollections
about Fabianus (*Contr.* II pr. 2) that it was assumed by the
Sextians, to whose *sanctis fortibusque praeceptis* (*ibid.* 1) he had
dedicated himself, that emotions ought to be suppressed; they also
taught that one should fight adversity with virtues (Sen. *Ep. mor.*
59.7). Both the Senecas, however, had their doubts whether such
an ideal was attainable by ordinary people, or indeed wholly admirable: on Lesbocles and Potamon the elder Seneca remarks,
*utriusque tamen adfectum temperandum puto: hic durius tulit
fortunam quam patrem decebat, ille mollius <quam> virum* (*Suas.* 2.
15), and his son, consoling Lucilius on his bereavement in *Ep.
mor.* 63.1, similarly feels it allowable for a man to succumb to

his emotions in moderation: *nobis autem ignosci potest prolapsis ad lacrimas, si non nimiae decucurrerunt, si ipsi illas repressimus. nec sicci sint oculi amisso amico nec fluant; lacrimandum est, non.plorandum*. These are commonplace sentiments no doubt, for it was hardly possible for a Roman to write about bereavement without reference to the conventional topics of *consolatio* – the poor younger Seneca cannot recall his deep grief at the death of Annaeus Serenus (*Ep. mor.* 63.14) without envisaging himself *inter exempla...eorum quos dolor vicit* – but it is interesting nonetheless to see how closely the attitudes of father and son correspond over this matter.

Distaste for contemporary luxury was so commonly expressed by thinkers, serious and not so serious,[12] in the early Empire, that nothing precise can be determined about the elder Seneca's philosophical position on the basis of his tirade on the subject in *Contr.* I pr. 7ff., but certainly both Sextius (Sen. *Ep. mor.* 108. 18) and Attalus (*ibid.* 23) held strong views on the subject. As for the respect in which the elder Seneca most differed from his second son, his non-participation in public life (whether the result of conscious choice or force of circumstances) and his approval of Mela's decision to live free from desires and thereby safe, to a large extent, from the whims of Fortune (*Contr.* II pr. 3: *perge quo inclinat animus, et paterno contentus ordine subduc fortunae magnam tui partem*), it is interesting that the career of the elder Sextius provided a classic precedent for the choice of such a life: *honores reppulit pater Sextius, qui ita natus ut rem publicam deberet capessere, latum clavum divo Iulio dante non recepit; intellegebat enim quod dari posset et eripi posse* (Sen. *Ep. mor.* 98.13).

Velleius Paterculus makes no mention of any great period of Roman philosophical writing in his remarks on the brief flowering periods of the literary genres. Probably he thought Rome's philosophical achievements totally unworthy of comparison with those of Greece; such a view would be in line with his opinion (I.16.4) that no Greek philosophers worth mentioning had flourished much after the time of Plato and Aristotle. Velleius does, however, express an opinion as to the limits of the great age of Roman

poetry: with the exception of tragedy and comedy which flowered
early (I.17.1), Rome's only poetry of note, he considers, had been
composed in those same seventy odd years, up to the death of Livy,
which had produced the best Roman historiography (*ibid*. 2: *nec
poetarum in antiquius citeriusve processit ubertas*). And in the
case of poetry as well as historiography none of the elder Seneca's
Latin quotations antedates that golden age whose limits Velleius
was so early able to discern.

The only Greek poet to receive mention in the elder Seneca's
extant books is Homer (set-book of the Greek grammarians).[13]
Homeric quotations and paraphrases were sometimes included in
Greek declamations (*Contr*. I.8.15; X.2.18; *Suas*. 1.12), and occasionally, it would seem, in Latin ones too (*Contr*. I.7.14).
Wits, Greek and Roman, made effective use of Homeric tags (*Contr*.
VII.7.19; IX.3.14; *Suas*. 7.14). But we find no real Homeric
criticism in the elder Seneca's books, unless we count Maecenas'
discussion of literary *magnitudo* in *Suas*. 1.12, which was initially
prompted by the failure of the declaimer Dorion to paraphrase
Homer without tumidity.[14]

In striking contrast to Cicero, the elder Seneca never quotes
from, or even (if we except Cassius Severus' reference to *Pomponium
Atellanarum scriptorem* in *Contr*. VII.3.9) alludes to, any early
Roman dramatists or epic poets. This can scarcely be because he
had not read them: his school-days belonged to a time when their
works, and not yet those of Virgil and Horace, were the staple fare
of the pupils of Latin *grammatici*, and from them, presumably, came
the verses which he memorized with such facility as a boy (*Contr*.
I pr. 2).

Several late Republican poets active within Velleius' 'less
than eighty years' receive mention, but all in passages where
Seneca is more or less certainly quoting other critics. Cicero's
poetry is contemptuously dismissed in *Contr*. III pr. 8 by Cassius
Severus: *Ciceronem eloquentia sua in carminibus destituit*. The
mimicus Publilius Syrus has his reputation vindicated in *Contr*.
VII.3.8f. by the same critic, who also mentions in passing Laberius, another mime-composer active in the late Republic (*ibid*.
9). In *Contr*. VII.1.27 Julius Montanus suggests that some fine

lines by Varro of Atax were the inspiration for some even finer
ones by Virgil, which Cestius had failed miserably to emulate in
prose:

Montanus Iulius, qui comes fuit <Tiberii>,[15] egregius poeta,
aiebat illum imitari voluisse Vergilii descriptionem:
  nox erat et terras animalia fessa per omnis
  alituum pecudumque genus sopor altus habebat. (*Aen*. VIII.26f.)
at Vergilio imitationem bene cessisse, qui illos optimos versus
Varronis expressisset in melius:
  desierant latrare canes urbesque silebant;
  omnia noctis erant placida composta quiete. (Fr. 8 Morel)

(Note that Montanus does not, as a modern commentator would, point
to Apollonius Rhodius, *Arg*. III.749f.,

οὐδὲ κυνῶν ὑλακὴ ἔτ' ἀνὰ πτόλιν, οὐ θρόος ἦεν
ἠχήεις· σιγὴ δὲ μελαινομένην ἔχεν ὄρφνην,

as the original which lay behind Varro's description of night.)
Words from poems by Catullus and Calvus, as we have seen,[16] are
quoted in the appreciation of the latter's oratory in *Contr*. VII.
4.7.

But the Latin poets most often quoted by the elder Seneca are
Virgil and Ovid. Of Virgil we are told by Cassius Severus that
his eloquence deserted him in prose, just as Cicero's deserted him
in poetry (*Contr*. III pr. 8). We are possibly indebted to the
elder Seneca rather than to his son for some remarks by Julius
Montanus on Virgil's delivery recorded in Donat. *Vit. Verg*. 29.
We certainly owe him a debt of gratitude for the evidence recorded
in *Suas*. 1.12 of how Maecenas appreciated Virgil's avoidance of
bombast. Seneca himself shows an admiration for Virgilian
beauties[17] of style when he expresses a preference for *Aen*. XI.
280ff. over lines on a related theme by one Abronius Silo, even
though these contained an imitation of a *sententia* by Latro, *si*
nihil aliud, erimus certe belli mora (*Suas*. 2.19):

postea memini auditorem Latronis Abronium Silonem...recitare
carmen in quo agnovimus sensum Latronis in his versibus:
  ite agite, <o> Danai, magnum paeana canentes,
  ite triumphantes: belli mora concidit Hector.
...sed ut sciatis sensum bene dictum dici tamen posse melius,
notate prae ceteris quanto decentius Vergilius dixerit hoc quod
valde erat celebre, 'belli mora concidit Hector':
  quidquid ad adversae cessatum est moenia Troiae,
  Hectoris Aeneaeque manu victoria Graium
  haesit.

Messala aiebat hic Vergilium debuisse desinere: quod sequitur:
　　　　et in decimum vestigia rettulit annum
explementum esse; Maecenas hoc etiam priori conparabat. (*Ibid.*
19-20 W)

Once again it seems that Seneca had heard a discussion of Virgil
in which Maecenas had participated. He praises Virgilian lines
again in *Suas.* 3.5, this time verses from the *Georgics* (I.427ff.),
which he considers to have been expressed *simplicius et beatius*
than the prose paraphrase of them which Fuscus had contrived in
the hope of pleasing Maecenas.[18]

　　Virgil, like Homer, was not only imitated by declaimers, as
for instance by Cestius (*Contr.* VII.1.27) and Fuscus (*Suas.* 3.1,
4f.), but was sometimes quoted by them verbatim, as by Fuscus
and one of his pupils about whom we are told an amusing anecdote
in *Suas.* 4.4f.:

declamitarat Fuscus Arellius controversiam de illa quae, postquam
ter mortuos pepererat, somniasse se dixit ut in luco pareret...
<cum> declamaret et a parte avi non agnoscentis puerum tractaret
locum contra somnia et deorum providentiam et male de magnitudine
eorum dixisset mereri eum qui illos circa puerperas mitteret,
summis clamoribus illum dixit Vergili versum:
　　　scilicet is superis labor est, ea cura quietos
　　　sollicitat.　　　　　　　　　　　(*Aen.* IV.379f.)
auditor Fusci quidam, cuius pudori parco, cum hanc suasoriam de
Alexandro ante Fuscum diceret, putavit aeque belle poni eundem
versum et dixit:
　　　scilicet is superis labor est, ea cura quietos
　　　sollicitat.
Fuscus illi ait: si hoc dixisses audiente Alexandro, scisses apud
Vergilium et illum versum esse:
　　　　　capulo tenus abdidit ensem. (*Aen.* II.553)

From this story and from the jokes in *Suas.* 3.6f. based on the
allegedly Virgilian phrase, *plena deo*,[19*] it emerges that Virgil
was already sharing the fate of Homer in providing useful quotations for the repertoire of wits.

　　Ovid, himself once a student in the schools of declamation
(*Contr.* II.2.8ff.), also in due course shared Virgil's privilege
of having his poetry imitated in declamatory prose. P. Vinicius,
a great admirer of Ovid, recommended that one should store in
one's memory *ad fingendas similes sententias* an *epiphonema* from
the *Metamorphoses* (XII.607f.):

　　　quod Priamus gaudere senex post Hectora posset,
　　　hoc fuit.　　　　　　　　　　　　　(*Contr.* X.4.25)

In *Contr*. III.7 *extra*, Cestius disapproves of a *sententia* by Alfius Flavus which he alleges to have been based on lines by Ovid:

Alfius Flavus hanc sententiam dixit: ipse sui et alimentum erat et damnum. hunc Cestius quasi corrupte dixisset obiurgans: apparet, inquit, te poetas studiose legere: iste sensus eius est qui hoc saeculum amatoriis non artibus tantum sed sententiis implevit. Ovidius enim in libris metamorphoseon dicit:
ipse suos artus lacero divellere morsu
coepit et infelix minuendo corpus alebat. (*Met*. VIII.877f.)

Ovid's poems, like Virgil's, provided wits with apt quotations. Thus Scaurus silences Murredius by quoting from one of his *Priapeia* (*Contr*. I.2.22).[20]

As we have seen,[21] there is much of interest to be learnt about Ovid both as poet and as declaimer from *Contr*. II.2.8ff. and other passages in Seneca's anthology. It comes as no surprise to be told in *Contr*. II.2.12 that he preferred *suasoriae* to *controversiae*, only declaiming the type of *controversiae* known as *ethicae* of which *Contr*. II.2 (about the suicide pact of a married couple) is presumably an example. We also learn that his argumentation in this *controversia* had no clear structure (*ibid*. 9: *sine certo ordine per locos discurrebat*) and that in general *molesta illi erat omnis argumentatio* (*ibid*. 12) - facts which are of interest to the reader puzzled by the strange order in which topics are sometimes presented in, for instance, the *Heroides*, though they should not necessarily always be relied on as a defence of the received text where hopeless disorganization seems to reign. An amusing anecdote is told in *Contr*. II.2.12 about Ovid's fondness for lapses of taste in his poetry:

verbis minime licenter usus est nisi in carminibus, in quibus non ignoravit vitia sua sed amavit. manifestum potest esse, quod rogatus aliquando ab amicis suis ut tolleret tres versus, invicem petit ut ipse tres exciperet in quos nihil illis liceret. aequa lex visa est; scripserunt illi quos tolli vellent secreto, hic quos tutos esse vellet: in utrisque codicillis idem versus erant, ex quibus primum fuisse narrabat Albinovanus Pedo, qui inter arbitros fuit:
    semibovemque virum semivirumque bovem (*Ars am*. II.24);
secundum:
    et gelidum Borean egelidumque Notum (*Am*. II.11.10);
<tertium: ...>[22]*
ex quo adparet summi ingenii viro non iudicium defuisse ad compescendam licentiam carminum suorum sed animum. aiebat interim

decentiorem faciem esse in qua aliquis naevos esset.
In addition, Ovid's taste for brevity in description is evidenced
by his suggestion, quoted in *Contr.* VII.1.27, that certain lines
of Varro's would benefit from pruning. His habit of composing
several consecutive *sententiae* on the same theme is seen from
Contr. IX.5.15ff. to have been criticized by his contemporaries
and to have had parallels in the speeches and declamations of
Votienus Montanus. Unfortunately Seneca does not make it clear if
the poet influenced the orator or vice versa, or whether their
resemblance was merely coincidental, for Scaurus, whose remarks on
the subject are quoted by Seneca, was as ready to refer to Montanus
as *inter oratores Ovidium* as he was to give Ovid's repetitions the
name of *Montaniana* (*ibid.* 17). That Ovid frequently included conscious imitations of Virgil in his poetry, *non subripiendi causa,*
sed palam mutuandi, hoc animo ut vellet agnosci (*Suas.* 3.7 W) was
attested by his friend Gallio.

Curiously lacking in Seneca's range of references to Roman
poetry is any direct quotation from Lucretius, the earlier el-
egists, or Horace. However, Seneca may well have had in mind the
lines of Lucretius,

> sed veluti pueris absinthia taetra medentes
> cum dare conantur, prius oras pocula circum
> contingunt mellis dulci flavoque liquore (I.936ff.= IV.11ff.)

when on one occasion he referred to the way in which children have
to be tricked into drinking medicine:

et quia hoc <propo>situm recta via consequi non potero, decipere
vos cogar, velut salutarem daturus pueris potionem. sumite pocula.
(*Suas.* 6.16 M)[23]*

At any rate Quintilian, wishing in III pr. 4 to use the same image,
actually quoted the Lucretian lines. Again, Seneca includes in
his criticisms of Haterius some words, *cum torrentis modo magnus*
quidem sed turbidus flueret (*Contr.* IV pr. 11), which remind one
of Horace's reference to the muddy flow of Lucilius, *cum flueret*
lutulentus (*Serm.* I.4.11).[24]

The elder Seneca's taste in modern poetry extended to an
admiration for several of the lesser epic poets of his day, including some who certainly or probably survived into the reign of
Tiberius. Julius Montanus, who is described as an *egregius poeta*

in *Contr.* VII.1.27 was actually a friend of Tiberius: the younger
Seneca, less enthusiastic about him than his father, calls him
tolerabilis poeta et amicitia Tiberi notus (*Ep. mor.* 122.11).

As for the types of modern epic poetry alluded to by the
elder Seneca, it is interesting that whereas there is one quotation (the one by Abronius Silo, Latro's pupil, deemed in *Suas.*
2.19 *bene dictum* but inferior to similar lines in Virgil)[25] which
comes from an epic concerned wholly or in part with the Trojan
Wars, his other four extracts from minor hexameter poets come from
epics about Roman history of the post-heroic era. Was the preference of Lucan foreshadowed in his grandfather's taste in modern
poetry?

Cornelius Severus is quoted on two occasions, once for lines
describing the Roman army on the eve of a crucial battle (*Suas.*
2.12) and again for a passage lamenting the death of Cicero (*Suas.*
6.26). Seneca has doubts whether the lines in *Suas.* 2.12 do justice to the greatness of the Roman people, but he admires nonetheless the poet's telling use of colloquial language.[26] He has
no hesitation in preferring this poet's lament for Cicero to any
treatment of the same theme by a prose historian, and, given his
high regard for historiography, this is praise indeed: *nemo tamen
ex tot disertissimis viris melius Ciceronis mortem deploravit quam
Severus Cornelius* (*Suas.* 6.25). A propos of one of the lines in
Severus' lament, *conticuit Latiae tristis facundia linguae*, Seneca
notes that it was inspired by another by one Sextilius Ena, a
Corduban poet whom he describes as *homo ingeniosus magis quam
eruditus, inaequalis poeta et plane quibusdam locis talis quales
esse Cicero Cordubenses poetas ait, <pingue> quiddam sonantis
atque peregrinum* (*Suas.* 6.27). Reciting this line, *deflendus
Cicero est Latiaeque silentia linguae*, in the house of Messala on
one occasion Ena had caused annoyance to Pollio, though he evidently pleased Cornelius Severus, who was also a member of the
audience:

Pollio Asinius non aequo animo tulit et ait: 'Messala, tu quid
tibi liberum sit in domo tua videris; ego istum auditurus non sum,
cui mutus videor', atque ita consurrexit. Enae interfuisse
recitationi Severum quoque Cornelium scio, cui non aeque displi-
cuisse hunc versum quam Pollioni apparet, quod meliorem quidem sed

non dissimilem illi et ipse composuit. (*Ibid.*)

A quotation from a poem by Albinovanus Pedo in *Suas*. 1.15 has as
its theme an episode of even more recent Roman history, the North
Sea voyage of Germanicus.[27]   Seneca regarded the lines quoted from
Pedo's poem as superior to any of the declaimers' attempts to
describe *Oceanus*:

Latini declamatores in descriptione Oceani non nimis viguerunt;
nam aut minus descripserunt aut <nimis> curiose. nemo illorum
potuit tanto spiritu dicere quanto Pedo... (*Ibid.*)

Both of the elder Seneca's extended quotations from epic, Cornelius
Severus' lament for Cicero and Pedo's description of the North Sea,
clearly belong stylistically to the beginnings of Silver Latin.[28]
That he praises both these quotations highly makes it questionable
whether he would have agreed entirely with Velleius' opinion that
no Roman poetry of note had been composed since the time, towards
the end of the second decade A.D., which was marked by the death
of Ovid as well as that of Livy, in Velleius' view Rome's last
great historian.

The almost total absence of references to early Latin literature in the elder Seneca's books probably reflects a decided modernity in his literary outlook. It is not safe to infer, however,
that such modernist disregard for the past in a man of his time
was the outcome of a preoccupation with contemporary school rhetoric. Seneca the Elder belonged to a generation which had received in the schools of *grammatici* all too thorough a grounding
in the Latin poetry of the third and second centuries B.C. Positive aversion to such literature was expressed most famously by
Horace, born in 65 B.C., that is, perhaps no more than ten years
before Seneca the Elder, and brought up on Livius Andronicus in
the school of the fearsome Orbilius (*Epist*. II.1.69ff.). There is
no record that Horace attended any school of rhetoric, and in
Epist. I.2.1ff. he seems anything but envious of Lollius, his
addressee, whom he imagines busy declaiming in Rome while he himself is re-reading Homer at Praeneste. Horace's preference for
modern over early Roman poetry was a conscious choice, which he
justified in *Epist*. II.1.18ff. in the face of opposition from
enthusiasts for the old poets, who included, it seems, not just

academic archaizers, but a large theatre-going public (*ibid.* 60-3).
Horace's view of the poems he had learnt at school was that,
though they did not deserve to be consigned to the bonfire, they
were far from being the flawless masterpieces people sometimes
made them out to be:

> non equidem insector delendave carmina Livi
> esse reor, memini quae plagosum mihi parvo
> Orbilium dictare; sed emendata videri
> pulchraque et exactis minimum distantia miror;
> inter quae verbum emicuit si forte decorum, et
> si versus paulo concinnior unus et alter,
> iniuste totum ducit venditque poema. (*Ibid.* 69ff.)

Thus, the elder Seneca was in good company if, in adult life, he
chose to turn his attention towards poetry more polished than any
he had learnt at school. Similarly, if he had no taste for early
Roman historiography, there were very respectable precedents for
such an attitude in the criticism of early annalists in Cicero's
De oratore (II.12.51ff.), and in Livy's disdain for archaizing
stylists (*Contr.* IX.2.26). In the case of Roman philosophy it
was hardly possible to argue by analogy with Greek literary history (cf. Hor. *Ep.* II.1.28ff.) that old was best, seeing that
philosophical Latin was so largely the recent creation of Cicero
and Lucretius. As for oratory, Cicero's *Brutus* provides ample
evidence that already among the literary men of the late Republic
interest in archaic Latin speeches was negligible. The only Latin
speeches known by Cicero to be extant which were earlier than the
elder Cato's were apparently *Appi Caeci oratio...de Pyrrho et non
nullae mortuorum laudationes* (*Brut.* 16.61), none of which he
imagines would appeal to his contemporaries. Even the speeches of
Cato, who died, as Cicero points out, '*annis LXXXVI ipsis ante me
consulem*', and whom it was therefore wrong to think of as belonging
to remote antiquity (*ibid.* 15.61), were very seldom read any
longer: *Catonem vero quis nostrorum oratorum, qui quidem nunc sunt,
legit? aut quis novit omnino* (*ibid.* 17.65). It is evident that
Cicero's researches into the oratory of the second century B.C.
did not represent a kind of activity normal among men of his time.
Yet nobody could mistake the *Brutus* for an archaizer's manifesto.
Cicero was perhaps the most firmly convinced of all late Republican
critics that modern Latin oratory, and especially his own, was

superior to all that had come before it. As we have seen,[29] he declares in *Tusc. Disp.* II.1.5 that the glory of oratory had risen *ab humili* till it had arrived in his own day *ad summum*.

The distaste for the archaic felt by modernists in the age of Augustus, as in the late Republic, was clearly the product of a positive and eminently justifiable pride in the excellence of recent Roman literary achievements. It did not owe its origins to narrowness in the teaching of *Latini rhetores*. However, considerably before the end of what Velleius considered to be the great age of Roman poetry and historiography, we can detect certain new tendencies in the writings of authors educated during or after the Civil Wars, which may surely be suspected of having originated in the schools of declamation. The elder Seneca's passing criticisms are occasionally helpful in confirming that it was indeed from the rhetorical schools that these tendencies are likely to have arisen.

It is a commonplace in the criticism of early Imperial literature that 'the most outstanding influence discernible in the Ist century, largely determining its character, is...the rhetorical element'.[30] Of course, no Roman writing with any pretensions to artistry had ever been entirely unrhetorical, but never before had techniques of deliberative and judicial rhetoric, employed with such an unremitting search after effect, been so generally prevalent in all the literary genres. Particularly characteristic of this new literature are tight argumentative sequences each capped by an *epiphonema*. In addition, moralizing *loci*, *exempla*, and *descriptiones* are repeatedly drawn from what one senses is a fairly limited stock-in-trade.

Probably these tendencies are to be explained largely by a change in educational custom.[31] Horace attended the school of a *grammaticus*, but there is no evidence that he went on to study with a *rhetor*. The latter stages of Virgil's education, according to Donatus' *Life* (§15), were devoted chiefly to the study of medicine and, more especially, mathematics. Rhetoric may have been among the *cetera studia* which he touched on, but Donatus tells us, immediately after his remarks on Virgil's education, that his one appearance as an orator was a failure. When Virgil and Horace were growing up it was probably still not thought normal to study

rhetoric unless one was destined for public life; the old Roman
attitude described by Antonius in the *De oratore* (II.13.55) may
well have still prevailed: *nemo...studet eloquentiae nostrorum
hominum, nisi ut in causis atque in foro eluceat.*

It seems, however, that in the generations which succeeded
that of Horace it became increasingly abnormal for a Roman with
any pretensions to culture to have been without a period of training in one of the schools of rhetoric. It was admittedly because
his father wished him to enter public life that Ovid, the leading
poet of the first generation to be educated under the Principate,
was made to study rhetoric (*Trist.* IV.10.21ff.). More remarkable
is the case of Fabianus who, some time after he had begun studying
rhetoric, decided that his mission in life was to be a philosopher.
Amazingly, even though the *praecepta* which he embraced were of a
kind which militated against the emotional ostentation required of
declaimers, he continued to declaim conscientiously for some
time after his philosophical conversion (*Contr.* II pr. 4). In
doing this, Fabianus indicated his acceptance of the educational
principle, in which Seneca the Elder (and doubtless many of his
contemporaries) firmly believed, that a rhetorical training - that
is, given the limited curriculum of early Imperial schools, practice in the declamation of *controversiae* and *suasoriae* - was of
value not only to the future orator, but also to students whose
intention was to distinguish themselves in *artes* quite remote from
the oratory of the forum: *facilis ab hac in omnes artes discursus
est; instruit etiam quos non sibi exercet* (*Contr.* II pr. 3). The
assumption, which had originated in Greece and particularly in the
school of Isocrates (see Cic. *De or.* II.13.55ff.), that rhetoric
could provide useful techniques for other types of writers besides
orators, was at last becoming accepted in Rome.

That did not mean that everyone agreed that declamation provided a good training even for prospective orators. As we have
seen, Seneca quotes two most virulent attacks on this assumption
in the third and ninth prefaces.[32] He also tells several anecdotes in which orators are recorded to have behaved as if they
were in a school-room rather than in a law-court, with results
ranging from the amusing to the disastrous. The bystanders at the

trial reported in *Contr.* II.1.34ff. were treated to a comic alter-
cation between counsel for the prosecution and the defence about
the rival theories of Apollodorus of Pergamum and Theodorus of
Gadara relating to *narrationes*; they expressed their appreciation
magnis...clamoribus.[33] No doubt among them there were many
habitués of the schools of rhetoric, interested, as Seneca the
Elder was, in the ingenious *colores* put forward by the defence in
this difficult and sensational case. Albucius felt obliged to
retire from his forensic activities after a *figura iurisiurandi* he
had incautiously used was taken literally by his opponent, who
thereupon secured his client's acquittal (*Contr.* VII pr. 7),[34] and
how out of touch with reality a *scholasticus* might become is
further revealed by the story, related in *Contr.* VII.5.12, that
when Votienus Montanus had a charge brought against him by the
citizens of Narbo, he greeted his prosecutor's speech with
pleasure, and singled out *sententiae* from it for special praise,
thereby prompting the wit Surdinus to ask, '*numquid putas illum
alteram partem declamasse?*' Such anecdotes, together with the
invectives of Cassius Severus (*Contr.* III pr. 12ff.) and the
critic quoted in the ninth preface, serve to prove that declamatory methods and attitudes were starting to infiltrate into the
law-courts.

It was the elder Seneca's view that a rhetorical education
could benefit a future philosopher (*Contr.* II pr. 3f.). Yet the
declamations which Fabianus so assiduously delivered in the school
of Blandus after his philosophical conversion were not the *theses*
which Cicero had considered the appropriate sort of themes for a
philosopher to practice upon in order to develop fluency:[35] they
were *controversiae* and *suasoriae*. There was certainly scope for a
certain amount of philosophizing in these types of themes: large
ethical questions were often raised in the *tractationes aequitatis*
in *controversiae*, and sometimes declaimers of *suasoriae* devoted
the whole of their argument to the consideration of such questions
as whether the gods intervened in human affairs (*Suas.* 3.3) or
whether it was possible to predict the future (*Suas.* 4.4). It
would not be fair then to suggest that the teaching of the rhetoricians in Seneca's day constituted a complete rejection of Cicero's

notion that the ideal orator should always seek to isolate the
abstract issue at stake in any dispute in which he had to partici-
pate (*Or.* 14.45: *a propriis personis et temporibus semper, si
potest, avocet controversiam*), even though Cicero's works on rhetorical theory seem to have had precious little influence on the
curriculum of the schools of that time.

However, the reason why Seneca the Elder believed declamation
could be of benefit to philosophers cannot have been that he considered there was scope in it for extensive practice in philosophizing. For, doubtless sharing with Latro (*Contr.* VII.7.10) a
general preference for tautness in the exposition of *loci*, he condemns in Albucius' private declamations *illa intempestiva in
declamationibus eius philosophia* which *sine modo tunc et sine fine
evagabatur* (*Contr.* VII pr. 1). From the anecdote which he tells
about Albucius and Cestius in *Contr.* VII pr. 8 we can see that
Seneca's view that philosophizing in declamation ought to be kept
within proper limits was not totally unreasonable:

nec in scholasticis tamen effugere contumelias poterat Cestii,
mordacissimi hominis. cum in quadam controversia dixisset
Albucius: quare calix si cecidit frangitur, spongia si cecidit non
frangitur? aiebat Cestius: ite ad illum cras; declamabit vobis
quare turdi volent, cucurbitae non volent.

Cicero himself, surely, would not have considered the subject of
Albucius' speculation a suitable topic for rhetorical treatment.
Nevertheless, *intempestiva* seems quite a strong word with which to
criticize the large philosophical element in this rhetorician's
declamations. It therefore seems appropriate to consider the
comment quoted from *Contr.* VII pr. 1 in relation to that anti-
Ciceronian tradition in Imperial rhetorical theory supported by
Aper in Tac. *Dial.* 19.1ff. and condemned by Quintilian in III.5.
12ff.

Aper argues that, now that philosophical knowledge had become
widely disseminated among the Roman public, the treatment of abstract issues in speeches would not have the same effect on
listeners as it had in the old days when, *si quis odoratus philosophiam videretur atque ex ea locum aliquem orationi suae in-
sereret, in caelum laudibus ferebatur* (*Dial.* 19.3). The representatives of this tradition met by Quintilian do not seem to have

presented nearly so intelligent a rationale as that of Aper for
their view that *universales quaestiones* were useless in oratory
(Quint. III.5.12). It was on a bogus authority that they placed
their reliance, namely some books falsely ascribed to Hermagoras
of Temnos (*ibid*. 14). They would have done better to have cited
the passage in the *De inventione* (I.6.8) where Cicero as a young
man had argued against the true Hermagoras' inclusion of θέσεις
within the province of rhetoric, even though he was later to
change his mind completely over this matter.[36]

   We see from *De inv*. I.6.8 that one did not need to be a hater
of philosophy to think it unsuitable to discuss purely abstract
issues in oratory and, though the followers of ps.-Hermagoras encountered by Quintilian were doubtless very narrow men, it is not
justifiable to assume that Seneca the Elder was like them in
every respect. After all, his sons received a philosophical as
well as a rhetorical education. It just seems that he thought
expansive philosophizing did not mix well with declamation.
Eloquence, on the other hand, seemed to him an excellent quality
in a philosopher: Attalus is praised in *Suas*. 2.12 as *magnae vir
eloquentiae*. Presumably the reason why he considered that rhetorical training had benefited Fabianus was that it had enabled him
to expound his precepts persuasively to a public accustomed to
ornate rhetoric, whose reaction to a crabbed style of dialectic
would have been that expressed by Antonius in Cicero's *De oratore*:

in philosophos vestros si quando incidi, deceptus indicibus
librorum, qui sunt fere inscripti de rebus notis et inlustribus,
de virtute, de iustitia, de honestate, de voluptate, verbum
prorsus nullum intellego; ita sunt angustis et concisis disputatio-
nibus inligati. (II.14.61)

   About the possible value of rhetorical training for a historian, such as he was himself, the elder Seneca says nothing
whatsoever, beyond praising one of Gallio's declamatory *sententiae*
in *Suas*. 5.8 as worthy of inclusion in a *historia*, though presumably history was one of the disciplines he had in mind when he
claimed in *Contr*. II pr. 3 that there was an easy path from rhetoric *in omnes artes*. He does, however, tell us several interesting
facts about certain historical fabrications which circulated in
the schools of rhetoric. He traces the origin of the theme of

Suas. 7, in which Cicero is faced with the choice of death or the burning of his books, to a malicious passage in Pollio's *Pro Lamia*:

nam quin Cicero nec tam timidus fuerit ut rogaret Antonium nec tam stultus ut exorari posse eum speraret nemo dubitat, excepto Asinio Pollione, qui infestissimus famae Ciceronis permansit. et is etiam occasionem scholasticis alterius suasoriae dedit; solent enim scholastici declamitare: deliberat Cicero an salutem promittente Antonio orationes suas comburat. haec inepte ficta cuilibet videri potest. Pollio vult illam veram videri; ita enim dixit in ea oratione quam pro Lamia edidit. (*Suas.* 6.14f.)

On the other hand it is the declaimers who are blamed for the invention of a story that Popillius, the man named by a few, but not all, historians, as the assassin of Cicero, had once been defended by the great orator when faced with a charge of parricide (*Contr.* VII.2.8).[37] However, as none of the historians known to Seneca took over the story of the parricide trial, we cannot use this intriguing piece of source criticism as evidence that fictions were being imported from declamatory themes into historical narrative at this date, as they certainly were to be later, in the *Gesta Romanorum*.[38] Seneca unfortunately leaves it unclear whether the story, which *was* accepted by some historians, that Popillius had been defended by Cicero on some lesser or unspecified[39] charge, was of declamatory or historical origin.

That poets were coming under the influence of rhetoricians is evident from his recognition of imitations of Latro in the verses of Ovid (*Contr.* II.2.8) and Abronius Silo (*Suas.* 2.19). It is not the case that the only qualities which Seneca the Elder admired in poetry were the declamatory virtues: he detects in Pedo's lines on the North Sea a certain *spiritus* which he did not find in any declamatory descriptions of Ocean (*Suas.* 1.15); he is sensitive, more sensitive than the *grammatici*, to the poignancy of a colloquialism in a poem by Cornelius Severus (*Suas.* 2.12); he prefers the simple felicities of lines in Virgil's *Georgics* to a convoluted paraphrase of them by Arellius Fuscus (*Suas.* 3.5). We are also reminded by Seneca that it was not only declamation that served in his time to encourage ostentatiousness among writers: the custom of *recitatio* to which he refers in *Contr.* IV pr. 2 and *Suas.* 6.27 was another important outlet for literary *ambitio*. The fact remains that Seneca does not make an exception of poetry when he asserts that rhetoric provides a training for 'all the arts', and that he seems not in the least disapproving when he recalls in *Contr.* II.2.8 Ovid's indebtedness to the *sententiae* of Latro.

It seems to be implied in the assertion, *facilis ab hac in omnes artes discursus est* (*Contr.* II pr. 3), that rhetoric is the central literary discipline, seeing that from it the other *artes* are approached by travelling in diverse directions. In a very real sense *declamatio* did occupy a central position in the literary culture of the elder Seneca's day. A rhetorical training seems to have come to be regarded as an essential tertiary stage in education, as it had not been in Rome at the dramatic date of the *De oratore*, and probably still was not when Virgil and Horace were boys. Some of the distinguished members of the older generation met by Seneca in the *auditoria* of the declaimers were little disposed, at least when engaged on serious writing, to change the stylistic habits which they had learnt in an earlier age, but writers of the elder Seneca's own and subsequent generations had been brought up from boyhood among the clangor of *sententiae* and the rant of standard *exempla* and *descriptiones*, with results which are widely apparent in the literature of the early Empire.

APPENDIX

Clausula usage of Seneca, Latro and Fuscus: a trial sample*

	pattern	Seneca	Latro	Fuscus
I	–∪––∪̲	16	12	13
II	–∪–∪̲	12	11	18
III	–∪––∪∪̲	10	13	15
IV	–∪–∪∪̲	6	13	12
V	––––∪∪̲	5	6	7
		49	55	65

Resolutions

		pattern	Seneca	Latro	Fuscus
I	R1	–∪–∪∪∪̲	10	3	4
	R2	–∪∪∪–∪̲	2	2	2
	R3	∪∪∪∪∪–∪̲	1	-	-
	R4	∪∪∪––∪̲	-	1	-
	R5	∪∪∪–∪∪∪̲	2	-	-
III	R1	–∪–∪∪∪∪̲	1	3	1
	R2	∪∪∪––∪∪̲	2	-	2
	R3	–∪∪∪–∪∪̲	-	-	3
IV	R	∪∪∪–∪∪̲	-	3	-
V	R1	–––∪∪∪∪̲	2	2	-
	R2	∪∪––∪∪∪∪̲	1	-	-
	R3	–∪∪––∪∪̲	1	1	2
	R4	–∪∪–∪∪∪∪̲	1	1	-
	R5	––∪∪–∪∪̲	-	1	1
			23	17	15

		Seneca	Latro	Fuscus
Also (cf. V)				
	‿‿‿‿‿	2	3	1
R1	‿‿‿‿‿‿	1	2	–
R2	‿‿‿‿‿‿	–	–	1
		3	5	2

Spondaic, dactylic and anapaestic rhythms

	Seneca	Latro	Fuscus
‿‿‿‿	16	13	6
‿‿‿‿‿	7	4	2
‿‿‿‿‿	1	3	4
‿‿‿‿‿‿	–	1	1
‿‿‿‿‿	–	1	–
‿‿‿‿‿‿	1	–	2
‿‿‿‿‿	–	1	3
	25	23	18
	100	100	100

Seneca the Elder: a man of his time

[1] This is the least garbled version of the title, preserved
e.g. by BV in the colophon to the *liber suasoriarum*; we have
no way of being sure that it is Senecan, but it is difficult
to imagine anyone much later than Seneca's time bothering to
draw attention to the fact that his work includes extracts by
oratores (i.e. amateur declaimers) as well as *rhetores*.

[2] This is as precise a dating as can safely be deduced from
Contr. I pr. 11, cf. Miriam Griffin, 'The elder Seneca and
Spain', *JRS* LXII (1972), 5, and *pace* L.A. Sussman, *The elder
Seneca* (Leiden, 1978), 20.

[3] See pp.104ff.

[4] See pp.107ff.

[5] The evidence is collected by S.F. Bonner, *Roman declamation*
(Liverpool, 1949), 16ff.; note particularly Cic. *De or.* II.
24.100, bearing in mind the dramatic date of the dialogue.

[6] Suet. *De gramm. et rhet.* 7.3ff. Brugnoli.

[7] For further discussion see pp.104ff.

[8] *Ad Q. fr.* III.3.4, cf. E.G. Sihler, 'θετικώτερον', *AJPh* XXIII
(1902), 283ff.

[9] Though he had heard an older contemporary, Arellius Fuscus,
talking about his master's treatment of *Contr.* I.7 (see §14),
and appears to accept that Cicero declaimed something very
like *Contr.* I.4 (see §7).

[10] On Corduba see M.T. Griffin, *JRS* LXII (1972), 1ff.; in particular on the difficulties of travel from Corduba to Rome in
43 B.C. see Asinius Pollio's letter to Cicero, *Ad fam.* X.31.

[11] See Sen. *Cons. Helv.* 19.2 on the younger Seneca's apparently
very early removal to Rome; PIR^2 A 611 on Lucan's childhood;
M.T. Griffin, *JRS* LXII (1972), 6 on the education of children
from leading provincial families in the late Republic.

[12] Ps.-Plut. *Vit. X orat.* 836a, 848c.

[13] Mrs Griffin, *JRS* LXII (1972), 6, and Sussman, *The elder*

Seneca 20f. argue otherwise. It is not possible to date the arrival of Seneca and Latro in Rome at all precisely. The earliest datable anecdote from Seneca's Roman days is the reference in *Contr.* II.2.9 to a declamation by Ovid, which presumably was composed before 24 B.C. when his formal education ended (*Trist.* IV.10.30), but, as I surmise (p.269), after the publication of Tibullus' first book in 27 or 26. However, it seems from *Contr.* II.2.8 that Latro was already well established as a rhetorician by this time. On the other hand, Sussman's inference (p.20) from *Contr.* I pr. 3 that Seneca reached Rome while still a boy (*puer*) is invalid.

[14] Suet. *De gramm. et rhet.* 7.3 Brugnoli.

[15] Most·Roman references to the blowing of a trumpet to mark the time refer to the night watches, as M. Winterbottom notes *ad loc.*, but maybe the practice of sounding the trumpet three times in the daylight hours mentioned, admittedly in a Greek context, in Sen. *Thyest.* 798f. was not unknown in Rome.

[16] *Contr.* IV pr. 2, cf. A. Dalzell, 'C. Asinius Pollio and the early history of public recitation at Rome', *Hermathena* LXXXVI (Nov. 1955), 20ff.

[17] Cf. M.T. Griffin, *JRS* LXII (1972), 5. N.b. It may conceivably have been in Corduba that Seneca first heard Pollio declaim (*Contr.* IV pr. 3), not in Rome as Sussman (*The elder Seneca* 22) and others have assumed.

[18] The text of this sentence is discussed further later, pp.12ff.

[19] *JRS* LXII (1972), 9; 'Imago vitae suae', *Seneca, studies in Latin literature and its influence*, ed. C.D.N. Costa (London, 1974), 5; *Seneca* (Oxford, 1975), 33f.

[20] As was pointed out to me by Mrs Griffin *per litt.* 24.2.75.

[21] To which we are obliged to resort for lack of any specialized lexicographical work on Seneca the Elder which can be trusted.

[22] *ThLL* s.v. I 3. See also n.48, p.337, on the failure of H.T. Karsten to prove his contention that Latro used *alioqui* in the sense *alio tempore*.

[23] *ThLL* s.v. II 1,2. There appear to be only three occasions besides *Contr.* II pr. 4 where the elder Seneca uses the word. In *Contr.* I pr. 11, *alioqui in illo atriolo...potui adesse*, it clearly means 'otherwise'. In *Contr.* IV pr. 8, *regi autem ab ipso non poterat; alioqui libertum habebat, cui pareret...*, Winterbottom obelizes *alioqui*, and clearly it does not serve to refer us to a time or circumstance different from that to which the state of affairs described in the preceding clause pertained; maybe, however, the reading *alioqui* is correct and has the meaning 'at any event' (see *OLD* s.v. 2b; *ThLL* I 1b). The exact meaning of *alioqui* in *Contr.* IX.5.11 is uncertain,

but cannot be 'at one time': *Gallio utrumque miscuit et hoc colore, qui videri potest alioqui thema evertere, paratius usus est.*

24 *Per litt.* 25.10.76. For the linking of weighty phrases of this type with *-que* cf. especially Cic. *Div. Caec.* 20.65: *quem actorem causae suae socii defensoremque fortunarum suarum potissimum esse voluerunt.*

25 Tac. *Ann.* XVI.53, XVI.17, cf. *Contr.* II pr. 3.

26 For a detailed account of the evidence see M.T. Griffin, *JRS* LXII (1972), 6-8. One of Mrs Griffin's general conclusions (12ff.) about the elder Seneca is that he seems less deracinated from his provincial background than his son the philosopher.

27 See L. Casson, *Ships and seamanship in the ancient world* (Princeton, 1971), 270ff.

28 See *Cons. Helv.* 18.9 for evidence that her father was still alive in the 40s A.D.

29 *Cons. Helv.* 19.2. Probably literally as a babe in arms, but on the ambiguity of *ferre* with reference to children going for long journeys see *Contr.* IX.6.13.

30 *Chronici canones* ed. J.K. Fotheringham (London, 1923), 251.

31 Not necessarily just before Pollio's death in A.D. 5 as Mrs Griffin (*op. cit.* 8) and Sussman (*The elder Seneca* 23) assume.

32 See M.T. Griffin, *loc. cit.*

33 *Contr.* II.1.33; 5.11,13; III pr. 2; VII pr. 5; X pr. 8; *Suas.* 3.6.

34 E.g. Tac. *Ann.* XV.73; XVI.17.

35 But see M.T. Griffin, *Seneca* (Oxford, 1975), 43ff. for a discussion of the evidence for the activities in public life of known connections of the Annaei Senecae in this period, and an attempt to account for the late début of Novatus and Seneca in politics.

36 The punctuation and the substitution of *tu* for the MSS reading *ut* were both suggested by E. Thomas, 'Schedae criticae novae in Senecam Rhetorem', *Philologus* Supptbd VIII (1900), 232f. Modern editors prior to Winterbottom sadly obscured the sense of the opening of the digression and the connection between praise of Mela and the pen-portrait of Fabianus, by misguided attempts to emend the words, *hoc unum ...studeas,* to suit their own preconceptions. See especially Müller's apparatus, and his own version: [*hoc unum con-*

*cupiscentem] nihil concupiscere <nisi> ut eloquentiae tantum
studeas.* Müller and the others must have been troubled by
the fact that Seneca here praises someone who has chosen
philosophic calm, whereas he is supposed, on the strength of
Ep. mor. 108.22, *Cons. Helv.* 17.4, to have hated philosophy.
They, and later writers on the elder Seneca, e.g. Bornecque,
Décl. 14, Edward, *Suasoriae* xxvi, Sussman, *The elder Seneca*
48, have wanted him to be praising Mela for single-minded
devotion to rhetoric. But this makes nonsense of the digression in its context.

37 *Seneca* (Oxford, 1975), 33f.; cf. *JRS* LXII (1972), 9.

38 'A propos d'un passage de Sénèque le Père (*Contr.* II pr. 4):
la psychologie d'un père ambitieux pour ses enfants au 1er
siècle ap. J.C.', *Latomus* XXXII (1973), 162ff.

39 Vassileiou, *Latomus* XXXII (1973), 162ff., sees in the bleak-
ness of the words, *te in portu retineo*, evidence that the
elder Seneca was less than enthusiastic about Mela's intentions.

40 So Winterbottom in his translation and *per litt.* 19.11.75.

41 *Per litt.* 25.10.76.

42 Cf., e.g., *Contr.* I pr. 21, *et in illo...; et nescio an...*
for Seneca's use of *et* to link what amount to whole sentences
with different subjects.

43 Cf. *Contr.* I pr. 4, *ita ex memoria...* for the opening of a
sentence with *ita* in a sense equivalent to *itaque.*

44 See p.9.

45 Cf. Sen. *Ep. mor.* 14.13, and, for a detailed treatment of the
theme, Seneca's *De otio.*

46 Unlike the *aridi declamatores* of whom he remarks in *Contr.*
II.1.24 that no figure or *sententia* would distract them from
keeping faithfully to their chosen *colores.*

47 Tac. *Ann.* XVI.17.

48 Sen. fr. 98 Haase (from the younger Seneca's *De vita patris*),
quoted pp.15f.

49 So Bornecque, *Décl.* 24; Edward, *Suasoriae* xxvi; M.T. Griffin,
JRS LXII (1972), 4, 11; Sussman, *The elder Seneca* 92.

50 Fr. Hist. 2 Müller, on which see p.17.

51 I.e. before the younger Seneca's exile (see *Cons. Helv.* 2.5).
Evidence for the place of his death discussed by Mrs Griffin
(*op. cit.* 8) is surely inconclusive.

[52] Sen. fr. 98 *init.* Haase inserts *scriptorum* between *puris* and *titulis*, unconvincingly. Could *puris titulis* perhaps mean 'whose memorials boast no *cursus honorum*'?

[53] The second part of fr. 98, continuing straight on from the extract quoted above. After *diem <perductas>* or the like seems to be required, cf. *Contr.* I pr. 13: *ad ultimum eius diem perductam familiarem amicitiam.* As it is, the phrase introduced by *usque ad* dangles too loosely.

[54] Much speculation there has been nonetheless. Sussman, *The elder Seneca* 137ff. provides bibliography and an introduction to the main arguments about its possible scope, time of composition and publication, content and sources.

[55] Mrs Griffin, *JRS* LXII (1972), 10, argued against the attribution of the historical fragments to the elder Seneca. Sussman, *The elder Seneca* 137 is more ready to accept them as remnants of the lost *Histories.*

[56] The elder Seneca was not wholly 'unspeculative' as Mrs Griffin (*loc. cit.*) suggests. What about his speculations on the decline of eloquence (*Contr.* I pr. 7)?

[57] Here I adopt Bornecque's conjecture *derigant, RPh* XXVI (1902), 373, as against Kiessling's *derigam*, preferred by Müller and Winterbottom. The MSS divide between those reading *redicam, redigam* ('full text' MSS) and *reducant, redigant* or the like (*excerpta* MSS). However, for arguments suggesting that the 'full text' MSS are in general more to be trusted than the *excerpta* see H. Hagendahl, 'Rhetorica', *Apophoreta Gotoburgensia V. Lundström oblata* (Göteborg, 1936), 299ff.; M. Winterbottom, 'Problems in the elder Seneca', *BICS* XXI (1974), 24ff.

[58] See p.35.

[59] E.g. Bornecque, *Décl.* 16ff.; Edward, *Suasoriae* xxvii ff.

[60] Edward's translation (xxvii) of a phrase in Sen. *Cons. Helv.* 17.3.

[61] Bornecque, *Décl.* 16. The assertion that Cato was his ideal rests on *Contr.* I pr. 9 (part of the tirade on the decline of eloquence) in which a famous dictum of Cato's, *orator est, Marce fili, vir bonus dicendi peritus* is quoted with hearty approval. But one does not deduce that Fortunatianus was steeped in early Republican ideals just because at the beginning of his *Ars rhetorica* (81.4f.) he adopts Cato's definition of *orator*; see p.83.

[62] Edward, *Suasoriae* xxviii; cf. also now Sussman, *The elder Seneca* 26ff.

[63] Cf. Ovid. *Am.* I.8.43, *casta est quam nemo rogavit.*

[64] Also compare *Cons. Helv.* 16.3 with Fabianus in *Contr.* II.5.7.

[65] See p.308. On Seneca's misrepresentation of his father in *Ep. mor.* 108 see now Sussman, *The elder Seneca* 27f.

[66] For the attitude cf. Juv. 6.434ff.

[67] E.g. Bornecque, *Décl.* 16; Edward, *Suasoriae* xxviii; Sussman, *The elder Seneca* 26f.

[68] Edward, *op. cit.* xxix; cf. Bornecque, *Décl.* 17; Bonner, *Rom. decl.* 147; Sussman, *The elder Seneca* 26.

[69] *JRS* LXII (1972), 12ff.

[70] Edward, *Suasoriae* xxix; Bornecque, *Décl.* 17; Bonner, *Rom. decl.* 147.

[71] See *Contr.* III pr. 17; IX.3.13.

[72] Cf. Quint. X.1.105: *oratores vero vel praecipue Latinam eloquentiam parem facere Graecae possunt: nam Ciceronem cuicumque eorum fortiter opposuerim.*

[73] Edward, *Suasoriae* xxix; Bornecque, *Décl.* 17.

[74] 'Basic rhetorical theories of the elder Seneca', *CJ* XXXIV (1939), 350.

[75] J. Buschmann, *Charakteristik der griechischen Rhetoren beim Rhetor Seneca* (Parchim, 1878), *Die 'enfants terribles' unter den Rhetoren des Seneca* (Parchim, 1883). In fact, in the opening pages of the first paper he helped to promote the error.

[76] Adverse criticisms of Greek declaimers, but by no means always severe ones, are included or implied in *Contr.* I.1.25; 2.23; 4.7, 10; 6.12 (Winterbottom deletes *et greca*); 7.12; 8.7, 11; II.3.23; 6.13; VII.1.25; 4.10 (where, however, Seneca is quoting other people's views); 5.15; IX.5.17 (reading *sed genere corrupto*); X.4.18, 22f.; 5.21-5, 27f.; *Suas.* 1.12f., 16; 2.14.

[77] For praise and other relatively favourable criticism of Greek declaimers see *Contr.* I.1.25; 4.7, 11f.; 7.18; 8.16; II.1.39; 6.12 (*ars inculta* uncharacteristic of those under Greek influence); IV pr. 7 (see n.80, p.334); VII.1.26; 5.14; IX. 2.29; X.4.18; 5.21f.; *Suas.* 2.14; 7.14.

[78] *Contr.* I.1.25; 2.22f.; 4.10-12; II.3.23; VII.1.25f.; 4.10; 5.14; IX.1.12f.; 5.16f.; X.4.18-23; 5.19-28; *Suas.* 1.13; 2.14.

[79] So Müller, following AB, which give the declaimer's name in Greek letters.

[80] Cf. *Contr.* X pr. 3: *hi caloris minus habent, neglegentiae non minus.* On *facultas* as a characteristic of the Greeks, rarely reproduced by Latin declaimers, see *Contr.* IV pr. 7; for *licentia* in Latin see *Contr.* II pr. 1; *Suas.* 2.10 (Arellius Fuscus); *Contr.* II.2.7 (Marullus); *ibid.* 12 (Ovid's poetry).

[81] See, e.g., *Contr.* X.5.28, quoted p.23.

[82] See p.54.

[83] See pp.308-10.

[84] See Cic. *De or.* III.24.94; cf. Suet. *De gramm. et rhet.* 25.1 Brugnoli.

[85] See pp.77ff.

[86] See pp.305-7; 310-19.

The declamatory anthology

[1] Cf. T. Janson, *Latin prose prefaces* (Stockholm, 1964), 7ff. and, for discussion of Seneca's use of prefatory conventions, Sussman, *The elder Seneca* 51ff.

[2] C.W. Lockyer, 'The fiction of memory and the use of written sources: convention and practice in Seneca the Elder and other authors' (Diss. Princeton, 1970), 195ff., gives further examples of this device in Roman literature.

[3] *Latin prose prefaces* 21.

[4] Cited by Janson, *op. cit.* 61.

[5] Quint. X.2.11, 24ff.

[6] E. Rolland, *De l'influence de Sénèque le père et les rhéteurs sur Sénèque le philosophe* (Ghent, 1906); C. Preisendanz, 'De Senecae rhetoris apud philosophum filium auctoritate', *Philologus* LXVII (1908), 68ff.; C.S. Rayment, 'Echoes of the declamations in the dialogues of the younger Seneca', *CB* XLV (1969), 51f., 63.

[7] It is conceivable, however, that the format of his work had been partially anticipated in some anthology of extracts from the ten canonical Attic orators in ten books with a preface to introduce each orator. Cf. Cic. *Opt. gen.* 6.17.

[8] See also *Contr.* III pr. 18; IV pr. 11; VII pr. 9; X pr. 16.

[9] There are a few exceptions, e.g. in *Contr.* I.5.1; I.7.10.

[10] Some *enthymemata* might consist of two contrasting rhetorical

questions or exclamations (see p.204); see also *Rhet. Her.*
IV.17.24 for *sententiae quae dupliciter efferuntur*.

[11] Bornecque's generalization (*Décl.* 33): 'les *Sententiae*, où
l'on cherche dans quelle mesure le cas posé tombe sous le
coup d'une loi donnée', does not cover all we find in the
opening extracts of Seneca's surveys.

[12] See pp.202ff. and Sussman, *The elder Seneca* 36.

[13] Analysed on pp.251ff.

[14] See also for example *Contr.* II.1.10-13; *Suas.* 3.1.

[15] H. Bardon, *Le vocabulaire de la critique littéraire chez
Sénèque le Rhéteur* (Paris, 1940), 68ff. On Bardon's attitudes
see my pp.68ff.

[16] Seneca rarely uses *color* in the Ciceronian sense of 'stylistic
colour'; see Bardon, *op. cit.* 19. On this different technical
usage, see my pp.166ff.

[17] As I argue in *CR* N.S. XX (1970), 11f., *hunc sensum Vibius
Rufus...nisi nox defecisset* should be transposed to fit
between *impleri argumentis* and *hunc sensum a Latinis iactatum*.
A similar case of displacement is perhaps to be found in
Contr. X.4.25. The words *P. Asprenas...fortassis pater est*
could very well have been placed originally after the
sententia by Blandus in *Contr.* X.4.20 which ends *hic fortasse
meus est*, but later have been omitted owing to a confusion of
like endings, and consigned to the end of the survey by a
corrector.

[18] As Edward (*Suasoriae* 156) assumes.

[19] They contain his latest historical allusion in the work
(*Suas.* 2.22), but there is no certainty that they were composed last; cf. M.T. Griffin, *JRS* LXII (1972), 11. On the
liber suasoriarum see now also Sussman, *The elder Seneca* 69ff.

[20] Cf. Janson, *Latin prose prefaces* 16, 25.

[21] G. Boissier, *Revue des deux mondes* XI (1902), 480ff. trans.
W.G. Hutchison in *Tacitus and other Roman studies* (London,
1906), 163ff.; Bonner, *Rom. decl.* vii.

[22] Vol. I x.

[23] Bornecque, *Décl.* 28f.

[24] 'Literary sources in Cicero's *Brutus* and the technique of
citation in the Dialogue', *AJPh* XXVII (1906), 197 n.1.

[25] 'Wirklichkeit und Literaturform', *RhM* LXXVIII (1929), 114f.

[26] Princeton, 1970. Sussman, *The elder Seneca* 75ff., whole-heartedly accepts Lockyer's conclusions.

[27] Lockyer, Diss. 170f.

[28] Cf. Lockyer, Diss. 42ff.

[29] *Ibid.* 142ff.

[30] Bornecque, *Décl.* 25ff. citing M. Sander, *Der Sprachgebrauch des Rhetors Annaeus Seneca*, 2 vols. (Berlin, 1877, 1880); H.T. Karsten, *De elocutione rhetorica qualis invenitur in Annaei Senecae Suasoriis et Controversiis* (progr. Rotterdam, 1881).

[31] A.W. de Groot, *Der antike Prosarhythmus* (Groningen, 1921), 106f.

[32] For example, unlike the analyst of verse metre, he has no certain way of telling whether a naturally short syllable before a mute + liquid is to be regarded as long or short, and he can never be sure whether the possibility of synizesis, hiatus etc. is to be discounted in particular cases.

[33] The samples were taken from the following passages: Seneca - *Contr.* I pr. 1-16; II pr. 1-5; III pr. 1-7, 18; Latro - *Contr.* I.1.1-3; 2.1; 3.1; 4.1; 5.1; 6.1; 7.1-2; 7.10; 8.1; II.1.1; 2.1; 3.1; Fuscus - *Contr.* I.1.6; 2.5; 3.3; 4.5; 4.8; 5.2; 6.7; 7.5; 8.2; II.1.4-8; 2.1; 3.3; 3.9; 4.4; 4.5; 5.4. In making this sample I aimed to select only sentence endings which corresponded to major breaks in the sense. In doing so I did not abide rigidly by the sentence division of any one editor, though I was probably influenced to some extent by the punctuation of Winterbottom, whose edition I used. Detailed statistics, which however are not to be regarded as providing more than preliminary soundings, will be found in an appendix on pp.326f.

[34] See de Groot, *Der antike Prosarhythmus* 106, from which all the figures given below for the frequency of *clausula* rhythms in Cicero's speeches and 'normal' Latin usage are taken. On de Groot's methods see L.P. Wilkinson, *Golden Latin artistry* (Cambridge, 1963), 139ff.

[35] In a study of a larger sample one would be able to take account of discrepancies in the frequency with which the less common *clausulae* occur, in addition to the distribution of the eight types considered here.

[36] *Décl.* 25f.

[37] See n.30 above.

[38] *Sprachgebrauch* I 1.

[39] Sander referred to Bursian's edition by page and line in his notes. I have omitted several apparently false references from among the instances of normal usages which he cites for the sake of comparison. I am indebted to Dr J. Mejer of Copenhagen for the gift of a photocopy of this dissertation.

[40] Sander, *Quaestiones* 5 n.4, adds: 'pro *idcirco* ceteri rhetores *ob id*, *ob hoc*' and refers us to another note, 38 (actually 36) n.1, in which he lists the following examples: *ob id* - *Contr.* I.1.13 (Latro's *divisio*), 14 (Gallio's *divisio*); *ob hoc* - *Contr.* I.1 *thema*; II.6.4 (Fabianus), 5 (Latro's *divisio*); VII.6.13 (Latro's *divisio*); *Suas.* 2.21 (Seneca paraphrasing a *thema*); *propter hoc* - *Contr.* I.5.3 (Pompeius Silo), 8 (Seneca reporting Fuscus); 7.16 (Cestius); X.1.10; *propter id* - *Contr.* I.8.8 (where *id* is conjectural).

[41] = Sander, *Quaestiones* 5 n.11: cf. *Suas.* 6.13 (Varius Geminus' *divisio*: *iniquum* + infin.); *Contr.* I.6.5 (Iulius Bassus: *aequum* + infin.).

[42] = Sander, *Quaestiones* 5 n.12: (for *licere* + infin.) cf. *Suas.* 5.4 (Seneca reporting Cestius); *Contr.* I.1.14 (Gallio's *divisio*); IX.2.17 (Pompeius Silo's *divisio*).

[43] Sander, *Quaestiones* 6 n.1, gives examples of *iubere* + infin. which it would be superfluous to reproduce.

[44] = Sander, *Quaestiones* 3 n.1: cf. *Contr.* VII.1.2 (Albucius: *aliter quam*); 2.13 (Romanius Hispo: *aliter non potuisse pacari rem publicam quam...*).

[45] = Sander, *Quaestiones* 6 n.4: (for *lex* + infin.) cf. *Contr.* I.1.5 (Asprenas); II.3.10 (Marullus).

[46] See n.30, p.336 above.

[47] *Eloc. rhet.* 11.

[48] At least in *Contr.* I pr. 11 Seneca uses *alioqui* not in the sense *ceterum* as Karsten suggests in his entry s.v. (*Eloc. rhet.* 16), but in the same sense, *alio casu*, in which Latro customarily uses it; in none of the examples cited by Karsten does it appear to bear the meaning *alio tempore*, as he claims it sometimes does in Latro's usage; there is a contradiction between Karsten's observation on p.10 'de peculiari significatione particulae *alioquin* apud Latronem' and the documentation on p.16 s.v., from which it emerges that Gallio and Hispo used *alioqui* to mean *alio casu*.

[49] I have unfortunately not had access to the work of M. Cerrati, *La grammatica di A. Seneca il rhetore* (Turin, 1908), but C.J. Fordyce's description of it in his review of H. Bardon, *Le vocabulaire de la critique littéraire chez Sénèque le Rhéteur* in *CR* LX (1946), 129 as 'useful, though not always accurate' does not encourage one to suppose that it has all the merits

lacking in the work of Sander and Karsten.

[50] As Sander (*Quaestiones* 6) and Karsten (*Eloc. rhet.* 10) observe. See my pp.245-51; 270-4.

[51] See pp.290f.

[52] *Contr.* IX.1.3,10,12; 2.11,13,18,19,22; 3.5,10; 4.5,11,14,15, 16; 5.3,6,16; 6.3,19; X.2.12; 3.16.

[53] O. Gruppe, *Quaestiones Annaeanae* (Diss. Berlin, 1873), 28.

[54] R. Hess, *Quaestiones Annaeanae* (Diss. Kiel, 1898), 4ff.

[55] Bornecque, *Décl.* 200.

[56] I.e. to discuss points of declamatory technique, rather than to deliver full declamations. For this use of *disputare* (distinct from that relating to philosophical discussion, examples of which are collected by G. François in his article, '*Declamatio* et *disputatio*', *AC* XXXII (1963), 513ff.) see *Contr.* VII.3.10, X pr. 15.

[57] W. Hoffa, *De Seneca Patre quaestiones selectae* (Diss. Göttingen, 1909), 33ff.

[58] See p.40 on the use of *aiebat* perhaps with reference to these writings.

[59] References to M. Valerius Messala Corvinus as an orator, critic and wit occur in *Contr.* II.4.8,10; III pr. 14; *Suas.* 1.7; 2.17,20; 3.6f.; 6.27. Iulius Montanus is mentioned as a critic in *Contr.* VII.1.27; also in fr. 3 Müller, which however may be by the younger Seneca (cf. *Ep. mor.* 122.11). It is unlikely that the name of Iulius Montanus unabbreviated could have been corrupted into Votienus Montanus in *Contr.* IX pr. 1: the name Votienus is so much the *lectio difficilior* as compared with Iulius, and it occurs twice in the one section. If we accept the hypothesis that someone other than Votienus Montanus was introduced at the beginning of the ninth preface, we have to account for the fact that almost all of the extant fragments of Votienus come in the ninth book. Perhaps they were equally numerous in the eighth book and, if the remarks in *Contr.* VII.5.11f. were not sufficient introduction, he had been mentioned in the preface to *Contr.* VIII. If this were so, the name of Votienus Montanus would have been familiar to the hypothetical early scribe who made the mistake, when he came to copy *Contr.* IX pr. 1.

The criticism

[1] Montaigne, *Essais* ed. M. Rat (Paris, 1962), I 36f.

[2] Cowley, *Essays and other prose writings* ed. A.B. Gough (Oxford, 1915), 179f.

[3] Jonson, *Works* Vol. VIII ed. C.H. Herford, P. and E. Simpson (Oxford, 1947), 590f.

[4] *Op. cit.* 591.

[5] *Op. cit.* 391. See also Jonson's use of *Contr.* IV pr. 7-11 in his prose criticism of Shakespeare, quoted and discussed by Sussman, *The elder Seneca* 170f.

[6] Sussman, *op. cit.* 95ff., now provides much fuller discussion of Seneca's pen-portraiture than any previously available.

[7] Or just conceivably a book; cf. the use of *aiebat* in *Contr.* IX.6.18.

[8] S.F. Bonner, *Dionysius of Halicarnassus* (Cambridge, 1939), 23.

[9] *Op. cit.* 24.

[10] See pp.245f.

[11] See pp.80f.

[12] Cf. G. Watson, *The literary critics* (Harmondsworth, 1962), 11ff.

[13] See W.D. Lebek, 'Zur Vita des Albucius Silus bei Sueton', *Hermes* XCIV (1966), 360ff.

[14] See F. Leo, *Die griechisch-römische Biographie nach ihrer literarischen Form* (Leipzig, 1901 repr. Hildesheim, 1965); W. Steidle, *Sueton und die antike Biographie* (Munich, 1951); A.D. Momigliano, *The development of Greek biography* (Cambridge, Mass., 1971).

[15] *Antigonos von Karystos* (Berlin, 1881), 82.

[16] *History of autobiography in antiquity* (London, 1950), I 299 = *Geschichte der Autobiographie*[3] (Frankfurt, 1947), I 312.

[17] Now edited by F. Wehrli, *Schule des Aristoteles*, Supptbd I (Basel, 1974).

[18] *Antigonos von Karystos* 82.

[19] For the neuter form see *ThLL* s.v. *epitaphius*.

[20] On the nature of this work see Momigliano, *Development of Greek biography* 96f.

[21] See p.93; n.68, p.346.

[22] *HRR* II 40.

[23] See n.68, p.346, on fr. 24*, but it is not certain exactly which of Nepos' works this fragment comes from.

[24] See W.D. Lebek, *Hermes* XCIV (1966), 360ff. Only sections 3 and 5 of the Suetonian *Life* are certainly derived from *Contr.* VII pr.

[25] But n.b. this work is not as comprehensive as it at first sight appears; for example it does not include by any means all the fragments of Nepos concerned with literary matters.

[26] Notably J.F. D'Alton, *Roman literary theory and criticism* (London, 1931), 546: 'His prefaces alone would win for him a high rank among Roman critics. It is probable that he would not have achieved so much, if Cicero had not smoothed the path for him, but his judgements are generally characterised by a freshness and spontaneity that we often miss in Cicero.'

[27] *CJ* XXXIV (1939), 347ff.

[28] 'The elder Seneca as a critic of rhetoric' (Diss. N. Carolina, 1969), 70ff.; *The elder Seneca* (Leiden, 1978), 115ff.

[29] See pp.151-239.

[30] See pp.246-96.

[31] Paris, 1940.

[32] *AC* XII (1943), 5ff.

[33] Notoriously, Bardon makes no use of Müller's edition; many other serious failings in his lexicographical method and conclusions were soon pointed out by reviewers of *Vocabulaire*, e.g. J. Marouzeau, *REL* XVIII (1940), 203ff.; A. Cordier, *RPh* XVII (1943), 220ff.; W. Stegemann, *PhW* LXIV (1944), 172ff.; C.J. Fordyce, *CR* LX (1946), 129. See also Sussman, *The elder Seneca* 103f.

[34] His chapter headings: II *Faiblesses: obscurités*; III *Faiblesses: Appauvrissement de certains emplois*; IV *Faiblesses: pauvreté du vocabulaire*, will give some indication of the tone of his work.

[35] *The Greek and Roman critics* (London, 1965), 179.

[36] Bardon, *Vocabulaire* 85.

[37] Watson, *The literary critics* 14.

[38] *Op. cit.* 28.

[39] Bardon, *Vocabulaire* 85.

[40] See E. Fantham, *Comparative studies in Republican Latin imagery*, Phoenix Suppl. Vol. X (Toronto, 1972), 137ff., on the *De oratore*.

[41] *Editio Commeliniana* (Heidelberg, 1603/4) *praef.* He was dissenting '*a viro docto, qui memoria nostra Senecam hunc Rhetorem leviter doctum, ac quasi proletarium appellat*'. Schott's judgement is cited with whole-hearted approval by Edward (*Suasoriae* x).

[42] Bardon lists a number of more or less inelegant expressions used by Seneca the Elder in his article, *AC* XII (1943), 5ff.

[43] For a comparison between the two Senecas' accounts of Fabianus' style see A.D. Leeman, *Orationis ratio* (Amsterdam, 1963), I 264ff.

Oratory and rhetorical theory up to his own time

[1] See pp.95ff.

[2] On the text see n.50, p.345.

[3] See pp.101f.

[4] Discussed further on pp.104ff.

[5] Cf. Edward and Winterbottom *ad loc.*

[6] Fragments collected by D. Matthes (Teubner, Leipzig, 1962).

[7] G.M.A. Grube, 'Theodorus of Gadara', *AJPh* LXXX (1959), 337ff. gives a well-balanced account of Seneca's references to their teaching, in relation to the more extensive data in Quintilian and the 'Anonymus Seguerianus' *Rh. Gr.* I.2 352ff. Spengel-Hammer.

[8] Cf. Anon. Seguer. 113ff. (*Rh. Gr.* I.2 372).

[9] The theme does not state explicitly whether the ex-prostitute who wishes to become a priestess has actually, as she claims, kept her virginity.

[10] Grube, *AJPh* LXXX (1959), 335ff. argues against the view that Theodorus favoured impassioned rhetoric free from rules, but does not cite *Suas.* 3.7 in this connection, as one might well do.

[11] Ἰδιωτισμός first appears in Philodemus, *Poet.* II.71, but is credited to earlier Stoic theory by Diog. Laert. (VII.59); μετάφρασις is not attested in Greek sources before Plut. *Dem.* 8.2. See n.14, p.342, for Senecan references.

[12] Used in several senses by Plautus and in the sense 'writer of comedy' by Cicero (Or. 55.184).

[13] Note how in Suas. 6.21 a transliteration is provided by a second hand in B, where AB[1] have Greek characters. Sometimes (e.g. in Contr. X.4.21f. M) even Greek declaimers' names have been transmitted in Greek letters.

[14] Except that the Greek words never seem to be metaphors for describing the critic's subjective impressions of the nuances of style. Most of them are technical terms referring to literary occupations and genres, themes for rhetorical or philosophical treatment, the major sections of a literary work, figures of speech or thought and elements of diction: anthypophora (Contr. I.7.17); cacozelia (Contr. IX.1.15; 2.28; Suas. 7.11); cacozelōs (Suas. 2.16); comicus (Contr. VII.3.8); echo/ἠχώ* (Contr. VII.7.19); enthymema (Contr. I pr. 23); epilogus (Contr. III pr. 10; IV pr. 8; VII.4.5*,6,8; 5.7; IX.6.12*,13); epiphonema (Contr. I pr. 23; X.4.25); ἐπιτάφιον (Suas. 6.21, see n.19, p.339); ethicōs* (Contr. II. 2.12); ethicōs (Contr. II.3.23; 4.8; Suas. 1.13); grammaticus* (Suas. 2.13); hendecasyllabi* (Contr. VII.4.7); hermeneumata (Contr. IX.3.14); (hexis - Bursian's conjecture in Contr. VII pr. 2); historia (Suas. 5.8; 6.15; 6.25); historicus (Suas. 2.22; 6.14,16); idiotismos (Contr. II.3.21; VII pr. 5); ironia (Contr. I.7.13); metaphrasis (Suas. 1.12); mimicus* (Contr. VII.5.15); mimus (Contr. VII.3.9); pantomimus (Contr. III pr. 16*; Suas. 2.19); phantasia (Suas. 2.14); philosophumenos (Contr. I.3.8; 7.17); phrasis (Contr. III pr. 7; VII pr. 2*); problema (Contr. I.3.8); prooemium (Contr. I.1. 25; VII.1.26; X.1.13); rhetor (Contr. VII.4.8,9; IX.2.26; X pr. 10,11; Suas. 2.12); schema (Contr. I pr. 23f.; II.1.24; 3.22; VII pr. 7*,8; IX.2.22; X pr. 10); schola (Contr. I pr. 24*; 7.18; III pr. 13*, 15f.*; IX pr. 5*; X pr. 11; Suas. 2. 15,21); scholastica (Contr. I pr. 12; II.3.13*; III pr. 12*; VII pr. 8; IX.5.15; X.5.12, see S.F. Bonner, 'Rhetorica', CR LXI (1947), 86); scholasticus - adj. (Contr. IX pr. 4*, 5); scholasticus - noun (Contr. I.6.10; 7.15; II.2.8; 3.13*,19; III pr. 16*; VII pr. 9; 5.12; Suas. 3.6); soloecismos (Contr. IX pr. 3; Suas. 2.13); syllaba (Contr. I.7.18*; X pr. 11; Suas. 7.11); tetracolon (Contr. IX.2.27); tetradeum* (Contr. X pr. 13); thema (Contr. I.2.14; IX.5.11); thesis (Contr. I pr. 12; VII.4.3); tragicus (Contr. VII.3.8); tragoedia (Suas. 3.7); tricolum (Contr. II.4.12).

Systematic lexicography will probably reveal that this list is not exhaustive. It contains merely the examples cited by Bardon in Vocabulaire, plus a few (marked with an asterisk) which I happen to have noticed to be missing from his Lexique.

[15] Contr. I.1.15; 2.16; II.1.23; 3.18; 4.9; 6.6; VII pr. 6; IX. 2.24; X.4.18.

[16] See especially Contr. IX.2.27f. for the interchangeability of these words; Seneca's use of them is discussed in detail on pp.214ff.

17 See n.14, p.342.

18 See p.5.

19 E.g. *Contr.* VII.6.17.

20 By contrast, the *Seianiani* were described as parricides for
their offences against the Emperor (*Contr.* IX.4.21), even
though Tiberius was never officially dubbed *Pater Patr̈iae*.

21 See Winterbottom's notes on these declamations.

22 *Contr.* VII.2.1 (Sepullius Bassus) cf. *Verr.* II.5.118; *Suas.*
6.3 (Latro) cf. *Verr.* II.5.161; also *Suas.* 6.11 (Varius
Geminus on Cicero and Sicily in general).

23 *Contr.* VII.2.10 (Marcellus Aeserninus) cf. *Cat.* IV.3 etc.;
Suas. 6.3 (Latro) cf. *Cat.* I.2 etc.; *Suas.* 6.12 (Varius
Geminus) cf. *Cat.* IV.3 etc.

24 *Suas.* 6.2 (Haterius) cf. *Mil.* 92,105; *Suas.* 7.3 (Cestius) cf.
Mil. 101; *Contr.* III pr. 15 (Cestius' declamation *in Milonem*).

25 *Contr.* VII.2.5 (Haterius) cf. *Phil.* II.64; *Contr.* VII.2.10
(Marcellus Aeserninus) cf. *Phil.* II.119 (where Cicero recalls
Cat. IV.3); *Suas.* 6.3 (Latro) cf. *Phil.* II.63-4; *Suas.* 6.4
(Pompeius Silo) cf. *Phil.* II.64; *Suas.* 6.5 (Triarius) cf.
Phil. II.67; *Suas.* 6.7 (Argentarius) cf. *Phil.* II.77 etc.;
Suas. 6.12 (Varius Geminus) cf. *Phil.* II.119 (with *Cat.* IV.3);
Suas. 7.2 (Cestius) cf. *Phil.* II.24; *Suas.* 7.5 (Pompeius Silo)
cf. *Phil.* II.20; 5 and 60.

26 Latro in *Suas.* 6.3 quoting *Cat.* I.2.

27 Words extracted from a sentence in *Cat.* IV.3 (cf. *Phil.* II.
119) quoted in *Contr.* VII.2.10 and *Suas.* 6.12.

28 *Suas.* 7.3 = *Mil.* 101 paraphrased.

29 *Phil.* I.38; *Marc.* 25 or possibly *Ad fam.* X.1.1.

30 Cf. Winterbottom, *BICS* XXI (1974), 26.

31 *Suas.* 1.5: *nos quidem illum deridemus, sed timeo ne ille nos
gladio* ἀντιμυκτηρίσῃ; *Ad fam.* XV.19.4: *scis, quam se semper a
nobis derisum putet; vereor, ne nos rustice gladio velit*
ἀντιμυκτηρίσαι.

32 Parallel noted by Winterbottom *ad loc.*; cf. his notes on
Suas. 6.4 (Cestius) and 6.8 (Latro) where *sententiae* are
compared with *Ad fam.* X.1.1; but the similarity is only a
general one.

33 *Contr.* IX.6.16.

[34] Winterbottom *ad loc.* also compares Vell. Pat. II.66.5; ps.-Quint. *Decl.* CCLIII (37.11 Ritter).

[35] Though perhaps also by Nepos, see p.65.

[36] See p.23.

[37] Though all or part of the digression on Antony's visit to Athens is perhaps Senecan.

[38] Cf. *Suas.* 6.4, where Winterbottom compares a *sententia* by Cestius with, among other passages, *Ad fam.* X.1.1.

[39] Pp.104ff.

[40] On certain vaguenesses in the exposition of the data in *Contr.* I pr. 12, which make it seem unlikely that Seneca was himself the scholar responsible for the underlying research, see pp.129f.

[41] On the question of how much, if any, of Cicero's correspondence was available for public perusal in Seneca's day see p.130.

[42] Cf. M.T. Griffin, *JRS* LXII (1972), 10.

[43] On the unreliability of arguments *ex silentio* see the discussion of Seneca's references to poets, pp.311ff.

[44] Quoted p.104.

[45] He taught Fabianus (*Contr.* II pr. 5); more than that cannot be said with certainty - the dating of Latro's departure from Rome to 15 B.C., and the assumption that he did not return, used by Bornecque (*Décl.* 194) in dating Blandus' birth, are baseless.

[46] Not that his vocabulary was entirely distinct from Cicero's; Bardon's *lexique* in *Vocabulaire* 11ff. lists many examples of usages shared by the two critics. But Sussman never adequately justifies his assertion (*The elder Seneca* 95) that 'Seneca's critical outlook substantially reflects the influence of Cicero...'

[47] *PACA* XII (1973), 11.

[48] But for another case where Cicero's name has surely been interpolated without any such provocation see Sen. *De clem.* I.10.1 where modern editors have let the following statement about Augustus slip past unemended: *iam Domitios, Messalas, Asinios, Cicerones, quidquid floris erat in civitate, clementiae suae debebat.*

[49] Cf. A.D. Leeman, *Orationis ratio* I 138ff.; W.D. Lebek, *Verba prisca* (Göttingen, 1970), 83ff.

[50] reget *A* riget *BVD*: viget *Jahn*. *Rigere* is not found in
Cicero's rhetorical works; nor does *rigidus* seem to be used
of literary qualities by the rhetorical theorists; *vigere*, on
the other hand, is used with reference to prose rhythm in
Cic. *Or*. 64.215. For another comparison of Calvus with
Demosthenes see Plin. *Ep*. I.2.2, quoted n.62, p.346.

[51] Here Müller prints his supplement *summisse*, which is also
adopted by Winterbottom, but *molliter*, suggested to me by Mr
Duncan Kennedy, seems more convincing.

[52] Cf. *ORF*[3] 492ff. for the testimonia relating to Calvus' oratory; Lebek, *Verba prisca* 88f. for a summary of modern
attempts to account for the disagreement over its merits.

[53] On the dating of this letter see D.R. Shackleton Bailey ed.
Ad familiares (Cambridge, 1977), *ad loc*.

[54] See p.99.

[55] *Orationis ratio* I 139. Cf. Lebek, *Verba prisca* 95f. on the
fact, recognized in later antiquity, that Cicero's manner was
quite far removed from that of Demosthenes.

[56] *ORF*[3] 494ff.

[57] A.W. de Groot, *Der antike Prosarhythmus* (Groningen, 1921),
107.

[58] *Handbook of antique prose rhythm* (Groningen, 1919), 196.
Unfortunately de Groot gives no figures for Lysias. He
regards Thucydides, with some reservations, as virtually
reproducing the 'normal' frequency of rhythms in Greek.

[59] *primum igitur eum tamquam e vinculis numerorum eximamus.*
sunt enim quidam, ut scis, oratorii numeri, de quibus mox
agemus, observandi ratione quadam, sed alio in genere
orationis, in hoc omnino relinquendi.

[60] *tum removebitur omnis insignis ornatus quasi margaritarum* etc.

[61] On the identity of the Roman *Attici* see A.E. Douglas, 'M.
Calidius and the Atticists', *CQ* N.S. V (1955), 241ff. especially 245f. where he excludes from the ranks of the
Atticists everyone but Calvus and, probably, Brutus; also
his *Cicero - Greece and Rome: New Surveys in the Classics* II
(Oxford, 1968), 38f. where he excludes Brutus as well,
following K. Barwick, intr. ed. *Brutus* (Heidelberg, 1949), 15,
who argues that Cicero would not have dedicated the Atticists
to Brutus if he had belonged to their movement (an invalid
argument, seeing that Caesar dedicated his *De analogia* to
Cicero, with whose views he was not in agreement), and F.
Portalupi, *Bruto e i neo-atticisti* (Turin, 1955), who sees
Brutus' style as the product of his philosophical training
and the natural austerity of his character. But the time has

come for a reaction against the type of reasoning which seeks
to eliminate from consideration as an Atticist any orator who
does not conform strictly to Cicero's prescription for the
plain style (or who, though conforming to it, may have had
extra-literary reasons for doing so). Future discussions of
Roman Atticism ought to take the fragments of Calvus, the one
Latin orator known to have aspired to the epithet *Atticus*
(Cic. *Brut.* 82.284), as their starting point. Lebek, *Verba
prisca* 97, is right to stress that there were diverse tendencies within the Atticist movement.

[62] Cf. Plin. *Ep.* I.2.2: *temptavi enim imitari Demosthenen semper
tuum, Calvum nuper meum, dumtaxat figuris orationis; nam vim
tantorum virorum, 'pauci quos aequus...' adsequi possunt.*

[63] And consequently not to conclude automatically that any
orator whose style is known to have been rhythmical must be
excluded from their number. The case of M. Calidius (cf.
A.E. Douglas, *CQ* N.S. V, 1955) needs to be reconsidered.

[64] Discussed by Lebek, *Verba prisca* 86 n.16. I accept the modern
convention of regarding $-\cup-\cup$ and $-\cup--$ as the same clausula
type. Note also Calvus fr. 27: *vehementissimē probārē.*

[65] W.H. Shewring, 'Prose rhythm and the comparative method II',
CQ XXV (1931), 12ff., esp. 13f.

[66] Note the successions of short syllables: *crēditē mǐhǐ, nōn
ēst tūrpē mǐsērērǐ.*

[67] Cf. p.54.

[68] N.b. A fragment of Nepos (*Exempla*, fr. 24*, *HRR* II 33) contains a Catullan allusion amongst miscellaneous information
about Mamurra.

[69] So Winterbottom; Müller prints his conjecture, *sceleratissimi
calumniatoris.*

The history of declamation

[1] On the textual problem here see p.95.

[2] For detailed discussions see: R.P. Robinson ed. Suetonius, *De
gramm. et rhet.* (Paris, 1925), 35ff.; H. Throm, *Die Thesis*
(Paderborn, 1932); W. Hofrichter, *Studien zur Entwickelungsgeschichte der Deklamation* (Diss. Breslau Univ. publ. Ohlau,
1935); W. Kroll s.v. *'Rhetorik'*, *RE* Supplbd VII (1940),
1039ff.; S.F. Bonner, *'Rhetorica'*, *CR* LXI (1947), 84ff.; *Rom.
decl.* 1ff.; M.L. Clarke, 'The *thesis* in the Roman rhetorical
schools of the Republic', *CQ* XLV (1951), 159ff.; E.M.
Jenkinson, 'Further studies in the curriculum of the Roman
schools of rhetoric in the Republican period', *Symbolae*

Osloenses XXXI (1955), 122ff.; S.F. Bonner, *Education in ancient Rome from the elder Cato to the younger Pliny* (London, 1977), 65ff.; Sussman, *The elder Seneca* 2ff.

3 This is a selection of the examples in Cic. *Part. orat.* 18.61ff., a passage which illustrates the appallingly complex way in which the different varieties of θέσεις were classified by ancient theorists. For a useful list of θέσις topics see Bonner, *Rom. decl.* 3-5.

4 On the part played by Aristotle and Theophrastus in promoting the θέσις see also Quint. XII.2.25; Theon, *Prog.* 69.1 (*Rh. Gr.* II Spengel).

5 See Cic. *De or.* I.11.45ff.

6 Cf. *De or.* III.18.67; *Brut.* 31.119f.; *Acad.* I.19; *De fin.* IV.5; Quint. XII.2.25.

7 See n.6, p.341.

8 Cic. *De inv.* I.6.8; Quint. III.5.5; 7ff.; 12ff. etc. = Hermagoras fr. 6a-e Matthes. Hermagoras' claim that abstract questions were included in the province of rhetoric was challenged by Poseidonius (Plut. *Pomp.* 42.5).

9 Though perhaps we should read *rebus*; see n.45, p.351.

10 Few papyri giving fragments of school exercises of any sort survive from before the Roman Imperial period. See R.A. Pack, *The Greek and Latin literary texts from Greco-Roman Egypt*[2] (Ann Arbor, 1967), nos. 2495-2559: oratory (including rhetorical exercises); nos. 2642-2751: elementary school exercises.

11 Lucian's *Phalaris* II is a *suasoria* (the Delphians deliberate whether to accept the bronze bull of Phalaris as a gift), his *Tyrannoktonos* and *Apokeryttomenos* are *controversiae*, the latter on the same theme as *Contr.* IV.5; the speeches of Aelius Aristides include show-pieces of the *suasoria* type e.g. LII. On sophistic declamations later than these see W. Morel, W. Kroll, s.v. *'Melete'*, *RE* XV.1 (1931), 496ff.; G. Kennedy, *The art of rhetoric in the Roman world* (Princeton, 1972), 553ff.

12 I accept that, as Bonner (*Rom. decl.* 15) points out: 'the illustrations of the various types of στάσις given in the rhetorical handbooks are remarkably like simple and straightforward declamatory exercises'.

13 One cannot regard the interest in deliberative oratory shown in Aristotle's *Rhetoric* or the *Rhetorica ad Alexandrum* as certain proof that school exercises of the *suasoria* type were in use when these works were written. Spengel's μελετῶν πολλάκις in *Rhet. Alex.* 1422a *fin.*, cited by Bonner, *Rom. decl.* 11, is conjectural.

[14] παραγγελματικῶς in Sext. Emp. *P.H.* I.204 has the meaning 'hortatively'; no other example is cited in LSJ.

[15] Cf. *Rhet. Her.* III.2.2 for other examples of multiple themes for deliberation.

[16] Though Philodemus (*Rhet.* I.134 Sudhaus) alludes to μιμήματα ...τῶν δικαν[ικῶ ν] κα[ὶ] συμβουλευτικ[ῶν κ]α[ὶ π[ρεσ]βευτικῶν λόγ[ῳ]ν.

[17] As we shall see, there is no need to share Bonner's doubts (*Rom. decl.* 12) as to whether judicial exercises more complex than mere type declamations such as 'against a rich man' or 'against a tyrant' could have existed as early as Aeschines' time.

[18] *Rhetorische Papyri* ed. K. Kunst (Berlin, 1923), 4ff.

[19] I accept that this, the MSS reading, is probably right (cf. *Contr.* X pr. 8) rather than Müller's *pro Pythodoro <reo> Messalae* (cf. *Suas.* 6.24), but I disagree with Winterbottom's inference that it was a very eloquent speech by Messala *pro Pythodoro* that Latro recited. Latro's recitation was provoked by an unkind remark which Messala had made about his style. The verb *recitare* is used of all three of these mock law-court speeches; this seems to suggest that they were more carefully prepared than the average *declamatio*, hence perhaps Seneca's curious use of the term *oratio* with reference to Latro's display speech.

[20] See K.J. Dover, 'The chronology of Antiphon's speeches', *CQ* XLIV (1950), 44ff.

[21] Bonner, *Rom. decl.* 12; cf. Clarke, *CQ* N.S. I (1951), 161.

[22] Murder: *Tetr.* I.1.2 τὸν φόνον; time and place: I.4 ἀωρὶ τῶν νυκτῶν...ἐν ἐρημίᾳ; slave still alive when found: 1.9 ἔμπνους γὰρ ἔτι ἀρθείς; no robbery: 1.4 ἔχοντες...τὰ ἱμάτια ηὑρέθησαν; the accused a rich man: 2.12, 3.8; enmity between him and the murdered man: 1.5 ἐκ παλαιοῦ...ἐχθρὸς ὤν; prosecution for embezzlement not yet heard: 1.6-8; date of crime: 4.8; identification by slave: 1.9 ἀνακρινόμενος ὑφ' ἡμῶν, τοῦτον μόνον ἔφη γνῶναι τῶν παιόντων αὐτούς; his subsequent death is assumed in, e.g., 1.4 οὐ γὰρ ἂν σὺν τῷ ἀκολούθῳ διέφθειρεν αὐτόν and his unavailability for interrogation under torture is a crucial issue discussed in 2.7, 3.4, 4.7.

[23] Contrast the comparative wealth of circumstantial detail even in such a simple speech as Antiphon's *Prosecution of the stepmother.* None of the allegations made about the rich enemy in addition to the charges outlined above, or statements made by him in self-defence, goes beyond the approved varieties of mud-slinging and white-washing described by ps.-Quintilian in *Decl. min.* CCCLI and CCCLII.

24 *qui...reum detulerat* cf. ps.-Quint. CCCXIX; *divitem inimicum*
cf. *Contr.* X.1; *peculatus* cf. *Contr.* IX.1 (for *peculatus* as
equivalent to ἱερῶν κλοπή see Bonner, *Rom. decl.* 106); *inter
moras iudicii* cf. ps.-Quint. CCCXIX; *cum servo*: for slaves in
controversiae see, e.g., ps.-Quint. CCCLXIV, *Contr.* III.9;
VII.6; *nocte* cf. ps.-Quint. CCLXXII; *processit* cf. ps.-Quint.
CCCLXIV; *occisus inspoliatus...inventus est* cf. *Contr.* X.1;
in solitudine cf. ps.-Quint. CCLXXXI; *servus...nominavit* cf.
Contr. VII.5: ...*pater familiae in cubiculo occisus inventus
est, uxor volnerata, communis paries perfossus* (hence my
nominative); *placuit propinquis quaeri a filio quinquenni,
qui una dormierat, quem percussorem cognosceret; ille
procuratorem digito denotavit; iuxta cadaver* cf. ps.-Quint.
Decl. mai. II; *et decessit* cf. *Contr.* II.4; *dives caedis
reus est* cf. ps.-Quint. CCCLXIV.

25 Actually this argument is not pressed as unsubtly as one
might have expected in the first *Tetralogy*; the emphasis is
on the improbability that ordinary robbers committed the
crime, rather than on the likelihood that the rich man was
responsible.

26 *De gramm. et rhet.* 25.9 Brugnoli, see p.116.

27 See pp.164f.

28 Dem. *Or.* XXIII 54, cf. 51 for ascription to Draco.

29 *CQ* XLIV (1950), 58.

30 On similarities to Attic law see especially U.E. Paoli,
'Droit attique et droit romain dans les rhéteurs latins',
Revue historique de droit français et étranger XXXI (1953),
175ff.; for an extremely archaic law used in connection with
controversiae see *Contr.* IX.4: *qui patrem pulsaverit manus ei
praecidantur* which, as Bonner notes (*Rom. decl.* 96), has an
exact parallel in the Code of Hammurabi of 2100 B.C. (§195) -
text and translation in G.R. Driver, J.C. Miles, *The
Babylonian laws* (Oxford, 1955), II. (This appears to be the
only parallel between declamatory law and this code.)
Whereabouts in the Greek world mock law-suits might have
originated remains to be traced; we may rule out any of the
Sicilian colonies where the Code of Charondas was used, for
this well-documented code (Arist. *Pol. passim*; Diod. Sic.
XII.11ff.) shows no particular affinities with known declamatory law. Sicily remains a possibility (Cic. *Brut.* 12.46),
but remember the sophists' diverse origins and wide travels.

31 E.g. *Contr.* I.7; II.5; IV.7; V.8; IX.4.

32 Note that, if the use of διαφθείρειν in *Tetr.* II, e.g. in
4.9, ἐὰν διαφθαρῇ, is taken to refer to the death penalty,
the legal situation in that *Tetralogy* is not identical with
Roman declamatory law, in which five years' exile is the
standard penalty for involuntary homicide (see Bonner, *Rom.*

decl. 98ff.). But need it be interpreted in this way?

33 See Philod. *Rhet.* II.97 Sudhaus, fr. VIII, for evidence of a dispute about the extent of Aeschines' education.

34 He was well aware of what constituted a *thesis*, see e.g. *Contr.* VII.4.3.

35 These exercises, with the exception of translation, all belong to the class which Greek rhetoricians called *progymnasmata*. In the Roman education of Suetonius' day they were dealt with by the *grammatici*, the Roman *rhetores* considering such simple exercises beneath them; the Greeks however seem always to have taken them more seriously (Quint. I.9.6). For an ancient account of the history of *progymnasmata* see Theon, *Prog.* 65ff. (*Rh. Gr.* II Spengel); for the individual exercises see this work *passim*; also for *dicta*... *exponere* cf. Quint. I.9.2; *narrationes...explicare* cf. Quint. I.9.3; II.1.8; 4.15ff.; *viros...vituperare* Quint. II.1.8; 4.20f.; *quaedam...ostendere* (*theses*) Quint. II.1.9; 4.24f. (cf. also Quint. II.1.11; 4.22f. on *communes loci*); *fabulis* ...*demere* cf. Quint. II.4.18f.

36 Brugnoli's text, except for the last sentence, where the obelizing is mine.

appellationes Graeci *OαKHUCS* (synthesis graeci eas appellationes *E*); appellationes Graece *WβMΩ* Roth, *Hofrichter, Bione, qui crucem anteposuit*; appellatione Graeca *Schott, Reiff.*; †appellationes† < > Graeci *Robinson*; appellationes del. *Brugnoli.*

syntasis *OB*; syntaxis *WNGDV Reiff, Hofrichter, Bione*; synthesis *L* (*corr.* syntaxis) *HE Roth*; sintaxis *IM*; sintesis *K*; sinthasis *UC*; sinthesis Δ; synthasis *Ω*; συνθέσεις *S*; συντάξεις *Stegemann*; συστάσεις *Bonner*; θέσεις *Gronovius, Bentley*; ὑπο- θέσεις *Wolf, Volkmann*; συντάσεις *Brugnoli.*

Despite Bonner's arguments in '*Rhetorica*', CR LXI (1947), 84ff., I find it hard to believe that the exercises were ever called *appellationes*, and am inclined to think the conjecture *appellatione Graeca* is right (cf. *appellatio...Graeca* in *De gramm. et rhet.* 4.1). As for *syntasis* etc., we should bear in mind that the earliest extant MSS of the *De gramm. et rhet.* belong to the fifteenth century and derive from a single archetype brought to Italy from Hersfeld by Enoch of Ascoli around the middle of the century. All but perhaps one of the manuscript readings recorded are therefore Renaissance conjectures or miscopyings. Clearly the word began with *syn-* or *sin-* in the Hersfeld *codex*, but we need not be so sure that the word Suetonius wrote began with this prefix as we would have to be if a wide range of medieval manuscripts were extant, all attesting such a reading. In addition, the Greek word seems to have been transmitted in Latin characters; uncomprehending western scribes could have distorted it considerably in the transmission of the text before the Renaissance. These facts need pointing out because the only conjecture which corresponds well with the known usage of

Cicero's time is ὑποθέσεις, rather remote from the MSS
readings. For ὑπόθεσις = *causa, controversia*, see pp.125f.
and especially Quint. III.5.7: *hae* ὑποθέσεις *a Graecis
dicuntur, causae a nostris*, and observe that Seneca in the
section of *Contr.* I pr. 12 parallel with the Suetonian
passage refers to the use of the term *causae*.

37 See pp.105f.

38 Cf. E.G. Sihler, 'θετικώτερον', *AJPh* XXIII (1902), 283ff.

39 This must be the conclusion even if, on the grounds that
theoretical works do not necessarily reflect accurately the
curriculum of contemporary schools, we prefer not to assume
that all the numerous imaginary legal situations cited as
illustrations of technical points in handbooks like the
De inv. and *Rhet. Her.* need have been actually used as
themes for declamation in the schools of the Roman Republic.

40 Including perhaps more of the type represented by the declamation about Leptines in *Berl. Pap.* P. 9781, on which see
p.110.

41 Cf. pp.144ff.

42 The expression is Cicero's: *Tusc. disp.* I.35.86.

43 Cf. the invectives against Cicero and against Sallust in the
Sallustian appendix, but R. Syme, *Sallust* (Cambridge, 1964),
314ff. for arguments against a late Republican dating for them.

44 Cf. Bonner, *Rom. decl.* 22, 29.

45 *Rebus*, suggested here in a marginal note in *Cod. O* (see
apparatus in K. Kumaniecki's Teubner, 1969, *ad loc.*) may be
preferable both in this phrase and the parallel one in §110
(quoted p.106 above) to the MSS reading *reis* printed by the
editors. *Rei* only figure in judicial rhetoric, whereas the
example of a *finita controversia* given here belongs to the
genus deliberativum, and *controversiae*, according to the
theorists being reported, could also be epideictic. Cf.,
however, Cic. *Or.* 14.46: *a propriis* personis *et temporibus*...

46 *mox controversias quidem* [sc. *vocabant*]*, sed aut fictas aut
iudiciales*. I am unconvinced by the interpretation of these
words assumed by Bonner, *Rom. decl.* 18f.

47 *Contr.* VII pr. 8; IX.5.15; Quint. IV.2.30; VII.1.14.

48 *'Rhetorica', CR* LXI (1947), 86.

49 Cf. p.95, on the text.

50 His source may have made the matter clearer.

[51] Contrast Bonner's arguments, *Rom. decl.* 28. But the fact that the *Auctor ad Her.* calls *declamatio* an exercise is irrelevant, for he is referring to voice-training, and in any case the traditional dating of the *Rhet. Her.* to the Sullan period has been called into question since Bonner wrote by A.E. Douglas, '*Clausulae* in the *Rhetorica ad Herennium* as evidence of its date', *CQ* N.S. X (1960), 65ff.

[52] Though Bake's conjecture *denuntiatio* is printed in the OCT.

[53] Cf. the use of *declamatio* in *Planc*. 19.47.

[54] As Clarke, *CQ* N.S. I (1951), 166, has pointed out.

[55] That the *thesis* alone is assigned to the pre-Ciceronian period in *Contr.* I pr. 12 is more easily explained if we imagine that Seneca's source gave some generalizations, similar to those in Quint. II.1.9 about the early use of abstract exercises, rather than a detailed list of *progymnasmata* such as we find in the Suetonian account.

[56] Quoted p.119. *Causa* is not used with reference to rhetorical exercises in the more famous autobiographical passage, *Brut.* 89.304ff.

[57] Cf. D.R. Shackleton Bailey ed. *Cicero's Letters to Atticus* Vol. I (Cambridge, 1965), 59ff.

[58] Clarke, *CQ* N.S. I (1951), 165f., notes how in Ciceronian theory general questions are regarded as prior logically to particular questions, and suggests that 'this supposed logical priority may have given rise to the belief in their historical priority'.

The decline of rhetoric in the early Empire

[1] See p.84.

[2] Cf. H. Caplan, 'The decay of eloquence at Rome in the 1st century', *Studies in speech and drama in honor of Alexander M. Drummond* (Ithaca, N.Y., 1944), 295ff.; L.A. Sussman, 'The elder Seneca's discussion of the decline of Roman eloquence', *CSCA* V (1972), 195ff.

[3] See Tac. *Dial.* 36.1, where we read after a lacuna: *eadem ratio in nostra quoque civitate antiquorum eloquentiam provexit*, and ps.-Longin. *Subl.* 44, which contains statements about the conditions provided for great literature by δημοκρατία in general, and ἐν ταῖς πολιτείαις in the plural (44.2-3). N.b. with J.W.H. Atkins (*Literary criticism in antiquity* (Cambridge, 1934), II 210ff.) and D.A. Russell (ed. Longin. *Subl.* (Oxford, 1964), xxii ff.), I think the treatise *On the sublime* belongs most likely to the first century A.D.,

pace G.M.A. Grube (*The Greek and Roman critics*, 340ff.) who argues in favour of a later date.

[4] Cf. Bonner, *Rom. decl.* 42ff.; Sussman, Diss. 191ff.

[5] Müller and Winterbottom print Thomas' conjecture, *pretium* but see n.8 below.

[6] Cf. *Contr.* II pr. 2; *Suas.* 6.9; *Contr.* II.1 *passim.*

[7] Cf. Quint. XII.1.1.

[8] Here, *pace* Thomas and the editors who adopt his conjecture *pretium*, I am content with the MSS reading *praemium*. If *gloria* (*Mil.* 13.34) and *laus* (*Off.* II.45) can 'fall' (*cadere*) in Cicero, as can almost any other abstraction in classical prose, there seems no reason why *praemium...cecidisset* is unacceptable Latin; see *ThLL* s.v. *cado* II 2.

[9] Cf. Aper's unorthodox arguments early in Tacitus' *Dialogus* (5.3ff.) to the effect that orators in his day were, unlike poets, well rewarded for their labours. Note especially his use of the term *voluptas* (§6 *passim*), and his rhetorical question in 7.3 (quoted p.139) about the glory won by orators. More in line with Seneca's view is Maternus' suggestion in *Dial.* 41.5 that his colleagues would have enjoyed *laus et gloria* if they had lived in an earlier age.

[10] H.I. Marrou, *A history of education in antiquity*, trans. (from ed.[3]) G. Lamb (New York, 1964), xiv = *Histoire de l'éducation dans l'antiquité*[6] (Paris, 1965), 20.

[11] Cf. Sall. *Iug.* 2: *omniaque orta occidunt et aucta senescunt.*

[12] See pp.83f., and pp.306ff.

[13] See pp.83f.

[14] Caplan, 'Decay of eloquence' 319; Bonner, *Rom. decl.* 42f.; Sussman, *The elder Seneca* 12ff. Contrast, however, the views of E.P. Parks, *The Roman rhetorical schools as a preparation for the courts under the early Empire* (Baltimore, 1945).

[15] Of course, ideally it should also be considered in relation to all the information given by historians and others about the senatorial debates and major trials of the period, but to make an adequate attempt at this task would be outside the scope of the present work. Parks, *Rom. rhet. schools*, provides much useful material.

[16] On the difficulty of the words, *Passienus, qui nunc primo loco stat* in this passage see D.R. Shackleton Bailey, *CQ* N.S. XIX (1969), 326, but the text has to stand: cf. *Contr.* II.5.7: *Passienus temporis sui primus orator.*

[17] Cf. Parks, *Rom. rhet. schools* 19ff.

[18] Dio LVI.27.1, Suet. *Calig*. 16.1, cf. M.T. Griffin, *JRS* LXII (1972), 14.

[19] Cf. M.T. Griffin, *Seneca* (Oxford, 1975), 48; but n.b. the association with Sejanus is only Tiberius' conjecture and too much weight cannot be placed on it.

[20] Though Seneca uses the scholastic term *color* in his analysis, it is clear that this was a real trial and not a *controversia*, as two *actiones* (see pp.164f.) and the non-scholastic procedure *calumniam iurare* are mentioned.

[21] The quotation is not necessarily indicative of Seneca's own attitudes.

[22] Cf. Parks, *Rom. rhet. schools* 19ff.

[23] See *Contr*. X pr. 5 (on Labienus): *libertas tanta, ut libertatis nomen excederet, et, quia passim ordines hominesque laniabat, Rabienus vocaretur. animus inter vitia ingens et ad similitudinem ingeni sui violentus et qui Pompeianos spiritus nondum in tanta pace posuisset*; cf. *Contr*. II.4.13.

[24] Cf. Bonner, *Rom. decl*. 71ff.

[25] Cf. the sarcastic allusions to declamation themes in Juvenal's *Satires*, especially 7.150ff., though the subject here is the unpleasantness of the rhetorician's job, rather than the decline of eloquence.

[26] See pp.299ff.

[27] Bornecque, *Décl*. 20; Edward, *Suasoriae* xii; Bonner, *Rom. decl*. 71f. But Sussman, Diss. 158ff., presents the evidence more accurately; see his remarks in *The elder Seneca* 17.

Inventio

[1] The orator was supposed to tackle the five parts of his work in the order given here, as Quintilian explains in III.3.10.

[2] See Winterbottom's edition, Vol. II, 635, Index II, s.v. 'advocates'.

[3] But cf. *Contr*. II.6.10.

[4] See Bonner, *Rom. decl*. 53.

[5] Cf. Sussman, Diss. 83.

[6] On *divisio* see Bornecque, *Décl*. 102-5; Bonner, *Rom*.

decl. 56ff.; Bardon, *Vocabulaire* 68ff.; Sussman, *The elder Seneca* 38ff., 111ff. Seneca does not suggest that a bare statement of disputed issues 'regularly occurred after the narration', as Sussman (p.111) asserts.

7 Supplied by J.B. Hall.

8 An issue, however, which raised a number of subsidiary lines of enquiry, see p.154, on Cestius' treatment of *Suas.* 3.

9 *Contr.* I.7.12; II.2.5; VII.4.3, 4.

10 *Contr.* II.5.14; VII.4.4; 8.8.

11 *Contr.* I.1.14; 2.14; 4.6; II.2.5; IX.1.9.

12 *Contr.* I.5.8; II.2.5.

13 The Roman schools of rhetoric were less important as promoters of *aequitas* than is suggested by e.g. Bornecque, *Décl.* 132, '...*le sentiment de l'équité, qui s'introduit vers cette époque dans le droit*', Parks, *Rom. rhet. schools* 76, who makes the suggestion that the declamations of Seneca's time 'may have contained the germs of one of the most important phases in Roman law, that is, the development of equity'. The concept of equity was in fact as well entrenched in the minds of Greek and Roman orators by Seneca's time as it would ever be; it hardly needed the schools to promote its 'development'. For equity in Cicero's writings see Bonner, *Rom. decl.* 46.

14 H. Bardon, in a chapter gloomily entitled '*Faiblesses: obscurités*' (*Vocabulaire* 68ff.) gives a very hostile account of Seneca's expression in his sections on *divisio*; I have aimed to provide something of a corrective to his strictures.

15 *etiamsi lex...idonea sit* is a question of *aequitas*.

16 *Vocabulaire* 69ff.

17 For the terminology of στάσις theory, Greek and Latin, see Hermagoras frs. 9-13 Matthes; Bonner, *Rom. decl.* 12ff. Note that Seneca never uses the adjectives which describe the other three types of στάσις: *definitiva, generalis, translativa* (Cic. *De inv.* I.8.10), nor indeed the terms στάσις, *status* or *constitutio*. See, however, also on *color* (pp.166ff.) for another apparently Hermagorean element in Seneca's critical vocabulary.

18 Here a question of fact is raised which was left ambiguous in the *thema*.

19 Cf. *Contr.* II.1.20: *Silo Pompeius sic divisit: coepit a vetere et explosa quaestione, an in omnia patri parendum sit.*

20 However, in *Contr.* II.6.5 we find Latro using this *volgarem*

quaestionem, quam solebat fastidire...

21 I.e. Pollio considers that Latro, if he wished to imitate the practice of the law-courts, should not have omitted to argue that the accused, however cruel, was not mad. I cannot accept, *pace* Winterbottom *ad loc.*, that the last sentence is Seneca's rather than Pollio's.

22 On whom see n.2, p.373.

23 E.g. *De or.* III.25.96; 52.199; Seneca himself uses the word similarly in *Contr.* X pr. 5: *color orationis antiquae.*

24 E.g. *De or.* III.25.100; *Brut.* 87.298.

25 See e.g. Hermog. *Stat.* 38.16ff. (*Rh. Gr.* VI Rabe); and for Latin expositions of the same theory, Cic. *De inv.* I.11.15; Quint. VII.4.7ff.

26 Possibly the explanation is that the term was taken from works misattributed to Hermagoras of Temnos, such as those deemed spurious by Quintilian in III.5.14.

27 See Hermagoras ed. Matthes, 73ff. (*index rerum*).

28 Diels/Kranz, *Vorsokr.*[6] II 367f.

29 *colores...qui non possunt coargui*: surely not just 'irrefutable' *colores* (so Winterbottom), for the adoption of these could hardly have been considered a *vitium* from any point of view.

30 The text of *Contr.* II.1.33 seems corrupt in several respects. The muddle in the MSS after *coargui: non ut omniasse ut non esse* (*-se* B) AB; *non ut omniā* (*-iaa* Dτ) *sseverent ut non esse* VD gives scope for such varied reconstruction that it seems a case for the obelus - Shackleton Bailey (*CQ* N.S. XIX (1969), 324) does not even accept the usual assumption that *somnia* or *somniasse* was in the original, and suggests that *non ut omniasse* is 'a dittography of *ut non esse*(t) with *non* added for good measure'. *Falsum* in the sentence, *sed ridiculum ...possit*, should surely be deleted. Read then: *illi enim colores probabant qui non possunt coargui* †*non ut omniasse ut non esset aliquo nomine offensus.*† *sed ridiculum est adfectari quod* [*falsum*] *probari non possit. non multum interest in causa sua falsum aliquis testem det an se: alteri enim credi non debet, alteri non solet.*

31 Cf. Bonner, *Rom. decl.* 60, on the 'swoon'.

32 Should the words *in hoc visum* be regarded as a mangled dittography of *invidiosum*, and deleted?

33 Cf. Quint. IV.2.28.

34 testem adducit *A. Augustinus.* As alternatives consider *ad testem ducit <controversiam>*, or (a suggestion of J.B. Hall) *ad test<imonium r>em ducit.*

Dispositio

1 Cf. Bornecque, *Décl.* 53f.; Bonner, *Rom. decl.* 54; Sussman, *The elder Seneca* 115ff.; for examples of complete *controversiae* see ps.-Quint. *Decl. maiores.*

2 References to some complete works of the *suasoria* type are given in n.11, p.347.

3 See p.80.

4 Cf. *Contr.* X pr. 15.

5 See pp.210ff.

6 *Rom. decl.* 58; cf. Sussman, *The elder Seneca* 116.

7 See the index of commonplaces, colours and rhetorical terms in Winterbottom's edition, Vol. II 635ff.

8 The words *luxuriam in multis* are attested only by the *Excerpta* MSS and, seeing that Gurges has already been mentioned as an example of *luxuria*, one would happily delete them as an inept interpolation, if it were not that Lucullus' name is more associated with luxury than avarice. At all events the text of the end of this sentence seems suspect.

9 See n.68, p.346.

10 On the dating of this work see J. Wight Duff, A.M. Duff, *A literary history of Rome in the Silver Age*[3] (London, 1964), 54f.

11 Cf. my analysis of Latro's treatment of *Contr.* II.7, pp. 251ff.

12 I accept that Kiessling and subsequent editors are right to transpose the words *in epilogis...Graecus* from *Contr.* VII.4.3 (after *passurum*) to a position before Latro's remarks on *epilogi.* It seems less certain that the declamatory quotation here assigned to Apollonius belongs to him, rather than some other declaimer whose name has dropped out. Perhaps *in epilogis...Graecus* came immediately before *Latro dixit...*

13 Cf. pp.96-7.

14 Cf. the translations of Bornecque: '*Le coupable doit disparaître dans la péroraison*', and Winterbottom: 'In the peroration the accused should be over and done with.'

[15] I recognize that, if my deletion of *Latro* were rejected, and
it could be argued that Fuscus was making a new point, the
question would have to be asked whether *debet...reus in
epilogo desinere* could not mean just the reverse, i.e.: 'It
ought to be the defendant who concludes the speech in the
epilogus.' But I suspect the declamatory Latin for that
would be: *debet...reus cum epilogo desinere* cf. *Suas.* 1.2:
tempus est Alexandrum cum orbe et cum sole desinere. For
desinere in cf. Sen. *De prov.* 4.14: *omnes considera gentes in
quibus Romana pax desinit, Germanos dico et quiquid circa
Histrum vagarum gentium occursat.*

[16] It might conceivably be regarded as part of Fuscus' critique
and be taken to mean (reading Bursian's *contexet*): 'but he
will weave the *epilogus* (i.e. his concluding accusations)
on to the defensive part of his speech as well as possible' -
but would there be any particular point in a smooth transition when the defendant is changing his tactics radically
and is eschewing the psychological advantages to be gained by
putting defence last?

Elocutio

[1] The fullest existing discussions of Seneca on diction are
those of A.F. Sochatoff, *CJ* XXXIV (1939), 347ff., and Sussman,
Diss. 113ff., 121ff.; *The elder Seneca* 118ff.; but none of
these is detailed enough to illustrate all the respects in
which Seneca differs from the stricter critics.

[2] See n.14, p.342.

[3] *Décl.* 121.

[4] *Priap.* 3.7f.: *quod virgo prima cupido dat nocte marito* | *dum
timet alterius vulnus inepta loci.*

[5] Cf. *Contr.* VII pr. 3 for inclusion of lamps among *res...
sordidissimas.*

[6] *Vocabulaire* 11ff. That is not to suggest, of course, that
there are *no* elements common to the vocabulary of the two
critics.

[7] P.248.

[8] Müller's conjecture, *plantaria*, has much to recommend it.
The context demands reference to something which could be
fancifully described as 'rising groves': *plantaria*, 'saplings'
or 'tree-nurseries', fulfil the requirement admirably.

[9] Though, to judge from Sen. *Ep. mor.* 114.4ff., Maecenas' own
prose was notoriously full of just this type of *licentia*.

[10] No lacuna is marked in Winterbottom's text, but surely a

Greek quotation is lacking at this point.

[11] On the text of this passage see pp.265ff.

[12] On the meaning of this word see pp.211f.

[13] See Dion. Hal. *De comp.* for a full treatment of this subject
in relation to Greek style by a near-contemporary of Seneca
the Elder. See also pp.43ff. on the *clausulae* preferred by
Seneca, Latro and Fuscus, and my review of Winterbottom's
Loeb, *JRS* LXVI (1976), 270ff. for a critique of Hagendahl's
statements about *clausulae* in the declamatory extracts.
Sussman's account of *compositio* (*The elder Seneca* 126f.) is
in several respects misleading: *(in-)fractus* does not mean
'choppy' in Seneca's usage (see n.44, p.360); I do not
believe that either *scholastici* or Atticists 'virtually
neglected' rhythmic considerations.

[14] See the analysis of *Suas.* 3.1, pp.246ff.

[15] See p.281.

[16] See pp.101-2.

[17] See appendix on p.326; the rhythm of the preceding *clausula*,
publicae securis acies (III R1 in my appendix) was not dis-
dained by Latro either.

[18] See p.268.

[19] Cf. Sussman, *The elder Seneca* 127ff.

[20] See pp.251ff.

[21] The name given by some theorists to the proof *ex con-
sequentibus*; see Quint. V.10.2.

[22] Much helpful information about the use of this term is given
by H. Schepers s.v. Enthymem, *Historisches Wörterbuch der
Philosophie* II (Darmstadt, 1972), 527ff.

[23] Cf. Cic. *Top.* 13.55; Quint. VIII.5.9; the recurrence of this
kind of remark about the high esteem in which such γνῶμαι
were held proves that there must be a degree of continuity in
the tradition between the theory of Aristotle's time and
Cicero's.

[24] Cf. the definition of *enthymema* as *sententia cum ratione*
mentioned by Quintilian in V.10.2.

[25] This observation may be Cicero's own. It is not justifiable
to infer (with Schepers, *op. cit.* 531) that ἐνθύμημα was so
used in any Stoic dialectical source used by Cicero, seeing
that he explicitly attributes the usage to rhetoricians.

[26] Cf. Quint. V.10.2 on the usage of Cornificius.

[27] For another example see *Contr.* X.4.25, quoted on p.313.

[28] Around IX.3.87 Quintilian starts to lose patience with the proliferation of types of expression classed as *figurae* by some critics of his day.

[29] Cf. Sussman, *The elder Seneca* 120ff.

[30] So the MSS in the only passage (*Contr.* II.4.12) where the singular occurs, but that is not to say it is certain, or even probable, that Seneca the Elder preferred that form to *tricolon*; he may even have written the word in Greek letters; see n.13, p.342.

[31] Pp.163f.

[32] See p.184.

[33] Actually, though, one cannot make a rigid demarcation between *descriptiones* and moralizing *loci*: a declamatory description of *amor* was bound to be moralistic in tone; the description of Xerxes in *Suas.* 5.1 could fairly be classed as a treatment of the *locus*, '*quomodo animi magnis calamitatibus everterentur*' (cf. *Contr.* I.7.17).

[34] See list of descriptions, pp.210f.

[35] Cf. Lucr. I.832: *patrii sermonis egestas* with which Winter-bottom (note on *Contr.* VII pr. 3) contrasts Cicero's belief, expressed, e.g., in *Nat. deor.* I.4.8, that the inferiority of Latin to Greek in *verborum...copia* was a thing of the past.

[36] See p.315.

[37] See pp.291f.

[38] See pp.176ff.

[39] See p.101.

[40] Quoted p.52.

[41] Quoted pp.181f.

[42] See pp.278-9.

[43] Cf. Quint. V.13.16 for the grouping: *contraria et supervacua et stulta*.

[44] Given that *compositio* is the standard Latin translation of σύνθεσις (ὀνομάτων). For the meaning of *fracta* see Quint. I.10.31 (on modern theatre music) *effeminata et impudicis modis fracta*; Demetr. *Eloc.* 189, σύνθεσις δὲ ἀναπαιστικὴ καὶ

μάλιστα ἐοικυῖα τοῖς κ ε κ λ α σ μ έ ν ο ι ς καὶ ἀσέμνοις
μέτροις, οἷα μάλιστα τὰ Σωτάδεια διὰ τὸ μαλακώτερον and
ps.-Longin. Subl. 41.1, μικροποιὸν δ' οὐδὲν οὕτως ἐν τοῖς
ὑψηλοῖς ὡς ῥυθμὸς κ ε κ λ α σ μ έ ν ο ς λόγων καὶ σεσοβη-
μένος, οἷον δὴ πυρρίχιοι καὶ τροχαῖοι καὶ διχόρειοι, τέλεον
εἰς ὀρχηστικὸν συνεκπίπτοντες...

45 There is no unanimity among Greek critics as to the scope of
κακόζηλον. In Demetr. Eloc. 186 κακόζηλον is the fault into
which the writer falls if he fails in an attempt at elegance
(τῷ γλαφυρῷ); it is distinguished from ὁ ψυχρὸς χαρακτήρ, the
fault which comes of failing to attain to grandeur (τῷ
μεγαλοπρεπεῖ). In ps.-Longin. Subl. 3.4 κακόζηλον is
associated with puerility (μειρακιῶδες), the fault which
results from striving after prettiness and sweetness, rather
than with tumidity (τὸ οἰδοῦν), the vice of unsuccessful
grand stylists. On the other hand in Hermog. Inv. IV.12 (Rh.
Gr. VI.202 Rabe) κακόζηλον is made to embrace even more
faults than it does in Quintilian's account: τὸ δὲ κακόζηλον
γίνεται ἢ κατὰ τὸ ἀδύνατον ἢ κατὰ τὸ ἀνακόλουθον, ὃ καὶ
ἐναντίωμά ἐστιν, ἢ κατὰ τὸ αἰσχρὸν ἢ κατὰ τὸ ἀσεβὲς ἢ κατὰ τὸ
ἄδικον ἢ κατὰ τὸ τῇ φύσει πολέμιον, καθ' οὓς τρόπους καὶ
ἀνασκευάζομεν μάλιστα τὰ διηγήματα ἐκβάλλοντες ὡς ἄπιστα.
Nor do the Latin grammarians who use the term agree as to its
definition. According to Diomedes (GL I 451.8ff.), cacozelia
est per affectationem decoris corrupta sententia, cum eo ipso
dedecoretur oratio, quo illam voluit auctor ornare. haec fit
aut nimio cultu aut nimio tumore. According to Sacerdos (GL
VI 455.12f.), cacozelia est, quae fit duobus modis, aut
magnarum rerum humilis dictio, aut minimarum oratio tumens.

46 There follow the examples of Murredius' tumidity quoted on
pp.208f.

47 The following instances of the use of these words have been
taken into consideration; those marked with an asterisk are
not included in Bardon's 'Lexique' in Vocabulaire 11ff.:
corruptus: Contr. III.7 extra*; VII.1.25; 4.10; IX.2.27*;
5.17; X.4.22,23; X.5.23*; Suas. 1.12,16*; corrupte: Contr.
II.1.26; III pr. 15*; IX.2.21; X.4.18,23; 5.28; corrumpere:
Contr. II.6.8 (conjectural)*; IX.5.17*; 6.11; insania: Contr.
II.1.25*; VII.3.8*; IX.2.26,28; insanus: Contr. II.1.25*;
insanire: Contr. IX.2.26*; X.4.22*; 5.27; Suas. 1.12,13;
2.16; furor: Contr. II.1.25*; IX.2.27*; furiose: Contr. X.5.
21,23; cacozelia: Contr. IX.1.15; 2.28; Suas. 7.11; cacozelōs: Suas. 2.16. It goes almost without saying that Bardon
is wrong in translating cacozelia as 'emphase, pathos' and
cacozelōs as 'emphatiquement'.

48 Quoted in full on pp.199f.

49 On verba impropria see Quint. VIII.2.2ff., where, after
citing the expressions Hibericas herbas and duratos muria
pisces contrived by orators in attempts to avoid undignified
expression, he avers that such departures from plain language

constitute a fault: *id apud nos inproprium,* ἄκυρον *apud Graecos vocatur, quale est 'tantum sperare dolorem', aut, quod in oratione Dolabellae emendatum a Cicerone adnotavi, 'mortem ferre', aut qualia nunc laudantur a quibusdam, quorum est 'de cruce verba ceciderunt'.*

50 Seneca's criticism is quoted in full on pp.208-9.

51 Others are quoted on p.199.

52 On hyperbole see Quint. VIII.6.67ff. With Maecenas' criticisms compare Hermog. *Inv.* IV.2 (*Rh. Gr.* VI.202f. Rabe) on Homer's avoidance of κακόζηλον in the passage which Dorion paraphrased.

53 Quoted in context on p.200.

54 See p.199.

55 Cf. Quint. VIII.6.23ff.

56 Cf. Seneca's remark on a similar *sententia* by Florus: *numquam Latro...tam incredibilis umquam figuras concipiebat ut in ipso triclinio inter lectos et †loco† et mensas percussum describeret (Contr.* IX.2.24 W).

57 Quoted on p.215.

58 *Contr.* X.5 *thema: Laesae rei publicae sit actio. Parrhasius, pictor Atheniensis, cum Philippus captivos Olynthios venderet, emit unum ex iis senem; perduxit Athenas; torsit et ad exemplar eius pinxit Promethea. Olynthius in tormentis perit. ille tabulam in templo Minervae posuit. accusatur rei publicae laesae.*

59 *Suas.* 2 *thema: Trecenti Lacones contra Xersen missi, cum treceni ex omni Graecia missi fugissent, deliberant an et ipsi fugiant.*

60 Cited by Quintilian, VIII.3.28. On Cimber and the notion of *Attica febris* see Leeman, *Orationis ratio* I 163; Lebek, *Verba Prisca* 160ff.

61 See pp.191ff.

62 E.g. Leeman, *Orationis ratio* I 187: 'the Atticist ideal and slogan of *sanitas*'.

63 For references to scholars sceptical of their authenticity see G.L. Hendrickson, 'Cicero's correspondence with Brutus and Calvus on oratorical style', *AJPh* XLVII (1926), 235ff. Hendrickson rejects their arguments, as does Leeman, *op. cit.* 140f. Testimonia relating to this correspondence are collected by W.S. Watt, *Ciceronis Epistulae* III (OCT, 1958), 168ff.

64 Cf. *Brut.* 13.51: *nam ut semel e Piraeo eloquentia evecta est, omnis peragravit insulas atque ita peregrinata tota Asia est, ut se externis oblineret moribus omnemque illam salubritatem Atticae dictionis et quasi sanitatem perderet ac loqui paene dedisceret. hinc Asiatici oratores non contemnendi quidem nec celeritate nec copia, sed parum pressi et nimis redundantes; Rhodii saniores et Atticorum similiores.*

65 N.b. the term κακόζηλον was not peculiar to extreme Atticists in Greek criticism. Demetr. *Eloc.* in which it occurs (186) is written in *koine* Greek with only occasional Atticisms; see G.M.A. Grube, *A Greek critic: Demetrius on style* (Toronto, 1961), 46ff., 133ff.

66 See K.M. Abbott, W.A. Oldfather, H.V. Canter, *Index verborum in Ciceronis rhetorica* (Urbana Ill., 1964).

67 E.g. *De or.* II.75.305: *ex quo etiam illud adsequor, ut si quis mihi male dicat, petulans aut plane insanus esse videatur;* *Brut.* 66.233: *C. Fimbria...qui omnia magna voce dicens verborum sane bonorum cursu quodam incitato ita furebat tamen, ut mirarere tam alias res agere populum, ut esset insano inter disertos locus;* *Or.* 71.236: *composite et apte sine sententiis dicere insania est; ibid.* 70.232: *quantum autem sit apte dicere, experiri licet, si aut compositi oratoris bene structam conlocationem dissolvas permutatione verborum; - corrumpatur enim tota res ut* [et] *haec nostra in Corneliana et deinceps omnia...*

68 This grouping of *stultum* with *contrarium* among the *rerum vitia* has some precedent in Cicero's remarks in *Part. orat.* 38. 133 on the unfortunate consequences which are inevitable when a defence counsel's interpretation of an ambiguous written statement is rejected: *fore uti multa vitia, stulta, iniqua, contraria consequantur.*

69 The following passages have been taken into consideration; those marked with an asterisk are not included in Bardon's 'Lexique' in *Vocabulaire* 11ff.: *stultus: Contr.* I.3.11; 4.12; V.2 *extra*; VII.5.10*; IX.4.22; X.5.25; *Suas.* 2.18*; 7.14; *stulte: Contr.* X.5.25; *stupor: Contr.* VII.2.14; 3.8; IX pr. 2; *Suas.* 2.21*; *fatuus: Contr.* VII.4.3; 5.15; IX pr. 2; X.5.25; *Suas.* 2.22; *ineptus: Contr.* I.4.7; 6.11*; II.3.13*; VII.3.10; 4.3; 5.10*, 11, 13; 7.14; IX.2.20; 6.11,12*; *inepte: Contr.* I.6.11*; IX.2.24*; X.1.12*; *ineptiae: Contr.* IX.6.10.

70 See p.215.

71 The part of the theme of *Contr.* VII.5 relating to the stepmother's wound is quoted on p.112.

72 Supplied by H.J. Müller.

73 Müller and Winterbottom here print conjectures.

[74] *CQ* N.S. XIX (1969), 321. See, however, the objections of L. Håkanson, 'Some critical notes on Seneca the Elder', *AJPh* XCVII (1976), 121ff., who proposes: *nam cum coepisset scholasticorum frequentissimo iam more, ut quam primum tantum tumeant quantum potest, a iureiurando, et dixisset multa, <ait> 'ita aut...*

[75] See p.224; compare also Pollio's remarks on Latro's elimination of *ineptae quaestiones* in *Contr.* II.3.13, quoted on p.162.

[76] See p.176.

[77] See *Contr.* II.4.12; X.4.23 for the expression; also pp. 174f. for *colores* running contrary to themes and to the declaimer's interests.

[78] In this *controversia* much hinged on the question whether the crime committed by the mutilator of beggars, however despicable, constituted *res publica laesa*.

[79] Here Müller prints Gertz' conjecture, *parilem*.

[80] On the stepmother's wound, see p.112.

[81] Here Winterbottom prints Shackleton Bailey's conjecture *licentissimi* (see *CQ* N.S. XIX (1969), 320), but the MSS reading *decentissimi* seems defensible. Seneca the Elder was capable of making such statements as *nihil est autem amabilius quam diligens stultitia (Contr.* VII.5.12). *Decentissimi generis stultam sententiam* can be viewed as one of a series of whimsical allusions to fatuity in *Suas.* 2: compare *sed si vultis historicum quoque fatuum dabo* (§22); *sed ne vos diutius infatuem* (§23).

Memoria

[1] Pp.37ff.

[2] On mnemonic techniques in antiquity, the Middle Ages and the Renaissance, see F.A. Yates, *The art of memory* (London, 1966). Sussman, *The elder Seneca* 131f. includes a brief discussion of Seneca's remarks on memory.

[3] Cicero (*De or.* II.88.359) mentions a system in which standard symbols are contrived to represent even conjunctions, but Quintilian (XI.2.25) considers such a system impracticable.

[4] So printed by H. Caplan (Loeb ed. 1954), on whose divergences from the editions of F. Marx see his introduction, xxxvii ff.

[5] Cf. p.37.

[6] See *Contr.* I pr. 18 and pp.184f.

[7] The standard example of great length in literature, cf. Tac. *Dial.* 20.1; Quint. XI.2.25.

[8] Note, however, *Contr.* I pr. 22, for evidence of his ability to improvise *sententiae* orally.

[9] Quintilian (XI.2.36f.) was appreciative of the usefulness of a well-constructed *divisio* as an aid to memory: *nam qui recte diviserit, numquam poterit in rerum ordine errare: certa sunt enim non solum in digerendis quaestionibus sed etiam in exequendis, si modo recte dicimus, prima ac secunda et deinceps, cohaeretque omnis rerum copulatio, ut ei nihil neque subtrahi sine manifesto intellectu neque inseri possit.*

Actio

[1] Sussman, *The elder Seneca* 132ff. includes a discussion of Seneca's remarks on delivery.

[2] Cf. *Contr.* VII.4.10 on uncritical applause in the schools.

[3] Cf. *Contr.* I pr. 14: *cum vero se silvis montibusque tradiderat, in silvis ac montibus natos, homines illos agrestis, laboris patientia et venandi sollertia provocabat et in tantam perveniebat sic vivendi cupiditatem, ut vix posset ad priorem consuetudinem retrahi.*

[4] Cf. *Contr.* VII.4.6: *Calvus, qui diu cum Cicerone iniquissimam litem de principatu eloquentiae habuit...*

[5] *Suas.* 2.17: *nam et servos nolebat habere nisi grandes et argentea vasa non nisi grandia. credatis mihi velim non iocanti, eo pervenit insania eius, ut calceos quoque maiores sumeret, ficus non esset nisi mariscas, concubinam ingentis staturae haberet.*

[6] Quoted in full on p.277.

Asianism, Atticism, and the styles of the declaimers

[1] E. Norden, *Die antike Kunstprosa* (Leipzig, 1898 repr. Stuttgart, 1958) I.152: '*Wir werden nun späterhin den Jahrhunderte lang dauernden Kampf dieser beiden Richtungen zu verfolgen haben, und zwar wollen wir dabei den Asianismus als den "neuen Stil", den Atticismus als den "alten Stil" bezeichnen.*' Norden's use of these terms is criticized in Wilamowitz' important article 'Asianismus und Atticismus', *Hermes* XXXV (1900), 1ff.

2 *Antike Kunstprosa* I 263-73.

3 See especially *Contr.* VII pr. 5, quoted on p.214.

4 See pp.200f.; 214; 238.

5 *Antike Kunstprosa* I 263-5.

6 Cf. p.238.

7 See pp.296ff.

8 N.b. such an expression as *cum esset ex Asia* would be con-
ceivable at least in colloquial Latin (cf. Plaut. *Bacch.* 472;
Rud. 737) but for the expression *ex Asianis* see *Contr.*
IX.1.12.

9 It is improbable that the minor declaimers Dionysius Atticus,
trained by Apollodorus of Pergamum (*Contr.* II.5.11), and
Antonius Atticus, criticized for extreme puerility in *Suas.*
2.16, were distinguished for their Attic preferences in
rhetorical style.

10 *Asianus* is Bursian's certain conjecture; the MSS have *asinius*.

11 *Lugent* is Haase's conjecture; Winterbottom reverts to the MSS
reading *legunt*, which for me, however, strikes a false note.
For funerary imagery in the prose of *cacozeli* and *Asiani* see
pp.218, 250.

12 Quoted in context on p.52.

13 E.g. Cic. *De or.* III.48.184, where the recommendation,
*orationem...non adstricte, sed remissius numerosam esse
oportere*, is attributed to Theophrastus.

14 Edward *ad loc.* actually suggests that this clause 'reads like
a marginal note inserted in the text'.

15 See pp.201f.

16 Normally confined to poetry at this date, though there was
precedent for its use in prose in Cic. *De or.* II.44.187.

17 P. Lunderstedt, *De C. Maecenatis fragmentis* (*Commentationes
Philologicae Jenenses* XI fasc. 1) (Leipzig, 1911). For
further bibliography relating to the text of these very
obscure fragments see the apparatus to L.D. Reynold's OCT of
Seneca, *Epistulae morales*, *ad loc.*

18 Contrast, e.g., Sen. *Nat. quaest.* V.3.1: *aer nubilo gravis
est.*

19 Strabo XIV.1.41: ὃς ἦρξε μάλιστα τοῦ 'Ασιανοῦ λεγομένου
ζήλου; cf. Cic. *Or.* 69.230.

[20] I 134-9.

[21] However, as Norden (*Antike Kunstprosa* I 138) notes, this phenomenon was already present in the style of Alcidamas, who is criticized for it by Aristotle in *Rhet.* III.3.3.

[22] Cf. p.186.

[23] Cf. p.158.

[24] Cf. *Contr.* I.6.12.

[25] Assuming that Wachsmuth was correct in transposing it to this point; see Müller's apparatus.

[26] Cf. p.226; p.364 n.77.

[27] Cf. p.209.

[28] The *excerpta* following those taken from the extant Latronian passage (*seram querellam...defendatur uxor*) seem to represent variant treatments of topics treated earlier in Latro's arguments, and are probably to be ascribed to other declaimers. Note that the *Excerpta* show that Seneca recorded at least one extract from the treatment of the *altera pars* of this declamation, and therefore did not confine his attention to Latro's treatment of the husband's case.

[29] Unless we accuse him of *contrarium* in §6; cf. pp.226f.

[30] I cannot accept the view of K. Büchner, 'Ein Stilwechsel Ovids', *Mus. Helv.* XIII (1956), 183, that the *diversum dicendi genus* referred to was poetry as opposed to rhetoric. When referring to literary genres other than rhetoric the elder Seneca uses the terms *artes* (*Contr.* II pr. 3) and *studia* (*ibid.* 4); Cassius Severus uses *opus* in a similar sense in *Contr.* III pr. 8. The term *genus dicendi* seems always to refer to a type of rhetorical style; see *Contr.* II pr. 1; III pr. 7; VII pr. 5; IX.5.17; X pr. 2.

[31] Quoted on p.245.

[32] Cf. p.5.

[33] Bonner, *Roman education* 20ff. discusses the various levels of tuition provided by Greeks in Roman households and, p.178, the amount of Greek required before a boy could profit from the Greek exercises and study of texts set by *grammatici*.

[34] See Jerome on Olympiad CXCI,4 (p.249 Fotheringham).

[35] See pp.117ff.

[36] See pp.245ff.

[37] See pp.110ff.; 165.

[38] See p.205.

[39] On Timaeus' style see also A.E. Douglas, ed. *Brutus* (Oxford, 1966) *ad loc.*

[40] Although Polybius quotes Timaeus in indirect speech up to this point, the lack of any marked change of style in the subsequent direct quotation shows that he is keeping close to the original from the outset.

[41] See *ORF*[3] *passim*. Admittedly sententiousness is not entirely lacking in early Ciceronian oratory, but it is not to be supposed that it need be the product of Asiatic influence. Compare, e.g., *Rosc. Am.* 89, *tempus hercule te citius quam oratio deficeret*, with Isocr. *Archid.* 81; Dem. *De cor.* 296. For similar *sententiae* in declamation see *Contr.* I.5.9.

[42] Why, for instance, if *iudices* so disliked having their time wasted and their intelligence insulted, did a plain style not become more generally favoured, and why did the treatment of philosophical and historical topics in rhetoric not become less, rather than more, trite?

[43] lite *Obrecht*: luce *MSS; Lehnert.*

[44] tandem *scripsi*: tamen *MSS.*

[45] *Tusc. disp.* II.8.20f. trans. Soph. *Trach.* 1060ff. Sussman, *The elder Seneca* 37, also recognizes that drama provided precedent for declamatory sententiousness.

[46] A. Dihle, 'Ein Spurium unter den rhetorischen Werken Ciceros', *Hermes* LXXXIII (1955), 303ff., argues that this work is not by Cicero.

[47] See pp.101f.

[48] P.101.

[49] Quoted on p.259.

[50] See p.106, on their attitude towards philosophy.

[51] See pp.166ff.

[52] See Philod. *Rhet.* II.216ff. Sudhaus.

[53] See Cic. *Brut.* 95.325; Suet. *Aug.* 86.3.

[54] I am unconvinced by the interpretation of this sentence proposed by K. Büchner, *Mus. Helv.* XIII (1956), 180: 'Natürlich ist sein zweiter Teil keine Begründung, sondern korrigiert wie so häufig eine Erwartung oder Vorstellung. Offenbar war

bekannt die Verbindung Ovids mit Latro. *Seneca sagt betont,
Ovid sei der auditor, der Hörer des Arellius Fuscus gewesen:
jawohl; denn die allgemein bekannte Verbindung mit Latro war
erst später wirksam.*' For objections to this last assertion
see n.30, p.367. Nor does it seem quite natural to interpret
it as Winterbottom does in his translation, 'I remember this
controversia being declaimed by Ovidius Naso at the school of
the rhetor Arellius Fuscus - Ovid being his pupil. He *was* an
admirer of Latro, though his style of speech was different.'
To take *nam Latronis admirator erat* to mean 'for his position
in relation to Latro was merely that of an admirer' places
too much strain on the Latin, given that the elder Seneca was
not merely chatting elliptically to his sons and other people
of his time who were perhaps already aware of Ovid's debt to
Latro, but was writing for posterity (*Contr.* I pr. 11).
Posteri could not be expected to take the words to mean anything other than 'for he was an admirer of Latro'.

55 See Müller's apparatus *ad loc*.

56 We have to suppose that a scribe, after copying *cuius auditor
fuit*, felt a certain compulsion to bring like closer together
with like and, skipping *cum...genus*, went straight on to copy
nam Latronis admirator erat. (It was perhaps at this stage
that the *excerpta* were compiled. They give the reading:
*Ovidius Naso apud Arellium Fuscum magistrum suum hanc contro-
versiam declamavit; nam Latronis admirator erat*.) Later a corrector noted in the margin the words omitted and the next copyist reinserted them incorrectly in the main body of the text.
For cases of transposition where a similar sequence of events
has to be postulated see, e.g., *Contr.* II.7.4/5 (Wachsmuth),
Contr. VII.4.3/5 (Müller), and n.17, p.335.

57 On Ovid's affinities with Fuscus see T.F. Higham, 'Ovid and
rhetoric', *Ovidiana* ed. N.I. Herescu (Paris, 1958), 35f.

58 *Op. cit.* 39; he cites as illustrations *Met.* I.292; II.263f.;
Pont. III.1.19f. Even where Ovid includes poetic descriptions of greater length, e.g. *Met.* XI.474ff. (shipwreck),
XII.39ff. (*Fama*), his style loses none of its characteristic
tautness.

59 Cf. Quint. IX.4.61: *neque enim loqui possum nisi e syllabis
brevibus ac longis...*

60 For examples of metrical snatches from all the best classical
prose stylists see Quint. IX.4.72-8.

61 N.b. later in *Contr.* II.2.8 it is reported that the
scholastici learnt a sentence from a *praefatio* by Latro
quasi carmen.

62 I am indebted to Dr J.B. Hall for this rendering. Experiment
along these lines was initiated by R. Ehwald in his *Ad
historiam carminum Ovidianorum recensionemque symbolae*

(Progr. Gotha, 1892).

[63] Pp.251ff.

[64] See, e.g., *Contr.* II.1.25f.: *hic controversiam postero die quam erat a Fabiano dicta declamavit; solebat* autem *sic ad locos pervenire, ut amorem descripturus paene cantantis modo diceret...*; VII pr. 3: *adfectus efficaciter movit, figurabat egregie, praeparabat suspiciose. nihil est* autem *tam inimicum quam manifesta praeparatio.*

[65] It includes two examples of *anthypophora* (anticipation of objection) and one *tricolon*, two of the very few kinds of *figurae* which the elder Seneca mentions by name (see pp. 208f.).

[66] For the theme see p.159.

[67] But n.b. such repetitions were not confined to the Fuscine descriptive manner. A Latronian example of repeated opening rhythm in conjunction with anaphora may be found in *Contr.* II.7.5: *quŏtĭēns ābsēntĭs viri nomen inploravit? quŏtĭēns, quōd nōn ūna peregrinaretur, questa est?*

[68] See Winterbottom's notes *ad loc.*

[69] For Fuscus' preferences see pp.326f.

[70] *...ēffŭgĭum sīt; ...āmnēsqu(e) ĭmĭtāntŭr.*

[71] *...cōrpŏrĭbŭs cōnstērnĭtŭr; ...prōxĭmūmquĕ dīvīnō gĕnŭs; ...pārrĭcĭdĭūm tāntī fŭīt; ...dīvĭtĭāe cōrrŭpĕrĭnt.*

[72] Cf. Leeman, *Orationis ratio* I 264ff. on the two passages. Leeman's supposition, however, that there was a difference of opinion between the two Senecas as to the necessary constituents of a *sententia* (266f.) can hardly be right: the younger Seneca's criticism, *deest illis oratorius vigor stimulique quos quaeris et subiti ictus sententiarum* (§8) is a paraphrase of his father's *deerat illi oratorium robur et ille pugnatorius mucro* (*Contr.* II pr. 2); the fact more likely is that whereas Fabianus' declamations often enough included *fere dulces sententias*, they were less common in his philosophical works.

[73] E.g. in the *Satires* and *Odes* of Horace, where he treats similar themes.

[74] See *ThLL* s.vv.

[75] See p.352 n.3.

[76] See also, however, p.294, on Moschus.

[77] See p.199.

[78] See p.238.

[79] See p.10.

[80] Perhaps a famous passage; at any rate Quintilian alludes to one sentence in it in IX.2.91. The theme of *Contr.* II.3 is as follows: *raptor raptae patrem exoravit, suum non exorat. accusat dementiae*; the legal position presupposed is that *raptor, nisi et suum et raptae patrem intra dies triginta exoraverit, pereat.*

[81] S.v. Iunius 77, *RE* X (1917), 1035ff.

[82] See Cic. *Brut.* 8.33 cf. *Or.* 50-51.169.

[83] So Winterbottom's translation after e.g. Quint. IX.4.22.

[84] Though n.b. the rhythmic sequence was not without parallel in the usage of Seneca and Latro; see appendix, p.326 (V R4).

[85] See *Contr.* III pr. 6.

[86] See pp.292f.

[87] *Orationis ratio* I 231.

[88] See n.34, p.367.

[89] See pp.54, 89.

[90] Bardon, *Vocabulaire* 33, is totally unconvincing in his definition of *floridus* as '*fleuri (c'est à dire: relevé d'images)*'; such a description certainly does not fit Pollio's declamatory manner. Probably Seneca meant by *floridior* something like *sententiis dulcior*. Cf. Quint. XII.10.60 on the middle (floridum/ἀνθηρόν) style: *medius hic modus et tralationibus crebrior et figuris erit iucundior, egressionibus amoenus, compositione aptus, sententiis dulcis, lenior tamquam amnis et lucidus quidem sed virentibus utrimque ripis inumbratus*, though n.b. Seneca's criticism is singularly deficient in references to the classical theory of three styles which is being described by Quintilian in XII.10.58ff.

[91] N.b. theorists on *compositio* advised against the use of too many short words in succession e.g. Dion. Hal. *De comp.* 12.

[92] See p.197.

[93] Given Albucius' fluency, Bursian's conjecture in §2, *non hexis magna*, can hardly be right.

[94] The remarks on Albucius' technique for manipulating emotions call for some elucidation. We have observed (p.208) that Quintilian regarded *figurae* as devices aimed at persuasion, not as mere ornaments, and that this view was shared by Latro;

hence the inclusion of *figurabat egregie* between two criticisms relating to persuasiveness. *Suspiciose* cannot mean *'de manière à éveiller les soupçons'* (so Bardon, *Vocabulaire* 56), seeing that the declaimer wants above all to inspire confidence in his hearers. Winterbottom's interpretation in his Loeb translation, 'He was...skilled at allusiveness in his preparation', seems the right one. *Praeparatio*, on which Seneca (*loc. cit.*) proceeds to comment, *nihil est autem tam inimicum quam manifesta praeparatio; apparet enim subesse nescio quid mali*, was the most common of the several varieties of the figure *praesumptio*/πρόλημψις recognized by the theorists; it is used *cum id quod obici potest occupamus* (Quint. IX.2.16) and consists of hints made usually in the *prooemium* as to the arguments which one is intending to use. Seneca (*loc. cit.*) also advises moderation to prevent one's *praeparatio* from turning into a *confessio*. A *confessio* was another variety of *praesumptio* in which one conceded a point to one's adversary before proceeding to argue against him on other counts.

95 Pp.163f.

96 See p.192. In §2 the words *magna...phrasis* seem suspect.

97 The whole passage is quoted on p.214.

98 The evidence of this preface has to be considered separately for reasons explained on pp.47ff.

99 Cf. pp.269f.

100 Here I have adopted Wachsmuth's transposition, *desinere... dicere*, whereas Müller and Winterbottom keep the MSS reading, *scire dicere quam scire desinere*.

101 See pp.276f.

102 Cf. Fabianus' description of Ocean quoted on p.271f.

103 *Ad Hor. Epist.* I.5.9.

104 *Valenter* is the reading of the *excerpta* MSS; the editors prefer the *lectio difficilior* of the 'full text' MSS, *violenter*, but it seems to me too difficult to accept that Seneca linked two expressions of opprobrium with *sed*. For the use of *valenter* with reference to Sparsus' model, Latro, see *Contr.* VII.7.10.

105 See p.239.

106 See pp.191ff.

107 See p.177.

108 On the theme of this *controversia* see p.172.

[109] Quoted on p.214.

[110] See p.245.

[111] See pp.283f.

[112] See p.245.

[113] See Norden, *Antike Kunstprosa* I 267.

[114] See pp.221ff.

[115] See pp.216ff.

[116] *Antike Kunstprosa* I 263ff.

[117] The parody is of a type of declamation which calls for much gesticulation; compare the passage of Iulius Bassus quoted on p.295, and Seneca's disapproval of his *actio* (*Contr.* X pr. 12). Such a rhythm as *dătĕ mĭhĭ dŭcēm...* (assuming *ducem*, deleted by K. Müller after Jacobs, to be in fact Petronian), might well have been considered by Seneca as a case of *emollita compositio*. Cf. *Contr.* VII.4.8, discussed on p.101, a passage which proves, incidentally, that even 'effeminate' rhythms were not a monopoly of the *Asiani*. See also p.261, for a comparison between the Petronian parody and the emotional rhetoric of Attic drama, as translated by Cicero.

118 See pp.101f.

[119] See pp.5f.

120 *Antike Kunstprosa* I 152.

121 Norden (*op. cit.* 265f.) dismisses Dionysius as '*ein falscher Prophet*', and his account of an Atticist revival as the wishful thinking of a *Stubengelehrter*.

Declamation and literary modernism in the early Empire

[1] See pp.292f.

[2] These *sequentes* are apparently given the alternative name of *novi declamatores* in *Contr.* I.1.14, but why Seneca should have classed some of the declaimers he does as *novi* (e.g. Cestius, *loc. cit.*) is mysterious since, as Hoffa (*Quaest. sel.* 7ff.) has observed, there is not always a chronological justification for describing them as new. It is on the basis of *Contr.* I.1.13f. that I make a very tentative suggestion in my forthcoming article, 'The elder Seneca and declamation', in *ANRW*, n.163, that the term might have originated in attempts by Latro to pose as a preserver of antique standards, in which he denigrated anyone who departed from his boasted

classicism as *novi*.

3 See pp.285f. But n.b. paradoxically we have noted certain seemingly archaic features in the declamatory fragments of Cassius Severus who was to be considered later (Tac. *Dial.* 19.1; 26.4) as the first of the moderns. Also bear in mind that Dionysius of Halicarnassus (*Rhet. vet.* 2) thought he detected an almost universal movement back to classicism among students of Greek rhetoric in his day.

4 See pp.77ff.

5 See pp.220f.

6 See Edward and Winterbottom *ad loc.*

7 *Epochs of Greek and Roman biography*, Sather Classical Lectures IV (Berkeley, Calif., 1928), 36. The most famous example of Thucydides' use of this device is the assessment of Pericles after the mention of his death in II.65.6; the brief appraisal of Nicias in VII.86.5 is certainly another example; the more extensive estimate of Themistocles' gifts in I.138.3 precedes, rather than follows, the narrative of his death. On the term ἐπιτάφιον see n.19, p.339.

8 See R. Syme, *Sallust* (Berkeley and Cambridge, 1964), 274ff.

9 See pp.14ff.

10 Cf. *Ep. mor.* 59.7: *Sextium ecce cum maxime lego, virum acrem, Graecis verbis, Romanis moribus philosophantem.*

11 Quoted on p.22.

12 See Winterbottom's notes on *Contr.* II.1 *passim*, and for declamatory examples his Index III (Vol.II 638ff.) s.vv. luxury, rich men, poor men.

13 See H.I. Marrou, *Histoire de l'éducation dans l'antiquité*[6] 246ff.; Bonner, *Roman education* 212f.

14 Quoted on pp.199f.

15 Cf. Sen. *Ep. mor.* 122.11, quoted on p.316.

16 See p.97.

17 Cf. Ovid's remark, *aiebat interim decentiorem faciem esse in qua aliquis naevos esset* (*Contr.* II.2.12), for the meaning of *decentius* in Seneca's appreciation of Virgil.

18 See pp.249.

19 The phrase does not occur in our texts of Virgil. See Edward and Winterbottom *ad loc.*; E. Fraenkel, *Horace* (Oxford, 1957),

199 n.1; F. Della Corte, 'Plena deo', *Maia* XXIII (1971), 102ff.

20 See p.195.

21 See pp.264ff.

22 Müller is more certain than Winterbottom that there is a lacuna here. Certainly it is possible, as Winterbottom observes *ad loc.*, that the third quotation was unknown to Seneca, but it seems a remote possibility, seeing how fond story-tellers always are of three-part narration. Seneca would surely have felt the need to apologize supposing he had forgotten the third *versus*.

23 Winterbottom prefers to delete the MSS' *si tam* before *recta via*. For a different reconstruction of this corrupt piece of text see D.R. Shackleton Bailey, *CQ* N.S. XIX (1969), 321.

24 C.O. Brink, *Horace on poetry: prolegomena to the literary Epistles* (Cambridge, 1963), 159, compares Callim. *Hymn to Apollo* 108f.:

  Ἀσσυρίου ποταμοῖο μέγας ῥόος, ἀλλὰ τὰ πολλὰ
  λύματα γῆς καὶ πολλὸν ἐφ' ὕδατι συρφετὸν ἕλκει.

25 See p.312.

26 See p.194.

27 Probably that of the younger Germanicus in A.D. 16. See Winterbottom *ad loc*.

28 See H. Homeyer, 'Klage um Cicero. Zu dem epischen Fragment des Cornelius Severus', *Annales Univ. Saraviensis (phil. Fak.)* X (1961), 327ff.; V. Bongi, 'Nuova esegesi del frammento di Albinovano Pedone', *Istituto Lombardo di scienze e lett. Rendiconti (Classe di Lettere)* LXXXII (1949), 28ff.; V. Tandoi, 'Albinovano Pedone e la retorica guilio-claudia', *Studi Italiani di Filologia Classica* XXXVI (1964), 129ff.

29 P.136.

30 So C.W. Mendell, *Latin poetry, the age of rhetoric and satire* (Hamden, Conn., 1967), 10.

31 Though n.b. some Republican *grammatici* taught a considerable amount of rhetoric. See p.5.

32 See pp.146f.

33 See p.80.

34 See p.209.

35 Cf. pp.118ff.

36 See p.118.

37 See pp.90f.

38 See L. Friedländer, *De Senecae controversiis in Gestis Romanorum adhibitis* (Königsberg, 1891); Müller's ed., introd. VIIf. n.1.

39 So Dio, XLVII.11.1.

BIBLIOGRAPHY

EDITIONS

The text in my quotations from Seneca the Elder normally represents
the consensus of the editions of H.J. Müller (Vienna, 1887, repr.
Hildesheim, 1963) and M. Winterbottom (Loeb ed. with English translation, Cambridge, Mass. and London, 1974). Where these editions
differ I indicate which of them I am following by means of the
letter M or W appended to the book and section reference, usually
only giving reasons for my preference or including any discussion
of textual matters in cases where the interpretation of Seneca's
criticism is at issue. Asterisks are used to indicate any notes
which contain discussion of problems in the text of Seneca the
Elder or other ancient authors.

Occasional mention is also to be found in this book of all
the other nineteenth- and twentieth-century editions of Seneca the
Elder, besides those of Müller and Winterbottom, namely those of:
C. Bursian, Leipzig, 1857
A. Kiessling, Leipzig, 1872, repr. Stuttgart, 1967
H. Bornecque, Paris, ed.[1] 1902 and ed.[2] 1932 (with French
translation)
W.A. Edward, *The Suasoriae of Seneca*, Cambridge 1928 (with
English translation and commentary).

Among earlier editions I cite only the *Editio Commeliniana* of
the two Senecas by A. Schott and M.A. Muretus, Heidelberg, 1603/4.
The preface by Schott from which I quote is also printed amongst
other introductory material in the important Elzevir edition,
Amsterdam, 1672, with commentaries by J. Schultingh and others.
Classification and description of the early editions is provided
in an article by H.D.L. Vervliet, 'De gedrukte Overlevering van
Seneca Pater', *De Gulden Passer* XXXV (1957), 179ff.

SECONDARY WORKS

No attempt is made here to do more than set down a list of works
(excluding those on non-literary matters) cited in this book. A
useful, though not exhaustive, bibliographical study is provided
in J.E.G. Whitehorne's 'The Elder Seneca: a review of past work',
Prudentia I (1969), 14ff. This will be supplemented in due course
by a detailed bibliography by L.A. Sussman, and my own article,
'The elder Seneca and declamation', both forthcoming in *Aufstieg
und Niedergang der römischen Welt*.

Abbott, K.M., Oldfather, W.A., Canter, H.V. *Index verborum in Ciceronis rhetorica* (Urbana, Ill., 1964).

Atkins, J.W.H. *Literary criticism in antiquity* (Cambridge, 1934).

Bardon, H. *Le vocabulaire de la critique littéraire chez Sénèque le Rhéteur* (Paris, 1940)

'Mécanisme et stéreotypie dans le style de Sénèque le Rhéteur', *AC* XII (1943), 5ff.

Barwick, K. ed. Cicero, *Brutus* (Heidelberg, 1949).

Boissier, G. 'Les écoles de déclamation à Rome', *Revue des Deux Mondes* XI (1902), 480ff.; trans. by W.G. Hutchison, 'The schools of declamation at Rome' in *Tacitus and other Roman studies* (London, 1906), 163ff.

Bongi, V. 'Nuova esegesi del frammento di Albinovano Pedone', *Istituto Lombardo di scienze e lett.: Rendiconti (Classe di lettere)* LXXXII (1949), 28ff.

Bonner, S.F. *Dionysius of Halicarnassus* (Cambridge, 1939).

'Rhetorica', *CR* LXI (1947), 84ff.

Roman declamation in the late Republic and early Empire (Liverpool, 1949).

Education in ancient Rome from the elder Cato to the younger Pliny (London, 1977).

Bornecque, H. *Les déclamations et les déclamateurs d'après Sénèque le Père* (Lille, 1902, repr. Hildesheim, 1967).

'Le texte de Sénèque le Père', *RPh* N.S. XXVI (1902), 360ff. and XXVII (1903), 53ff.

Brink, C.O. *Horace on poetry: prolegomena to the literary Epistles* (Cambridge, 1965).

Büchner, K. 'Ein Stilwechsel Ovids?', *Mus. Helv.* XIII (1956), 180ff.

Buschmann, J. *Charakteristik der griechischen Rhetoren beim Rhetor Seneca* (Progr. Parchim, 1878).

Die 'enfants terribles' unter den Rhetoren des Seneca (Progr. Parchim, 1883).

Caplan, H. 'The decay of eloquence at Rome in the first century', *Studies in speech and drama in honor of Alexander M. Drummond* (Ithaca, N.Y., 1944), 295ff.

Cerrati, M. *La grammatica di A. Seneca, il retore* (Turin, 1908).

Clarke, M.L.   'The *thesis* in the Roman rhetorical schools of the Republic', *CQ* XLV (1951), 159ff.

Cordier, A.   Review: Bardon, *Vocabulaire*, *RPh* 3me sér. XVII (1943), 220ff.

D'Alton, J.F.   *Roman literary theory and criticism* (London, 1931).

Dalzell, A.   'C. Asinius Pollio and the early history of public recitation at Rome', *Hermathena* LXXXVI (Nov. 1955), 20ff.

Della Corte, F.   'Plena deo', *Maia* XXIII (1971), 102ff.

Dihle, A.   'Ein Spurium unter den rhetorischen Werken Ciceros', *Hermes* LXXXIII (1955), 303ff.

Douglas, A.E.   'M. Calidius and the Atticists', *CQ* N.S. V (1955), 241ff.

'*Clausulae* in the *Rhetorica ad Herennium* as evidence of its date', *CQ* N.S. X (1960), 65ff.

ed. Cicero, *Brutus* (Oxford, 1966).

Cicero: Greece and Rome, New Surveys of the Classics II (Oxford, 1968).

Dover, K.J.   'The chronology of Antiphon's speeches', *CQ* XLIV (1950), 44ff.

Duff, J. Wight, Duff, A.M.   *A literary history of Rome in the silver age*[3] (London, 1964).

Ehwald, R.   *Ad historiam carminum Ovidianorum recensionemque symbolae* (Progr. Gotha, 1892).

Fairweather, J.A.   'A transposition in the text of Seneca the Elder, *Contr.* I.5.9', *CR.* N.S. XX (1970), 11f.

Review: M. Winterbottom ed. and trans. *Seneca the Elder*, *JRS* LXVI (1976), 270ff.

'The Elder Seneca and declamation', forthcoming in *Aufstieg und Niedergang der römischen Welt*.

Fantham, E.   *Comparative studies in Republican Latin imagery*, *Phoenix*, Suppl. Vol. X (Toronto, 1972).

Fordyce, C.J.   Review: Bardon, *Vocabulaire*, *CR* LX (1946), 129.

Fraenkel, E.   *Horace* (Oxford, 1957).

François, G.   '*Declamatio et disputatio*', *AC* XXXII (1963), 513ff.

Friedländer, L. *De Senecae controversiis in Gestis Romanorum adhibitis* (Progr. Königsberg, 1891).

Gerth, K. s.v. *'Iunius'* 77 (Iunius Gallio), *RE* Xi (1917), 1035ff.

Griffin, M.T. 'The elder Seneca and Spain', *JRS* LXII (1972), 1ff.

'Imago vitae suae', *Seneca: Studies in Latin literature and its influence*, ed. C.D.N. Costa (London, 1974), 1ff.

Seneca (Oxford, 1975).

de Groot, A.W. *Handbook of antique prose rhythm* (Groningen, 1919).

Der antike Prosarhythmus (Groningen, 1921).

Grube, G.M.A. 'Theodorus of Gadara', *AJPh* LXXX (1959), 337ff.

A Greek critic: Demetrius on style (Toronto, 1961).

The Greek and Roman critics (London, 1965).

Gruppe, O. *Quaestiones Annaeanae* (Diss. Sedini, 1873).

Hagendahl, H. 'Rhetorica', *Apophoreta Gotoborgensia V. Lundström oblata* (Göteborg, 1936), 299ff.

Håkanson, L. 'Some critical notes on Seneca the Elder', *AJPh* XCVII (1976), 121ff.

Hall, J.B. 'Seneca, *Controversiae* I praef. 12', *PACA* XII (1973), 11.

Hendrickson, G.L. 'Literary sources in Cicero's *Brutus* and the technique of citation in the dialogue', *AJPh* XXVII (1906), 185ff.

'Cicero's correspondence with Brutus and Calvus on oratorical style', *AJPh* XLVII (1926), 235ff.

Hess, R. *Quaestiones Annaeanae* (Diss. Kiel, 1898).

Higham, T.F. 'Ovid and rhetoric', *Ovidiana*, ed. N.I. Herescu (Paris 1958), 32ff.

Hoffa, W. *De Seneca Patre quaestiones selectae* (Göttingen, 1909).

Hofrichter, W. *Studien zur Entwickelungsgeschichte der Deklamation* (Diss. Breslau Univ., publ. Ohlau, 1935).

Homeyer, H. 'Klage um Cicero. Zu dem epischen Fragment des Cornelius Severus', *Annales Univ. Saraviensis (phil. Fak.)* X (1961), 327ff.

Immisch, O.   'Wirklichkeit und Literaturform', *RhM* N.F. LXXVIII
    (1929), 113ff.

Janson, T.   *Latin prose prefaces* (Stockholm, 1964).

Jenkinson, E.M.   'Further studies in the curriculum of the Roman
    schools of rhetoric in the Republican period', *Symbolae
    Osloenses* XXXI (1955), 122ff.

Karsten, H.T.   *Elocutio Rhetorica qualis invenitur in Annaei
    Senecae Suasoriis et Controversiis* (Progr. Rotterdam, 1881).

Kennedy, G.   *The art of rhetoric in the Roman world* (Princeton,
    1972).

Kroll, W.   s.v. *'Rhetorik'*, *RE* Supptbd VII (1940), 1039ff.

Lebek, W.D.   'Zur Vita des Albucius Silus bei Sueton', *Hermes* XCIV
    (1966), 360ff.

    *Verba Prisca: Die Anfänge des Archaisierens in der lateinischen
    Beredsamkeit und Geschichtschreibung* (Göttingen, 1970).

Leeman, A.D.   *Orationis ratio* (Amsterdam, 1963).

Leo, F.   *Die griechisch-römische Biographie nach ihrer
    literarischen Form* (Leipzig, 1901, repr. Hildesheim, 1965).

Lockyer, C.W.   *The fiction of memory and the use of written
    sources: convention and practice in Seneca the Elder and
    other authors* (Diss. Princeton, 1970).

Lunderstedt, P.   *De C. Maecenatis fragmentis, Commentationes
    Philologicae Jenenses* XI fasc. 1 (Leipzig, 1911).

Marouzeau, J.   Review: Bardon, *Vocabulaire*, *REL* XVIII (1940),
    203ff.

Marrou, H.I.   *Histoire de l'éducation dans l'antiquité*[6] (Paris,
    1965); trans from ed.[3] by G. Lamb, *A history of education in
    antiquity* (New York, 1964).

Misch, G.   *Geschichte der Autobiographie*[3] Vol. I (Frankfurt, 1947);
    trans. Misch and E.W. Dickes, *A history of autobiography in
    antiquity* (London, 1950).

Momigliano, A.D.   *The development of Greek biography* (Cambridge,
    Mass., 1971).

Morel, W., Kroll, W.   s.v. *'Melete'*, *RE* XVi (1931), 496ff.

Norden, E.   *Die antike Kunstprosa* (Leipzig, 1898, repr. Stuttgart,
    1958).

Pack, R.A. *The Greek and Latin literary texts from Greco-Roman Egypt*[2] (Ann Arbor, 1967).

Paoli, U.E. 'Droit attique et droit romain dans les rhêteurs latins', *Revue Historique de Droit français et étranger* XXXI (1953), 175ff.

Parks, E.P. *The Roman rhetorical schools as a preparation for the courts under the early Empire*, Johns Hopkins University Studies in Historical and Political Science, Series LXIII no. 2 (Baltimore, 1945).

Portalupi, F. *Bruto e i neo-atticisti* (Turin, 1955).

Preisendanz, C. 'De Senecae rhetoris apud philosophum filium auctoritate', *Philologus* LXVII (1908), 68ff.

Rayment, C.S. 'Echoes of the declamations in the dialogues of the younger Seneca', *CB* XLV (1969), 51f., 63.

Robinson, R.P. ed. Suetonius, *De Grammaticis et Rhetoribus* (Paris, 1925).

Rolland, E. *De l'influence de Sénèque le père et des rhêteurs sur Sénèque le philosophe* (Ghent, 1906).

Russell, D.A. ed. 'Longinus', *On the sublime* (Oxford, 1964).

Sander, M. *Quaestiones in Senecam rhetorem syntacticae* (Diss. Greifswald, 1872).

Der Sprachgebrauch des Rhetors Annaeus Seneca, 2 vols. (Berlin, 1877, 1880).

Schepers, H. s.v. 'Enthymem', *Historisches Wörterbuch der Philosophie* II (Darmstadt, 1972), 527ff.

Shackleton Bailey, D.R. ed. *Cicero's letters to Atticus* I (Cambridge, 1965).

'Emendations of Seneca "Rhetor"', *CQ* N.S. XIX (1969), 320ff.

ed. Cicero, *Ad Familiares* (Cambridge, 1977).

Shewring, W.H. 'Prose rhythm and the comparative method', *CQ* XXIV (1930), 164ff. and XXV (1931), 12ff.

Sihler, E.G. 'Θετικώτερον', *AJPh* XXIII (1902), 283ff.

Sochatoff, A.F. 'The basic rhetorical theories of the elder Seneca', *CJ* XXXIV (1939), 347ff.

Stegemann, W. Review: Bardon, *Vocabulaire*, *PhW* LXIV (1944), 172ff.

Steidle, W. *Sueton und die antike Biographie* (Munich, 1951).

Stuart, D.R. *Epochs of Greek and Roman biography*, Sather Classical Lectures IV (Berkeley, California, 1928).

Sussman, L.A. 'The elder Seneca as a critic of rhetoric' (Diss. Chapel Hill, N. Carolina, 1969).

'The elder Seneca's discussion of the decline of Roman eloquence', *Cal. Stud. Class. Antiq.* V (1972), 195ff.

The elder Seneca (Leiden, 1978).

Syme, R. *Sallust* (Berkeley and Cambridge, 1964).

Tandoi, V. 'Albinovano Pedone e la retorica guilio-claudia', *Studi Italiani di Filologia Classica* XXXVI (1964), 129ff.

Thomas, E. 'Schedae criticae novae in Senecam rhetorem', *Philologus* Supptbd VIII (1900), 159ff.

Throm, H. *Die Thesis - Ein Beitrag zu ihrer Entstellung und Geschichte*, *Rhetorische Studien* XVII (Paderborn, 1932).

Vassileiou, A. 'A propos d'un passage de Sénèque le Père (*Contr.* II praef. 4): la psychologie d'un père ambitieux pour ses enfants au Ier siècle ap. J.C.', *Latomus* XXXII (1973), 162ff.

Watson, G. *The literary critics* (Harmondsworth, 1962).

von Wilamowitz-Möllendorff, U. *Antigonos von Karystos* (Berlin, 1881).

'Asianismus und Atticismus', *Hermes* XXXV (1900), 1ff.

Wilkinson, L.P. *Golden Latin artistry* (Cambridge, 1963).

Winterbottom, M. 'Problems in the elder Seneca', *BICS* XXI (1974), 20ff.

Yates, F.A. *The art of memory* (London, 1966).

INDEXES

GENERAL INDEX

Bruttedius Niger,80,306

Buteo,224,236

cacemphaton,215

cacozelia, cacozelos,82,215-
24,243-4,249,302,342 nn.14,
16,361 nn.45,47,362 n.52,
363 n.65,366 n.11

Caesar, *see* Iulius

calamistri,278,302

Calidius, M.,345 n.61,346 n.63

Caligula (C. Iulius Caesar
Germanicus),15

Callimachus,375 n.24

Callisthenes,79

Calpurnius Flaccus,113

calumniam iuro,354 n.20

canticum,215-16,218,238

causa,104,116,125,130-1,350 n.
36,352 n.56; *see also* [*hypothesis*]/ὑπόθεσις

Capito,40,88,102,295

Cassius Dio,354 n.18,376 n.39

Cassius Longinus, C.,87,89-90

Cassius Severus,7,15,50,53,57,
58,78-9,85-8,102,138-40,142,
146,180,190,201,207,210,216,
232-4,237-8,278-83,307-8,
311,321,367 n.30,374 n.3

Catiline, *see* L. Sergius
Catilina

Catius Crispus,220

Cato, *see* Porcius

Catullus, *see* Valerius

Catulus, *see* Lutatius

Celsus, *see* Cornelius

Censorinus,142

Cestius Pius, L.,7,10,23,26,
32,45,53,54,85-9,110,146,
154,158,164,170,174,179-82,
187,196,211,213,226,232,

263,281,283-5,291,297,313,
322,337 nn.40,42,343 nn.24,
25,32,344 n.38,355 n.8,373
n.2

characterization,151,176-8,
194,213

chauvinism ascribed to the
elder Seneca,23-6

children in rhetorical themes,
174,185,195,285

chria,31,116-17,350 n.35

χρῶμα and associated Greek
terminology,166-7,356 n.26

Cicero, *see* Tullius

Cineas,92,228

circumlocution,217-18,249-51,
293,367 n.21

circumstantial detail excluded
from rhetorical themes,111,
114,121,348 n.23

Civil Wars,5,8,77,165

civilis applied to language,
213

class barriers broken by men
of letters,93

Claudius Caecus, Appius,318

Claudius Marcellus Aeserninus,
7,165,188,286,343 nn.23,25

clausulae,42-4,98-101,201-2,
273-4,281,326-7,345 n.58,
346 n.64,359 nn.13,17,370
nn.69-71,371 n.84

Clodius Turrinus (the elder),
94,142,296

Clodius Turrinus (the younger),
94,296

codices used by declaimers,
228,289

cogitatio in relation to
memory,234

cognitio (in classification of
theses),104

colloquialism,60,144,193-5,
316,324

INDEX OF PASSAGES CITED